Comeback

The Restoration of American Banking Power in the
New World Economy

Roy C. Smith
Professor of Finance and International Business,
New York University and Limited Partner,
Goldman, Sachs & Co.

Harvard Business School Press
Boston, Massachusetts

Published by the Harvard Business School Press in hardcover, 1993; in paperback, 1994

Library of Congress Cataloging-in-Publication Data

Smith, Roy C., 1938–
   Comeback : the restoration of American banking power in the new
world economy / Roy C. Smith.
      p. cm.
   Includes bibliographical references and index.

   ISBN 0-87584-326-3 (acid-free paper) (hc)

   ISBN 0-87584-567-3 (pbk)

   1. Investment banking—United States.   2. Investment banking—
European Economic Community countries.   3. Investment banking—
Japan.   4. Banks and banking, International.   I. Title.
HG4930.5.S57   1993
332.1'5—dc20
                                                                    92-237⁵
                                                                       CII

Printed in the United States of America
98 97 96 95 94   5 4 3 2 1   (pbk)

The paper used in this publication meets the requirements of the American
National Standard for Permanence of Paper for Printed Library Materials
Z39.49-1984.

Contents

Acknowledgments

I n writing this book I have relied on many sources, most of them people. I am especially indebted to Professor Ingo Walter of New York University and INSEAD, with whom I co-teach a constantly changing course for MBAs called Global Banking and Capital Markets, and with whom I have co-authored two academic volumes on the subject. Professor Walter is also my partner in a London-based consulting firm, Large, Smith & Walter, which has now completed its second year of working with senior executives of British, Swiss, Japanese, and German financial institutions on the formulation and implementation of effective strategies. Every aspect of the issues explored in this book has been the subject of lengthy discussion between us as we have labored to understand (and stay up to date on) all the fine points of global financial services.

I am grateful too for many lessons learned from our other partner, Andrew Large, formerly a senior general manager of the Swiss Bank Corporation, and now the head of the Securities and Investment Board, the chief securities regulatory body in the United Kingdom. Andrew was always ready to de-Americanize our viewpoints and enlarge our perspective. He was also a great source of introductions to interesting clients and friends throughout Europe.

Although I retired as a general partner of Goldman, Sachs & Co. in December 1987, I am still a limited partner of the firm and remain in touch with many of my former international colleagues and partners. I declare a bias toward the firm, but have not attempted to apply its strengths and virtues as I know them to the investment banking industry as a whole. It wouldn't be accurate to do so. I am especially grateful to my partner (and former international colleague) Michael Coles for reading the manuscript and offering many valuable suggestions. I have also had much support from former colleagues William Brown, John Ehara, Gene Fife, Henry James, and others. I am appreciative of the invaluable and uncomplaining support of Mary Elizabeth Poje and the Goldman Sachs research librarians.

Finally, I am blessed with a large circle of friends on the faculty at New York University and other academic institutions in Europe and Japan; they have taught me a great deal. I received much help from Professors Larry White, once a member of the Federal Home Loan Bank Board; Tony Saunders, an active consultant to Poland on banking issues; David Rogers, the author of *The Future of American Banking*; Jean Dermine of INSEAD, editor of *European Banking in the 1990s*; Jonathan Story, also of INSEAD, an expert on the metamorphosis of Soviet-style communism; Horst Siebert, president of the Kiel Institute for World Economics and a member of the German Council of Economic Advisors; Clas Wiborg of the University of Gottenburg; Ernst Kilgus, director of the Swiss Banking Institute of the University of Zurich and his associate director Christine Hirszowicz; and Tad Kobayashi and Yui Kimura of the International University of Japan.

Any errors, of course, are all mine.

PART I
THE UNITED STATES: SURVIVING THE DECLINE

The past decade has been an extraordinary one for American banking and finance, perhaps comparable only to the years just before and after the crash of 1929. During that time, a small number of large and powerful banks rode a wave of easy money and good times into a brief period of frenzied overspeculation, which was followed by a market break and a long, painful decline in the real economy. These events brought great distress to the banking system, which was radically reformed by Congress as a result. The large banks, which were much criticized at the time for their role in the crisis, had their freedom sharply curtailed and were turned into regulated public utilities.

Forty years later, in the 1970s, the banks remained much the same as they were after the passage of the Banking Act of 1933. Regulation restricted their activities and the rates they could pay for deposits. Banks were safe, but dull. The large ones concentrated on competing with each other for domestic corporate loans and international business. Some complained that they were missing out on opportunities to expand their businesses into other states and into other services such as investment banking and insurance. But Congress was not interested in bank reform, and proposals for change found little support.

In the 1970s, however, the stable financial environment of the United States began to change drastically. In 1971, the fixed relationship between the dollar and gold was broken, and exchange rates were allowed to be set by the market. Inflation accelerated and the dollar weakened, pressuring interest rates upward. The oil price shock of 1973 pushed both inflation and interest rates well into double digits for the first time in memory. The banks began to recycle huge deposits from the oil-producing countries into term loans for third world countries staggered by the rising cost of imported oil. High inflation destabilized monetary controls, and the volatility of financial market instruments increased considerably.

1

The bank regulatory structure governing deposit rates no longer worked. Mutual funds, which paid market rates of interest, were established, and bank and savings and loan depositors flocked to them. Money was soon being sucked out of the traditional savings institutions. The large S&L industry was the first to be squeezed, and it responded by appealing to Congress. Regulations were passed that allowed the S&Ls to pay competitive interest rates on their government-insured deposits and to invest in higher-returning, but riskier, assets.

The banks too were permitted to pay higher rates on deposits, though this cut into their profits. They began to rely on what they hoped was better management and smarter (i.e., riskier) lending to overcome unprofitability. Meanwhile, many bank clients were issuing commercial paper and other securities in the New York and London capital markets at lower costs than the banks could offer, a practice that pressured banks on the lending side of the balance sheet.

The changed economic landscape created the disintermediation, weakened the banks and S&Ls, and eventually drove them into dangerous lending practices. Government regulators, of which there are a great many, failed to understand what was going on, or were powerless to prevent the situation from getting worse. The management of many of these institutions was either unaware of the problems or unable to control them. The result was the destruction of much of the S&L industry by the end of the 1980s, at an all-in cost to the taxpayer of about $500 billion, or about $2,000 for every person in the country. No wonder the deposit insurance system has been described by economist Ingo Walter as a clever program "to provide for the privatization of profits by the socialization of risk."

The damage was not confined to the S&Ls. Many commercial banks also failed or had to be rescued by the government, more than at any time since the 1930s. The Federal Deposit Insurance Corporation's (FDIC) resources were soon exhausted and had to be replenished from the Treasury. Most banks, of course, survived without FDIC assistance. But those banks that only narrowly escaped being closed down or sold became mere shadows of themselves. Mighty American money-center banks, not long ago the largest and most respected in the world, also fell. Their profits and credit ratings deteriorated sharply, curtailing their ambitions and their global reach. Their places were taken by powerful foreign institutions, whose access to capital and profitable businesses seemed to have increased while their U.S. counterparts were sinking. British, German, French, Swiss, and, most of all, Japanese banks began to encroach on the U.S. market, by investing in American banks and by increasing the size and aggressiveness of their U.S. lending efforts. By 1992, according to a report by Robert McCauley and Rama Seth published by the Federal Reserve Bank of New York, foreign banks accounted for approximately 45% of all commercial and industrial loans made to U.S. borrowers.

The banks had another problem. While they were strapped and not expanding very fast, the capital markets were growing at exceptional rates. Traditional bond and stock market activity rose sixfold during the 1980s, but that was modest in comparison to the growth in mutual funds, commercial paper, and mortgage-backed securities, the direct consequences of disintermediation. The largest growth in capital market activity, however, was in the government securities sector, which expanded by $3 trillion to finance the ever-growing federal budget deficit. Although banks could participate in the government bond market, they were prohibited at the beginning of the 1980s from competing in all other sectors of the securities market. Even though healthy banks gained regulatory relief by the end of the decade, during one of the greatest periods of capital market expansion ever, banks remained on the sidelines.

This extraordinary growth in capital market activity was a response to several virtually simultaneous developments. Deregulation of foreign exchange and capital controls around the world led to the formation of a global capital pool, which in turn led to substantial market integration. Advancing computer technology allowed firms to process greater transaction volumes and to develop innovative securities and financial instruments such as interest rate and currency swaps, financial futures and options, and asset-backed securities. Tax cuts associated with the Reagan economic plan produced a burst of economic growth and a buoyant stock market, which tripled during the 1980s. Stock market activity, among other factors, fostered a merger boom, which was nourished by several potent and particularly American creations: junk bonds, leveraged buyouts, and other highly leveraged transaction loans.

U.S. investment banks were the prime beneficiaries of these developments. Their profits soared; they expanded rapidly and spread into many new businesses such as real estate, foreign exchange, and large-scale money management.

The banks' share of the market for financial services was declining, but the share attributed to investment banks was shooting ahead. Some of the Wall Streeters, of course, bungled this opportunity, dropping out of the top ranks because of scandal or mismanagement. Still, during the 1980s, several leading investment banks increased their influence and market power. Several carried more assets on their books than did many of the top ten commercial banks, a circumstance that would have been unthinkable a decade earlier. And the trading-oriented investment banks turned over all of their assets every day or two, not once a year as did most commercial banks.

All in all, the banks were losing serious ground to money market funds, the commercial paper market, foreign competitors, and investment banks. They were also losing to their former clients, large industrial corporations such as General Electric, American Express, Ford Motor Company, and

Sears Roebuck, which had acquired or beefed up financial subsidiaries that were now offering competitive products and services.

Some banks, overwhelmed by this competition, failed and were closed down. Others, including several once-great banking names like Continental Illinois, First National Bank of Dallas, and Bank of New England were forced into financial restructuring at the FDIC's expense. Still others, like Bank of America, retrenched through downsizing and specialization. Some reorganized through mergers with other large banks. And some, such as J.P. Morgan and Bankers Trust, moved into the mainstream of capital market activity and investment banking after the Federal Reserve finally cracked and allowed bank participation in the securities business. This participation was permitted through a loophole in the Glass-Steagall Act—a piece of legislation that was still on the books after almost 60 years, despite a concerted, but ultimately unsuccessful, attempt by Congress in 1991 to repeal it.

Most of the larger American banks have had to restructure themselves. As their capital was eroded by loan losses, it had to be replaced—in many cases, again and again. Management changes, asset sales, massive staff layoffs, and branch closings were everyday events. Virtually every bank in the country was forced to remake itself, often radically, in ways that would never have been considered in the 1970s.

The first thesis of this book is that the turning point has finally been reached—that the U.S. banking industry is on its way to recovering its power and influence. What has emerged, however, is a vastly changed industry, one that has reshaped itself to maximize its competitiveness and long-term chances of survival. Bankers of all types have learned to respond to exceptional competition from outside their own sector of the industry, something few industries do successfully. The industry's people are different too. High-level American bankers today are hardened survivors, veterans of arduous restructuring programs, cost-cutting efforts, and substantial retraining. They are performance-oriented and profit-minded, and many are optimistic about the future.

The new configuration of retail banking in the United States is that of a large, state-of-the-art transactions-processing factory, which handles a broad mix of imaginative and well-marketed consumer financial products at very low cost. Impressive economies of scale are found in these organizations. Funds generated from deposits or the sale of investment products are recycled into credit card and other high-return consumer loans, or into small and mid-sized commercial loans. Branches are out; automated teller machines (ATMs), banking by phone, and various new forms of plastic are in. Expensive international operations are unnecessary for the success of the business because retail banking is not global, but national or regional. Large corporate customers are ignored because there is no money to be made from lending to them.

The new shape of wholesale banking is also radically different. Its principal orientation is toward global capital markets, where client transactions are executed with investors, not carried on the bank's books. Proficiency in capital markets requires real-time knowledge of all the world's major financial markets, as well as trading skills, distribution capability, and the ability to manage and hedge all kinds of financial risks. Size (beyond a considerable minimum amount of capital and personnel) is not important. Talent, adaptability, resourcefulness, and networks are. Tomorrow's wholesale banking is today's investment banking with better manners, more client services, and longer-term relationships. Needless to say, U.S. commercial banks, long denied access to investment banking services, are at a disadvantage in competing with the major Wall Street and City of London houses for wholesale business; but for those that are determined enough, such as Bankers Trust and J.P. Morgan, the disadvantages should not be overwhelming or long lasting. Nevertheless, the number of top U.S. investment banks has been winnowed down to fewer than a dozen as a result of a decade of tough competition and emphasis on market performance. To this number will be added another three or four from the ranks of those commercial banks seeking to specialize in wholesale finance. The businesses of the top investment and wholesale banks will surely converge, but only a small number of each will survive today's competitive battering in the wholesale markets.

Power and influence in the new banking configurations will be measured, as it always has been, in terms of dollar volume of transactions arranged, processed, or dealt with at competitive prices in the market. Power in finance comes with market share and concentration.

In retail banking, concentration is beginning to occur in meaningful ways as banks cross state borders, credit cards are distributed nationally, and various forms of electronic banking proliferate. Before long, a few retail "super banks" ought to emerge in the United States, each handling a much larger share of the total national market than ever before. Having a dozen or so large national retail banks would lift banking concentration ratios in the United States toward the levels found in Europe and Japan, increase the influence of these banks on the market as a whole (and vice versa), and add to their stability, without diminishing market efficiency and competition.

Wholesale banking power is also a reflection of concentration. The present relatively high levels of concentration in the U.S. investment-banking industry (the top ten firms represented about 60% of combined new issue and merger and acquisition volume in 1991) will not be much affected by adding the top half-dozen or so syndicated loan arrangers to the full list of competitors making up the market. There are still more than 12,000 banks in the United States, but only a handful have serious ambitions to become top wholesale bankers in the near term. The main area of change in wholesale banking market-share concentration, however, lies in the international arena.

This brings us to the book's second thesis—that as American banks are recovering from the problems of the past few years, the principal European and Japanese banks are just beginning to experience many of the same problems.

As a result of disintermediation, regulatory changes, new competition, and large exposures to bad loans at home and abroad, many large and once-aggressive international banks are pulling back from global competition to repair the damages. Indeed, these banks must not only restore their balance sheets and capital positions, but also begin to learn from the U.S. banking experience. American banks now know that the competition created by open markets tends to force traditional corporate wholesale business off the balance sheets of banks into securities markets. This business in turn tends to be replaced with lesser-quality corporate, real estate, or other loans, which can lead to problems later on, especially during recessions. European and Japanese banks, therefore, must learn to compete in securities markets with top investment banks from the United States and the United Kingdom for the business of their own clients. This will not be easy.

The process of adjustment in the international community has begun, but it cannot move swiftly in large, bureaucratic, change-resisting banks that have been protected by domestic regulation from the main force of global competition. In Japan adjustment is further impeded by regulatory restrictions that still prevent banks from having fully competitive access to the securities markets.

In today's American wholesale market, banks and investment banks are virtually the same thing. This is not so in continental Europe, despite traditions of universal banking, where most wholesale business with corporate clients is still in the form of bank loans and where securities market activities are considered less important. Also, despite efforts at "Europeanization" on the part of many large European wholesale banks during the past five years in the run-up to 1992, only five Europeans were among the top fifteen providers of international wholesale banking services in 1991. Nine of the leaders were U.S. banks or investment banks; one was a Japanese securities firm. In Japan, scandals and huge loan losses related to the collapse of the stock and real estate markets have also significantly weakened the competitive capability of the leading banks and securities firms, at least for the time being. No one, of course, should underestimate the potential of the Japanese to make a powerful recovery; though to do so would be a substantial achievement.

As we find our way into the 1990s, we'll discover what we mean by the "new world economy." We do not now know how this will emerge, but we do know that it will have resulted from many profound changes having been worked upon the old world economy.

The effort to create a single European market for all goods and services, operating on the principles of free-market capitalism, will bring many changes, not all of which can easily be foreseen. It is likely to increase opportunities for American firms, which have already been extremely successful in penetrating indigenous wholesale European markets. The new free-market notions have many regulatory implications, mostly of the sort that threaten to strip away market practices that protect insiders against outsiders, and various forms of privilege that have long been the rights of controlling shareholders. After these obstructions have been removed, the winners will be those firms that get there first with the best service at the best price. Today, not all European business is awarded that way, especially in financial services. Indeed, some European financial institutions are concerned enough about events back home to want a "second leg" in North America.

The other uncertainty in Europe is how the economic development of Eastern Europe will unfold. It is inconceivable that the world's governments will supply even the minimal amount of capital required to bring this vast area into alignment with the rest of the world. The combined $24 billion Russian relief program announced by President Bush in April 1992 was far less than the Russians claimed they needed, and the International Monetary Fund (IMF) noted that it was well short of the $44 billion it estimated was needed annually by all of the states of the former Soviet Union. Somehow private capital will have to play the major role in rebuilding what was once communist Europe, a role that can only be filled by the world's major wholesale banking organizations.

For example, Goldman Sachs is already involved, though perhaps only on a preliminary basis, as adviser to the Russian Republic in its search for Western investment capital. Today we may think that such an undertaking is next to impossible, considering the dire straits of the Russian and the other ex-Soviet economies. But for most of the 1980s, many observers (including me) said the same thing about Mexico. Yet by 1992, several large Mexican privatizations had taken place, led by U.S. wholesale banking firms and involving extensive recapitalization of entire industries, merger and acquisition transactions, and public offerings of billions of dollars of securities. Surely the new world economy of the 1990s will have to rely more on these kinds of wholesale banking skills than on low-cost loans from large Japanese or European banks. Along with that shift in reliance, much of the perceived power in the banking world will also shift.

One of my colleagues at New York University, Robert Kavesh, is regarded by many members of the faculty as one of the institution's great teachers. He once explained to me the secret of his success. "Students have a hard time understanding the significance of anything," he said, "unless they realize, first, that everything that happens is related to something that happened in the past, and second, that everything that happens is also related to everything else that is happening at the same time." To understand where banking is going in the 1990s, we have to understand it in the 1980s and before. But we also have to understand how it relates to what else is going on in the main competitive playing fields of Europe and Japan.

Accordingly, this book is divided into four parts, the first three of which deal with the background, evolution, and current state of the banking and securities industries in the United States, Europe, and Japan. Part II examines the many aspects of European financial systems that are dissimilar to those in the United States, and illustrates the rich variety of possible strategies that European banks have so far identified. Part III brings out the enormous differences in de facto financial market regulation among Japan, the United States, and the EEC, and emphasizes that convergence with the rest of the world is likely to be unavoidable, but painful. Part IV analyzes what it takes to compete effectively in the present and the new world economies. Here I discuss how effective strategies are created, how they are implemented and, finally, how competitive success is to be measured.

1
LEGACIES OF THE 1980s

Banking and finance in the 1990s has been greatly affected by the many dramatic political, economic, and marketplace events of the 1980s. Much that we see in financial markets, products, and competition today are legacies of the 1980s.

The legacies of the 1980s in domestic affairs are closely interrelated: Reaganomics and its twin deficits, a speculative era in finance and real estate that produced a boom in mergers and acquisitions but ended in the world's greatest market crash, the devastation of the savings and loan industry, and, at the decade's end, a nasty economic slump and crises in the banking and insurance industries. The decade also brought important changes for U.S. firms in the international scene, as they discovered that the world of finance was more closely linked across international borders than ever before and that these linkages exposed Americans to the threat of large amounts of unstable foreign investment, which could come and go with the fate of the dollar. Globalization of financial markets not only produced new opportunities for American firms, but also left them vulnerable to tough competition from large, modernizing European universal banks and from the new banking and investment banking colossi of Japan.

The 1980s began in a recession, which followed a frightening period of rising inflation that peaked at about 14% in early 1981 and pushed interest rates on three-month Treasury bills over 16%. There was also deep discouragement abroad at the fumbling efforts of the Carter administration to provide leadership in economic policy and foreign affairs. In November 1979, Iranian revolutionaries held U.S. embassy personnel as hostages, and Iran cut off oil shipments, which raised the price of crude to $19 a barrel, 70% higher than a year earlier. And in December 1979, in apparent disregard of the will or the capacity of the United States, the Soviet Union invaded Afghanistan. The price of gold (long an index of worry and dread) shot up to $850 per ounce, more than four times its level of a year before.

Contracts covering the sale of 17 million tons of grain to the Soviet Union were canceled. The dollar sank in foreign exchange markets.

The Federal Reserve Board brought about the recession. Led by Paul Volcker, its chairman since July 1979, it took the usual steps to combat inflation by raising interest rates. But these efforts were not successful, so in a sudden move on October 6, 1979, the board reversed its traditional practice of trying to manage the money supply through the setting of interest rates to one in which the volume of the money supply itself would be managed and interest rates could go where the market took them. William Greider referred to the change as "one without precedent in modern experience":

> In a few short months, the Fed had nearly doubled the price of money. Despite the technical complexities, that was the essential meaning of Volcker's operating shift—the dramatic ratcheting upward in interest rates. A few months before, the governors had been arguing over half-percent increases. Now the Fed was pushing the Federal Funds rate from 11% towards 20%. And other short-term rates followed in step.[1]

The Fed raised the discount rate from 11% to 12% on October 6. Bond and stock markets plunged in their heaviest single day of trading since the 1929 crash. The result was an instantaneous leap in interest rates and bond market volatility. In the week between October 5 and October 12, one-year Treasury rates leapt from 11.02% to 12.50%. Subsequently, "real" interest rates (i.e., nominal rates minus the inflation rate), which actually had been negative before the policy switch, began to turn positive, reaching 3% to 4% in 1981 before beginning to stabilize. These steps brought the economy to a halt.

A year later, in November 1980, when Ronald Reagan was elected president, the economy was still being wrung dry. GNP growth over the past year had declined to minus 0.2%. Unemployment was 7.6%, up from 5.8% only one year before. The dollar was trading near its lowest postwar values against the Deutschemark, the Swiss franc, the yen, and even the pound, where reaction to the first full year of Margaret Thatcher—during which taxes had been cut, foreign exchange controls removed, and harsh free-market economic policies put to work—was extremely positive. It was a tough backdrop to a re-election campaign. Carter went on television to talk about the "national malaise" that had sapped American spirits; he gave every impression that his spirit was the most sapped of all.

Reagan had been considered a radical from the far right during his previous try for the presidency, but people were getting used to his soft voice and unthreatening, homey touch, which sounded better as conditions grew worse. It was time for a change, even if it meant electing as president a right-wing movie star who most people thought was an intellectual weakling.

REAGANOMICS: VISION OR VOODOO?

Reagan's campaign floated on a tide of old-fashioned personal values and fundamentalist economic ideology. Though his ideas were portrayed as conservative, many were in fact radical and even populist. They appealed to blue-collar workers as well as to conservative philosophers. The Reagan platform consisted of three basic ideas: Americans should have more personal liberty and attempt to recover their traditional values; America's power in the world had to be strengthened substantially, especially with regard to the Soviet Union; and the American economy had to be returned to the private sector where it could perform better, free of growth-killing government interference.

These ideas, simple enough in broad concept (if not in execution), spawned the series of economic policies that came to be called "Reaganomics." Large tax cuts and a substantial defense buildup were enacted within the first several months of the Reagan administration, when the president's popularity was so great that even the Democrats hoped for some reflected glory. The package involved a 27% personal tax cut over a three-year period, higher depreciation allowances for corporations, an approximately 14% annual increase in military spending, and an effort to limit other government spending without making substantial cuts in existing programs. It was clear at the time that these policies, in combination, would produce a record budget deficit, initially in the area of $70 billion (the White House had a much lower estimate). So large a deficit was unheard of, and surely would have been condemned as the work of an irresponsible radical, had it not been brought about by the most conservative American to occupy the office of president since Herbert Hoover. It helped, of course, that the economy was in deep recession.

From the Supply-Side

Still, the Reagan team had to have some justification for taking such a large risk with the economy. It did. It was the theory of "supply-side" economics, which claimed that tax cuts would produce a surge of capital investment that would increase the supply and quality of goods and services in the economy, and the increased supply would lower prices enough to stimulate the demand for the goods. Increased demand, produced this way, would give rise to noninflationary growth in the economy. Tax reduction would also give workers a greater incentive to earn money because they could keep more of it. Therefore not only was there basic new growth to be gained, there was a bonus—citizens would work harder and productivity would increase. This doctrine has a respectable intellectual pedigree, going back to Adam Smith, John Stuart Mill, David Hume, and other classical economists. It has also drawn support from such well-known conservative economists as Milton Friedman, Arthur Burns, Herbert Stein, and Murray Weidenbaum. Most modern economists did not like the idea very much, however, and they held to the doctrine established by John Maynard Keynes: the way to make the economy grow was to stimulate the demand side of the macroeconomic equation. Supply-side economists, incidentally, did not necessarily endorse huge deficits; in general they viewed the remedy as beneficial only in the right dosages.

Modern supply-side thinking can be traced to Robert Mundell, an economist from the University of Chicago and later Columbia University, whose disciple, Arthur Laffer, became the new faith's most effective promoter. One day in 1974, supposedly during excited discussion of supply-side policies with future Reagan policy advisers at a Washington restaurant, Laffer sketched a graph showing the effect on government tax revenues of increasing tax rates. When you start at zero tax and increase it to 100% of income, the result is a curve that shows revenues ascending from the lower left, peaking, and then descending sharply to the lower right as tax rates approach 100%. This was the famous "Laffer Curve." It meant that if tax rates were higher than the rates at which the maximum amount of tax revenues occurred (the peak of the curve), then a reduction in tax rates could actually increase tax revenues. The notion of supply-side economics as a whole was considered extremely simplistic by many prominent economists. MIT professor Paul Samuelson, a Nobel Prize winner, and then perhaps the dean of Keynesian economists in America, wrote a paper in the 1970s entitled "Why They Are Laughing at Laffer." Harvard professor Martin Feldstein, a chairman of the Council of Economic Advisors during the middle period of the Reagan administration, also derided supply-side thinking in a paper presented to the American Economics Association in 1987 called "Old Truths and New Claims." Things just didn't work that way in our complex, modern economy, the traditionalists said, even though there was clear evidence that in the early 1960s a similar tax cut had produced a six-year period of uninterrupted economic growth.

Nevertheless, a cohort of supply-siders soon emerged to take up the fight for the Laffer Curve. This original group included Irving Kristol, a conservative intellectual associated with the quarterly publication *The Public Interest* and New York University, journalist Robert Bartley of *The Wall Street Journal*, and Jude Wanniski, a free-lance commentator. The emerging political dynamo Jack Kemp and his sharp-witted and articulate economic adviser, Paul Craig Roberts, were also charter members. The group promoted the idea of a tax cut zealously and persuasively. Ultimately their efforts came to the attention of Ronald Reagan, who endorsed the Kemp-Roth tax reduction bill, then stalled before Congress.[2]

As a candidate for the 1980 presidential nomination, George Bush sided with the traditionalists, labeling the president's supply-side ideas "voodoo economics," suitable only for the fanatical and the superstitious. In ideological terms, Senator Daniel Patrick Moynihan described the supply-side crowd "as being to conservatives what anarchists were to liberals."

Within seven months of taking office, according to Moynihan, the agenda of the Reagan administration had effectively ended—its main work on tax and defense policy was done, and there was no money left for anything else. Moynihan is a worthy observer, one whose first career was spent as a Harvard professor and author and whose second has been in political office, both appointed and elected. Reaganomics, he said, "had a hidden agenda":

> It came out in a television speech sixteen days after President Reagan's inauguration, when he stated "There were always those who told us that taxes couldn't be cut until spending was reduced. Well, you know we can lecture our children about extravagance until we run out of voice and breath. Or, we can cut their extravagance by simply reducing their allowance." The President genuinely wanted to reduce the size of the federal government. He genuinely thought it was riddled with "waste, fraud and abuse," with things that needn't or shouldn't be done. He was astute enough to know that there are constituencies for such activities, and he thought it pointless to try to argue them out of existence, one by one. He would instead create a fiscal crisis in which, willy-nilly, they would be driven out of existence.[3]

Reagan did not offer to cut government spending in the beginning; there was a catholic belief that the revenues would be made up from forced reduction in the rate of future spending and from the Laffer effect. The administration's first budget submission showed a deficit of $27 billion for fiscal 1981, a balanced budget in 1983, and a $93 billion surplus in 1985, even without full achievement of its spending reduction goals.[4]

Moynihan noted that, contrary to what voters expected, "Mr. Reagan made big government cheap." His programs were so popular because "for seventy-five cents worth of taxes, you got a dollar's worth of government programs." Moynihan added that the Reagan team knew perfectly well what they were doing; they would give the country a welcome tax cut, boost defense spending, blame Congress for the deficit that followed, and take away a major political bonus: Congress would be paralyzed. It could create no new programs and would have to dismantle some of its more liberal works from the past. The Democratic party would fall apart, having nothing to offer its traditional constituency of labor, liberals, minorities, and the poor.[5]

The Reagan Revolution

"It was the greatest economic expansion in history," claimed Martin Anderson, one of Reagan's longest-serving, truest-believing economic advisers, who worked with him on his early campaigns in the 1970s, and served in his first administration until 1982. "Wealth poured in from the factories of the United States, and Americans got richer and richer. During the five years between November 1982 and November 1987 more wealth and services were produced than in any like period in history."

Anderson believes that Reaganomics was a great success: investment in military preparedness paid off, excessive reliance on the welfare state was cut way back without destroying necessary and appropriate programs, attitudes about work and productivity changed, inflation dropped, and market prices of securities rose. Confidence was restored to the economy and in the American government. The dollar rose sharply until it had to be restrained and turned around in 1985.

Free-market economics was given a boost as never before. Gradually, throughout the world, people were expressing greater confidence in the private sector than in the public sector. Governments were coming to be viewed as wasteful and inefficient. Left alone, democratic capitalism was seen to produce superior results. The essence of the "Reagan Revolution," according to Anderson, was the belief that the free market, with all its faults, works better than any alternative. This notion would survive, he declared in 1988, even though the Reagan deficit admittedly had become too large and an economic slowdown loomed ahead. For the revolution to continue, Anderson added, the economic policies of the Reagan administration would have to be continued, but there would need to be a balanced-budget amendment to the Constitution, a movement toward sounder money, and a greater role for gold.

The alternatives to these free-market policies were central economic planning, typical of socialist states, and national industrial policies, used by the industrial democracies, especially in Europe. These policies had created a web of subsidies, government ownership of industrial properties, and stifling regulation. By the end of the 1970s, it was clear that such policies were suppressing growth and national income. People began to look more closely at the Reagan and Thatcher approaches, in which the "market" (i.e., the private sector) allocates where the money goes according to basic economic laws of supply and demand. The system was working in Thatcher's Britain, where she had gone a step further by selling off government-owned industrial holdings to make them more competitive. The French had a try at it too, then others followed suit. In 1985, the European

Economic Community (EEC) adopted a plan for large-scale deregulation, which would create a "single market" for goods and services within Europe by 1992.

Also, in 1985, Mikhail Gorbachev came into office and had to face a high-tech arms race with the United States that his crumbling economy simply could not cope with. The result was a radical change in Soviet international policies. By the time of Reagan's departure from office, Gorbachev had orchestrated new disarmament initiatives, as well as devolution of political authority within the Soviet Union and its Eastern European satellites. Ultimately, this led to the collapse of Soviet-led communism in Eastern Europe and the end of the 45-year Cold War, clearly a major policy success of the Reagan administration. Only in China did communism still prevail, and even there it had been highly transformed by graftings of regional capitalism and entrepreneurship.

Deficits, Deficits

Revolutions, like new cars, have to be sold, and never were there more skillful promoters and makers of illusion than within the Reagan White House. We were alerted to this in December 1981 by the premature public confessions of David Stockman, Reagan's first budget director, who claimed that Reaganomics was a fraud designed to benefit the rich and that horrendous deficits would last for "as far as the eye could see." The Reaganauts claimed to have a magic theory to make the numbers work out, but, according to Stockman, who controlled the Washington numbers factory at the time, they were making things up as they went along.

Stockman claimed that the president was a "terminal optimist" who, supported by a cadre of true believers like Marty Anderson, would permit no deviation from the original supply-side ideas. After 1983, Stockman added,

> the case for a major tax increase was overwhelming, unassailable, and self-evident. Not to raise taxes when all other avenues for raising revenues were closed was a willful act of ignorance and grotesque irresponsibility. In the entire twentieth-century fiscal history of the nation, there has been nothing to rival it.[6]

Sometimes we learn how important a president's propaganda support is only when the machine is turned off and the power is used to bolster his successor. Out of office, Reagan no longer seems a credible economic statesman or theorist. Reaganomics, now undefended, is judged by tangible evidence to be a hopeless tangle of debt and a host of unsolved economic problems rather than an enduring legacy which will affect us well into the next century.

The only enduring part seems to be the large deficit, which has nullified many of the supply-siders' hopes for lasting respectability. The Laffer effect did not occur. The administration came to depend on Congress for spending cuts, which did not materialize to the extent needed. Congress did cut some programs, but not enough to prevent the deficit from growing much as Stockman said it would. An increase in social security withholding in 1986 produced a surplus in the social-security trust fund, which the government has used to reduce the amount of government borrowing needed to fund the deficit. But still the deficit grows and grows in absolute terms. For the fiscal year that ended in September 1992, eleven years after the Reagan tax cut, estimates made in January 1992 showed the deficit reaching $400 billion (even after applying $60 billion or so of social-security trust fund surpluses), yet another record. Their estimate was $120 billion greater than Budget Director Richard Darman's predictions of a year earlier, and was completely out of line with expectations following the much-touted White House–Congressional budget negotiations during the summer of 1990, which were to provide a cumulative deficit reduction of $500 billion over five years. Darman expressed "shock" at the enlarged deficit estimate and blamed the difference on the recession and "technical re-estimates by the Treasury." Mr. Darman and his deficit seemed to be made out of "Teflon," said *The Wall Street Journal.*

With the deficit at this level, equal to about 6.3% of GNP (double the level three years earlier, and the highest since World War II), across-the-board spending cuts required under the Gramm-Rudman-Hollings Budget Balancing Act would have been necessary. Gramm-Rudman was passed in 1985 as a major effort to curtail the deficit. Though crude, it at least frightened Congress into restricting spending programs to avoid triggering the mandatory, pro-rata cuts. But the law was rescinded during the deficit reduction negotiations in 1990. Now, there is nothing to hold the budget in check. Despite strong evidence that the deficit is now out of control, tax relief for the middle class and other vote-getting spending proposals by both parties were abundant during the election campaigns of 1992.

The deficit has to be financed by increasing the national debt. During the eight Reagan years, the national debt tripled from the level it had taken 192 years to reach. The money has to be borrowed (or, some would say, just printed) in the government bond market, where it has the double effect of soaking up about three-fourths of all private sector savings and keeping real long-term interest rates high. During the tax-cut-led expansion of the 1960s, the government only absorbed about 10% of savings and real interest rates were nominal. The combination of low savings and high interest rates has become America's economic Achilles' heel. It strangles the new capital investment in plant and equipment needed to invigorate and sustain the economy. This is why some economists, such as Harvard's Benjamin Friedman, claim that the deficit is "ruining the country."

But after ten years, Americans appear to be used to high deficits, and most financial commentators feel it is useless to keep complaining about it. Apparently no one cares anymore.

The deficit (technically, the "fiscal deficit") is also responsible for the *other* deficit, the "trade deficit." The United States's early burst of economic growth in 1982–1985, while the rest of the world's economies were flat and the dollar was rising, sucked in an extraordinary amount of imports. The U.S. imbalance between its exports and its imports, about $25 billion when Reagan took office, topped $100 billion four years later before peaking at $153 billion in 1986. In 1990, the trade deficit was still above $100 billion, despite a weak dollar and the U.S. recession.

As the trade deficit grew, more dollars flowed abroad to pay for the difference between exports and imports. In time these dollars found their way back into the country in the form of investments, usually in government securities. These investments were very attractive to foreigners, who actually bought more than they had trade-generated dollars for, tapping into savings to do so and buying the dollars in the foreign exchange market. The fiscal deficit heightened the importance of this diversion of excess foreign savings (especially from Japan and Germany) to bolster depleted U.S. savings in financing the budgetary imbalance. In time, U.S. financial markets became "addicted" to foreign capital to finance the deficit. The term is apt, but overstated: it only means that without the foreign money, public and private borrowings would have to occur at somewhat higher interest rates to clear the market.

The trade deficit has to be funded, however, and each year Americans pay out more than $30 billion in interest to foreign creditors, which drains the domestic savings pool further. Payments to foreigners are not automatically reinvested in the United States, as interest payments to domestic creditors are. Foreigners may decide to keep the money in a bank outside the country, or buy Eurobonds with it, but ultimately the dollars will find their way back to the United States. What goes out must come back, though not necessarily promptly. Also, if the United States appears to be an attractive place to invest money, foreigners may withdraw their domestic savings and add to the investment flow generated by the trade account. Such discretionary investment funds, however, can be withdrawn from the U.S. market on very short notice.

So far, the world has continued to invest in the United States and until recently has not appeared to be especially concerned about its level of foreign debt. In the period 1985–1989, foreign portfolio investment in the United States exceeded disinvestment by about $400 billion; however, in 1990, there was a sharp drop in such investment, forcing the current account to be balanced in other ways.

In 1982, the United States was the world's largest creditor. By 1985, because of the trade deficits, it had become a debtor nation, and by 1987, it was the world's largest debtor, passing Brazil. To keep the foreign finan-cial situation in balance, U.S. interest rates have to be high enough to attract investment away from foreign markets, which means American monetary policy has become hostage, in an unprecedented degree, to for-eign influences and pressures.

The Inflationary Undertow

The vast amount of debt has created a powerful inflationary undertow. Residual budget deficits in the range of 5% to 6% of GNP are extremely worrisome to those who fear that the only real enemy the U.S. economy has is its own mismanagement. The U.S. economy can be destroyed only from within, according to this view, by inflation; and continuing large def-icits contain a dangerous inflationary bias. Among the people who share these views are members of the Federal Reserve Board, now led by infla-tion-hater Alan Greenspan. The only way to offset the stuck accelerator in the car, he figures, is to keep the brake stuck too. The resulting ride may not be smooth, comfortable, or fuel efficient, but at least it will prevent the car from exceeding the speed limit and killing all the passengers. To coun-teract the Reagan deficits, the Fed has given us high real interest rates, which remain at 4% or so more than a decade after the get-tough policy change effected by the Fed in 1979. Such high levels of real rates have kept growth rates low: in 1982–1986, annual real growth of GNP averaged 2.8% (or 4.5%, if, like Martin Anderson, you drop eleven months of the reces-sion year 1982 and include eleven months of 1987), but for the next five years, in 1987–1991, the average growth rate fell to about 1.7%.

Reaganomics was an experiment that worked in some respects and didn't in others. It was pushed for political advantage as well as to support an economic theory. Theories affecting economic policy, however, are dif-ficult to test through experimentation. Too many other events have inde-pendent effects on the test for the results to be conclusive, and you can't run the world twice. Does the free market work more efficiently than a state-controlled system? Sure, but in the United States, the comparison must be made between a mostly free market and a somewhat freer one, not between an unfree market and a totally free one.

We are aware by now that real free markets can be cruel to a great many people. Cut out government spending on mental institutions, for example, and the number of homeless people sleeping in the subways increases. Make industry supercompetitive and no one makes any money for a while, so companies lay off thousands of workers, many over forty, thus sharply increasing the number of people receiving unemployment or welfare pay-ments. Cut off funding for universities and tuitions become unaffordable. In the end, as columnist George Will says, society in America prefers a mild socialistic bias to its economic affairs. Reaganomics preached tough economic discipline, but softened it with inflationary deficits to float the economy over the difficult parts. It is inconceivable to most of us what the 1990–1991 recession would have been like without the huge federal deficit to counter its harsher aspects. Forcing a balanced budget on the country today would put it through a wringer like the one Poland has just gone through.

In any event, a decade after Reaganomics the economy was back where it started—in recession, with unemployment above 7% and financial casualties all over the place. The Reagan government, in the words of the London *Economist*, did a leveraged buyout of the country. A big dividend in the form of the tax cuts was financed by a vast increase in borrowing. In buyouts, the debt level becomes crippling (if not terminal) unless it is reduced substantially within a few years through cash flow and productivity improvements provided by the buyout. Certainly, there is no room for waste or frills, but beyond that, something basic has to change to produce more revenues so the debt can be reduced quickly, before it hardens. If this does not happen, the buyout is a failure. So far, by buyout standards, Reaganomics is a failure.

But maybe things take a bit longer where governments are concerned. The deficit was shrinking as a percentage of GNP until 1990, when the recession and the refunding of the federal deposit insurance funds caused it to surge upward again. Perhaps it will begin to decline again when these temporary problems pass by. Total debt in the hands of the public rose during the Reagan years from 25% of GNP to more than 50% in 1992, but it had been higher than that at times during the 1950s. The problem with the economy, President Bush announced before the 1992 New Hampshire primaries, is the Fed's tight money policy, which restricts bank lending. Although the Fed has pushed interest rates to levels not seen in years— and rates may drop lower still—it is certainly not clear that what the economy needs is more debt.

As it recovers, the private sector will have a chance to present the second act of its play, in which thinned down, more competitive survivors start to produce productivity growth, create new jobs, and reverse the decline in the U.S. standard of living, as measured by per capita income. Most economists and financial people believe this will be the case, all things being equal, which they almost never are.

At present, however, we are still in a financial bind. There's no money left in the till for foreign aid to Eastern Europe, or for fighting the Iraqis again. (Perhaps Bush's most brilliant tour de force during the Persian Gulf War was to get other countries to pay for all but about $7 billion of its $60 billion cost.) Nor is there any money for fighting crime and drugs at home, or health insurance, or for education. Most of the burden for social services has been passed to state and local governments, many of which face either bankruptcy or unpopular tax hikes. These events come at the political expense of local officials, not at President Bush's, though he has had to eat his own memorable words about taxes. Fiscally paralyzed, governments have had to shrink, as Senator Moynihan predicted, making things very difficult for those who represent the Democratic party at the national level. They can only propose new programs if they also suggest tax increases, which experience to date indicates is politically suicidal. A poll taken during the summer of 1991 by the *New York Times* and CBS News showed that those claiming allegiance to the Republican party had grown since 1980 from 22% to 31%, while those claiming to be Democrats had declined from 42% to 34%, despite current economic conditions. On the other hand, polls taken a year later, after the Democratic Party Convention in July 1992, indicated that George Bush was blamed for the weak economy, that voters wanted more substantive actions to be taken to revive it, and that they were somewhat more willing to see tax increases if they could be sure that the money would be used to improve the country's long-term future.

Agent of Change

Thus Reaganomics has endowed the president of the United States (whoever he is) with an increasingly impecunious and declining public sector. Sooner or later, however, the earth will stir and tax increases will be proposed again so services thought necessary can continue. This is already happening at the state level, where a growing proportion of these services are now administered, and where the relative political importance of governors and state legislatures is also increasing, at the expense of federal officeholders.

One thing that can certainly be said about Reaganomics is that it was a fantastic agent of change in the field of finance. Market forces were released into the private sector, where they had a series of dramatic effects on financial communities in the United States and elsewhere in the world: 1) the United States' fiscal policies led directly to an explosion of government bond trading, financial market volatility (the trader's friend), and hedging with sophisticated new financial futures and options; 2) inflows of foreign capital accelerated the rate at which financial markets became globally integrated, creating both new opportunities and competitive problems for American financial firms; 3) growth in the economy created 18 million new jobs and $20 trillion of new goods and services,[7] though much of the profits were invested in securities and real estate rather than new productive assets; 4) stock prices tripled and bond prices surged as interest rates dropped after 1981; 5) the SEC permitted substantial deregulation of new-issue registration requirements, and competition for securities market and investment banking business intensified, leading to an era of unprecedented financial innovation and new technology, which greatly acceler ated trends toward securitization of financial assets previously held by banks and S&Ls; 6) Reaganomics supported deregulation, which led to restructuring of the banking, transportation, telecommunications, and other regulated industries; 7) deregulation also reduced the level and scope of antitrust enforcement, and accordingly, mergers and acquisitions proliferated, supplemented by leveraged buyouts, hostile bids, and junk bonds, all of which occurred without SEC interference; and 8) the spread of free-market economic policies to Western Europe, the third world, and, most recently, Eastern Europe and the Soviet Union has created an eager market for the financial skills developed in the United States during the 1980s.

Nothing grew as fast during the 1980s as financial transactions. These indeed owed a great deal to Reaganomics, and may be one of its least recognized but most lasting legacies.

MERGERS, BUYOUTS, JUNK BONDS, AND GREED

In June 1991, the Harvard Business School class of 1971 assembled in Soldiers Field for its twentieth reunion. On this occasion, the reuniting classmates organized a panel on leveraged buyouts (LBOs) and asked several of their number to contribute comments. A friend of mine named Brody, a senior investment banker from a highly respected firm, spoke first. He defended the LBO as a useful financing technique that had helped many companies increase productivity and shareholder value. He also pointed out that, as happened in speculative periods in the past, the LBO movement had run to excess and many failed companies were the result. He conceded that the fees paid out to bankers like himself might have been excessive, but, if so, things were now coming back to normal. The audience stirred restlessly. Brody asked for a show of hands: How many thought LBOs were bad for the economy? More than half did.

Brody was followed on the panel by another member of the class, a journalist who claimed he couldn't help but point out that Brody was "mea-culpa-ing" all the way to the bank. The journalist added that he found this to be a common attitude among his friends on Wall Street, who would say almost anything for a buck. The audience murmured agreement.

Then came a question period. Brody got creamed. Most of the questions were of the incriminating type, like "How could someone as smart as you possibly believe these deals could survive?" or, "Wasn't greed the main incentive for your getting involved with them?" Brody tried to defend himself, at first perhaps sounding a bit patronizing:

"Most of these deals were initiated by our clients, who asked us to represent them. We have a duty to help our clients and did so. We were able to assist them in making the most out of the deals they wanted to do. Naturally, we charged the market rate for our services, which our clients willingly paid."

The debate grew more heated. Brody's morals were questioned. He, his firm, and his industry were blamed for all of the abuses of the 1980s. He tried to explain:

"Look, these are transactions in a market. A market is just a place where people come to buy and sell things. Markets are not animate beings, they are neither ethical nor unethical. Humans who participate in markets are, of course, and they either trade or they don't depending on the individual circumstances. If they don't trade, for ethical reasons for example, they shouldn't be blamed for the actions of someone else who does trade."

The audience wasn't buying it. The smart guys down on Wall Street could squirm their way out of anything. Brody became progressively more uncomfortable. Finally the session ended, and he stepped down off the stage. There he saw a friend, a former colleague at his firm, who suggested that he was probably pretty glad that it was over.

"Peter," said Brody, "these people don't like me very much. And this is the Harvard Business School. What do you suppose the rest of the country thinks?"

The journalist, Jeff Madrick of NBC, added some comments in an op-ed piece in the *New York Times*. The basic point, he said, was that the group was envious, afraid, and angry. They were envious of the money their Wall Street classmates had made without having contributed much to the economy beyond shuffling paper around. They were afraid of the mess in the "real" economy, where so many of their own contemporaries were being laid off and where their own children starting out in business couldn't find good jobs. And they were angry at what had been left behind when the glory days were over. There was too much debt. Productivity was weak. Business investment was low. The educational system had gone to the dogs. Law and order were gone. The country had lost competitiveness. They themselves, graduates of the famous Harvard Business School, were doubtful of their own futures now and pessimistic. They were no longer the bright-eyed optimists of twenty years earlier. For this they were angry and wanted to blame someone.[8]

An Elusive Search for Perspective

The 1980s were at once dynamic, extravagant, and unreal. They were years of growth and change and controversy, but they were not unique when considered in historical perspective. They ended, predictably, in a slump—with the economy weakened by the speculative excesses and bankruptcies that inevitably follow roaring bull markets. The future never looks good from the bottom of a slump, which more than partly explained the anxieties of the class of 1971.

In some respects the market adjustments that ended the LBO and junk bond boom were crueler than previous ones. Companies no longer carried any fat to cushion against bad times. Heavy debt loads left little room for error during a recession. Performance alone was valued, though it could only be assessed in the short term. Loyalty and long service were no longer important. The free market, so glorified during the 1980s by the upwardly mobile class of 1971 and many others, can be pretty ugly when it turns against you.

The class of 1971 seemed to believe that the whole economy had been wrecked by unbridled speculation and the behavior of a comparatively small number of greedy, amoral individuals who, acting from positions of power, put their own interests ahead of those of society as a whole.

Could this be so? A $5 trillion economy of 250 million people wrecked by a handful of greedy Wall Streeters? Most of the things that make economies successful and competitive have to do with fundamentals such as the work ethic, the use of technology, the availability and cost of skilled labor and capital, and so forth. Financial techniques can indeed make a difference in both the availability and the cost of capital. Actually, during the 1980s, the availability of capital (as measured by the volume of completed corporate financings) increased sixfold, and the cost of capital (as reflected by the incremental cost of debt and equity) decreased considerably. The financial market, in other words, did its job—it generated an ample supply of capital, at a decreasing cost, for industry to invest during a time of growth. As during other similar periods in American history, there was some waste of capital in the process. Most of those who speculated excessively were rewarded with financial losses, but many innocent bystanders were also hurt by bankruptcies and layoffs.

Big Boom in Mergers

There was the merger boom, of course, replete with hostile takeovers and LBOs sponsored and advised by Marty Siegel* and others of Madrick's classmates from Wall Street. Whether it was healthy or unhealthy for the economy as a whole, the boom was certainly disruptive. But this was not our first, nor our most significant merger boom. There were three others in this century, one in 1887–1902, another in the 1920s, and a well-remembered one in the 1960s.

The first of these booms followed the great period of buccaneer American capitalism of the last few decades of the nineteenth century—when a true free market existed. There were no rules, and corruption was commonplace. This was the time of the "robber barons" and the first trusts, the era Mark Twain scornfully called the "Gilded Age." It was a swash-

---

*Martin A. Siegel, HBS class of 1971 and former head of mergers and acquisitions at Kidder, Peabody & Co., admitted to insider trading and aiding Ivan Boesky in his activities in 1986 and served time in jail.

buckling period of scandals and wild speculation that began with the Grant administration in 1869 and did not falter until the depression of 1893–1896.

This merger boom has attracted a great deal of attention from scholars. Ralph Nelson compiled the statistics, which showed more than 2,600 transactions in the manufacturing sector aggregating more than $6.3 billion in value (in 1900 dollars). The first merger boom thus involved a much higher percentage of total American manufacturing, and represented a larger sum per unit of GNP than occurred during the peak merger period in the 1980s.[9] Alfred Chandler, the business historian, concluded that this period of merger activity is explained by the need for major industries to organize their businesses on a national (or regional) basis for the first time, something that could only be done by acquisition. The biggest deal ever (until RJR Nabisco in 1989) was concluded during this period. In 1901, Andrew Carnegie merged his steel company into a consortium of nine other steel operators advised by J.P. Morgan in a transaction valued at $1.4 billion (perhaps $20 billion in 1990 dollars). Morgan visualized the new nationwide steel giant as being worth more than the sum of its parts. He organized the consortium, and raised the money to finance it by underwriting issues of debt, preferred stock, and common stock in the United States and Europe. Morgan's fee, taken in stock, proved to be worth $12 million then, more than $100 million today. The transaction was thoroughly blasted in the press in New York and London—it was called "monopolistic," a "menace to commerce," a "triumph of the millionaire," and was labeled as a product of excessive concentration of power in Wall Street (not Pittsburgh).[10]

The boom in the 1920s corresponded with the formation of the electric power, and to a lesser extent the automotive, industries. This was a period when investment trusts were formed, leveraged, and sold to retail investors so they could purchase shares of utility holding companies that were acquiring telephone and electric companies. Samuel Insull, of Commonwealth Edison of Chicago, was a leading figure of the times. Insull rose to great heights from which an equally great fall was to follow on the collapse of his pyramid of utility holding companies. This boom period ended with the stock market crash of 1929 and the beginning of the Great Depression. The role of Wall Street during all of this was again found to be wanting, and the Banking Act of 1933 (containing the Glass-Steagall provisions which separate commercial and investment banking) and the Securities Acts of 1933 and 1934 were the results.

The next merger boom had to wait out the lean 1930s, the warring 1940s, and the conservative 1950s until it could get started in the 1960s. This time the boom was led by growth-oriented stock market investors, now coming to be dominated by public and private pension funds, mutual funds, and other financial institutions. As a group, these institutional investors accounted for 5.2% of all U.S. financial assets in 1950. By 1960, their share of market had increased to 12.5%, and by 1970, to 16.2% (today they represent 24%). Their people were smart, well educated, and aggressive. They were also young, and they displaced the retiring members of the cautious, caretaker, 1940s generation on Wall Street. They were called "gunslingers" because they shot from the hip. They were interested in growth in earnings per share from new technology and savvy management, and their favorites became the glamour stocks of the day such as IBM, Litton Industries, Polaroid, Texas Instruments, and Xerox.

Growth was king, but growth was difficult to achieve in double-digit figures from regular business operations, even when well managed. And it was not easy for companies to acquire businesses they knew much about because antitrust enforcement was then at its height. The best way to grow was to use financial skills to buy companies in different industries on a basis that would increase earnings per share. LTV Industries, led then by James Ling, became the master of the technique of creating earnings per share growth through acquisition, and then creating more growth through spin-offs and recapitalizations and other exotic financial transactions. Applied financial engineering as we know it today was born in the 1960s, and has been used ever since. Leveraged buyouts began then, as did widespread issuance of subordinated debentures and other high-yield securities, exchange offers, and hostile tender offers. These developments culminated in the formation of numerous multi-industry companies, called "conglomerates." Because of the flexible structure of their businesses, the conglomerates claimed to be able to grow at 15% or more indefinitely. The merger market took off: the players would buy anything, and could often get financing to do so on an unfriendly basis. LTV, for example, began as an electrical supply company and later acquired, among other things, an airframe manufacturer, a meat packer, a sporting goods company, an insurance company, and finally a large, second-rate steel manufacturer.

Ultimately, the conglomerates suffered severe gastrointestinal complications because of their inability to digest all they had eaten, and had to take to their beds for a long recuperation. Their troubles helped trigger the collapse of the market. This too was a time of great speculation and excess, for which Wall Street was given most of the credit.

Merger booms require several conditions before coming to life. There must be some sort of industrial rationale to act as a motivating force, government regulations (or market practices) must allow transactions to be completed at market prices, there must be money available to finance the deals, and entrepreneurs willing to risk all in the hope of lasting success must appear on the scene. There never seems to be a shortage of these entrepreneurs; in 1873, Walter Bagehot, then editor of *The Economist*, described them as the "New Men" of capital, who appear when opportunities exist to make a fortune or to become famous (or both). Bagehot used the New Men to illustrate how a brave young man willing to borrow heavily to trade in the markets against risk-averse "old capitalists" will ultimately drive the latter into retirement. The New Men are the risk takers, the change agents, and the unruly (and often unsuccessful) *enfants terribles* of all periods of intense financial activity. All they need is credit. The merger men of the 1980s preferred to be called "new American entrepreneurs," a label much more admired than the traditional "corporate raider" or "asset stripper." Later in this book, we will see New Men emerging to take important roles in Europe in the 1990s.

Landmarks of the 1980s

Several unusual features of the 1980s boom make this period somewhat different from the earlier ones. Antitrust enforcement policies of the 1960s had been reversed by Reaganomics, and many deals between companies in the same industry took place. Indeed, it could be argued that antitrust policy became so lax that many companies not especially interested in acquiring others had to act in order to protect themselves from the market-consolidating actions of competitors, or to take advantage of a major opportunity that could not have been realized before, nor perhaps would be again in the future.

The logic behind the extensive restructuring of companies that took place in the 1980s began with the idea that the companies were substantially undervalued. The market as a whole, dominated by institutions, valued stocks at about the same prices in 1980 that it did in 1970, though many of these companies had increased earnings and cash flow and substantially reduced borrowings during the period. Leverage was low—corporate borrowings were about the same percentage of total capital in 1980 that they had been in 1957.[11] The 1970s, to be sure, had been a depressing period, filled with oil shocks, political scandals, runaway inflation, increased volatility of market prices, and ferocious competition from the Japanese and other foreigners. During this time, many companies had become large, conservative, bureaucratic institutions run by insiders who did not feel especially accountable to their boards of directors or their shareholders. Often these companies substantially underperformed their competitors, but no one could do anything about it.

Many companies hung on to old ways despite ample evidence that changes were needed in their business strategies, mix of assets, and cost structure. They preferred gradual change and harmonious, coordinated responses to external events. Multi-industry companies, such as conglomerates, were now completely out of fashion and were especially vulnerable to undervaluation. Some of these companies, as in the case of closed-end investment companies, traded in the market at a significant discount from the net asset value of all the investments held.

During the 1980s, Michael Jensen of the Harvard Business School was especially critical of sleepy American management. He pointed out that in the previous merger boom, companies traded in the market at prices approximately 20% to 30% below their acquisition value (i.e., the value someone else would pay for control of the company). In the 1980s, however, companies traded at prices 50% to 60% below their acquisition value. Institutional apathy was partly to blame for this, but Jensen claimed mismanagement was really to blame for the "destruction" of 20% to 30% of shareholder value.

Jensen also had something to say about the dynamics of acquisitions from the buyer's perspective, which he called the "free cash flow theory." He noted that companies have to decide among three alternatives in spending their surplus cash flow (i.e., cash left over after all necessary capital expenditures have been made): they can increase dividends, buy their own stock in the market, or acquire other companies. Dividends are not tax effective, so the practical choice usually is between acquisitions and buy backs. In time, this assertion became the basis for the "restructuring" theories of the 1980s, in which management sought to maximize shareholder value by treating the business as a constantly changing portfolio. Cash-generating assets should be bought and sold, changed, and managed differently if necessary, leveraged and subjected to sophisticated new techniques to achieve the highest sustainable market value possible. Market value was what counted, not continuity or corporate culture. For many companies, especially those committed to what they thought of as traditional values, this was a highly disagreeable idea.

The New Men, and other entrepreneur-raiders, sought out undervalued companies that could be restructured profitably. Because of the relatively low stock prices at the time, the raiders often found companies that could be bought for not much more than their book value, even after paying a substantial premium over the market price to induce shareholders to sell. By borrowing money to make the acquisition, the entrepreneurs increased their financial leverage and earned a higher return on investment than the old shareholders had received. By using superleverage, as in an LBO, they could earn even higher returns. By invigorating the company with new, highly motivated management (who would have large financial incentives to succeed), they had a good chance of making operations more efficient. And by disposing of selected parts of the business to buyers that valued those individual parts highly, but did not want to own the rest of the company, they could realize some early return of capital. As time went on, subsequent re-restructurings would occur in order to maximize continually the values of the properties owned and the cash extracted.

Acquisitions, then, occurred when the restructured value of the company was likely to be greater than the all-in cost of acquiring and financing it. There were many such companies available in the early 1980s, though acquisitions diminished their number. Some of the early entrepreneurs such as Kohlberg, Kravis & Roberts (KKR) capitalized on their success by selling participations in large LBO funds to institutional investors. However, once the institutional money came in (from pension funds, insurance companies, and banks), it came in torrents and swamped the market for LBOs. By the end of 1988, institutions and other investors had contributed $30 to $40 billion to LBO equity investment funds, which, leveraged ten to one, could potentially yield takeover power in the area of $300 to $400 billion, amounts vastly in excess of the supply of good deals. Prices for companies went sky-high as competition for deals became intense, and the expected returns diminished accordingly. By the late 1980s, few deals were attractive to experienced players; only the incurably acquisitive and those playing with large supplies of other people's money stayed in the game. It is hardly surprising that the deals done late in the cycle have turned out so poorly.

To finance the LBOs subordinated debt was needed. The banks wisely preferred to stick with senior debt in the form of bridge and term loans, so another source of subordinated capital had to be found. The development of a public market for extremely large issues of junk bonds in 1985 was thus a watershed event, giving big-league, multibillion-dollar striking power to small-time raiders, entrepreneurs, and LBO fund managers. This, of course, was the work of Michael Milken (Wharton MBA class of 1970) and Drexel Burnham Lambert, who built a market for these junk bond issues originally from a group of New Men investors and later from insurance companies, S&Ls, and mutual funds. It is clear that under normal circumstances, a large company in the same industry as a target company can pay more for the acquisition than can a stand-alone LBO operator. This is because the corporate buyer will be able to realize many economies of scale, cost reductions, and management synergies not available to the LBO firm. The only way the LBO firm can manage to pay more for a target than a corporate buyer is when it is willing and able to borrow more money to complete the transaction; and the banks will only lend so much, secured by the tangible assets of the company. In the mid-1980s, bank debt, plus the equity the LBO operators were prepared to put up, was still nowhere near enough to compete with a corporate buyer. The extra money that was needed could only be raised through unsecured, subordinated, high-yield debt (junk bonds). As long as someone such as Drexel was willing to issue these bonds in large amounts, the raider was in business. Without it, he was not. In the case of the 1986 Beatrice Foods buyout, $2.5 billion of junk bonds were sold to finance the transaction; in RJR Nabisco, $5 billion. Without junk bonds to fund these large public deals, they would not have happened. As the junk bond market has now been discredited (though it has also recovered), these sorts of mergers are not likely to happen on a similar scale for some time.

Soon after the merger boom began, it became clear that takeover rules were sufficiently lax that any financed cash offer could expect to succeed. Investors, especially institutions, were all too happy to accept a 30% or 40% premium over market value for their stock, either from the buyer or by selling the stock in the market to arbitrageurs. This made many companies feel exposed to being picked off in a turkey shoot whenever market prices were low or earnings were under pressure. Two results followed.

First, a greater effort was made to construct takeover defenses that could withstand a sudden but lowballed offer. The most effective of these devices was the shareholders' rights plan, or *poison pill*. This plan revolved around the idea that if a raider acquired more than a threshold amount of a company's stock, previously distributed stock purchase rights would automatically come into effect, authorizing all shareholders except the raider to acquire additional shares at an exceptionally low price. The purpose of the poison pill was not to prevent takeovers altogether, but to require the raider to enter into negotiations with the board of the target company, which was seeking to assure shareholders that no deal would be offered to them, unless the board believed it reflected a fair and adequate price for the company. The board was considered to be objective enough to render reasonable judgments on these matters because the majority of its members were "outsiders" who were not affiliated with management and who had the benefit of their own legal and financial advisers. Since the SEC had chosen not to interfere in the free market for corporate control, the resolution of the numerous disputes arising from the takeover process was left to the courts, usually those in the state of incorporation of the target company. These courts, after a ten-year period rich in case law, laid out rules for establishing a level playing field for mergers and acquisitions. Directors have special duties to their shareholders. They must react differently to ownership issues than to enterprise issues and impose different and higher standards so as to ensure that managers do not put their own interests ahead of shareholders'. It may not be perfect or pretty, but it now works fairly well; most observers would agree that the current system for keeping the field level is much better than the one that existed in 1980.

The second result of companies being exposed to takeovers was self-restructuring. Many companies decided that if they could not be sure of beating the raider, then they would undertake themselves the restructuring actions that the entrepreneur would seek to perform in order to increase the market value of the company. The management of some such companies decided to take themselves private by tendering for all of their own stock. Others increased leverage, cut costs and expenses, sold off divisions, increased dividends, and performed various steps that their bankers told them would capture value for their shareholders. The net effect, after a decade, is some form of restructuring for almost all publicly owned companies—restructuring that has made them more efficient, more dynamic, and more competitive.

Assessing the Damage

About the same time that the class of 1971 was grilling my friend Brody, the class of 1966 was conducting a panel discussion about the 1980s. I was the moderator of this group; the others were senior Wall Street bankers and investors. We were talking among ourselves; there were no victims of the recession or op-ed writers among us.

The panel agreed, almost at once, that the merger boom had run to excess, as these things tend to do (excesses are unpreventable, really, in a free market). This had resulted in an accumulation of too much debt on the part of most LBOs, and these companies were suffering accordingly. In the relatively short *three*-year period 1986–1988, 232 large LBOs (each more than $100 million) were completed, totaling $150 billion in value; in addition, there were 84 other large deals totaling $120 billion that were offered but not completed. This compares with 92 deals totaling $47 billion that were completed during the *six*-year period 1980–1985. The deals were financed by LBO funds and issuances of junk bonds. The investors were predominately large financial institutions.

"The LBO market was a pretty good thing before the institutions got involved in it," said a prominent venture-capital fund manager. "Restructuring made a lot of sense for many companies, and in the right proportions, good returns could be had. But the institutions flooded money into the market and swamped it, paying too much for deals, almost guaranteeing failure. They were into junk and LBO funds and into venture capital and real estate too during the eighties. They should have stuck to their standard common stocks instead."

"The main body of corporate America, those companies that survived the merger boom of the eighties, is not especially overleveraged," said another, an investment banker. "The excess debt is concentrated in the 1986–1988 LBOs, where probably two-thirds are in trouble." Throughout the eighties, LBOs accounted for only about 15% of completed mergers, 25% during the peak year of 1988. In 1980, total corporate debt as a percent of capital (debt plus shareholder's equity) was 33%; in 1989, debt had increased to 57%, high but not unmanageable. Of course, these figures include the big LBOs in which debt ratios of 90% were not uncommon.

"When companies are overborrowed they have two problems," added another member of the panel. "First they are vulnerable to insolvency, especially during a recession such as we have now, and everybody knows it. This makes it hard to get along day by day. There is no planning. Management is by crisis intervention, and far from efficient. Under such conditions short-termism at its worst comes into play. Second, expenditures that are important for long-term viability are postponed or ignored. There is no money to spend on developing new products, research, or markets. The company is in the intensive care ward; if it recovers, fine, but if not, it's going to face an early death.

"This is hardly a prescription for a healthy, competitive industrial sector," he added.

"Fact is, though," another wanted to point out, "not too many companies are in such bad shape. In 1990, the junk bond default rate was 8.7%, a record for the eighties, but not all that high when you consider the terrible deals that were done, like Campeau's purchase of Federated Department Stores, the sorry state of a number of industries like the airlines and banking that really were not in on the LBOs at all, the corruption in the junk bond market, and the recession." The default rate increased slightly in 1991 to 9.0%.[12] Many observers felt it would peak at about this level—in the first half of 1992, it was about 6.0%. Most of the outstanding junk bonds (by volume) are LBO connected, and most are still paying off. The cumulative default rate for the whole ten years is about 40%, of which investors have recovered about 40% of their claims. Many companies are being restructured after bankruptcy, and have a decent chance for the future. "Most of the so-called debt problem has already happened," the panelist added "or soon will have, and its victims are being rebuilt. For companies that were not involved in LBOs, debt problems are not especially important at all."

"I do believe some good came out of the period," a banker interjected. "Certainly the tightening up and self-restructuring that went on increased corporate efficiency and productivity. A lot of fat was trimmed away, voluntarily or otherwise—just look at RJR Nabisco now, or General Electric, or Philip Morris, all big companies that were actively involved in the merger boom on one side or the other.

"And I think we have a better attitude about stockholder-management conflicts. Now outside directors take charge and prevent management from stonewalling or hiding takeover possibilities, or from launching stupid deals of their own. The situation is far from perfect, but it's much better now, more balanced."

And finally, a comment from the head of a large brokerage firm: "Market prices are much higher than at the beginning of the eighties, and much closer to the real value of companies. There's less incentive to take them over now, and at higher stock prices, many companies are taking advantage of the situation to sell new stock, reduce debt, and lower their cost of capital. That's a positive development. Whereas the eighties were the 'debt decade,' I think the nineties will be the 'equity era,' and I am very optimistic about the future." The others said they were too.

Out of merger boom periods some good does come along with the bad. Disruption of the status quo is not always contrary to the interests of the system. In the 1980s, companies had to be on guard constantly against a predatory attack. The best defense against such an attack was a high stock price, but this could only be achieved through superior quarter-to-quarter earnings improvement. This situation gave rise to short-term thinking, a condition that makes business and government leaders despair (and that is used by some as an excuse for Americans' lack of competitiveness), but it also produced efforts to improve management and productivity.

Disruption, in that sense, had a cleansing effect on the system. The targets for attack were those that needed cleansing the most, as demonstrated by such conditions as stock prices trading well below the "true" (or cleaned up) value of the company. Many such misalignments of value, as measured by relative price/cash flow ratios, market to book value ratios, and return on investment, existed at the beginning of the 1980s, but the values were realigned by rising stock prices.

However, during the 1980s the purchasing in the market that drove prices upward was done by corporations, which acquired over $500 billion of common stocks (in acquisitions and buy backs) during the five years between 1986 and 1990. They were interested mainly in fundamentals like cash flow, market share, new products, and synergies with their own businesses. The sellers capturing the benefits of these premium transactions were the institutions, which were motivated by modern portfolio theory (in which share values were held to be a function of the volatility of their market prices, or "betas"), by the desire to beat the averages, and to attract more funds to manage. They were not optimists about American stocks during the 1980s, acquiring only $115 billion during the 1986–1990 period, an acquisition rate that was about half of what it had been during the 1970s. They looked for other investments, ones that promised higher rewards for sophisticated risk taking. So they ventured into those investment areas that promised 30% to 40% returns such as junk bonds and LBOs. Since they are not likely to increase these investments further during the 1990s, it may be that they will come back to basics and buy stocks again. Early indications are that they have.

THE DECIMATION OF THE S&Ls

Certainly one of the more memorable and enduring legacies of the 1980s will be the S&L debacle, in which the federal agencies insuring depositors' funds experienced losses approximating $250 billion. This estimate is before interest payable on thirty years of borrowing to fund the obligation, which, if included, would put the cost of the S&L mess at about $500 billion. Taxpayers will ultimately have to pay virtually all of this amount.

Though the FDIC now insures deposits of both the banks and the S&Ls up to a maximum of $100,000 per account, the insurance premiums are not intermixed, i.e., healthy banks, which have been required to pay for refinancing the Bank Insurance Fund (used to recapitalize unhealthy banks), do not pay for unhealthy S&Ls. The S&Ls are treated separately.

The taxpayer bill for the S&Ls has yet to be presented in full, and it won't be for a long time. In February 1992, Treasury Secretary Nicholas Brady asked for an additional $55 billion on top of the $105 billion already spent on the S&Ls. Even then, he said, this $160 billion may not be enough. The FDIC also has a borrowing facility of another $70 billion to cover deposit insurance losses of commercial banks. The Treasury will borrow the money and lend it to the FDIC to disperse as necessary. The loss-absorbing process will continue as other banks and S&Ls are closed, and as asset sales from previously closed banks prove to be less than expected, until the problem is completely resolved. At the end of 1991, only about 55% of assets taken over by the FDIC had been sold. Certainly another wave of refinancing of the FDIC is probable in the future, though it is likely to be done by increasing the government's total amount of borrowing as needed rather than transferring a large chunk of money out of the current budget. In other words, the taxpayers may know they are stuck with the bill, but it will simply be put on the credit card to be dealt with later on.

The amounts to be paid by the taxpayers in the 1990s, ironically, are in the same ballpark with the aggregate amount lost by small depositors in the banking collapse of 1931–1934 ($22.8 billion in 1934 dollars, maybe ten times that in 1991 money) when 9,000 commercial and mutual savings banks were closed.[13] Franklin Roosevelt's first act as president was to declare a bank holiday and to begin work on the Banking Act of 1933, which, among many other things, provided federal insurance of bank deposits (for up to $2,500) for the first time. Too many little people, decent, regular folks just trying to make a living and put something away for a rainy day, were hurt by the banking failures of the 1930s. It would not be allowed to happen again. It hasn't because this time around the little people are being "bailed out" by the FDIC, which is itself being bailed out by taxpayers, big and little. Certainly the bailouts do not benefit the owners of the S&Ls, as is sometimes thought. The only beneficiaries of the government's involvement in the current mess are depositors, whose life savings have been protected. Most people believe they should be protected.

S&Ls are deposit-taking thrift institutions that predominantly invest in home mortgages. "Thrifts" include savings banks and savings and loan corporations. They have long played an important part in the convoluted history of American finance. In 1816, the first mutual savings bank (which was owned by its depositors, like a co-op) was formed in Philadelphia to collect and protect personal savings of individuals who had nowhere else to put their money. Some years later, it began to make some mortgage loans, but most of its investments were in government securities, rather like a mutual fund. Similar institutions sprang up throughout the Northeast. In time commercial banks began offering retail services, and the mutuals stopped growing, though plenty of them are still around today.

The first S&L, modeled on the British building societies of the time, was established in 1831 for the express purpose of financing home mortgages for its members. This was the Oxford-Provident Association of Frankford, Pennsylvania, which was dissolved ten years later when everyone had a mortgage. The idea was soon copied, however, and the new industry flourished, as it served an important need in a growing economy.[14]

Thrifts grew to perform a dual function in their communities: they were safe places to deposit small sums in passbook accounts, and they were a source of credit to their depositors (and other customers) for financing homes. A high political priority of the Roosevelt administrations was encouraging families to buy their own homes; consequently, there was government support for thrift activities. In 1938, the Federal National Mortgage Association (FNMA) was established to buy mortgages from thrifts to recycle mortgage money through the system faster. At the end of the 1920s, there were more than 12,000 thrifts throughout the country. After the 1930s, when failures and consolidations took place, the industry was reconstituted; by 1979, the number had declined to 5,100. These organizations accounted for about 30% of all deposit liabilities in the United States in 1989. Most important, almost every little town had one or two thrift institutions; and dozens were in each congressional district.

Hazardous Morals

In Frank Capra's 1946 film, *It's a Wonderful Life*, the banker George Bailey (played by Jimmy Stewart), in a moment of frustration, called his S&L a "penny ante, nickel and dime business," which it was. But it was also a safe and steady business for at least forty or forty-five years after federal deposit insurance was provided in 1933. Before this, guys like George had to face the possibility of a run on the bank—their worst nightmare. They knew that most of their money was invested in house mortgages. If depositors panicked and demanded their money back, there would never be sufficient liquidity in the bank to pay out all the deposits. Runs on banks occurred frequently during the 1920s and at other times before that. But when Roosevelt provided deposit insurance, that ended the nightmare. In fact, because of deposit insurance, George slept better at night. He became a Democrat and helped finance local campaigns for pro-thrift candidates. Today he would be a Republican.

However, George knew that deposit insurance had another benefit: if he really wanted to get rich, all he had to do was crank up the deposits and make more loans, even much riskier loans—if they failed, the government would have to pay them off, not George. However, George thought it might be immoral for him to do this—to enrich himself by increasing the hazards that the government would be exposed to by insuring his deposits, so he passed up the opportunity.

Economists call such a situation a "moral hazard," and they recognize it as a flaw in the deposit insurance scheme, one they believe can only be controlled by examination and supervision of the insured banks. "Well," said George, "you're absolutely right about that; if the government is going to insure the deposits, then the government ought to check the books. But, Gosh! We'd never try to pull a fast one on the government, what kind of people do you think we are?"

But lurking in the night was another bad dream, a monster George and his colleagues had never thought of before. What would happen, the monster asked George, if, all of a sudden, your depositors were offered interest rates several percentage points higher than what you were offering? What if interest rates, which had been stable for decades, were suddenly pushed up by rising inflation or some other economic pressure?

"I'd have to match 'em, or I'd soon be out of business," he replied. "I've got a lot of loyal customers, but even they won't stay here for 200 basis points (2.00%) less on their money.

"But if I raise deposit rates by 200 basis points, I'm going to lose money, because the mortgage rates I've been charging are only 100 basis points more than my current deposit rates, and those mortgage rates are fixed. If the situation should keep up for any appreciable length of time, the losses will eat up my capital, which is only about 5% of assets anyway. Right now, I've got $2 million in mortgage loans, $1.9 million in deposits, and $100,000 in capital. If I start losing 1% on my mortgages, after paying the depositors, I'm going to lose $20,000 a year instead of making that much, which means I'm dead in five years.

"'Course, I could sell off some mortgages, though I probably wouldn't get 100 cents on the dollar if market interest rates had gone up 2% over a short period. Say I'd get 85 cents, then I'd have to take a loss, and I couldn't do too much of this or I'd still be in the soup. But, you know, I could sell off about $300,000 of mortgages at a loss of 15 cents on the dollar, which would cost me about $45,000. This I would claim was an extraordinary item, and charge it directly against my capital (not as an operating loss). Then with the $255,000 I'd clear on the sale of the mortgages, I could invest in higher-yielding assets, like commercial real estate, high-yield bonds, stocks, whatever. But I'd have to clear 6% over my mortgage lending rate just to break even, which I admit might be pretty hard to do without taking on some really risky loans. At least I could hold the fort, though, until those darn interest rates come back down to where they ought to be, or maybe until the government puts a limit on them. After all, the government has an interest in this too. If it doesn't do something, then I'm going to have to increase its 'hazard.' I'll have no choice, it'll be the government or me."

Comes the Storm

In the latter part of the 1960s, pressured by the inflationary effects of the Vietnam War, market rates rose; three-month Treasuries increased from 3.4% in April of 1964 to 5.4% by the fall of 1966, when mortgage rates were 4.5% to 4.75%. George started to get nervous. He and his colleagues passed along their concern to the government, which patched over the problem by passing the Interest Rate Control Act of 1966. This act fixed the maximum interest rates that thrifts could pay on deposits. The Federal Reserve also adopted similar interest-rate ceilings for banks (Regulation Q). The problem went away, mostly, because three-month Treasury bill rates stayed mainly within a 4%-6% band from 1966 to 1979 (except for 1973–1974, when they went to 8%), ceiling rates were adjusted (upward) periodically, and small-time investors had nowhere else to go with their money. Treasury bills and large certificates of deposit (CDs) of commercial banks paid money market rates, but savers had to put up $10,000 to buy just one certificate. The patch worked until early 1979, when passbook ceilings were 5.25% but three-month Treasuries rose to 9.36%; later in the year, the Treasury rates went up to 10.72%, while passbook rates were actually cut to 5.20%. The difference was 5.5%. George's depositors, who would walk for 200 basis points, would fly for 550 basis points.

So George was in trouble. He faced the interest rate risk associated with a *maturity mismatch*. All the S&Ls did, because they took in short-term deposits to fund a long-term mortgage portfolio, in direct violation of the first rule of banking: never borrow short to lend long. Commercial bankers didn't have this problem (so much) because most of their assets were short- to medium-term bank loans, not thirty-year mortgages. Their loans were also at interest rates that fluctuated relative to a base rate (the "prime" rate) that each bank would post daily, not at fixed interest rates for the life of the mortgage.

"OK," said George, "we'll get out of this one by offering only short-term mortgages, and we'll make the interest rates adjustable so if deposit rates change, the mortgage rates will too."

Of course, nobody wanted five-year mortgages with crushing monthly payments, and Congress strongly opposed switching to adjustable-rate mortgages (ARMs). On several occasions during the 1970s, the Federal Home Loan Bank Board (the federal S&L supervisor) proposed regulations to permit federally chartered thrifts to offer ARMs, but each time congressional leaders shot it down—because they were afraid that S&L operators would abuse the system at the expense of the innocent consumer.[15] The opponents of ARMs thought that the mismatch problem was overstated and argued that depositors really had nowhere else to go with their money except to banks or S&Ls, which were both covered by the ceilings. Only large depositors would pull out their money and put it into government bonds, and large depositors in S&Ls were rare. Just wait it out, they said.

The trouble was that an enormous gap between deposit rates and market rates settled in on the market in 1979. Before, there was not much incentive for depositors to withdraw. Although money market mutual funds, which took in small investments and commingled them in order to buy government bills and other high-rate money market securities, had been formed in 1973 (when gaps of 1.0% to 2.5% existed), they were slow to take hold. In 1978, however, with a fairly permanent 2.0% gap, assets in the funds nearly tripled to $9.5 billion from $3.3 billion the year before. In 1979, the gap more than doubled and fund assets quadrupled, to $43 billion, then rose again to $77 billion in 1980 (they are now more than $500 billion). This asset growth came predominantly at the expense of banks and S&Ls; their deposits were being sucked out. Many S&Ls had to sell mortgages to cover the redemptions. The sales generated losses because a 4% mortgage in a 10% market was only worth about fifty cents on the dollar.

By the end of 1979, the S&Ls were in bad shape; a third were losing money and overall industry profitability had fallen. A year later, nearly three-fourths of all thrifts were unprofitable. At the end of 1981, more than 90% were in the red, and industry accounting practices greatly understated the real losses. Larry White, an economics professor at New York University, who was a Home Loan Bank Board member from 1986 to 1989, points out that "a proper recognition of the writedowns and capital losses from the sale of assets during these years would have shown industry losses of $6.9 billion instead of $4.6 billion in 1981 and $22.2 billion instead of $4.2 billion in 1982."[16]

Congress to the Rescue

Thrift regulators and their congressional counterparts became concerned. In 1979, ARMs were finally allowed. Beginning in 1980, during the Carter administration, interest rate ceilings were phased out, and thrifts were allowed to expand greatly the types of loans and investments they could make: credit card and consumer loans could increase to 30% of assets, secured commercial real estate loans to 40% of assets, commercial loans to 11%, and direct equity investments up to 3%. Some state thrift regulators were even more lenient. At the same time, Congress bumped up the deposit insurance coverage to $100,000 for all accounts, including those deposits provided by brokers.

Thus, over a two- to three-year period the industry had been almost totally deregulated and thrust right into the midst of market forces. Now, if they wanted to, thrifts could alter their asset portfolios from 90% mortgages to only 16%, with the rest of the assets being made up of new types of investments with which S&Ls had no experience. And they could fund these investments with market rate deposits fully insured by the government. These actions were not wholly the work of Ronald Reagan; some preceded him, though he endorsed the steps taken. His major role came later.

It was now evident that market forces could be extremely powerful and could force regulatory changes even against the will of the regulators. No one really wanted these changes; they were made because the gap between regulated rates and market rates was so large that competitive alternatives to bank deposits were created, and the S&Ls were hemorrhaging. Since the government had agreed to insure the deposits of the S&Ls, Congress (which had always had a strong interest in the S&L industry because of its political potency) became involved in the solution to the problem: fully deregulate it to close the interest rate gap and allow S&Ls to compete freely in the market. If this had not been done, the S&Ls clearly would have bled to death, at the government's expense.

Was this the right response? Professor White, who came on the scene long after these events, thinks so.

> The major deregulation actions were fundamentally sound and sensible. A number of commissions and studies during the previous decade had called for wider powers for thrifts and for the end of Regulation Q. The authorization to offer ARMs was essential for thrifts to deal with their interest rate risk problems, and the opportunity to diversify their portfolios, if done prudently, could strengthen their profitability and reduce their overall riskiness. . . . The increase in the insured amount to $100,000 . . . was a sensible step, since a larger insured deposit amount lessens the vulnerability of a depository to a run by nervous depositors.[17]

The problem for the government, as White also emphasized, was that the moral hazard alarm bell was ringing like mad. Honest S&L operators would have to diversify into areas they knew nothing about. Dishonest operators would have an enormous scope for their activities. And New Men would swarm in to exploit the gap created by the deregulation: with very little money down, entrepreneurs could borrow all they needed at government insured rates in order to invest in risky deals with high-profit opportunity if they worked, and hardly any downside for the dealmakers if they didn't.

Screwing It Up

The only way the new economically deregulated system could work was for it to be accompanied by strict regulation of safety and soundness conditions. The deposits' insurer, if no one else, would need better information about the loan portfolios, tighter scrutiny and examination, higher capitalization standards, and probably a better, risk-based system for charging for the insurance provided.

Virtually none of this was forthcoming, despite the fact that S&L performance data were terrifying. By the end of 1983, the net worth of all insured thrifts had declined to 0.4% of their assets, down from 5.7% in 1979. By comparison, the net worth as a percentage of assets of commercial banks had not changed at all, but remained 6.9% during this period. There was nothing left holding up the S&Ls by 1983, except the government. Or, put another way, deposit insurance had never been intended as a substitute for sound capitalization and operations of the thrifts—only as a vote of confidence to prevent runs. The insurance risk to the government would be minimal if the insured banks were well capitalized and well run, but they were not. Instead of serving as an ancillary support, deposit insurance had become the principal load-bearing beam in the structure. The stage was set for disaster.

And it came. In the comparatively short period from 1983 to 1985 (the same superconfident, optimistic time that saw the rapid rise in leveraged buyouts and junk bonds, which peaked in 1988), the industry was wrecked.

Again, market forces were involved—lucrative opportunities had been created, supervision was lax, and opportunists from the "market" were eager to exploit the available incentives. First, there was growth in all insured thrift assets, which more than doubled in 1983 to 18.6%, then rose to 20% in 1984 before settling back to 10% in 1985. In Texas and California, asset growth was even greater, more than 30% in both 1983 and 1984 in Texas and nearly that in California. Commercial bank-asset growth during these years averaged about 6%.

Then, there was diversification—by 1985 nonhome mortgage assets for all thrifts had risen to 20% of all assets, from 10% in 1982. For the fastest-growing thrifts, nontraditional assets averaged 47% of total assets. Large brokered deposits also grew disproportionately during this time, as thrifts used national securities firms to find more and more deposits. De novo thrifts expanded rapidly, as did conversions of mutuals to stock companies to provide opportunities for capital gains for entrepreneurs.

At this point Reaganomics entered the picture, but only for a walk-on role. The federal agencies involved with thrifts were subject to budget squeezes, and examination schedules suffered. Also, many government officials of this era believed that deregulation was supposed to be just that, not reregulation. Interfering in the free market (through bureaucratic controls, reports, and such) was anathema to the Reagan ideology. But Congress really controlled the destiny of the S&Ls, more so than either the administration or the Federal Reserve Board. And Congress, never very efficient, was subject to all sorts of pressures and inducements. Some of these were improper, and their exposure led to the resignation of Speaker Jim Wright and the dramatic episode of the five U.S. senators who were compromised by S&L heavyweight Charles Keating.

The number of *disposals*—liquidations or forced placements of thrifts by the government—helps us chart the troubled history of these institutions. Significant thrift insolvencies, reflecting interest rate mismatching, occurred in 1981 and 1982, when insured assets disposed of rose to 2.1% and 2.5%, respectively, of all thrift assets, ten times the level of 1980. But then as interest rates receded, the disposals dropped off to between 0.5% and 0.6% for 1983–1986. After that, however, the disposals ran amok, reaching 7.5% of all thrift assets in 1988. They lagged the period of greatest troubles because government examinations were running late, accounting information was inaccurate (especially the ersatz accounting rules Congress allowed to cover up the thrifts' financial difficulties), delaying tactics of well-connected thrift owners were effective, or simply because the regulatory system was inefficient.

In 1985, the government began a series of policy steps to clean up the mess. Regulatory resources were expanded, accounting and capitalization standards were strengthened, the Federal Savings and Loan Insurance Corporation (FSLIC) was recapitalized and merged into the FDIC, which in turn was recapitalized a few years later as banks shared some of the same difficulties of the S&Ls.

The pace of disposals was accelerated in 1988, when an ambitious program for selling off 205 failed thrifts—principally in the Southwest—to a wave of New Men resulted in the transfer of $30 billion of assets. This was a very controversial step because many observers thought that the government negotiators had been out-traded by such skillful capitalists as Robert Bass, Ronald Perelman, and William Simon. The idea the FSLIC stuck to was to auction off the insured assets and accept only those bids that, even after tax benefits and various contingency payments, would produce a higher realized disposal price than FSLIC could get on its own. This issue continues to be controversial, and as a result further large disposals at auction have not occurred.

In 1989, Congress passed the Financial Institutions Reform, Recovery, and Enforcement Act, reflecting input from the pragmatic Bush administration and further finger pointing by Congress. The act abolished the FSLIC and the Home Loan Bank Board and set up the Office of Thrift Supervision and the Resolution Trust Corporation. It tightened regulations further, increased insurance premiums, and established new enforcement and financial recovery measures.

Applying Hindsight

Looked at in hindsight, we can probably conclude the following about the thrifts: 1) most of them are solvent and operating profitably under deregulated conditions and in compliance with all the new rules; 2) there still is a need for regionally dispersed deposit collectors and mortgage makers, a business not too many of the big banks have been eager to enter, so S&Ls in one form or another will continue to exist; 3) government regulation of interest rates in only some sectors of the financial economy, but not others, cannot work because the market will find ways to arbitrage the gap; 4) there will always be entrepreneurs to exploit easy opportunities in periods of lax supervision (White was surprised that only a hundred or so such entrepreneurs appeared on the scene, but there were many similar, or better, opportunities for New Men at the time); 5) governments can lose a huge amount of money quickly when market forces and necessary safety and soundness provisions are ignored; and 6) no regulatory system can work if the accounting information is inaccurate or untimely, as "historical cost" as opposed to "market value" accounting for financial assets will invariably be.

The S&L industry never bothered anybody before the early 1980s. It was fairly inconspicuous, as financial industries go, but it nonetheless accounted for about 30% of all insured banking assets in the United States. Subject to severe restrictions on its activities by regulation, the industry resembled a public utility—highly specialized, local, slow, and unsophisticated outside of its own field. Such industries are poorly equipped to deal with the ravages of rare sudden change in market economics.

Many other financial industries in the United States were subjected to radical change in the 1980s, changes that would determine their survival or their disappearance during the 1990s.

One of those industries was commercial banking.

2
BANKING AT THE BRINK

In 1970, Chase Manhattan was America's third-largest bank, trailing the leader, Bank of America, by less than $5 billion in total assets. First National City Bank, now called Citibank, beat it out for second place by a small margin. Chase was also the third-largest bank in the world, employing 24,000 people in 150 domestic and 70 international branches in 30 countries. Trailing it in various places on the list of the world's top thirty banks were Manufacturers Hanover (6), Morgan Guaranty (8), Chemical Bank (10), Bankers Trust (21), Continental Illinois (26), Security Pacific (28), and First National Bank of Chicago (30); all told, ten of the thirty were American. U.S. banks dominated the world. It was a time of expanding world trade and financial innovation, especially in the area of offshore currency deposits and internationally syndicated bank loans.

I was in Tokyo trying to develop investment banking business with Japanese clients during 1970. It wasn't easy, so I went around to see my compatriots at the big banks for advice, marketplace gossip, and introductions. The Chase branch, large and impressive, was located in the Marunouchi district, then Tokyo's premier banking location. The branch manager was friendly and we had hit it off on a previous visit. He invited me to his home for dinner, thanking me for the excuse to take a night off from the Tokyo banker's continuous cocktail and dinner party circuit. His limousine was ready when we left his office for the short trip to his home. He explained on the way that he had been busy that day confirming arrangements for his chairman, David Rockefeller, to visit with the prime minister the following week, and for a round of dinners and receptions that Chase was arranging in his honor.

"These things are important in Japan," he said. "Everything is based on relationships, obligations, and prestige. Banks are very important in this country—they make all the financial decisions for their corporate customers, and they're prepared to trade off some of their influence with Japanese companies for banking know-how and market access in the United States and in Europe. Naturally they look to us for help, and up to us in everything related to banking as a profession. They know who our *Fortune* 500 customers are, and what sort of access we have back home, and they're impressed. So our business is very profitable here."

I thought about this as we drove up to his large, modern house in the middle of a beautiful ten-acre garden in central Tokyo. The house, owned by Chase, was worth millions, even then. "It's got ten bedrooms, marble floors, a dining room that seats thirty, and a full staff. It's a bit much for my wife and our little daughter and me, but the last guy here was older and had lots of big parties for senior Japanese bankers and clients. Rockefeller likes his branch managers to socialize with important locals, and of course we're having a big bash while he's here next week. In a social sense, I'd say we were pretty competitive with the U.S. Embassy."

To the Japanese, Chase was like a little U.S. government, a financial state within a state, with which they had to have good relations in order to get ahead. Chase was prestigious, triple-A solid, and very knowledgeable about global banking, and it had great American corporations for its customers. That was enough for the Japanese. "We don't have to do much marketing here," added the branch manager, "unless having these damn dinners is marketing. The Japanese just come up and give us their business.

"For that matter, it's not just the Japanese that do that, our American customers do too, really. They're kind of locked in: they've got to get their working capital and term loans from someplace, and because of Regulation Q, all the banks pay the same for deposits and post the same prime lending rate. We all charge our customers the same rates and require pretty much the same compensating deposits.[1] And besides, most large companies need relationships with several banks because they want to be able to borrow more than our maximum lending amounts, which cannot exceed 10% of our capital. So we all syndicate our big loans among a group of other big banks. Therefore, it's hard (and probably foolish) to cheat on lending rates to steal business away from a competitor.

"We don't really compete on price, we compete on the basis of service and relationships. Service involves such things as economic research, credit information, handling international payments, and assistance with foreign exchange transactions. Advice is helpful too, especially about complex international stuff the customers don't know too much about, but the key is relationships with decision makers at the companies—the chief financial officer, the treasurer, and the assistant treasurer who handles banking.

"Consequently, most of our top guys are the strong, personable types who can develop relationships and keep 'em stroked—big-picture bull-shitters. They keep the front office happy and think up new services, but the back-office types make all the money on good credit analysis and by processing transactions efficiently."

The system worked very well. In 1970, Chase Manhattan reported profits of $138 million, a 12.2% return on shareholders' equity. Its stock price had traded as high as 11.2 times its earnings per share and 1.65 times its book value. Dividends were $1.80 per share, an annual yield to investors of 3.8%. Not brilliant results, perhaps, but quite respectable, and very steady. Net interest income was 80.6% of the bank's total revenues. Deposits made up 87% of its funding, and 57% of these were noninterest-bearing demand deposits. Loan loss reserves were equal to 30% of shareholders' equity.

Twenty years later, Chase reported the worst year in its history—losing $334 million because of increases in loan loss provisions of $1.2 billion. Loan loss reserves as a whole now equaled 60% of shareholders' equity, and nonperforming loans were 115% of equity. Moody's had dropped Chase Manhattan Corporation's senior bond rating to Baa-3, just one notch above a junk bond. Deposits now accounted for 72% of total funding, and only 18% of these were demand deposits. Its stock, which had traded at $45 during the last quarter of 1989, had dropped to as low as $9.75 per share, only 32% of its book value. Its dividend was slashed 52%, and it reported plans to lay off 5,000 employees, contrary to long-standing Chase policies of providing job security. And, to emphasize the determination of the board of directors to turn things around, Chairman Willard C. ("Bill") Butcher, a Chase man for forty-three years and CEO for a decade, would take early retirement.

FALL FROM GRACE

Chase was not alone in its misery—most of its major money-center competitors also suffered. Citicorp, Chemical Bank, and Manufacturers Hanover had all cut dividends; they and many other banks reported large increases in delinquent loans. "Nineteen ninety was the worst year for banking since the Great Depression," said Thomas Hanley, a top-rated banking industry analyst then at Salomon Brothers. Profits had fallen sharply because of problem loans, which had risen to 3% of industry assets—a post–World War II high—and now equaled the minimum amount of primary equity capital (3% of assets) that banks then had to maintain. Profits of all commercial banks averaged a miserable 0.54% of assets in 1990, down from 0.80% the year before.

Commercial real estate loans were the principal cause of the 1990 losses, but continuing losses on loans to third world countries and new losses on loans to highly indebted companies filled out the list of problem areas.

Bad loans had been the curse of the decade, a plague that had infected most large U.S. and many other banking institutions. There had been a dramatic increase in loan write-offs (those actually charged off against earnings, as opposed to reserved against). Lowell Bryan, a McKinsey banking industry expert, calculated that total bank write-offs from 1948 to 1982 were $28 billion. But during the four-year period from 1986 to 1990, a time of sustained growth in the economy, $75 billion of write-offs were taken. In 1990 alone, the charge-offs were $30 billion, and expectations for 1991 were for double that amount because of the effects of the recession on real estate and highly leveraged loans.[2] The charge-offs and the increases to bad debt reserves had hobbled growth in the banking industry for the past decade, limiting it to about 3% per annum for the industry as a whole. They had also eroded the capital of the banks, ruined their credit ratings, and cost them their position of preeminence in world banking. In 1990, only one American bank holding company, Citicorp, then ranked eighteenth in assets, was among the world's thirty largest banks.

The FDIC estimated that at the end of 1990, banks with assets of $408 billion, or 12% of the industry total, were vulnerable to failure, and this was after a substantial number of banks had already gone under. The Bank of New England failed early in 1991, and its $20 billion of deposits had to be protected. New England proved in 1990–1991 to be as disastrous a banking region as Texas had been a few years before. And Texas had been a true disaster area, with nine of its ten largest banks having to be rescued or reorganized. The FDIC's insurance fund was depleted by $4 billion in 1990 and Chairman William Seidman anticipated a $5 billion loss for 1991. He argued that the fund, which contained $11 billion for insuring deposits of banks and S&Ls at the beginning of 1990, needed urgently to be recapitalized before it ran out of money entirely.

Old Wounds and Memories

There were no American banks in colonial times, as the British didn't permit them. After independence a few were founded by merchants and lawyers to accommodate the local requirements of commerce. Roger Morris founded the Bank of Philadelphia in 1780, which became the Bank of North America a year later. Alexander Hamilton established the Bank of New York, and Aaron Burr organized a predecessor of the Chase Manhattan Bank in 1784. Hamilton was chosen as the first Secretary of the Treasury in the Washington administration, during which time the Bank of the United States, modeled on the Bank of England, was established in Philadelphia to aid government financing and to provide national banking and credit facilities for commerce. The idea of a national bank imposing harsh terms on the availability of credit and usurping regulatory powers intended for the states was repugnant to many at the time. In the end, Congress agreed to charter the bank for only twenty years, after which it would have to be renewed. The charter was not renewed when it expired in 1811.

In 1816, a successor, the Second Bank of the United States, was chartered, again for twenty years, to finance debts from the War of 1812 and to stabilize the currency. In 1816, there were about 250 state-chartered banks in the country. The Second Bank of the United States was well managed, but because it subjected its correspondents in the rural, capital-starved western states to unwelcome disciplines, its activities were thought to be monopolistic and to involve favoritism and special treatment of the eastern rich. The renewal of its charter became an issue in Andrew Jackson's political campaign for re-election to the presidency. Jackson and the western Democrats won the election and the bank's charter was not renewed, triggering a prolonged period of chaos in U.S. financial affairs.

Any hope for regulated national banking within the United States, a sensible practice followed in all other Western countries, died with the charter of the Second Bank of the United States. There was another effort in 1863 to establish national banking to help finance the Civil War, but these banks were too subject to local restrictions to become powerful institutions operating throughout the country. Political opposition to strong centralized banking controls and capital allocation has been a part of the financial history of the United States since its beginning.[3]

An unintended effect of hobbling national banking, however, was to allow the financiers of New York to pick up the pieces and to form a large, European-backed money pool in Wall Street. This left the rest of the banking system—the country part—as a spread of small, unregulated local outfits that tried to attract deposits by issuing their own banknotes as currency, which were accepted only at a steep discount. There was little safety in the system (banks collapsed all the time), little money, and less service, until the organization of the Federal Reserve system in 1913. Even then, banks outside the money center cities still put up substantial opposition to interstate branching, which they feared would damage their local franchises. This opposition, finally cemented into the McFadden-Pepper Act of 1927, explains why we still have more than 12,000 banks in this country today.

The system depended on the market to regulate itself. Good customers would avoid bad banks, and good bankers would avoid bad customers. Market forces would require bankers to be honest and fair. As J.P. Morgan explained to the House Committee on Money and Banking in 1912 ("the Pujo Committee"), commercial credit was not based on money or property, but on "character, which came before money or property or anything else . . . because a man I do not trust could not get money from me on all the bonds in Christendom."

During the 1920s, banks benefited from a decade of prosperity, but the boom was followed by a sudden collapse of the financial markets and the banking system. The stock market crash of October 29, 1929, brought to light abuses in the securities markets, including market rigging, insider dealing, and misuse of bank monies. On many occasions these abuses involved top officers of commercial banks, which had securities market subsidiaries that were prominent players in the bull market of the 1920s.

There were also abuses in the gathering of retail deposits, mainly by smaller, opportunistic banks that mismanaged or stole the funds they lured in. The panic that followed resulted in the permanent closing of thousands of banks throughout the country.

There was also a wave of foreign bond issues during the 1920s. Most were underwritten by the big New York banks for Latin American governments whose creditworthiness in those days was shabby to nil. These were the junk bonds of the times. The banks did not retain any of these bonds, but they did peddle them, mainly to small individual investors and country banks that were attracted by the high interest rates offered. Following the worldwide trade collapse of the early 1930s, which was greatly aggravated by the passage of the Smoot-Hawley Tariff Act in 1930, every Latin American borrower defaulted except Argentina, and its bonds traded at 25% of what investors had paid for them. The original investors in these securities were wiped out.

The banks were blamed for the Great Depression, and as a result the industry was brutally shaken by several pieces of tough regulation. The Banking Act of 1933 strengthened the Federal Reserve system, provided for deposit insurance, and, through its Glass-Steagall provisions, totally separated commercial and investment banking. The Securities Acts of 1933 and 1934 reorganized the way new issues of securities were to be handled and how secondary markets could operate. Banks had to decide whether they would resume business as an insured deposit-taking commercial bank, or as an investment bank dealing in marketable securities. Almost all chose to remain commercial banks, spinning off their investment banking subsidiaries.

The effect of these regulations was to scrap entirely the self-regulated, freewheeling banking industry in the United States, and to replace it with something resembling a tightly controlled public utility industry, in which rates and risk exposures were regulated. There were various bank regulators in the new system, to accommodate state and nationally chartered organizations and the differences between large and small banks, but the regulators were supposed to act in concert and apply common standards throughout the system. Banking "safety and soundness" (a favorite term of central bankers) were to be ensured, for the first time in American history, by comprehensive regulation. The crooks were gone and laws were passed to prevent their return. Securities markets too would now be honest. The public breathed more easily.

The system worked well for quite a long time, thirty or forty years, during which there were very few bank failures, not a single depositor lost any money, and the FDIC built up its insurance fund to comfortable levels. When Bill Butcher joined the Chase in 1947, a banker's life was a good one:

regular hours, relatively undemanding work, local respectability, and the opportunity to play a lot of business golf. You didn't get rich working for a big bank, but you didn't take any risks either. It was a bit dull, but if you kept your nose clean, employment with periodic promotion was guaranteed, and you could retire at sixty-five with a nice pension.

Escaping the Chains

In the mid-1950s, however, some discontent with the banker's paradise was beginning to appear at First National City Bank. Its chairman, Stillman Rockefeller, felt frustrated and boxed in by regulation. He cast his eyes abroad, where the regulations did not apply, and began building up a large, unregulated banking business outside the United States. He asked George Moore to take on the job, and Moore looked for the best man he could find to run the bank's London operations. He found Walter Wriston, and between them, the two came up with an aggressive, fast-moving plan to capture a large share of the market in international financial services, which was expanding rapidly as countries dug themselves out from under wartime conditions and world trade expanded. Their strategy was to aim at basic commercial banking services but to make their mark by innovative, hard-driving, smart-thinking American business practices. Moore became president of the bank in 1959, and Wriston head of international business. Under Wriston's leadership, the international sector blossomed; by 1967, when Moore became chairman and Wriston president and CEO, it was an important contributor to the bank's earnings, with a network of 148 branches and 93 affiliates overseas that accounted for about 30% of all loans. Soon foreign loans would exceed 50%.[4]

There were many profit opportunities in overseas banking just waiting for New Men Moore and Wriston to exploit. The bank, of course, would follow its major customers abroad to provide financial services not offered by local banks. But in addition, there were opportunities in the Eurodollar market, then just coming together, and in accelerating growth by "purchasing" deposits in the marketplace and relending the money to various U.S. and non-U.S. clients. There were also numerous case-by-case opportunities in indigenous markets such as Japan, Brazil, the Philippines, Indonesia, and others. And there were attractive business possibilities in the fast-growing field of foreign exchange and money market trading. They went after everything.

Citibank was so successful in the international business that it bypassed the Chase in the 1960s to become the second-largest U.S. bank. This attracted the attention of the other banks, which soon began to emulate its activities abroad. David Rockefeller (Stillman Rockefeller's cousin) headed international activities at the Chase, and wanted to advance them at the cost of certain, less-profitable domestic business. George

Champion, the chief executive, was more cautious (as most bank chairmen then were) about leaping into unknown waters. Champion restrained Rockefeller until the latter became chief executive in 1969. After that, Rockefeller began a determined effort to challenge Citibank's top international position, a goal he did not achieve. Citibank was just too far ahead.[5]

Walter Wriston became by far the most influential banker of his time. When other bank heads seemed like bureaucrats, Wriston stood out as his own man. He did his own thinking, formed his own conclusions, and let the world know it. He fought the regulatory status quo as long as he was at the bank and was responsible for much of its erosion through legal and other victories. He sponsored innovation, technology, and retail banking when everyone else wanted to give up on it, meritocratic appointments of very young senior executives, and a Darwinian survival-of-the-fittest working environment for executives. Wriston and his colleagues at Citibank were the leaders of American banking in the 1960s and the 1970s, and all the rest were the followers.

In the early 1970s, Wriston began claiming that Citicorp (Citibank's holding company) was a growth company, like many high-priced technology companies, and therefore its stock price should be higher. Citicorp was growing at 15% per year, he would say, and could keep it up indefinitely. This being the case, it ought to have a price-earnings ratio of 15 to 20, typical of growth stocks, rather than a pathetic 5 to 6, which was typical of public utility companies.

This was a radical thought. Why should a highly regulated, geographically hemmed-in banking business be confused with a growth stock?

Because, Wriston would argue, Citibank management was able to improve the profitability of permitted activities and to add new ones to the portfolio, and even more important, because the possibilities for growth in financial services throughout the world were completely unconstrained. International banking opportunities would proliferate, he added, in a world shorn of fixed exchange rates (as it had been by the collapse in 1971 of the Bretton Woods Agreement), where capital transfers could be made free of controls and profitable markets in new floating-rate foreign exchange would soon develop.[6]

Citibank's international earnings became the dominant source of the bank's profits—they would exceed 80% of total profits by the end of the 1970s—and by 1973, the market bought Wriston's line, when Citicorp stock reached its all-time high P/E ratio of 25. Other money-center bank stocks rose too.

Thanks to Wriston, the banking industry had the best of both worlds in the early 1970s: all the advantages of being both a public utility and a growth stock. But these two identities were in serious conflict.

Perils of the Growth Game

Despite Citibank's persuasive example, a growth strategy for an insured depository institution was inconsistent with its requirements to ensure safety and soundness. It is because of these requirements that the banks were regulated, and to be safe and sound means to be cautious and risk averse. The FDIC, by insuring deposits on behalf of the banks, had a right to insist on this, and the FDIC put the taxpayer on the line if the insurance fund was insufficient to cover claims.

The purpose of a growth stock, on the other hand, was to increase share-holder value by energetic managerial efforts and enlightened risk taking. To be a growth stock meant you had to grow. And if you were a bank in the 1970s, that meant increasing the size of your assets, upon which your *lending spread* (the difference between the bank's lending rates and cost of deposits) was made. To increase your assets, however, you had to increase not only your loans and other investments, but also the deposits you used to fund them. For profits to grow at 15%, the standard for growth stocks in the 1960s, you had to increase your balance sheet by that amount too. For example, for Chase's profits to grow at a compound rate of 15% for five years after 1970, its net income would have to grow by $140 million, and its loans and deposits would have to grow at approximately the same rate, i.e., *they would have to double every five years*. For Chase this would mean creating $25 billion of new assets over five years, all of which would have to meet the bank's standards for exposure to *credit risk*, i.e., the risk of default. It would also have to raise approximately $12 billion of new deposits, without excessively increasing its exposure to *funding risk*, i.e., the ability to renew deposits in the future so the same lending spread would apply. This could not be done by passively waiting for business to appear. It meant having to go out and get it, to hustle business and to take it away from competitors. It also meant increasing the moral hazard inherent in the banking business when deposits were insured by the FDIC.

Thus there was to be tough competition for loans, with the most aggressive lender winning the game—but only if interest and principal were fully paid on time and stable funding for the new loans found; otherwise, the winner would be a loser.

The situation made the bigger money-center banks, the ones playing the growth game, very dependent on large borrowers and on large depositors. The former were mainly large multinational corporations; the latter were also large multinational corporations and financial institutions.

However, the large multinational corporations with which the banks had such good relations were being wooed away by alternative, nonbanking methods of financing. Commercial paper had become a much cheaper source of short-term working capital, as well as a higher-yielding short-term investment for excess cash. Selling commercial paper to a dealer (or directly to the market in the case of large issuers) was an efficient way of raising short-term, unsecured funds for working capital. Simple one-page promissory notes with no further documentation were handed over, and same-day funds were credited to the issuer's bank account. Interest rates were set by the market, usually close to the federal funds rate at which banks dealt with each other and the Federal Reserve. Commissions were 0.125% or less, producing a net cost of funds substantially below the bank prime rate, even without considering compensating deposits. It was possible for a corporate borrower to issue thirty-day commercial paper and make money by buying a thirty-day large CD with the proceeds. As in the case of the S&Ls, when there is a substantial difference between market rates and administered rates, the money will flow to the more advantageous rate. Bankers call this process *disintermediation*.

Although many corporations continued to be loyal to banks during this period, Lowell Bryan believes that "high-grade borrowers were paying much more for services than their costs justified. These customers were subsidizing the system during the seventies and kept it running." In time, they saw the light and shifted huge quantities of their working-capital financing requirements to the commercial paper market. This represented a loss of important, core business to the banks. Commercial paper outstandings increased four times during the 1970s to $124 billion, and four more times in the 1980s to $570 billion as of December 1990. By contrast, the Federal Reserve reported all money center banks' commercial and industrial loans at that time to be only $322 billion.

A second form in which disintermediation appeared was through retail deposit transfers to money market funds, which began in the early 1970s and grew like wildfire thereafter, financing much of the growth in the commercial paper market. This problem was shared with the S&Ls at the time. Demand and low-cost savings deposits were being stripped away and had to be replaced in the money market by selling certificates of deposit to large investors at full market rates.

By the end of the 1970s, banks were being squeezed three ways. First, their basic, bread-and-butter short-term lending business for major corporations was uncompetitive with market rates, and this business was being lost. Second, the cost of funding loans was rising sharply because of competition with the money market funds. And third, as their cost of funding rose, the interest rates they charged on loans had to rise also in order to maintain their lending spread. At these higher levels, banks' lending rates were no longer competitive enough to attract top-quality borrowers, and banks were forced to seek business from lower-grade borrowers. But for lower-grade borrowers, the lending spread should have been increased to compensate the banks for the greater risk. Competition for loans prevented this from happening, however, and the "insurance premium" that the banks were receiving to cover their exposure to losses was thus insufficient. In the long run, being underinsured for risk exposure could be fatal to banks or any other financial institution.

Rescued by Recycling

Profits began to wobble as a result of these factors, so the large banks looked for other places to do business. They were saved, or so it seemed at the time, by the oil shock of 1973. Huge amounts of savings from all over the world were being transferred to Saudi Arabia, Iran, Kuwait, and other oil-producing countries. These countries were financially unsophisticated and conservative. They liked to keep large liquid deposits in banks, but only in the top thirty or so of the world's largest and safest banks. The big banks were therefore inundated with deposits. Even lowering the rates that they paid on them did not diminish the flow. The banks faced the problem of what to do with all the cheap, lendable funds which the windfall had brought to their doorsteps.

The trouble was, the oil shock squeezed most of the industrial countries into a highly inflationary business slowdown. Large multinational corporations did not need money and were not borrowing. Those who were borrowing were the less-developed countries, which had been hard hit by the oil price increases—countries like Brazil, Argentina, Zaire, and the Philippines. They wanted to borrow large amounts to keep their economies going, mainly in three- to five-year unsecured loans, to be used by the borrowers as they saw fit. Fearful of economic collapse throughout the third world, officials of the U.S. government and of the development institutions (e.g., the World Bank and IMF), encouraged the large banks to do the statesmanlike thing and lend the money, recycling the petrodollars to these countries. The first round of borrowers paid large spreads over their bankers' costs of funds, but they were happy to have the loans on any terms. They inspired a second round of borrowing by third worlders, including countries such as Mexico, Venezuela, Indonesia, and Nigeria, some of which had oil of their own but wanted the money for development or other purposes.

"Aren't you getting a little heavy with third world loans?" Wriston was asked.

"Nah," he said, "these countries don't go bankrupt, they just refinance, like the U.S. Treasury." To complete one of the most-famous-last-words ever uttered, he added, "Only companies go bankrupt."

Both the markets and the regulators believed Wriston, as they often did. Initially the profits of third world loans were very attractive (and provided suitable compensation for the risks they were taking). The volume was sufficient to meet growth-stock growth targets. They were just what the banks needed, early players thought. Other banks thought so too, however, and soon hundreds of banks were seeking their share of these juicy third-world loan participations.

The oil shock also created a boom in oil and gas properties located in politically "safe" countries, especially in the United States. Banks began to direct their newly aggressive lending officers to the "oil-patch" in Texas, Louisiana, and Oklahoma, where independent oil and gas wildcatters bought and sold deals. Their oil in the ground was now worth a lot more than it used to be, but money had to be raised to invest in production. The banks were ready and willing—the oil price bonanza looked like a permanent thing to them.

So did the inflation that the oil price rise triggered. The banks preferred to lend against inflation-proof assets such as real estate. So they increased their exposures to various forms of residential and commercial real-estate financing. Led by Chase, several banks plunged into Real Estate Investment Trusts (REITs), which transferred the bank's real estate loans and investments into an investment trust that was sold to the public so the little people and smaller institutions could participate in the boom too.

During the 1970s, most of the major banks pursued strategies based on asset growth, international diversification, and aggressive lending to non-mainstream sectors. Bank of America and Citicorp quadrupled their assets from 1970 to 1980, thereby sticking pretty close to the 15% targeted growth rate. Chase managed only to triple its assets, and thus grew at about 12%. Profitability of the banks actually declined, but this was not fully clear until the nonperforming loans came home to roost later on. There had already been some problems with the loans to the REITs. The recession of 1973–1974 ruined real estate values, but it was not until five years later that the Chase Manhattan Mortgage and Realty Trust Company was forced into bankruptcy when over $1 billion in construction and development loans went bad. This was the biggest of the REITs, nine of which finally went bankrupt. Though the failure of its REIT was expensive and embarrassing to Chase, the bank (like most of the money centers) was still regarded as safe and sound and retained its triple-A ratings.

During the 1970s, the large banks followed one another like lemmings in the search for new strategies. Competition was so intense that none could afford to lag behind. If one bank chose a growth-stock strategy, based initially on international growth, so did the others. All made LDC loans, many up to their maximum permitted amounts. All wandered into the oil patch, all into real estate. One or two banks, particularly Morgan Guaranty, exercised some self-restraint, but they were the exceptions.

The greater the number of banks chasing after a strategy that might once have been a good thing, the sooner the economics deteriorated—spreads would decline and default risks rise. Third world borrowers, offered money right and left by more and more bankers eager to lend, simply borrowed more than they could repay and invested it poorly. The countries played one bank off against another to bring the lending spreads down; first the Americans, then the Europeans, then the Japanese. They rarely told anyone how much their total borrowings were, and their repayment projections were never very hard or accurate. It was all doomed to fail, but at the time competitive factors colored the picture so much that reality was obscured. Gradually, the banks began to back off, having had enough, but by then the damage was done.

Inflation, the second oil price rise in 1979, corruption, and poor management of their affairs pushed borrowers in less-developed countries into the red zone by the end of the 1970s. The *restructuring* of loans to the worst cases began then. After 1982, when Mexico announced it could not repay its loans, the party was officially over and the era of debt restructuring and giant increases to loan loss reserves had begun. Restructuring meant that the loans would be extended over longer maturities so that principal payments would not have to be made; and interest due would be capitalized into new loans. This process was completely painless to the borrowers, but it seemed to satisfy regulators that all was well. In worse cases, the banks would transfer some of the current year's profits to their reserve for losses. In a few of the very worst cases, write-offs would occur.

Many people now recalled Wriston's remarks about third world borrowers. He was wrong in assuming that the borrowers could just roll over maturing debt as the U.S. Treasury did when it continually refinanced the federal deficit. The LDC borrowings were in the markets and currencies of other countries. If these markets lost confidence, there would be no rollovers, and the borrowers would actually be obligated to pay back what they owed. They couldn't redeem outstanding loans by just printing new ones, as they (and the U.S. Treasury) could do at home. Wriston was right, however, in that the countries didn't go bankrupt. There were no courts you could go to for protection: if the countries didn't pay, you couldn't make them. They knew that, so they offered to restructure their loans on a basis that would not require much in the way of cash repayments. In the end, the banks had to make up the difference between the value of these limp restructured deals and the original cost of the loans they had made. A secondary market in the old debt developed, in which quotes above forty or fifty cents on the dollar were rare, even for the best of the LDCs.

The large U.S. banks lost ground to their non-American competitors during the 1970s. Several of these had emerged and benefited from the depreciation of the dollar relative to currencies like the yen, the Deutschemark, and the Swiss franc. In 1980 there were only five Americans among the world's top thirty banks ranked by assets. Bank of America had dropped to second place, Citibank to fourth, and Chase to tenth.

Sturm und Drang

As the 1980s progressed it became clear that the large banks' failing health made them increasingly less competitive. Their debt ratings were cut back, and their funding costs increased further, despite the FDIC insurance on deposits. Aggressive Japanese and European banks (then with triple-A ratings) had entered in the United States in a big way, offering low-cost loans to the U.S. banks' customers. By the end of 1990, foreign banks had increased their share of onshore commercial and industrial loans by money center banks in the United States to 22%; when foreign offshore loans were added, the share was increased to 41%.[7]

When the S&Ls first began to encounter difficulties, a new market emerged in *collateralized mortgage obligations* (CMOs), which were marketable securities backed by a pool of residential mortgages. S&Ls, and later other holders of mortgages, sold a huge amount of these securities during the 1980s, which led to the proliferation of securities backed by different types of assets—automobile and credit card receivables, for example, or other more imaginative assets such as airplane spare parts. The process of transforming an illiquid asset from the balance sheet of a bank or other lending institution into a liquid asset that can be traded in the securities market is called *securitization*. During the period 1986–1990, more than $500 billion of mortgage and approximately $100 billion of other assets were securitized. In addition, certain types of high-risk, high-return loans that banks made to finance takeovers, project financing, and commercial real estate were also subject to securitization. During the 1980s, the merger boom prompted the issuance of more than $200 billion of high-yield securities (junk bonds), which in previous merger booms had been financed by bank loans.

Most of the volume of securitized transactions was drawn from business that would otherwise have been on the books of banks, S&Ls, or insurance companies. The volume moved, of course, because of disintermediation—cheaper financing alternatives being presented by the market. Together with business lost to commercial paper, disintermediation had swept about $1 trillion out of the banking system and into the securities markets by 1990. Even at today's low return on assets realized by banks, somewhere between $10 and $20 billion of retained earnings was thus lost to the system during the decade (mainly taken from the large money-center banks) when it badly needed them.

As the banks' credit quality deteriorated, however, they came under increased scrutiny from the marketplace and from regulators. The strategy of growth through asset expansion was discontinued. By 1990, Bank of America's total assets were $109 billion; in 1980, they had been $104 billion. Chase's assets had grown to $97 billion from $72 billion, reflecting an annual growth of only about 4% for the decade, about the same as the inflation rate. Most money-center banks grew at about that rate for the ten-

year period. Citibank, less cautious, increased its assets more aggressively
to $214 billion from $97 billion, a growth rate of about 11%. A large portion
of Citibank's assets was in profitable consumer loans, an area in which the
bank had developed a considerable technological advantage.

The weakening position of the banks was of course recognized by their
regulators—a collective phrase for the Federal Reserve, the FDIC, the
Comptroller of the Currency, and state banking authorities. The regulators, however, were concerned that if they tightened the money supply
significantly, then customers of the banks would simply go offshore for
funds, ultimately passing along the need for tightening to the whole
world, or at least to the important banking countries. So in 1986, the U.S.
regulatory authorities and the Bank of England began to discuss proposals
for a common international measure for bank capital adequacy. In January
1987, they announced an agreement to adopt risk-adjusted capital adequacy standards based on those devised by the Banking Regulations and
Supervisory Practices committee of the Bank for International Settlements
(BIS), an international central-banking institution based in Basel, Switzerland. This group is often called the Basel Committee, and the regulatory
standards it produced, the "BIS capital requirements."

The Basel Committee's approach was to seek a convergence of the various regulatory methods used by the Group of Ten (industrialized) countries, plus Switzerland and Luxembourg; its aim was to encourage international uniformity of standards, maintain levels of capital in the banking
system suitable for the types of risks undertaken by individual banks, and
eliminate competitive inequality deriving from lower regulatory standards.
Amazingly, these standards were adopted by all of the countries involved,
and went into effect in the United States in January 1989. Under the new
system, each type of banking asset was given a risk-adjusted rating for the
amount of capital that the bank had to maintain to support such an asset.
Capital was divided into two "tiers," the first being "core" capital (i.e.,
tangible equity) and the second "supplementary" capital, which included
subordinated debt and reserves. The guidelines included a schedule for
implementation: by the end of 1990, total capital to risk-weighted assets
had to be at least 7.25% (of which at least 3.25% had to be tier 1 capital).
By the end of 1992, a ratio of 8% (of which 4% had to be tier 1) had to be
in effect. These regulations forced many banks in the United States to hus-
tle to find additional equity capital.[8]

The markets were on to the troubles the banks were having, however,
and as a result, bank-funding rates increased and stock prices declined.
The market's onetime favorite bank, Citibank, had long since fallen from
grace—in 1982, its stock traded at an ignominious five times earnings, *lower*
than many public utilities.

The substantial slowdown in asset growth and the banks' many other
problems also led to a retreat from overseas operations and foreign lending, on which the risks appeared to be high and the returns low. Many

banks closed their London branches and came home. Almost all thinned out their foreign branches and affiliated companies. Both Chemical and Manufacturers Hanover had already cut their international operations to the bone. When asked about the international ambitions of the new Chemical Bank, after announcing its merger with Manufacturers Hanover in the summer of 1991, Walter Shipley, old Chemical's chairman, said, "The merged bank will be primarily a domestic bank, but we expect to have the strength at home to be a bigger presence abroad." In other words, we don't amount to much now in the international game, but maybe later. This rather tepid assertion did not suggest a leading global role for America's third-largest bank. The same would be true of the second-largest bank, Bank of America, which only recently had begun to recover from the terrible effects both it and Security Pacific (which it acquired in 1992) had experienced from foreign loans. NationsBank, the country's fourth-largest bank, was formed through the merger in 1991 of two regional banks that had never been much involved with international business, and therefore was not a global player.

CLEANING UP THE MESS

The various developments of the 1970s had disastrous (and in some cases, terminal) effects on banks in the 1980s. Restructuring on a very large scale took place as the banks adapted to the reality of their situation. They were no longer growth-oriented. They were forced to concentrate on survival instead. Disintermediation in its various sinister forms had shrunk the market for traditional banking services to an alarming degree. Having fallen into serious economic difficulties, they found on one hand that their cost of capital was rising to uncompetitive levels, and on the other, that the regulatory limits on their activities prevented them from migrating to the more profitable ground of investment banking and nationwide branching. Relationship banking as they had once known it no longer counted for very much with the big corporate customers. They were left with smaller, higher-risk customers instead. It was an unstable, dangerous time for many banks.

Continental Illinois, a glamour bank of the late 1970s and early 1980s, was the first important victim. At year end 1981, Continental, with $45 billion in assets, was the sixth-largest bank in the United States. It had averaged asset growth over 13% since 1974, when it had ranked eighth. Roger E. Anderson had become chief executive in 1973 and immediately inaugurated an ambitious plan to make Continental a world-class bank. His plan was to specialize in commercial and industrial loans, especially loans to the energy sector (which became 20% of all loans and leases), and to large mid-western corporations whose credit quality had been squeezed by economic conditions. The bank was reorganized following a McKinsey recommendation that to escape excessive bureaucracy and conservatism it ought to "push lending authority down to the lowest possible levels in the organization." The stock market loved what it heard, however. *Dun's Review* named Continental one of the five best-managed corporations in the United States in 1978. *Institutional Investor* featured Anderson on its cover in 1980, and many securities analysts wrote glowing reports. It was very profitable and very aggressive. Its ambition was to become "one of the top three banks lending to corporate America." Its market price-to-book-value ratio was a third again as high as its banking peer group average.

The Mother of All Restructurings

Continental was limited by Illinois banking laws to operating throughout the state from only one branch. Its ability to collect retail deposits was effectively limited to the Chicago area, and it was not possible for these to keep pace with its asset growth. Deposits had to be purchased from the money market (by selling CDs or borrowing in federal funds) at substantially higher interest rates than it paid on retail deposits. At the end of 1981, Continental was purchasing more than 70% of its total deposits, and more than half of these were acquired in the London Eurodollar CD market. Thus, its net lending spread was considerably lower than that of its peer group, despite somewhat higher interest rates on its industrial loans, and its funding capacity was almost totally dependent on the markets.

Six months later it all seemed a bad dream. A tiny bank based in a run-down shopping center in Oklahoma City, called the Penn Square Bank, had defaulted, leaving Continental with an unbelievable $1.1 billion of nearly worthless oil and gas loans it had purchased from a "motley band of horse traders and promoters wearing chrome-studded cowboy shirts and gold chains." Penn Square had sold participations in its own dubious loan portfolio to larger banks, including Continental, Seattle First (a later fatality of the period), and Chase Manhattan, all of which were eager to get a piece of the Oklahoma oil play.[9] The loans were not bought by the banks' highly experienced oil and gas departments (which generally knew nothing of them), but by special investments groups that dealt with participations in loans originated by others.

Shocked to learn of its exposure, the top management of Continental had the presence of mind to arrange $20 billion of facilities with the Chicago Federal Reserve, in anticipation of a run on its deposits by its institutional investors. Though this did not happen, the event dried up the U.S. market for deposits in Continental, which forced the bank to replace them in the Euromarket.

For the next year or so, Continental announced one nonperforming industrial loan after another: International Harvester, Massey-Ferguson,

Braniff Airlines, Nucorp Energy, Dome Petroleum, and others. The markets were already uneasy about Continental in early May 1984, when a rumor in Tokyo that it was soon to file for bankruptcy set off panic in the Eurodeposit market. The bank and the Fed stepped in to stabilize the situation in various ways. At this point the Federal Reserve declared that it and its sister regulators would "guarantee all depositors and general creditors of the bank," including those U.S. and foreign institutions that had purchased deposits in excess of $100,000, the statutory limit on deposit insurance. Thus the Fed finally proclaimed the "too big to fail" policy that market participants always believed would be invoked if needed to save the financial market from collapse. This was a precedent that could not easily be discarded in the future without causing a rush for the exits. In other words, deposit insurance could be assumed for all large banks because otherwise the system might fail. Even second-rate banks would continue to have first-rate access to deposit markets, regardless of their own credit standing or lending and investment practices. Moral hazard had found a place at this bargaining table too.

Within two weeks of the Tokyo rumor, $20 billion of deposits had run off. Various emergency measures were taken, but in the end, Continental was taken over by the FDIC, its shareholders lost their investment, its management was replaced, and the FDIC purchased $3 billion of problem loans in order to get them out of the way. It was then possible to restart Continental through a public offering of shares in a new "good" bank.

Anderson and his colleagues admitted to poor supervision of credit exposures and funding policies of the bank, but the real problem was that pressures for growth and profitability overshadowed the traditional banker's concern with safety and soundness. The shareholder was put before the depositor, but the depositor didn't care because he knew his deposit was guaranteed by the government. Large depositors, especially European and Japanese depositors, were confident that the bank would not be allowed to fail, and that they would be paid out. These depositors, however, could easily change their minds if circumstances changed. Management piled on risky loans and funded them with risky deposits, and no one knew until it was too late. No one, in this case, meant the market and the regulators. Historical information and book value accounting gave no advance indication of the difficulties to come.

The Fed acted as it did, according to Comptroller of the Currency Todd Conover, because had Continental failed and depositors and creditors lost money, "We could very well have seen a national, if not an international, financial crisis the dimensions of which were difficult to imagine. None of us wanted to find out."[10]

The action taken was in response to a crisis that blew up suddenly. There had been no precedent for such events in decades, and the regulators chose to step in broadly to protect the whole financial system. The regulators had also allowed many S&Ls and some large banks to continue to operate despite being technically insolvent. They overprotected the system, in the view of George G. Kaufman of Loyola University, by voluntarily insuring foreign depositors and large U.S. correspondent banks and sophisticated investors. The broad backstop policy has evolved since into a more narrowly focused one in which insolvency can now be declared and all creditors of bank holding companies whose banks are in trouble can expect to incur losses. Kaufman calls the "too big to fail" belief a myth that exaggerated the risks of collapse and correspondingly has resulted in too high a cost for the safety net underneath the banks. Based on his study of the Continental and other large bank failures, Kaufman finds that "private market discipline is weakened and greater risk taking is encouraged when the penalties for insolvency are not severe," and that smaller banks are discriminated against in the process.[11]

The FDIC took over Continental in July 1984, and extended $4.5 billion to stabilize the bank and to purchase some of the "bad" assets. It insisted on a change in the management and board of directors, and gradually began to sell off its shares in the "good" Continental Bank to the public. Continental as of December 1990 had assets of $27 billion and ranked twenty-seventh in the United States. Now led by Thomas C. Theobald, a dynamic former vice chairman of Citicorp, the bank has adopted a new corporate strategy, which Theobald describes as based on an exceptionally narrow focus:

> Not only are we a business bank, which is unusually focused for a bank, but we concentrate primarily on only a portion of the business market—companies with sales larger than regional banks serve, and smaller than the principal customers of Wall Street competitors. That focus gives us a huge advantage over institutions that try to serve every market.[12]

Continental was a large regional bank that adopted a growth strategy, stumbled over a series of ill-advised loans to U.S. corporations, outran its local deposit base and became dependent on purchased deposits, experienced an institutional run, and was scooped up by the FDIC to prevent chaos in the system. The FDIC restructured the bank into good and bad parts, refloated the good and slowly worked off the bad. The reborn bank changed its strategy, its management, and with a different outlook began to find its place in the market. It was not easy to rebuild the bank's franchise and profitability, but little by little, management began to do it. Its stock price gradually rose, permitting the FDIC to sell off its remaining holdings at a capital gain. As a result of this method of recapitalization through equity participation, the FDIC was able to reduce the actual costs of the rescue from about $1.7 billion to an estimated $800 million.

Continental thus became the model for the restructuring process for overreached regional banks during the 1980s.

Overexposure to the oil patch and to local real estate brought down all of the large Texas banks in the mid-1980s, as it had the Texas S&Ls a few years before. The five largest Texas bank failures would cost the FDIC more than $8 billion. The restructuring pattern, based on that of Continental Illinois, involved leaving the worst of the assets with the FDIC, and then selling off what was left. In order to minimize the uncertainty of the cost to the FDIC and to accelerate the return of its funds, merger partners were sought as an alternative to selling the shares in the reconstituted bank to the market. Acquirers willing to take risks on the bulk of the assets of the bank could purchase it for a modest down payment, with the rest being paid back to the FDIC over a period of years. They would then subject the acquired bank to heartless profit improvement programs.

The once-proud Texas Commerce Bank was forced by the regulators to merge. It was acquired by Chemical Bank in 1987, at what it then thought were opportunistic terms. Chemical has since subjected Texas Commerce to rigorous restructuring and returned it to profitability. The First National Bank of Dallas, then part of a powerful statewide holding company called InterFirst Corporation, was likewise forced to merge in 1987—in this case with its arch rival RepublicBank Corporation. The two formed First RepublicBank Corporation, the largest bank in Texas, with $33 billion in assets. First RepublicBank failed nonetheless fourteen months later. The regulators arranged the sale of the corpse to North Carolina National Bank (NCNB), now NationsBank.

Later in 1987, First City Bancorp of Houston met a similar fate, failing and then being acquired, this time by a private investor group headed by Robert Abboud, a former chairman of First Chicago who was subsequently fired when his turnaround efforts proved to be unsuccessful. And MCorp, a holding company formed in 1983 that combined Texas's fifth- and sixth-largest banks, also failed in 1989 and was resold to Banc One, an aggressive, Ohio-based regional bank holding company.

Before these events, only Texas-incorporated banking companies could control Texas banks, which before 1985 were considered extremely valuable banking franchises. Today no Texas-incorporated bank holding company controls a bank with more than $15 billion in assets; and the majority of Texas banking assets are now part of the national banking system.

The Texas banking disaster was repeated in New England in 1990–1991. Overinvestment in speculative real estate loans during the construction boom brought about the downfall of one of the most dynamic banks in the region, the Bank of New England, which failed in January 1991 with assets of $23 billion outstanding. The bank was one of the region's fastest-growing institutions, a kind of regional banking conglomerate, with the growth coming from acquisitions of smaller banks in the area. As a result, it was highly exposed to a relatively small geographic area, and to commercial real estate ventures within the region. Its fate was shared by other banks and savings banks in the region. According to an analysis by Veribanc Inc., a Massachusetts banking advisory firm, as of July 1991, the fifteen banks in the United States with the largest amount of problem loans in excess of capital were all in the Northeast—seven commercial banks and eight savings banks. Estimates by the FDIC in early 1991 anticipated losses from failures of banks in the Northeast to equal the cost to the insurance fund of the Texas failures in 1988 and 1989.

The FDIC handled the disposal of the Bank of New England much as it had dealt with the Texas banks. It retained $7.7 billion of bad loans, the deposits behind which were allowed to run off. It set up an auction for the remaining $13.4 billion of assets and liabilities. In this case, however, it allowed one of the largest banks in the New England region, Fleet/Norstar, to bid with a financial partner, leveraged buyout specialist KKR. This required special treatment to allow KKR's investors to acquire stock purchase rights and $283 million of nonvoting preferred stock, convertible into a 15.7% interest in Fleet/Norstar without violating the Glass-Steagall Act. Fleet/Norstar estimated that it could achieve $150 to $200 million in earnings from the Bank of New England within eighteen months and provide a strong stimulus to the sluggish New England economy. Necessity was becoming the mother of deregulation.

America's Bank

The Continental paradigm, though often repeated, was not the only model for major bank restructuring during the 1980s. The mighty Bank of America, the world's largest bank in 1970, also stumbled badly, both because of funding mismatches for its huge fixed-rate residential mortgage portfolio and because of large increases in loan-loss reserves, mainly from delinquent South American and California real estate loans. The bank had appointed 42-year-old Samuel Armacost as chief executive in 1981, replacing autocratic A.W. ("Tom") Clausen, who was designated by President Carter to head the World Bank. Armacost stepped into the job just as things started to fall apart. He found the bank's long-isolated California culture extremely resistant to change; the bank found Armacost indecisive and weak. Like most of the large banks then, it reversed its worldwide asset growth policy of the 1970s and adopted austerity instead. Profits plunged, as huge write-offs were taken. The bank's credit quality—once the best in the country—deteriorated rapidly. Its bond ratings dropped from Aaa to Baa-3 in just a few years. Sunk to such levels, the bank attracted unfriendly takeover efforts in 1985 from BOA's much smaller Los Angeles rival, First Interstate, and former American Express vice chairman and Shearson Lehman Brothers head, Sanford I. Weil. Though these efforts were not successful, its board of directors, horrified by these events, fired Armacost and rehired the 63-year-old Clausen, whose World Bank appointment was to end in 1986. Still slumping, the bank's tier 1 equity-to-assets ratio dropped to 2.66% in 1987.

For the next three years, Clausen abandoned his past ambitions of global preeminence; he slashed costs, sold assets, and replaced management. He recruited Richard Rosenberg to revive the California retailing franchise. Rosenberg was the former retailing chief at Wells Fargo Bank, who had moved on to Seattle's SeaFirst Bank (which BOA purchased in 1983 to avert its collapse). Rosenberg was known for marketing energy and consumer innovations, like putting scenery on checks and opening the bank on Saturday. Wholesale banking was substantially ignored, along with the asset growth strategy of the 1970s, and the bank concentrated on what it had done best since the days of its celebrated founder A.P. Gianini: it serviced profitable retail banking customers in California. BOA ended the 1980s with the same total assets that it had going in, though of course that meant a big drop in U.S. and international rankings. *The Economist* explained Bank of America's recovery somewhat differently:

> Bank of America had the good fortune to nearly go belly-up in the mid 1980s, and so was spared later wild lending to property developers and overborrowed companies. As a result it was not burdened with the bad loans that hurt New York's banks; its balance sheet was stronger than almost all its rivals.[13]

Rosenberg's contribution to the recovery—improved technology and new products across the branch network—was sufficient for him to be named Clausen's successor when Clausen retired for the second time in 1990. The bank has since recovered its profitability, logging in more than $1 billion in net income for the years 1989, 1990, and 1991, with a return on assets for each of the three years of 1.0%, well above the industry average. By the end of 1991, Bank of America's capital ratios had returned to solid ground, with a tier 1 capital-to-assets ratio of 6.9%, and total risk-based capital ratio of 10.6%. Its bond rating had been raised to A and the bank was generally considered strong enough again to expand its activities into other states, unlike some of its major retailing competitors. It focused its expansion on consumer banking in the western states. Before acquiring the ailing Security Pacific, its second-largest competitor in California, for $4.5 billion in Bank of America stock, it invested nearly $500 million in acquisitions of smaller banks and S&Ls in Nevada, Oregon, Washington, Arizona, Hawaii, and California. It has also acquired some properties in Texas, and was one of the bidders for the Bank of New England.

Bank of America announced the Security Pacific deal in August 1991. By all accounts, the combination promised to be America's most profitable and most highly valued banking institution. It passed Citicorp in terms of pre-tax earnings before loan loss provisions. It also topped J.P. Morgan's market capitalization of $9.8 billion by nearly $3 billion. It became the largest domestic bank in the United States, with the largest number of branches. Citicorp leads only in total book value of assets held, a figure that connotes size but not quality. Security Pacific, of course, was gutted—the bank announced plans to lay off 10,000 people, and a loan loss provision of $1 billion was taken for Security Pacific loans. Nearly $7 billion in deposits were sold, and a new "bad" bank was set up to hold $4.4 billion of the worst of their loans, and spun off to shareholders. Security Pacific also put its U.K. brokerage firm, Hoare Govett, up for sale. By midyear 1992, bank analysts all seemed to agree that the digestion of Security Pacific was somewhat ahead of expectations. In July 1992, Bank of America's market price-to-book value ratio had increased to 130%.

Salomon Brothers estimated that the combined banks, after cost cutting and pruning of overlapping operations, would increase after-tax earnings to more than $2 billion within two years. Some analysts claim that the highly retail-oriented Bank of America may provide a blueprint for one of the first efforts to create true national banking in the United States, which Rosenberg predicts will occur by the mid-1990s.[14]

Rosenberg's management team today contains many veterans of the Wells Fargo team that acquired the ailing Crocker Bank from Britain's Midland Bank in 1985, ruthlessly stripped it of most of its costs, and turned Wells Fargo into one of the banking success stories of the late 1980s. Led by Carl Reichart, this group put together the best example of same-city consolidation that has yet occurred. They dumped Crocker's wholesale business and troubled loans, preserved the retail customer base by integrating it into an efficient Wells Fargo back office, and laid off most of the staff. The savings were estimated at nearly 30% of combined overhead, which provided a considerable boost to cash flow and earnings. Crocker disappeared, Wells Fargo flourished. Despite its share of problems with bad loans, Wells Fargo achieved the highest vote of confidence possible when investment guru Warren Buffett, representing Berkshire Hathaway, acquired a friendly 22% interest in the bank in mid-1991. To do this, Buffett voluntarily forswore (to the Fed) any attempt to exercise control over the bank, as KKR had also done earlier in the year when it acquired its interest in Bank of New England together with Fleet/Norstar.

Restyling the New Yorkers

The principal casualties in the banking industry in the 1980s, other than the S&Ls, were in the large, regional money-center banks such as Continental Illinois, Seattle First, the Texans, Bank of New England, and Security Pacific. In contrast, the large New York banks, though staggering, were still standing. They had suffered the bulk of the business drain from the several forms of disintermediation, as well as their share of the credit-quality deterioration that had plagued the industry. They were also the banks most severely hampered by the binding restrictions of the McFadden Act and Glass-Steagall.

Limitations on asset growth also put the New York money-center banks in a bind. The third world loans weren't being reduced, but good-quality corporate loans were. The soggy part of the portfolio was getting larger, and the run-off of good loans was hard to replace with equal-quality paper because the banks' lending rates were no longer competitive. Meanwhile, the banks needed income badly, to replace capital lost to write-downs.

The banks had to look for new borrowers to whom they could lend money at high rates and still restore the quality of the loan portfolio. There weren't many such customers around—most of the outfits that wanted to borrow from the banks were in worse shape than they were, many with debt ratings in the junk bond category. There were five ways to escape the difficulty: 1) increase the emphasis on consumer products, especially credit card lending, in which interest rates of 19% could be charged. Citibank was the leading consumer bank, but Chase and Chemical also benefited from this approach; 2) increase trading, fee, and other noninterest income businesses to boost revenues without increasing credit risk. Morgan Guaranty and Bankers Trust were especially advanced in this and in the effort to increase their permitted investment banking business; 3) use sophisticated financial engineering and credit analysis to generate new types of lending businesses such as takeover and leveraged buyout lending, to participate directly in the merger and acquisition boom that was under way. Citibank, Bankers Trust, and Manufacturers Hanover were known for their skills in this area; 4) originate these types of loans so they could be syndicated and the bank's own position sold down, allowing the bank to retain a management fee but very little of the exposure. The big players, however, still managed to retain large exposures to such operators as Murdock, Maxwell, and Trump, and ended up with default rates in their HLT portfolios of 17% to 19% of total loans; and 5) concentrate on middle market and local and regional business, especially in the commercial real estate area, which was booming during most of the 1980s. Chase, Chemical, and Manufacturers Hanover were particularly aggressive in the mid-sized company and real estate markets.

The last of these strategies has not worked out for most of the banks that used it, because of the devastation to the commercial real-estate market at the end of the speculative period on Wall Street. Real estate values followed the stock market, and a recession followed them. At the end of 1991, Citibank had $13 billion of real estate loans on its books, of which $4.4 billion were nonperforming.

The rest of the strategies seemed to work, however, and gave the banks time to build up their reserves and raise new capital. The banks were too big to be ruined by a collapsing local economy. But their nonperforming loans were still a reality, one that left them nursing their wounds. The real solution to their problems, most thought, was to change the rules. Free us, they said, from the regulatory limitations that have forced us into difficulty and we will free the FDIC and the other regulators from having to worry about us.

Citibank, the largest and most aggressive bank, with the greatest exposure to all the problem loan areas, came under close scrutiny. Its profitability had declined sharply as a result of write-offs, its balance sheet was weakening, and mergers of other large banks were encroaching on its turf. "How long can John Reed last?" was a question heard everywhere during 1991. Reed, a very smart computer man, had risen to fame by persuading Walter Wriston to invest billions in a technology plant that would permit Citibank to develop a competitive edge in retail banking products. Though Wriston had to wait a few years for the results, they finally came in, and Citibank's basic pre-write-off margins soared. Wriston became a believer in the idea that the future of banking was in technology and picked Reed, then forty-five, to succeed him in 1984. Having little background in third world debt, commercial real estate, or LBOs, Reed was somewhat overwhelmed by the surge in these problem loan areas, which were mainly the result of wholesale lending policies that preceded him. Reed's own remoteness, frequent management changes, and a running amok of the aggressive Citicorp corporate culture ("We're the best, let's kick ass and do deals") during the wild and wooly 1980s contributed to the bank's loss of control over its credit operations. Other banks had problems too, in one area or another, but Citicorp turned out to be overexposed to all the problem areas.[15]

Reed had a plan, however, to even the keel. It was based, not on merging with another weak bank, but on the idea that prewrite-off margins had to be high enough for the bank to "be able to eat sustained credit losses and still add to retain earnings." When the bad loans are finally passed out of the system, profits will explode, and Citibank will return to glory. The only way that high margins can be assured without taking on commensurate lending risk (this risk certainly was underestimated in the 1980s) is to reduce expenses, increase retail business (the highest margins), and raise new equity to reduce capital costs and to restore the balance sheet. In mid-1991, having already cut 5,000 jobs (reducing the payroll to 90,000), Reed announced plans to be completed during 1992 to thin management ranks, sell peripheral businesses, and reorganize to chop another 10,000 positions and $1 billion of costs. During 1991, Citicorp did manage to raise $2 billion of new equity through two overseas private placements and by disposing of its Ambac municipal-bond insurance unit. First-quarter 1992 earnings were well ahead of analysts' estimates, and they began to recommend the stock (which had doubled between December 1991 and March 1992) again. However, tier 1 capital was still only 4.06% at the end of March 1992, only slightly ahead of the 4.0% required by the end of 1992.[16] Nonetheless, analysts began to refer to Citibank as having the "strongest appreciation potential" of any of the major banks.

Regulatory Relief

The New York banks had been arguing the case for banking deregulation for a decade. The industry is changing, they said, and if we are not allowed to adapt to market forces like securitization, we will not be able to remain competitive, either with the rest of the U.S. financial industry or with international banks that have already supplanted us in terms of world financial power. And if we are not competitive, sooner or later you are going to have to pay for our funerals at the taxpayer's expense.

Congressional committees were impressed by this argument, but the securities industry and regional bankers argued that there had been good reasons for the original legislation in the 1930s. They said that the large banks would overwhelm their smaller, more efficient competitors, and that they would lose their shirts competing in securities markets with top trading houses such as Salomon Brothers, Goldman Sachs, Morgan Stanley, and others.

The Bush administration favored the free-market solution, however, and Secretary of the Treasury Nicholas Brady pulled together an omnibus bill for banking reform based on four principles: 1) the FDIC had to be recapitalized and the economics of taxpayer-guaranteed deposit insurance revisited. "Firewalls" would be established to guarantee that insured deposits were used only for legitimate bank loans, and not, for example, to finance securities inventories; 2) well-capitalized banks (based on the BIS standards) would be free to have securities, mutual funds, and insurance affiliates, and would generally be subject to less strict regulation; 3) banks would be subject to substantial disincentives to becoming undercapitalized, including more stringent regulatory controls, supervision, and examination, as well as to higher costs for deposit insurance; and 4) nationwide branch banking would be permitted. There were also a couple of nonstarters—proposals for allowing commercial enterprises to own banks and for restructuring the regulatory system to bring a substantial portion of the bank holding companies under the control of what Brady called the "political arm of the government." Brady added that the reforms were necessary not only to save the banks, but also to conform to international practice, with which his proposals were generally in line. The only major exception was in Japan, and reforms in the United States would probably result in changes there too.

These proposals were aimed at permitting national, European-style *universal banking*, in which the stability of the banks was enhanced by the diversity of the services they were permitted to offer, to flourish in the United States. The existing banking system had worn out; it no longer fit the times or the markets, and changes had to be made to avoid having the banks, hollowed out by disintermediation and competition from nonbanking financial services suppliers, falling over half dead into the arms of the government's safety net. The government's plan assumed a blank sheet of paper, on which whatever new ideas were needed could be sketched in, to design an optimally effective system that would be both safe and competitive.

Not everyone was happy with the proposals. Congressman John Dingell, chairman of the House Energy and Commerce Committee (which had a subcommittee that dealt with securities markets), expressed reservations based on the deregulation of the savings and loan industry a decade earlier. While his committee was studying the Treasury proposals, he remarked:

> Brady says, "Oh, give them these powers and they will have a golden era and you don't have to worry about it." Someone else said the same thing a few years ago with the S&Ls. I didn't believe it then, and I don't believe Brady now. The same people who promised a golden era with the S&Ls are now making the same claim with the banks.[17]

Dingell was an old veteran of the banking-securities industry wars. Dingell's father had been a congressman when the Glass-Steagall provisions were approved in 1933; he had voted for them. Banks ought to be public utilities, Dingell thought. They served the public, and the public insured their deposits. Why did they have to get into risky businesses like underwriting and stock market trading? Let's solve the problem of safety and soundness by limiting what they can do, not increasing it. He had taken this line the last time the issue of banking reform had come up, in 1988, and had managed to create a stalemate between his committee and the House Banking Committee that could not be resolved before Congress adjourned.

In 1991, the banking reform issue was hot again. The Treasury and the Federal Reserve (and the other bank regulators) were in favor of most of the Brady plan. So were the House and Senate banking committees, and much of the banking industry. Smaller banks weren't crazy about the plan, however. Nor was the securities industry, though it said it would go along if the firewalls between banks and their investment banking subsidiaries were big enough. The issue came down to the size of the firewalls. Would they be sufficient to avoid giving the banks a competitive advantage in being able to fund their securities activities with government-insured deposits? Dingell's committee proposed very substantial walls, and the banks objected.

There was another aspect of regulatory change to be considered—in the accounting area, where discussions among the auditing profession, the banks, the regulators, and the SEC have been going on for years. Long-accepted accounting practices for banks permit recording the value of loans based on their historical cost, which does not reflect any deterioration in value caused by changes in market rates or the ability of the debtor to repay the loan. The alternative to historical cost accounting is market value accounting, in which the loans are recorded at their known or estimated market value, or the price at which the loans could be sold. Securities firms use market value accounting, and indeed mark their inventories to their market price every day, recording the change in the unrealized value of their assets against current profits or losses.

It is not practicable or necessarily useful, banking traditionalists say, to look to market prices for assets that are going to be held until maturity, and for which such prices would be simply inaccurate estimates of the true value of the loans. The other side argues that current accounting practices always give wrong and misleading information about the loan portfolio, which could be marked to market daily if the bankers wanted to find a way to do so.

If a bank had used market value accounting in the mid-1980s, the amount to be written off (as market values started to be reflected for many of the Latin American loans) would in some cases have exceeded all the capital that the bank had. Such write-offs might have caused a major loss of confidence in the deposit market. Thus, proposals to change accounting practice made the Federal Reserve Bank and the FDIC very nervous, even though they were aware that market information would serve as a better early warning of a bank's difficulties than their present examination reports. The spectre of depositor panic made the banking industry unwilling to institute accounting reform, even though it was clear that integrating securities affiliates into a bank holding company would only increase the demand for across-the-board market value accounting. Perhaps accounting reform will happen when the banks are a little farther along the way to recovery. In the meantime, the accounting profession (through the Financial Accounting Standards Board) and the SEC are increasing the pressure on banks to provide more meaningful information about their true financial condition. The SEC wants the banks to be required to report market-to-market values for marketable debt and equity securities, as well as related liabilities and off-balance-sheet contracts such as interest rate swaps. The FASB proposed a simpler, less comprehensive approach, suggesting that assets other than bank loans for which market values exist be recorded at those values. The banking profession and its regulators complained that this would be misleading because only assets, and not liabilities, would be marked to market. The FASB, though having promised to study the matter further in March 1992, approved the modified rules in July, noting that they "probably won't make anyone happy."[18]

TERRA NOVA

As it turned out, Congress was not in the mood for banking reform in 1991. Congressman Dingell's objections at the end of the process again created a stalemate over the reform issues. The money center banks finally announced that they would rather have no bill than the one Dingell was marking up, and that's what they got. All of the administration's proposals for liberalizing bank regulation—abolishing the Glass-Steagall and McFadden Acts, allowing insurance and corporate ownership—failed to be passed before Congress adjourned.

A bill was passed, however—the Federal Deposit Insurance Corporation Improvement Act of 1991. This act recapitalized the sinking Bank Insurance Fund (for banks only, not S&Ls), which otherwise would have been in the hole by $10 to $14 billion by the end of 1992. The recapitalization was paid for by increasing the insurance premiums paid by healthy banks.

The act clearly came down on the side of protecting taxpayers from having to foot the bill for future banking problems. Depositors would be protected in the future, but the banks themselves might not be, if (as in the case of several large S&Ls, where FDIC takeover was delayed) doing so might increase the cost of deposit insurance in the end. The act contained several new restrictions on regulators that limit their ability to protect uninsured depositors (under the "too big to fail" doctrine) or to aid banks in other ways when they run into trouble. Banks also are now subject to tough capital-adequacy classifications that impose mandatory penalties on those banks that fall below minimum levels.

William Dudley, an economist from Goldman Sachs, believes that the new burdens imposed by the act will accelerate the reduction in the role played by U.S. banks in the financial system. In 1975, depository institutions provided 57% of national financial-sector assets; in 1991, this share had declined to just over 35%. The cost of restoring the Bank Insurance Fund will require that banks pay a significantly increased deposit insurance premium for a long time. Also, regulatory forbearance will decrease because of the forced attention to capital adequacy classifications, thereby indirectly increasing the capital constraints under which banks must compete for business with nonbanks. The effect of these changes will be to increase the cost of money lent by banks, and decrease interest rates paid on deposits. The economics of banking, relative to nonbanks, foreign banks, and other financial services providers, are adversely affected to such an extent that banks will begin to sell off assets and go into other businesses. This will diminish the role of banks in the financial services sector even further. As this happens, Dudley asserts, the "ability of the Federal Reserve to assess the efficacy of monetary policy is likely to be impaired as the relationship between money supply growth and economic activity becomes more difficult to evaluate.[19]

Banks, however, were not completely felled by the new legislation. Those that wanted to do so could set up special subsidiaries under Section 20 of the Glass-Steagall Act to conduct "nonpermitted activities" (i.e., underwriting of corporate securities) as long as the nonpermitted income in those subsidiaries did not exceed 10% of the revenues of the subsidiary. This sounds tight, but the subsidiaries could have a lot of revenues if all of a bank's government bond and foreign exchange trading and various other permitted securities activities were put into them. Banks could also get exemption from the McFadden Act with permission of the states involved. A number of banks promptly took advantage of this opportunity to make out-of-state acquisitions, usually involving the rescue of a distressed bank. More such acquisitions are probably to be expected.

However, because the act tilted toward preserving and enforcing safety and soundness provisions at the expense of decreasing competitiveness considerations, it was not easy to plan bold new initiatives in either investment banking or interstate acquisitions. Capital adequacy requirements were stiff, especially during times of large write-offs. For banks to expand significantly into these other activities through the back doors left open for them would still require a lot more capital than they had. The banks now had some de facto rights to compete more broadly, but they did not have the capacity to take advantage of them. How to achieve it became the next question.

Siren's Song

Large banks considered consolidation as a solution to their competitive problems, but at first everyone wanted to be the buyer and no one the power-losing seller. When, in 1987, Bank of New York Chairman J. Carter Bacot approached Joseph A. Rice, his counterpart at Irving Trust, and proposed that his bank acquire Irving, his proposal was bluntly refused. A bitter, year-long takeover battle ensued, the first one ever involving money center banks. Bacot ultimately won, and consolidation into the fourteenth-largest bank in the United States (assets of $39 billion as of December 1991) has progressed smoothly, though not too aggressively, as only about 15% of the combined overheads of the two banks has been eliminated. The acquisition left Bank of New York with too little tangible equity capital, so a program to boost it began with asset sales and shrinkage, expense reduction, and perhaps an acquisition of another, overcapitalized bank. Thomas Hanley, then a Salomon Brothers analyst, described Bank of New York in April 1991 as one of the "bears" in an article about bank acquisitions entitled "Which Are Bears and Which Are Bear Meat?"

Medium- and smaller-sized banks, however, had a different view. For them it was an opportunity to combine several smaller banks into powerful regional holding companies that would develop substantial market share. Such combinations could enjoy economies of scale, and would be able to compete effectively against the large money-center banks when regulation would no longer keep them out of their regions. Powerful banking businesses began to grow out of solid core banks in the South, the West Coast, the Midwest, the middle Eastern states, and New England. The top thirty American banks now include such regional banks as San Francisco's Bank of America (second ranking in the United States with assets of approximately $180 billion after the acquisition of Los Angeles-based Security Pacific in 1992); NationsBank (third ranking with assets of $112 billion after the 1991 merger of Charlotte, N.C.-based NCNB and Atlanta-based C&S/Sovran Corporation); Banc One (seventh ranking with $72 billion in assets after five announced acquisitions in 1992 through April 15) of Columbus, Ohio; Fleet/Norstar Financial of Providence, R.I. ($46.4 billion in assets after the absorption of the failed Boston-based Bank of New England in 1991); PNC Financial ($45.5 billion in assets) of Pittsburgh, Pa.; Suntrust Banks ($33 billion) from Atlanta, Ga.; Barnett Banks ($32 billion) of Jacksonville, Fla.; First Wachovia ($25.8 billion) of Winston-Salem, N.C.; and CoreStates Financial ($23 billion) from Philadelphia, Pa. Many of these banks are among the country's most profitable and are well regarded by stock market analysts. Banc One, run by a third generation of the founding family, based its success on service, retailing focus, imaginative marketing, aggressive acquisitions, and tough-minded common sense. At the end of February 1992, when many banks its size and larger were trading below book value, Banc One, the new stock market favorite, was at 240% of book.

During the 1980s, regional concentration in banking increased substantially. The market share of medium and large commercial banks increased to 46% from 25% during the 1980s. With more than 12,000 banks in the United States, there is room for a great deal more consolidation. Richard Rosenberg of Bank of America predicts that the number of banks will be reduced to 5,000 from 6,000 by the end of the 1990s.[20]

This trend toward consolidation has been evident to banking industry analysts for some time. Lowell Bryan has forecasted a compression of the country's 125 banks representing $3.2 trillion in assets into 10 or 15 powerful new banking groups. Such consolidation, Bryan claims, would save the industry $10 billion a year in operating costs.[21] In July 1991, Chemical and Manufacturers Hanover proved that concerns about who was acquiring whom, and who would be on top, could be handled by a "merger of equals." In August 1991, NCNB was able to persuade C&S/Sovran of the same idea (having been rebuffed two years earlier after launching a hostile takeover bid for Citizens & Southern Bank of Atlanta, forcing it to merge with Sovran Financial Corporation). Bank of America's acquisition of Security Pacific was the third large bank deal announced over a six-week period in the summer of 1991. These combinations had everyone speculating as to the next giant deal. Banks that were not yet involved in acquisition discussions faced mounting pressure to take part. As one officer of First Interstate (rumored to be the main target of Wells Fargo) put it: "This is becoming a tidal wave, and the stock market responses are so strong, that you get left further and further behind if you do nothing. The pressure is on Wells [to acquire First Interstate],"[22] something Well's has not yet done.

Chemical and Manufacturers were both in sad shape at the time of their merger, with combined nonperforming loans being 5% of combined total assets, the same percentage of assets represented by the banks' combined capital. The two had a combined market value of $3.9 billion (after the merger announcement), which was 9.7 times their combined 1990 net income of $410 million. Both banks were rated Baa-3 by Moody's (Standard & Poor's rated them a bit higher). Chemical said that 17% of its $6.7 billion of real estate loans was nonperforming; 11% of the $3.5 billion Manufacturers real estate portfolio was nonperforming. Between them they had 660 branches and 45,000 employees, of whom 6,200 (15%) would retire or be terminated. A restructuring charge of $550 million (later increased to $625 million) would cover expenses associated with the downsizing. The two banks said they expected these changes to enable them to save $650 million (later increased to $750 million) a year in operating costs. After the merger, the banks said they would raise approximately $1.2 billion in new equity, which would increase the combined bank's tier 1 capital to 6% of assets, well above the 4% required under the international regulations taking effect in 1993.

Walter Shipley, old Chemical's chairman and new Chemical's president, recognized that "what seems like a great concept will prove to be a bad idea unless we can implement the cost reductions we have in mind. We are committed to do so."[23]

On the other hand, cautioned John B. McCoy, chairman of Banc One, "They better not just be tying up to the same boat-rope, because if they are they'll just be going down at the same speed together."[24]

The stock market appeared to like the idea of continued bank consolidations. During 1991, the index of 100 bank stocks maintained by Goldman Sachs rose relative to the S&P 500 index by 40%. A hot rally in bank stocks broke out at the end of the year, which drove Chemical Bank's share price from 19 to 29 in less than six weeks. Chemical was smart enough to use this rally for the new share issue it had promised to make, and in doing so exceeded all expectations, raising more than $1.5 billion of new tier 1 equity. The rating agencies were sufficiently impressed to upgrade the bank's rating back into the A range. During 1991 and the first half of 1992, the extremely active new-issue market for equities allowed approximately $10 billion of new capital to be raised by banks.

In the past, however, large bank acquisitions have spelled disaster more often than not; serious problems not known to exist at the time of the acquisition often appeared later. Indeed, in a study of 400 large bank mergers in the 1980s, a New York firm of banking consultants concluded that four out of five failed miserably, to the point of destroying value in the acquiring bank.[25]

Sellers often are persuaded to come to the bargaining table only because they sense the extent of their own problems. Cultural problems too get in the way of meshing separate organizations. The successful deals have been those in which a hard-eyed winner is free to cut and slash as needed, not when both sides intend to do a merger of equals in which survivors will be chosen jointly, based on their skills. Mergers rarely involve equals, no matter what the press conference is like. Manufacturers Hanover, which was suffering from deteriorating loans and reduced ability to obtain capital, finally saw that it would be better off being absorbed into Chemical than hanging on indefinitely or trying to find someone it could acquire. Though it had to settle for a modest (16%) premium over its market price and the disappearance of its hallowed name from the market, its chairman, John F. McGillicuddy, became chief executive of the new bank, with Chemical's Shipley to replace him in 1994, if not sooner.

New Configurations

By early 1992, after the write-offs, the cost cutting, the voluntary and the involuntary restructurings, the consolidations, and the regulatory changes, the banking industry in the United States was beginning to settle down. Those who were still employed at the banks—the survivors—began to see some grounds for optimism. All they needed was for the recession and the real estate slump to end, then they could really start to move ahead. The next few years would involve further industry consolidation through acquisitions, both to extend banking franchises into new territories (as Bank of America and Banc One have done) and to save expenses by combining operations under one roof (Chemical–Manufacturers Hanover). Gradually, further recapitalizations will occur, both by banks raising more equity capital and by the FDIC taking over and selling off or refloating weak banks. Gradually, what Tom Theobald calls the "overcapacity" of the industry will be reduced, and reasonable economics will return.

However, the new environment will be very different. The United States is not destined to have universal banking as it exists in Germany and other parts of Europe. In that system a bank can offer whatever financial services and make whatever investments it wants, all subject to a single overall regulatory control, which is predominantly based on strict capital adequacy tests. This was the objective of many of the larger banks while regulatory reform was in discussion, but it was not to be.

The system that the banks must live with for the foreseeable future is not as free, but for those meeting the capital adequacy tests there are still opportunities to engage in most of the financial services businesses of universal banks. Rosenberg still intends for Bank of America to become a large, national bank offering retailing services from coast to coast. J.P. Morgan and Bankers Trust still plan to become leaders in the securities industry. All of the major banks today also offer a variety of investment management, securities processing, and support services. The only services that universal banks offer that U.S. banks do not (or could not) are insurance services. U.S. banks also cannot own more than 5% of the shares of a nonbanking corporation. Neither of these two prohibitions are thought to represent a serious barrier to U.S. banks in competing effectively at home or abroad.

Banks today are hampered less by government restrictions than by their own inability to compete. Effective competition requires being able to manage risks better than the banks have done for the past twenty years. The banking environment has grown a great deal harsher. If banks are not competitive in the service areas they choose, they will fall prey to the "bears," or end up in the hands of the FDIC. Therefore, apart from the general need for consolidation in the industry to eliminate overcapacity and cut costs, there is also a need for banks to specialize in what they do well, to improve their competitive capabilities. Universal banking may be a great idea for the Europeans (as we shall see), but it is probably not a very practical idea for any U.S. bank at present, when capital is short, balance sheets are weak, and the government is getting tough.

The United States is a vast country (the size of all of Europe) with a highly developed financial system that now allows nonbanking institutions to compete directly with the banks, often on more favorable terms. The idea of having several all-powerful universal banks in the United States is, at least for the next decade, an idea incapable of implementation. A fantasy. Instead, we can expect a period of banking specialization along service lines, and consolidation within the specialty. Banks will then choose among the following service businesses.

Retail banking. In this type of business, banks provide consumer services and small to mid-sized commercial banking services. Deposits collected for loans and investments are provided with FDIC insurance. Economies of scale readily apply to retail banking, so there are natural incentives for forging large regional, and ultimately national, banking franchises based on advanced technology and product innovation. Such banks will become large factory-like establishments, heavily dependent on the continuing quality of their information technology and marketing abilities for success. The greater opportunities and competitive priorities in this business are essentially domestic, as consolidation and competition for local market share build up. For those with sufficient managerial and technological capacity to offer it abroad, the market potential could also be attractive, especially in Europe. For the most part, however, basic banking is not a global business, and, like many prominent European and Japanese banks, future U.S. retail banking leaders will not necessarily have to be involved with international activities at all. Citicorp, Bank of America, and Banc One will be the role models for this type of bank.

Wholesale banking and securities. This business represents the convergence of large corporate banking and investment banking. It is principally a business based on the price delivered to the customer. It is a function of market values of securities and involves considerable activity in market making and trading, product innovation, and global linkages. Increasing amounts of large-scale wholesale banking assets will be converted into marketable instruments through securitization. The application of *derivative products* (swaps, futures, and options that enable the creation of synthetic securities and various hedging instruments) helps link capital markets in all major countries and thus provides an efficient global trading environment. Only a few large firms (the large investment banks and some wholesale-oriented commercial banks) will find it feasible to provide the full range of these services, which are not entitled to the benefits of deposit insurance and are subject to separate capitalization requirements and regulation by the Securities and Exchange Commission and its counterparts abroad.

Finance and investment company operations. These involve investment activities for a bank's own account in a large variety of investment instruments and vehicles, as well as those that the bank manages, or distributes, or processes for others. The spectrum of this type of activity is broad, ranging from the activities of General Electric Capital Corporation (assets in 1990 in excess of $80 billion) to those of Fidelity Fund Management Group (combined assets under management in 1990 of $120 billion). This is the field in which nonbank competitors have in the past encroached far into the preserves of the banks. With greater permitted involvement in the securities area and in market making, banks now have an opportunity to compete more effectively for this business. Many banks have considerable skills in private placements, project finance, leasing, portfolio management, discount brokerage, and a variety of custodial services. These activities have deep global roots; e.g., investment portfolios need to include a substantial portion of non-U.S. securities and amply utilize synthetic securities in order to achieve optimal results.

U.S. banks, now restructured, streamlined, recapitalized, reregulated, and ready to go, can play where they want. Each market, however, involves different competitors and competitive conditions, some of which are new to the old banks. In particular, the securities industry has changed a great deal during the 1980s, at the expense of the banks, and has become the principal challenger to wholesale banking services.

3
THE NEW WHOLESALERS

One of the last, and most controversial, of the great leveraged buyout deals of the 1980s was the acquisition of 59.3% of the stock of Warner Communications Inc. by Time Inc. in July 1989, and the subsequent merger of Warner into a wholly owned Time subsidiary renamed Time Warner Inc. As a result of the merger, Time Warner became the world's largest media and entertainment company.

It also became one of the world's most heavily indebted companies, with more than $11 billion of debt outstanding, representing 64% of capitalization and requiring annual interest payments of more than $1 billion, which together with preferred stock dividend requirements, ate up more than 75% of the company's cash flow. Standard & Poor's responded with a junk bond rating of BB. For 1990, the first full year after the acquisition, Time Warner reported a net loss of $227 million.

But that wasn't the controversial part.

Time's shareholders were furious at the company's management and directors because of the way the Time Warner deal had been stuffed down their throats. The shareholders were not opposed in principle to a merger with another media giant. Trends in the industry had been toward global colossi and Time had a number of alternatives. In March 1989, however, Time announced an acquisition of Warner for Time shares, the majority of which, after the merger, would be in the hands of Warner shareholders. The event was considered by some to be the equivalent of selling Time, therefore the action taken by its board was tantamount to putting the company in play in a game in which others could be free to approach the company with higher-valued bids. Time's stock price, $105 per share before the Warner announcement, rose to $122 in anticipation of a better deal. Such a deal did emerge at the last minute. Paramount Communications (the new name for the 1960s conglomerate, Gulf + Western) offered $175 in cash for all the Time shares.

"Lookin' good," said some Time shareholders. "The arbs are piling in," said another. The arbs, or arbitrageurs, are Wall Street firms and other investors who would purchase shares at, say, $160 per share, hoping to tender them to Paramount for $175 or more. The Warner deal had to be approved by shareholders on June 23, 1989, and all the arbs would vote against the merger so the Paramount deal could go through instead.

So Time and Warner regrouped. They withdrew the original proposal and replaced it with a plan in which Time would offer to purchase about half of Warner's shares for $70 cash, and then merge the rest into Time for shares. This plan would not be subject to a shareholder's vote, and was protected by Time's *poison pill* (shareholders' share-purchase rights plan that functioned as an antitakeover device). Paramount countered this move with a raised offer of $200 per share, which drove the stock to a high of $182 3/4. Management rejected this offer too, and ignored its shareholder's complaints ("mostly arbs," they said).

The matter came before the Delaware Chancery Court, which presides over mergers and acquisitions cases involving companies incorporated in Delaware. At issue was Paramount's complaint of unreasonable opposition to a bona fide offer that was in the shareholder's interests. The court ruled that directors of Time did not have to be hindered by short-term shareholder hue and cry if it meant the firm's important long-term strategic issues, such as Time's long-standing plans for a combination with Warners, would have to be sacrificed as a result. The Time Warner deal could and did proceed. The stock fell like a stone, first to $123 1/4, later closing out the year at $118 1/4. The court's ruling, which seemed contrary to prior decisions aimed at ending management entrenchment and favorite son deals, was one of the last nails in the coffin of the LBO movement of the 1980s. It argued that directors could favor long-termism over short-termism, a popular idea among LBO haters, and that directors were not obligated under the law "to follow the wishes of the holders of a majority of the shares." This idea appeared to some as an unwarranted infringement of the right to private property.

THE EQUITY ERA

By the end of 1989, the last large LBO had been attempted (United Airlines) and had failed, the junk bond market had collapsed, ultimately taking Drexel Burnham Lambert with it, and the euphoria of the 1980s was officially over. Few people were more aware of this change than Time Warner shareholders, whose stock continued to sink, finally bottoming out at $66 1/8 near the end of 1990, a 37% discount from the price at which Time stock had traded before the original Warner deal was announced, and about a third of what it might have been if the Paramount deal had been allowed to proceed. Time shareholders were extremely grumpy, especially the institutional shareholders, who began to attend conferences on corporate governance and shareholders' rights.

Then, to rub it in, the news media began featuring stories about America's highest-paid executives. Steven Ross and N.J. Nicholas, Time Warner's co–chief executives, were right at the top. Ross's income for 1990, from salaries, bonuses, and stock sales, was reported to be more than $70 million.

But worse than that, the LBO wasn't really working out. For it to have done so, Time Warner would have had to reduce debt quickly and substantially from the proceeds of asset sales or refinancings. But the market for noninvestment-grade debt was completely shattered (Time Warner's own securities were trading at huge discounts), and the merger market into which promising subsidiaries might have been sold for cash was also in trouble, following the post–United Airlines backlash.

The Rights of Time

The company needed cash, Ross and Nicholas figured. Their discussion of the crisis must have gone something like this:*

"We might be able to raise cash by selling new stock," Ross said.

"We'll need to sell a lot," said Nicholas, "so why not make it a 'rights offering' in which our shareholders can subscribe for the new stock, and therefore can avoid being diluted. The stock would have to be sold at a discount from the market price [then back to about $110] to encourage participation, but if every shareholder bought his pro rata portion of the offering, then the company would have more capital and each shareholder would continue to own the same percentage of the company."

"Good idea, but our shareholders have been kind of surly lately. Do you really think they'll subscribe?"

"Maybe not, but we can 'incentivize' them to," said the Merrill Lynch man Ross had called in for advice. Merrill was the top U.S. underwriter and represented lots of aggressive firms like Time Warner. "We can offer a subscription price of $105, a 4.8% discount, if everybody subscribes—or a lower subscription price, if they don't. For example, we can have a sliding scale down to, say, a price of about $60 if only 60% subscriptions occur."

"You mean, if I don't like the deal and don't want to subscribe, I'll have to anyway or else some other bastard will buy up my stock at $60, a 43% discount?"

---

*The dialogue that follows is entirely fictional, though it is closely based on the facts of the Time Warner stock issue.

"You got it. They'll subscribe to a deal they don't like in order to prevent someone else from getting a good deal. That's the American way."

"But the stockholders won't know what price they're subscribing for until after the subscription is over. They might find a difference between $105 and $60 to be pretty important."

"Well, we've taken some soundings," said the Merrill man, "and think you can probably expect about 85% to come in at about $90; that will mean raising $3 billion of new equity, the biggest [U.S.] stock deal ever."

Ross decided to give it a try. But it bombed.

The market was outraged when the variable exercise-price rights offering was announced on June 6, 1991. The stock dropped dramatically, from $105 to $89 3/4 on July 12, reflecting the anticipated per-share dilution resulting from an increase in the number of shares outstanding by 60%, but it ended up just about where Merrill had predicted. Large institutional shareholders were angry. They complained to the SEC, which showed more than a little sympathy. The SEC finally told Time Warner to scrap the variable-price feature if they wanted the rights offering to be cleared.

Ross and Nicholas had a second fiasco on their hands. Then a call came in from a top man at Salomon Brothers, another investment bank they knew well.

"Look," said the Salomon man, "your deal's a disaster and it has to be scrapped. But raising the equity is the right thing to do, so you should proceed anyway, but with a fixed-price rights issue. A lot of your shareholders want out, and this offering gives them the chance they've been looking for.

"So, here's what we'll do. You reset the subscription price to $80, a $2.76 billion deal. Salomon Brothers by itself will underwrite one-half of the deal, $1.4 billion, and will line up underwriters for the other half within twenty-four hours. We don't succeed, we're out of the deal. We do, we run it. What do you say?"

"What about Merrill?" asked Ross. "They've been working on this deal for months."

"They screwed up, so screw them. We'll invite them to join our syndicate if they want, but that's it. It's them or us."

"OK, but how about a higher subscription price, like $90?"

"Nope. The market needs a better-looking deal than the first one, it's $80 or nothing."

Ross and Nicholas decided to take Salomon's offer. Within twenty-four hours, Salomon recruited institutional powerhouse Goldman Sachs and two eager newcomers to stock underwriting, BT Securities Corporation (affiliated with Bankers Trust) and J.P. Morgan Securities, Inc., plus eleven other firms (including Merrill); together they would not only underwrite the other half of the deal, but take some of Salomon's exposure as well.

The underwriters charged a customary 3% for standing by to purchase any shares that were not subscribed by shareholders.[1]

The issue was a success; holders of 98% of the stock participated. Of the total rights exercised, however, 42% were exercised by the underwriters, which bought rights in the market from shareholders not wishing to subscribe. The underwriters were entitled to subscribe for shares at a 3% discount, or at a price of $77.60. Thus they could suck up loose rights by bidding a small premium for them. Shareholders had to choose between exercising—which meant capturing a $4 per share discount (the stock price was then at $84, the subscription price at $80) but owning more Time Warner as a result—or selling their rights to the underwriters for $4.50, if they wanted out, as 42% ultimately did. The underwriters would then exercise the rights for a combined price of $82.10 ($77.60 + $4.50) and lay the stock off to other institutional customers at $84 for a $1.90 per share profit, or a total of $27.6 million. This sum would be added to their 3% standby underwriting commission of $82.8 million, for a total of about $110 million. This was divided among the eleven underwriters, three of which, however, accounted for 84% of the total. The canceled variable-price deal was not to have been underwritten—instead dealer-managers would solicit the exercise of rights, in which case a maximum of $145 million in commissions could have been earned. In both cases the fees would total about 4% of the amount raised by the company, or 9% if the subscription discount was included as a cost. This is not necessarily a high percentage for raising nearly $3 billion in stock for a sickly LBO starved for capital with which to refund debt. And in this case the underwriters also served to replace many of Time Warner's unhappy, pre-offering shareholders. Most public offerings of shares in the United States involve underwriting commissions of 3% to 7%, and large rights issues in the United Kingdom (where they are the most common form of new issues) involve discounts, fees, and commissions totaling about 7% to 12%.

Footprints to Follow

The first big U.S. stock issue of the 1990s, then, left a number of footprints. First, it was a large refinancing of an LBO on terms that substantially diluted the original investors, reducing whatever profits they expected to earn. Many similar stock issues occurred, and still others are expected, as the heavy shadow of old LBO debt passes over us. Second, it involved an ill-considered structure that had to be withdrawn and replaced by a conventional deal, which in turn was successful only because it was priced so much lower than the original attempt. The fiasco had enjoyed the blessing of Merrill Lynch, whose true strength was in retail not in institutional distribution, which clearly was needed here. The replacement of Merrill as lead manager by Salomon and Goldman Sachs, two quick-moving, aggressive institutional firms, demonstrated the limited amount of client loyalty that could be expected when things go wrong. Salomon certainly showed a lot of moxie in offering to take half of the deal itself. The addition to the underwriting group of two bank-owned securities affiliates offered a poignant taste of the post-Glass-Steagall world that was to come. Despite the huge size of the issue, the underwriting syndicate was limited to eleven firms, a forecast perhaps of how future deals would be handled. The deal also included, at the underwriter's insistence, an *international tranche* or special allocation of a modest portion of the underwriting to a parallel syndicate abroad (in this case run by the European affiliate of Salomon Brothers) to tap foreign demand for the shares. Almost all large syndicates for equity issues now include an international tranche. Finally, the fees were very attractive to those few firms that shared the bulk of them. The three major underwriters would each earn in the area of $30 million for their efforts, the eight lesser firms about $3 million each, everyone else, nothing. The new issue business had become extremely concentrated.

The Time Warner deal signaled the arrival of a new era of equity issues. For the past decade, in every year but two, corporate acquisitions or stock repurchase plans had taken more shares off the market than had been issued by all U.S. corporations combined. Public equity capital for American industry had been shrinking at an alarming rate, a drain of $552 billion in seven years. Also, as corporate debt had been increasing during this period, the heyday of the merger boom, debt ratios were rising sharply. By early 1990, it became evident that some recapitalization of U.S. industry was necessary. The stock markets cooperated, and a surge of new issues took place. In 1991, the trend reversed dramatically: $75 billion of new equity issues was brought to the market, yielding a net figure (after mergers and retirements) of $58 billion, the first positive number in eight years, and the largest infusion of new equity capital ever. New share issues during the first half of 1992 continued the trend. The equity cushion of corporate America was being reflated.

This development meant that something new had come along to replace the enormous, but unstable investment banking profits of the late 1980s, when mergers, LBOs, and merchant banking ruled the firms. The year 1991 was a fine year for Wall Street, with record profits of more than $5.5 billion reported, an impressive recovery from the $500 million of losses in 1990, the street's worst annual earnings performance in history. Wall Street business is highly cyclical and extremely difficult to predict. One year's source of glory is the next year's disaster area. A competitor's new angle— whatever it is—has to be duplicated right away for fear that something big might come out of it and leave you in the dust. By the early months of 1991, the race for new equity issues had already begun.

THE VOLATILE LIFE

Nineteen ninety was a dreadful year for just about anyone in the investment banking industry with a price to pay for prior excesses, misjudgments, and loss of operational control. Reflecting the end of the merger boom, investment banking fees reached a six-year low of $1.9 billion, down nearly 40% from the previous year.[2] Drexel Burnham, the street's most profitable firm in 1987, disappeared into bankruptcy, and its principal figure, Michael Milken, was sentenced to jail for ten years (later reduced to two years). Drexel was an independent firm with no place to hide when it got into trouble. However, three other major firms, Shearson Lehman, First Boston, and Kidder Peabody, probably would have succumbed to the same fate had they not been rescued by parent companies with deep pockets. For four of the top ten firms to vanish in one year would have been a shocking testimony to the inherent instability of the investment banking industry. It almost happened.

As it was, Shearson Lehman lost $966 million in 1990. First Boston and then Kidder Peabody sold their portfolios of highly depressed bridge loans (short-term LBO financing that had to be replaced by junk bonds) to their parents. First Boston, which lost $587 million, ended the year merged into a new $1 billion recapitalized international investment banking conglomerate controlled by Credit Suisse, one of the big three banks in Switzerland. Kidder was also subjected to substantial streamlining by its parent, General Electric. Prudential Bache took a $260 million loss for the year and its parent, Prudential Corporation, decided to abandon its much-touted plan to become a major investment banking presence. PaineWebber lost $55 million for the year. Merrill Lynch, which undertook a huge restructuring charge in 1989, earned less than half in 1990 of what it had earned in 1987. However, Goldman Sachs, Morgan Stanley, and Salomon Brothers, all heavyweight wholesalers of investment banking and securities market products to financial institutions and corporations, avoided the trend, reporting very profitable results. Yet even these firms joined the rest in harsh cost cutting and staff reductions. These measures had been going on since the stock market crash in 1987, when securities industry employment in the United States totaled 260,000. By the end of 1991, this total had shrunk by 50,000, with many of the layoffs occurring at the more expensive end of the payroll.

Investment banking profit margins, long among the financial services industry's highest, have been in decline since 1982, when pre-tax returns on shareholder's equity averaged 40.5% for all securities firms (55% for large investment banks), as compared to an average for the years 1987–1990 of 5.1% for all firms (10.5% for the large investment banks).

Not only that, but 1990 was also a rough year in two other respects. Public perception of the securities industry reached its lowest point in fifty years. Insider trading convictions, general disgust at the selfishness and greed that seemed to suffuse the industry, and the cumulative effects on public attitudes of such bestsellers as *The Predator's Ball, Liar's Poker, Barbarians at the Gate,* and *Den of Thieves,* as well as the movies *Wall Street* and *Working Girl,* reinforced a picture of Wall Street values and practices that was generally unattractive if not repulsive. These attitudes affected client relationships and the recruiting of top talent.

They also affected the political support that was needed to combat a major offensive by the banking industry to secure the repeal of the Glass-Steagall Act and give commercial banks unrestricted entry into the securities industry. Though this effort failed in 1988, the pressure was building, and Wall Street was running out of defenders. So the Securities Industry Association changed course and announced the end of its opposition to Glass-Steagall reform, insisting instead on the erection of firewalls, the higher the better.

Wall Street life, however, has always been volatile. In the early 1950s, the Justice Department brought an antitrust suit against the seventeen leading investment bankers. Not included among the defendants were Merrill Lynch and Salomon Brothers. Goldman Sachs (according to recollections of its senior partner at the time, Sidney J. Weinberg) barely made it onto the list, to the great relief of its partners. Today only two of the original seventeen (Morgan Stanley and Goldman Sachs) are still in business under their own names as independent firms.[3]

In the 1960s, four firms were so powerful as syndicate originators that they demanded and received special treatment by the rest of the industry. They constituted what was known as the "special bracket," because they appeared before all the other firms. These firms were Dillon Read (until 1991 wholly owned by Travellers Insurance), First Boston (now part of CS Holdings), Kuhn Loeb (now vanished along with a dozen other firms into Shearson Lehman Brothers, which is wholly owned by American Express), and Morgan Stanley. Dillon Read has long since disappeared from the special bracket; so has Kuhn Loeb, although Lehman Brothers sometimes appears there; the rest have been joined by Goldman Sachs, Merrill Lynch, and Salomon Brothers.

In its 1980 annual report, Goldman Sachs attempted to summarize the effects that the incredible events of the 1970s had on its business. This was a decade in which floating exchange rates were adopted, Penn Central— the nation's largest railroad—went bankrupt, oil prices quintupled, Watergate shocked the country, inflation surged to third world levels, and interest rates went through the roof. The Dow Jones index, which just exceeded 1000 in 1970, sank well below that level and did not recover until 1980. At Goldman Sachs, two successive senior partners, Sidney Weinberg and Gustave Levy, both strong leaders, died unexpectedly, and the investors in Penn Central commercial paper sued the firm for $80 million, twice the amount of its capital at the time. The annual report noted that though the firm began the decade with confidence and optimism, if it had known what was coming it might well have preferred to liquidate and let the partners take their money home.

But, for Goldman Sachs the 1970s was a decade of enormous growth, market share improvement, and profitability. The events and changes that were fatal for many firms became exceptional opportunities for Goldman Sachs, which was able to take advantage of the new conditions by adapting quickly (as were Salomon Brothers and Merrill Lynch, among others). Without all these changes in the business environment, Goldman Sachs would have had to fight the status quo and could have expected at best only slow, hard-won improvement of its market position.

The Volcanic 1980s

The numbers tell part of the story of the 1980s: during the decade, real growth of U.S. GNP was a bit less than 4%. The government deficit rose from $73 billion in 1981 to $277 billion in 1990, reflecting a compound growth rate of 14%. Most of the deficit was financed by the issuance (and subsequent rollover) of new Treasury securities—a total of $13.5 *trillion* of marketable securities were issued by the federal government from 1981 through 1990.[4] This volume contributed to the rise in activity in the futures and options markets, as did the development of new hedging and speculating techniques. The volume of futures and options contracts traded during the 1980s nearly tripled.

Corporate financing (through both public offerings and private placements of debt and equity securities) was also active, growing from $74 billion in 1980 to more than $500 billion in 1989 and $444 billion in 1990, reflecting an annual growth rate of about 20%. The Dow Jones Industrial Average nearly tripled, and the dollar value of trading volume on the New York Stock Exchange increased three and a half times. Financial institutions came to dominate markets, accounting for 70% of all stock trading and well over 90% of corporate and government bond trading in 1990. Mutual fund assets (stock, bond, and money market funds) increased nearly tenfold, totaling more than $1 trillion in 1990.

The decade was also the first in which capital markets around the world became closely integrated. The exuberance of the U.S. markets was shared in Europe, Japan, and certain developing countries. Global (stock) market value increased from $4.6 trillion in 1985 to nearly $10 trillion in 1990, though the U.S. share declined drastically during that period from more than 50% to 32%. Japan had been the star performer in the global market surge (exceeding the U.S. share of world market value in 1989) until the more than 60% decline in its stock prices that began in early 1990. Cross-border portfolio investment also grew at remarkable rates: total foreign purchases and sales of U.S. stocks and bonds increased twentyfold during the decade, and total worldwide securities purchases and sales in cross-border transactions grew at an average annual rate of more than 18%.[5]

In addition to these market activities, the United States experienced a major merger boom in which corporate transactions totaling $1.5 trillion were completed in 1985–1990, and peak volume of $362 billion was reached in 1988. About 20% of this volume involved foreign participants, and about 15% involved LBOs.[6]

Whatever else they were, the 1980s were certainly overweighted with respect to financial market transactions.

Total revenues of securities firms increased at a compound rate of about 12%, and total capital invested in the industry at about 15%, though the growth rate was faster at the leading firms. The top ten firms shared total capital of $22.5 billion in 1990, up from $4.3 billion in 1981. This capital was leveraged approximately 20–25 times by the firms, resulting in assets on their books of about $500 billion. These assets, predominantly securities held in trading inventories, are carried at their market values, not as in the case of commercial banks at historical cost. (The total assets of the top ten commercial banks as of the end of 1990 were approximately $900 billion, and their capital was leveraged about 13–17 times, reflecting total capital-to-assets ratios of 6% to 8%.)

Hard-Muscle Trading

Most of the major Wall Street firms benefited from the expansion of securities activity in the 1980s, but none more than Salomon Brothers, the quintessential Wall Street traders, the true "masters of the universe," described by Tom Wolfe in *Bonfire of the Vanities*. Salomon was founded as a money broker in 1910. It began trading in foreign government bonds in 1915, and became the second authorized dealer in U.S. government securities in 1917. The partners were niche players, specialists in a particular sector of the market. They were not included among the great German Jewish firms established in the nineteenth century, nor among the investment banks known for their corporate clients, of which the early Salomon had few, if any. They were not especially visible until the late 1960s, when they decided to expand into corporate bonds and stocks, using their trading know-how to bid aggressively for large, wholesale blocks of business with institutional investors or with corporate issuers. In 1967, Salomon ranked fourth among all underwriters of U.S. securities; in 1977, second, and ten years later, first.

In 1981, Salomon shocked Wall Street by announcing that it was selling out to Philip Brothers (later Phibro Inc.), a large publicly owned commodities trader, for $550 million in cash and convertible securities. The deal was thought to have been pushed through by John Gutfreund, the firm's

chairman since the retirement in 1978 of William ("Billy") Salomon, Gutfreund's predecessor and mentor. Billy and the other retired partners were
only told of the deal after it had been struck. They would not receive any
share in the $250 million premium paid by Phibro over Salomon's book
value. Gutfreund and David Tendler, CEO of Phibro, were to become co-
CEOs of the new firm. The Phibro side, however, soon fell apart as commodities profits dwindled. Tendler was forced out, and Gutfreund, a onetime English major at Oberlin College and son of a golfing friend of Billy
Salomon's, became sole CEO in 1984. The culture at Salomon, traditionally
unsophisticated but paternalistic, became rougher and more political
under Gutfreund, who believed it was his role to delegate great authority
and influence to those who could be competitive and make money. Salomon's internal atmosphere was considered by many of its competitors to
be substantially more savage than most. Michael Lewis, a former bond
salesman at Salomon, portrayed the firm in his book *Liar's Poker* as a kind
of Animal House for delinquent millionaires.

Trading dominated the firm. Those who didn't trade (or at least sit on
the trading floor) were considered paper pushers, secondary players. The
firm's culture valued boldness, flare, innovation, initiative, and perhaps
most of all, street smarts. It disparaged pedigree, affectation, timidity, and
hesitation. The culture was binding and almost all of the firm's senior people were lifetime employees. They believed that to make a mark you did
something dramatic, like offering to buy $1.4 billion of stock from Time
Warner and worrying about the consequences later. Sometimes you would
get it wrong, and lose a bundle, but if you knew what you were doing you
would make a bundle more often than not. If you didn't know what you
were doing, you'd be out of there fast. If you knew your markets and had
the courage to "bite the ass off a bear," as Gutfreund put it, then you
would make money. In a marketplace overflowing with new Treasury and
corporate securities, the Salomon crowd made out very well.

Salomon had another advantage which it used to propel its position
upwards in the early 1980s—its contacts with the S&L industry. As bond
market specialists, Salomon had taken the trouble to cultivate hundreds of
S&Ls as customers for their government securities business. When the
S&Ls got into trouble because of rising interest rates, they asked Salomon's
advice. The firm was quick to propose using *interest rate swaps* as a way of
converting some of their fixed-rate mortgage exposure to a variable-rate
exposure. Salomon would agree to enter into a contract with the S&L in
which it would swap 1) an obligation to receive a fixed rate of interest from
the S&L for a specified amount, for 2) an obligation to provide the S&L
with a variable rate of interest for the same amount. Thus the S&L could
pass on its fixed-rate income flow from certain mortgages to Salomon and
replace it with a variable-rate income flow instead, which could in turn be
matched against a variable-rate funding cost. Salomon would then lay off

the other side of the transaction, say to a Japanese bank that owed fixed-rate payments on a Eurobond issue but wanted instead to make variable-rate payments to match its variable-rate income from bank loans. Using its vast network of bond market customers and its own willingness to position the swap until it could be resold, Salomon was able to capture a large amount of this business. It therefore became more familiar with the S&L and mortgage industry than anyone else.

The next step for the firm was to develop the collateralized mortgage obligation, the second in a series of mortgage securitization products that began with the mortgage *passthrough,* in which the cash flow from a segregated pool of mortgages was passed on directly to investors every month. This was an awkward security to own, because you never knew how much you would receive in any month, as principal repayments of mortgages were unpredictable. The CMO, developed with the help of sophisticated computer programs, streamlined and rationalized the pass-through into a real, institutional-grade investment vehicle that traded at a modest interest-rate premium over U.S. Treasury securities. The CMO soon became a gold mine. Mortgage-backed securities grew at a compounded annual rate of 67% from 1978 to 1987, when the total volume of new issues reached nearly $100 billion. By 1991, the volume was over $250 billion. Salomon's profits from this new product line alone totaled several hundred million dollars, or more than 25% of Salomon's net income during its most profitable years in the mid-1980s.

The CMO business finally receded in profitability, as competitors piled into this market segment, and Salomon seemed to lose interest in it. But the firm had learned several important lessons from its experience. Aggressive trading and computer technology were a dynamite combination. Trading skills could bootstrap Salomon into the top of the underwriting league tables, where new issue fees could be added to trading profits from aftermarket dealing. New products could be extremely profitable, at least for a few years until competitors caught on and took the juice out. But to come up with great new products took more than just courage and street smarts. It took real brains too, the sort that Ph.D.s in mathematics from MIT and the University of Chicago have. Salomon hired dozens of them.

Meanwhile the large established markets were volatile and extremely competitive, and the advantages went to the firm with the best information. The best-informed firm was one that saw the whole order flow and saw it early. Sources, speed, and global reach were essential. But so was knowing what to do with the information once you had it. There was no money to be made in brokering a trade of government securities between two institutional investors. Money was made by positioning the firm for an expected market shift, say by borrowing $5 or $10 billion to invest in government bonds and making an informed guess that the prices of the bonds would go up within a few days. Buying on margin, you can control $5 billion of Treasuries with only $50 million of capital. If the price goes up fifty basis points (.50%) and you sell out within a week, you've made $2.5 million, before your financing costs, if any. That's equivalent to an annualized return on investment of 260%. Exposure of this type, however, can be very expensive if it goes wrong (what if prices instead go down by 1.0%?), so new ways of managing risk by hedging positions had to be found.

The Salomon traders led the way in exposing the firm to huge market risks, developing new hedging techniques, and broadening the range of instruments traded. Through the acquisition of Phibro they expanded into oil trading, foreign exchange, and most other commodities. They developed ways to arbitrage market inefficiencies, and paid those who developed the profits a percentage of the take. Though Salomon earnings declined by 36% in 1990 (to $303 million) and top officers took pay cuts, two successful traders cleaned up: Andrew Hall, president of Phibro Energy, which produced pre-tax earnings of $492 million, earned $20 million in 1990; and Lawrence Hilibrand, a 31-year-old MIT economist who had developed a proprietary, black-box program for bond arbitrage, earned $23 million. "We reward people based on their performance," said John Gutfreund, whose own compensation in 1990 was $2.3 million.[7]

Solly's Folly

By the end of 1990, Salomon had pushed its trading revenues to more than 80% of total, as compared to 57% in 1987. Its nontrading results were quite acceptable, finishing up in fourth place in U.S. underwriting and third in mergers and acquisitions, but trading was driving the firm now more than ever. And driving the trading was Salomon's Government Securities department. This group personified Salomon at its best and at its worst. Its brilliant, aggressive, workaholic young professionals were devoted to preserving Salomon's number one position and powerful reputation. They were also arrogant, ruthless, and so obsessively focused on beating the competition and making money that they lost sight of everything else. As Floyd Norris of the *New York Times* put it, "At Salomon Brothers, trading has always been a form of war in which the opponent is entitled to no pity and rules are viewed as impediments to be side-stepped, if possible."

Before any government auction, the firm's traders endeavor to estimate what the winning rate level will be and how much of the paper can be sold. They try first to build a book of orders from customers and then make their bid. At the time, only firms designated by the Federal Reserve as *primary dealers* could submit bids for new issues. There were about forty such dealers, who had the benefit of pre-bidding discussions with the Treasury to exchange views about the market. The dealers would aggregate their own bids for bonds with those of large institutional customers that had authorized them to do so, in order to present the largest possible block of orders to the Treasury. To minimize their position risks, dealers would sell (short) the as-yet-unissued bonds to customers at a price that they hoped was a good bet. The dealers would then have to count on being allocated bonds in the auction to supply these customers with the bonds they had sold them; any shortfall would have to be covered by purchasing bonds in the market.

Aggressive traders often bid for more bonds than they have orders for, and at a higher price. The more orders they have at the highest price, the more bonds they are allocated. The more they are allocated, the more they control. According to one former Salomon trader:

> If you build a book of $3 billion, $5 billion, $8 billion, then you really control the situation. Then you use your muscle, your big war chest of dollars, to force the thing with a drop-dead bid.[8]

The idea is, in effect, to control, or corner, the market—to make other dealers, and those covering short position, buy from you at whatever price you wish to set. However, cornering the market in Treasury securities is not allowed, though technically it was until July 1990, when the Treasury imposed limits on how much any firm could bid for a single issue. The problem had never come up before then—the Treasury market was just too large, and no single firm was big enough to be able to purchase a market-cornering position. In March 1990, however, Salomon and its customers successfully, and legally, purchased 75% of a two-year issue. A few months later, Paul Mozer, Salomon's 36-year-old managing director, who was head of the government-bond trading desk, astonished Treasury officials by bidding for 100% of an issue of thirty-year bonds. The Treasury rejected the bid and imposed a limit on bidding to 35% of any single issue.

In August 1991, Salomon admitted that its trading activities had become too aggressive, and that it had made several illegal bids in auctions for government securities between December 1990 and May 1991. A Treasury official had been suspicious about these auctions and had commenced an investigation of Salomon's bidding activities. When Mozer learned of the investigation, he came clean with his boss, John Meriwether, and in April admitted to falsifying a customer order that Salomon had presented at a February auction. This and other phantom orders had put more of the notes being auctioned into Salomon's hands than the 35% maximum that the government's rules allowed. Thus Salomon had established a small corner on the market for these notes. Having such a large position in the notes would enable Salomon to control for a few days the prices at which the notes were later sold to customers and other dealers. This way, Salomon could rig the market.

Meriwether was Salomon's top trading boss, the now legendary character, who supposedly (according to Michael Lewis) countered John Gutfreund's 1986 challenge to a hand of liar's poker—"one hand, one million dollars, no tears"—with an offer to play for "real money instead, ten million, no tears." Gutfreund apparently thought ten million was too much to bet on the serial numbers on a dollar bill, so he backed off. Salomon folklore uses this event to illustrate the "right stuff" of the trading floor, to show that even powerful, high-placed executives can't really measure up against the cool-hand Lukes of the trading room.

Right stuff or not, once Mozer had explained what he had done in February, Meriwether knew that the firm had a big problem and so informed John Gutfreund and Salomon president Thomas Strauss. These three, plus the firm's general counsel, decided that the practice had to be discontinued and that the infractions should be reported to the Treasury, but no one was assigned to make the report and no one did. Within a month of this meeting, Salomon violated the rules again. At the May 22 auction of two-year notes, "Salomon and its customers collectively purchased approximately $10.6 billion out of $11.3 billion in notes that were to be available for purchase by competitive bidders."[9] Salomon thus controlled 94% of the notes put out to bidding. In the process, the firm bid $2 billion for at least one customer, and simultaneously repurchased $500 million from the customer at the auction price while "inadvertently" failing to disclose its own position. Dealers charged that Salomon forced up prices of the notes after cornering the market to squeeze competitors. These competitors—other dealers—had sold notes short to customers in the when-issued market with the intention of covering their positions in the auction, as was the usual practice. But there were no notes available for them to purchase in the auction, so they had to go to Salomon, which forced them to pay a much higher price. The squeeze was no secret: many dealers were complaining openly, and the Treasury's price data showed abnormal patterns, provoking an inquiry.

In June, the SEC and the Justice Department issued subpoenas to Salomon and certain clients. One Treasury official, noting Salomon's arrogant disregard of the bidding rules, said that it was shocking that Salomon "could do it at the February auction, learn about it in April, not tell us, and do it again in May."[10]

The scandal was too much. The Treasury and the Federal Reserve were outraged and suspended Salomon from participation in government auctions. Salomon's board asked for the resignations of Gutfreund, Strauss, Meriwether, Mozer, and some lesser figures on August 16. The Salomon stock price dropped 30%. Many of the firm's government securities customers announced that their relationship with Salomon was subject to review. The firm was suddenly threatened with civil lawsuits, fines and penalties, and possibly criminal charges. Its eighty-year reputation for integrity and fair dealing was severely strained. No matter what the firm did to correct the errors, and to prevent their recurrence, it would have to pay a heavy price for them.

Warren E. Buffett was the chairman of Berkshire Hathaway, an extremely successful insurance and investing firm and a 16% stockholder in Salomon Inc. (the firm's largest). Buffett was also a Salomon director, and he took over as interim chairman and chief executive of the firm and resolutely began the process of putting it back together. To help him do so, Buffett selected 43-year-old Deryck C. Maughan as chief operating officer in charge of day-to-day activities. Maughan, until a month prior to these events, had been head of the firm's highly successful Tokyo operations. He was not a trader, not an American citizen (an Englishman, he had been an official in the British Treasury for ten years), and had had nothing to do with government securities. Maughan was seen as a good choice to look at matters objectively.

Buffett told Salomon employees that the firm would be taking fewer risks in the future and that it would not be operating as close to the edge as it had in the past. Compliance was to be emphasized. He would be "ruthless" in protecting the firm's reputation. He was able to convince the Treasury and the Fed to allow Salomon to participate in auctions for its own account (but not for the accounts of customers), and as the year progressed, the scandal settled down. But John Gutfreund, 61 years old and at the peak of his 38-year career, was out. A tough guy to the end, Gutfreund reportedly told his top executives at a closed-door meeting: "I'm not apologizing for anything to anybody. Apologies don't mean shit. What happened, happened."[11]

Ultimately the scandal died out. In May 1992, the firm settled with the government, agreeing to a payment of $290 million for fines and compensation to investors suffering losses because of its actions. It will remain a primary dealer, and was permitted to resume bidding at Treasury auctions on behalf of customers after August 1, 1992. The firm, however, still faced a battery of civil lawsuits in connection with the scandals. His nine-month work done, Buffett returned to Omaha to much applause from the press and from Wall Street, leaving Maughan in charge as CEO of Salomon Brothers.

As the scandal died down, Wall Street asked itself how this could have happened. Salomon was warlike, domineering, and arrogant, but few thought the firm was actually venal or dishonest. Or stupid, which is what you'd have to be to think you could get away with illegal manipulation of Treasury auctions. Part of the answer seemed to lie in the out-of-date auction process itself, which was governed by the Treasury Department, not the Fed or the SEC, which had market regulatory powers and experience. The process allowed bidders to submit their own bids together with bids for customers. It allocated all bonds to be sold among same-price bidders. There were a large number of rules related to bidding, and these changed often, complicating compliance. There were generally no penalties imposed for rule violations, which the firms themselves were required to report on a voluntary basis, although a firm's status as a primary dealer could be jeopardized by misconduct. The bidding process and the Treasury market regulatory environment had long predated the surge in market activity during the 1980s and badly needed to be re-examined and reformed.

The extent to which Salomon and other firms failed to police themselves also created potential for problems. The control function within the firms (the ticket processors, record keepers, and compliance officials) should be totally independent of the traders. Mozer and his chief clerk had the authority to change orders and confirmations and to alter their own paper trail, something that was clearly undesirable. A control group that had the authority and the testosterone to stand up to the top traders (a rarity within trading firms) might have saved Mozer and Salomon from themselves. But Wall Street glorifies its successful traders, not its compliance departments. Good compliance surveillance is expensive, and not always thought to be worth the money, though as the Mozer episode demonstrates, a strong, independent compliance group may be the Wall Street trader's best friend.

Of course, the fall of human beings from positions of high esteem is an old story. Wall Street has long been a crucible for self-destruction. The much-publicized round of convictions for insider trading and market manipulation is but a recent example. To know why the best and the brightest do such things to themselves requires an understanding of literature and religion, not finance. The temptations are surely there—money, power, recognition—and the Wall Street game being what it is, there seems never to be a shortage of those who, perhaps inherently susceptible to ruin from such things, have their heads turned. The young are especially vulnerable, being inexperienced and perhaps myopic, but Gutfreund was not young.

Salomon, however, proved capable of weathering the storm, once the Treasury agreed not to press federal criminal charges against the firm. In July 1992, Salomon Inc. announced a solid second-quarter earnings increase, based on an exceptional $647 million pretax operating profit at Salomon Brothers, after an additional charge of $185 million for settling civil charges related to the Treasury bond scandal. One Wall Street analyst, Guy Moskowski, said, "This shows pretty clearly that the notion that it's not the same old Salomon—that its earnings power will be severely impaired—is silly."[12]

They Have Seen the Future

Salomon's exceptional success in trading during the 1970s and early 1980s attracted the attention of its competitors. As more joined in the lucrative but risky game of making markets in various securities and instruments, the dealer spreads declined, arbitrages disappeared, and the risk exposures grew. The increased volume of securities in the market and their turnover offset these tightening conditions, but the business became much tougher and more intense. The profits were there for those who could survive in the huge volume, tiny spread, macho-man trading environment, but it was certainly nerve wracking for those involved. To make money now, traders have to be quicker, better informed, and more aggressive than their competitors. They have to try to outguess the other players in a market in which all disguise their moves—the Fed included. The Treasury market was based on the idea that forty or so highly experienced, licensed, professional dealers would police themselves and create as perfect a market as one can. Most of the traders, including those who scrupulously obey every regulation, know that to succeed they have to be right up against the edge or they will lose out to someone else who is. Ironically, in this respect, really free markets encourage cheating, because it is so difficult to make money the old-fashioned way—i.e., from large trading spreads in inefficient markets.

In inefficient markets, money can be made through arbitrage such as the buying and selling of the same security in different markets (e.g., London and New York) at the same time. In efficient markets, there is not much difference in the various prices of the same security, so trading profits have to be earned some other way, mainly through risk taking.

Another way to make money, of course, is to come up with something new, a new product or a new black-box discovery of market relationships that only mathematicians can uncover. Then you have a *proprietary product*, which can be used to trade profitably for the firm's own account (or for a few good customers) as long as it is kept quiet. Proprietary products don't last long, but they can improve the economics of trading for a while by lowering the risk exposure or improving the spreads. Naturally, everyone looks for these golden nuggets, but they are difficult to find and a certain amount of claim jumping occurs. In recent years, almost every firm has followed Salomon's lead in hiring a bevy of Ph.D.s and other very smart people to look for and polish the nuggets.

Because of the volumes involved and the increased volatility in the markets, trading as a whole is now vastly more important to firms than it was a decade ago. Enormous amounts of leverage are available to well-established traders to increase their market power. This market power draws increasing amounts of new business into the securities markets from banks and insurance companies, and enables prominent dealers to penetrate other businesses. Salomon started as a bond trader, fortified its position, and used trading skills to move into stocks, underwriting, and corporate finance, as Steve Ross of Time Warner could testify. Goldman Sachs and Morgan Stanley started as corporate finance houses with strong ties to institutional investors, and they have used these relationships to generate trading activity. Both firms moved into proprietary trading, index arbitrage trading, and trading in foreign securities, foreign exchange, oil, and certain other commodities during the 1980s. First Boston and Bear Stearns have had similar experiences. Trading revenues, including commodities and foreign exchange, are now in the range of 60% to 70% of total noninterest revenues at Goldman Sachs, and 40% to 50% for Morgan Stanley, half of which in Morgan's case are reportedly derived from proprietary trading. Bear Stearns was also in the 40% range for 1990. So too were Bankers Trust and J.P. Morgan, both long-standing traders of government securities and foreign exchange intent upon combining their trading skills with their new investment banking powers to establish leading market positions in corporate securities. Even retail-dominated wire-houses Merrill Lynch and Shearson Lehman Brothers showed trading revenues of more than 20% in 1990. The ability to trade freely in the market with the end users on both sides—the issuers of securities and their ultimate investors—has created a market access that did not exist before the 1980s and has resulted in major changes in the relationships between banks and their customers.

COME THE FREE MARKETS

Nothing affects finance and business more than the government. A small change in tax laws, antitrust enforcement, banking regulations, or foreign exchange controls can make a lot more difference to the profits of a firm than years of hard work from even brilliant employees slogging away night and day. A particular regime of government regulations sets the environment in which transactions take place at prices established by the market, but contained by the regime. This is no problem for competitors, really, if all are part of the same regime and must play by the same rules. If regimes overlap, however, and if players subject to a different set of rules enter the market, then the best policy, many economists agree, is to remove the regulations that are hampering the original players. Then you have a truly free market.

Free markets are not the same as free enterprise. Free enterprise permits you to own a bank, and me to operate a mutual fund, subject to our respective regulatory regimes. As long as the only people offering retail financial services are banks, then the relative effects of the cost of regulation (e.g., interest-free reserves on deposit with the Fed, insurance premiums paid to the FDIC, and the annual cost of bank examinations and reports) don't affect your deposit rates any more than any other bank's. The market for deposits is where you set it after taking into account all the regulatory cost factors. Mutual funds, not being banks, are not subject to such regulatory costs. So if one of my bright young folks comes up with the idea of a money-market mutual fund, with check-writing privileges, I can offer your customers bank-like deposits at a higher rate than you can. When you discover that I plan to do this you complain.

Either the regulators will listen, and kill off my fund (thereby protecting their insurance fund), or they won't, in which case, sooner or later, you will lose deposits to my mutual fund. Then they will have to reduce the regulatory burdens so you can compete on a more even basis with my fund. When you can do so, you're in a free market.

Conflicts of policy between banking and nonbanking regimes have dangerous loose ends. The collapse of the S&L industry is certainly an example of this. The banking industry, of course, faces similar problems, as illustrated by the steadily shrinking share that banks represent of national financial sector assets.

During the last two decades, U.S. economic policies have evolved toward free markets, on the theory that markets not interfered in by the government are usually more efficient. This changed attitude has involved more deregulation than most people would have thought possible—but after all, there has been much to deregulate. Nothing has changed the financial services industry more than the cumulative effect of continuous deregulation, not just in the United States but, over recent years, in the rest of the industrialized countries as well.

Loosening the Government's Grip

After the events of 1929–1933, federal regulation of financial services was extreme—everything was locked up tight. Wartime pressures required further regulation of national funds flows. The financial regulatory regime, with every piece in its own box, worked very smoothly during the 1950s. In the 1960s, however, the United States developed a balance of payments problem that, though small by today's standards, was distressing. It involved the shipment of U.S. gold reserves abroad when foreign holders of dollars presented them for payment, as they were entitled to do. Americans were not allowed to own gold themselves, and they did not want to see the hard-earned contents of Fort Knox emptied. Under the Bretton Woods Agreement negotiated among the World War II allies, the dollar was pegged to gold, and other currencies were pegged to the dollar. The trouble was, the exchange rates were all based on 1946 economic conditions, which were quite out of date twenty years later—the price of gold was set at $35 per ounce. In an attempt to stem the loss of gold reserves, the United States imposed strict controls on the export of dollars by corporations and institutions. Most other industrialized countries had had such controls since 1946, but the mighty United States had not.

Naturally these controls did not work very well because they affected only part of the problem, the exporting of capital. They did not address the importing of goods, because the United States had a free-trade policy. As the true value (not the official value, which was regulated) of other currencies rose relative to the dollar, and inflation set in, even more dollars flowed abroad in exchange for foreign goods. The holders of these over-valued dollars naturally wanted to exchange them for undervalued gold as long as they could. So the queue at Fort Knox grew longer. Market forces had gotten inside the regime and were wreaking havoc. Finally, President Nixon decided to close the gold window unilaterally. No more gold would leave the country. If you wanted to sell dollars, you could do so in the foreign exchange market, accepting whatever price was available. The fixed gold-dollar exchange ratio ceased to exist and the entire Bretton Woods fixed-exchange rate system collapsed overnight. Since then, cur-rency rates have fluctuated in the foreign exchange markets around the world, introducing unheard-of levels of volatility to foreign trade and investment.

We got used to it and foreign commerce did not die off—it tripled. We still have a large current account deficit, but it is not settled by shipping gold, it is balanced by financial inflows of portfolio and direct investments.

President Nixon did not want to bring the system down, but he had to do it. It was impossible to maintain two values for the dollar at once—two regimes—and the market forced the issue. It did the same in the case of Regulation Q (deposit rate ceilings) versus money market funds, which started the disintermediation that threatened to ruin S&Ls and banks unless they were given commensurate privileges and freedom to invest in different assets.

A form of deregulation occurs when the government does nothing in the face of a challenge to an existing institution by market forces. Another occurs when the government goes out of its way to remove a regulatory obstacle to free-market activity. The repeal in 1974 of the U.S. capital con-trols (no longer strictly necessary since the adoption of floating exchange rates) is an example of the latter. Britain also removed its capital controls as one of the first acts of the new Thatcher government in 1979, and other European countries and Japan gradually followed suit.

Another form of deregulation occurs when a sacred cow is slaughtered. In 1975, the New York Stock Exchange, very much against the wishes of its members, withdrew its policy of requiring all trades to be done at fixed minimum-commission rates. Trading on the exchange had increased enor-mously as institutional investors became active in common stocks. These investors traded in large blocks of shares, say 10,000 at a time. Such a block, valued at about $400,000 at the average share price then, would require a commission of about $4,000—twice that if the broker handled both sides of the trade as was often done. Brokerage commissions repre-sented about half of the total noninterest revenues of Wall Street firms before 1975 (they are now 16%).

Some aggressive institutions decided to challenge the exchange, and sued it for restraint of trade. The SEC joined in sympathy. In time, the free market won and fixed rates were abolished. Thenceforth, commissions were negotiated, and volume soared. Today the New York Stock Exchange is the world's most efficient and least expensive marketplace for trading equity securities. Britain deregulated the London Stock Exchange in 1986, and most other European exchanges now have negotiated rates.

A similar example occurred when the government supported efforts by unions and others to change corporate pension-fund rules. This led to the passage of the Employees Retirement Income Security Act of 1974 (ERISA), in which corporations, against their will, were required to keep pension plans fully funded and to invest the money prudently—that is, not entirely in the company's own stock. The result was that pension funds became more independent, and they hugely increased the volume of investment in common stocks; pension funds are now the single largest investor in common stocks in the United States. Again, the example has been judged a success by pension fund regulators in other countries.

In the Carter administration, the government advanced deregulation of the airlines and certain other industries. Reaganomics, as we know, picked up on the theme and was especially influential in cooling down antitrust enforcement, which helped inspire the merger boom. LBOs and junk bonds were not opposed by the SEC or the Federal Reserve or by many of the state insurance regulators, so they proliferated, until the market came to its senses and applied realistic values to them.

Financial markets, however, have been especially affected by two pieces of regulation that the SEC developed on its own initiative. In 1982, the dollar was strong and interest rates were falling. Bond prices were rising, and investors, including foreign investors, wanted to participate in the U.S. bond market. But in the United States, bonds are only sold in *registered form*—the names of the bondholders are registered, and payments on the bonds are made only to the registered holder. This procedure offers security against theft and aids tax collection. In Europe, however, investors often prefer Eurobonds, which are offered in *bearer form,* allowing payments to be made to whomever presents the bond. U.S. companies can issue Eurobonds, and investors like to buy them. Most Eurobond investors won't buy registered bonds in the United States for fear that the IRS will give their names to their local tax authorities.

Eurobonds are not regulated by any government, but only by the market participants that have kept it tolerably straight for more than thirty years. U.S. companies issued Eurobonds whenever the interest rate was lower than the rate they would have to pay at home. Such issues could be brought out at a moment's notice, as there was no requirement to file a registration statement with the SEC and wait a month or so for it to declare the issue eligible for sale.

In 1982–1984, with the dollar rising, creditworthy U.S. companies found financing cheaper in Europe than at home. The unregulated (i.e., free) market was cheaper than the regulated market, so business flowed to it.

The SEC worried that this trend might become permanent and weaken U.S. capital markets in general. It decided to revise its basic securities new-issue regulations to allow U.S. companies to preregister issues so they could come to the home market without delay. This change was incorporated in Rule 415. The IRS would not budge on bearer securities, which were popular with drug dealers and their money launderers, so preregistration (usually called shelf registration) was the best that could be done. When the dollar started to fall in mid-1985, Europeans were less eager to buy Eurobonds, whose price advantage disappeared. But the two markets were now even as to speed of market access, a consideration of growing importance to U.S. corporate treasurers, who had been learning to live with greater interest-rate volatility since the Volcker-instigated monetary policy change at the Fed in 1979.

Rule 415 stemmed the tide, but the change was not entirely voluntary on the part of the SEC. Market forces outside the control of the United States had necessitated the change.

The SEC also had another ambition—to attract foreign new-issue business to the U.S. capital markets, away from the Euromarkets. This would demonstrate the importance of the United States in global finance and create more business for U.S. firms. Foreigners, however, did not generally wish to file cumbersome and expensive registration statements with the SEC, particularly when they could float unregistered issues in the Eurobond market instead. Some private placements of foreign securities had already been arranged directly with U.S. institutional investors, which were not required to register these issues, and the SEC decided to open that door wider. In August 1990, it approved Rule 144a, which permits, in effect, anyone selling a new issue of securities to professional investors with $100 million or more under management (of which there are hundreds in the United States) to do so on an unregistered basis, subject only to private placement rules. If you are an American company, you might prefer for legal reasons to issue securities under Rule 415, but if you are a foreigner, you can now sell to a pretty big market of knowledgeable investors in the United States on the same disclosure basis as in your home country. Through the end of 1991, Rule 144a attracted $22 billion of foreign issues of debt and equity securities (19% of all private placements) that would not have been sold in the United States otherwise.[13] The U.S. market has now become user-friendly to foreigners for the first time since 1933.

Where Have All the Boundaries Gone?

The principal result of two decades of deregulation has been the removal of the boundaries that have separated players from different regimes. Before 1980, American companies chose an investment banker much as they would a legal or accounting firm, expecting it to give advice and handle transactions when the need occurred, which was not often. To prepare a registration statement for filing with the SEC, a company would ask its investment banker to join a team of its own executives and lawyers. Once filed, the registration statement would have to be reviewed by the SEC, a process that might take a month or more. Only then would the issue be ready for pricing, based on market conditions then prevailing. There was very little room in the process to search for an alternate issue or a better price from a different banker. Prior relationships were subject to mild competition from other bankers, but those in place were left respectfully alone. The total volume of corporate finance was modest in comparison to what it became by 1990, so the pressure to meet high transactional performance standards was not great.

All of this changed during the 1980s as a result of increased financing requirements, government regulatory reform, and the globalization of capital markets.

"Uh, Charlie, we're looking for some ten-year money and hoped you might be able to help," said the treasurer of a well-known A-rated *Fortune* 500 company.

"Thanks for calling to tell me, Bob," replied his investment banker of many years standing, a managing director of a well-known firm. "We'll be glad to take care of it for you. Right now, I'd say the rate level looks like about 90 basis points over ten-year Treasuries."

"That so? A fellow called me yesterday from London, said the market looked good over there for some of our paper. Said he would bid 85 basis points over Treasuries for a $100 million issue right now, on the phone, or if he could have twenty-four hours, he would try to syndicate a deal overnight in Japan at 80 over."

"Well, I guess we could match the 85, Bob, but it would be a stretch. Below that, I don't know. The deal might bomb. Maybe you ought to just let us handle it, as we always have, knowing we will do the best job we possibly can."

"I know you would do your best, Charlie, but I'm not so sure you guys are either the most knowledgeable about worldwide markets or the most aggressive group in the world. I don't want you to lose money on this deal, but I have to look after our shareholders too. Somebody offers me 80 I oughta take it; if it bombs, it blows up on the other guy, not me."

In the old days, before Rule 415, Bob would not have been able to price and sell his securities until the issue had been cleared by the SEC. By then, he would have long since committed to an underwriting firm. He would have issued Eurobonds only if Charlie had mentioned them as an alternative. But now he could go to market anytime, anywhere, with anyone who called with a good idea. Bob was no longer a captive market for his longstanding investment banker. Once the London man called, Bob wondered who else might contact him, and he began to cultivate relationships with other firms—not only other U.S. investment banks with known capabilities in particular areas, like Merrill Lynch, or Salomon Brothers, but Swiss, German, and Japanese firms too. And some of the big American commercial banks, such as Morgan and Bankers Trust, called almost every day.

At first Bob told the group what he was looking for and asked for their best bids. He selected the lowest price and felt happy. But he began to wonder whether he had missed something. Maybe he wasn't asking the right questions. Maybe he should let the group come to him with whatever ideas they had. Soon they were talking about issuing Swiss franc-denominated bonds and passing on the foreign exchange risk through a currency swap. Or issuing bonds with warrants attached to buy other bonds, or stock, or even gold. They all had ideas, and brought them around. Bob started to select the best idea to get the best rate, sometimes playing with the pieces, and ended up doing business with several firms. Once it was clear that Bob was not wedded to any single firm, he got even more calls. One day Charlie called.

"Bob, you've done five deals in the last year, none of them with us," he began. "By our figuring, no one made much money on any of these deals. You've come out OK, but you're pushing your relationships pretty hard, maybe too hard. Who can you count on to come to bat for you when you really need help?"

"Glad you called, Charlie. Gives me a chance to explain our new policy regarding investment bankers. We've had a great relationship in the past, and I hope we can keep it great. But it can't be exclusive anymore. No one firm always has the best ideas or rates. So we decided to spread our business around a little. We're going to have a core of four or five bankers that we regard as on the inside track. When we do plain vanilla deals we'll ask this group for their best rates. All of you will be briefed from time to time as to our needs and thinking, so you can keep your knowledge of the company up to date. We'll take proprietary ideas from any one of you, without revealing them to the others. Occasionally we'll bring other banks into the group, but only after they have done something to earn it. If we do a merger or something, we'll pick whichever our CEO thinks can help the most at the time, or doesn't have a conflict. We figure there are enough bankers around so that there will always be a couple who want to do business with us. Actually, all these issues we have been doing lately have taught our own people a lot, and we're not as dependent as we were on bankers to tell us what's going on.

"That OK with you, Charlie?"

Deregulation had diluted and downgraded Charlie's historical relationship. The doors had been opened to unlimited competition. Rising in importance was the need to be price competitive, totally up to date on all markets in the world, and innovative. Those things cost a lot of money, and with the competition for the business being what it was, it was hard to see how Bob's account could earn enough to pay the costs of servicing it, let alone hold up the profits of Charlie's department. You'd have to be a pretty big firm, with powerful global trading and distribution capability to be able to afford what it would take to win Bob's business and still make money.

Maybe we ought to give up Bob, thought Charlie, and look for smaller clients that won't get so much competitive attention. But that's why we went after Bob's business three years ago. The heavyweight competition is moving downmarket. Hell, this business is getting to be as bad as wholesale banking!

The benefits of wholesale financial services have moved from producers to consumers. Increased competition does that. If the supply of a service goes up, the price comes down. Because wholesale financial markets are now globally integrated through the Eurocurrency market, as well as through the bond and stock markets and swaps, the number of competitors and the quantity of innovation being offered have greatly increased.

"What's worse," said Charlie, having thought over the problem, "in the long run this disease is going to spread to all of our products. Only an innovative blockbuster, or a frenzy in mergers or equities, or something, can save the old-fashioned corporate finance business. Neither innovations nor market surges last for long, and if they can't be repeated, the firm's margins go to hell. And more and more of the competition are these new characters—banks and foreigners—that don't mind low-margin business because they are used to it. Those guys don't work on the basis of their individual performance, but instead on some sort of shoe-clerk salary.

"Maybe we ought to just run down the traditional investment banking business and all become traders."

As a result of deregulation and globalization, a substantially free market for large blocks of securities traded among sophisticated investors has emerged in the United States. This market is very efficiently linked to wholesale markets in Europe (Eurobonds and some national bond markets) and Japan (where private placements do not have to be registered). Through interest rate swaps, fixed-rate instruments are integrated with floating-rate instruments, and through currency swaps, interest rate obligations in convertible currencies are linked together. Arbitrage transactions will bring these rates back into line if any of them get too far from parity rates. It is now possible to say that the wholesale market for financial services is large, free, global, and efficient.

Firms like Charlie's have had to rethink their strategies. There is no more easy business from new issues, where you go to work when the phone rings. Investment banking is breaking up into capital market activity (such as new issues), and financial advisory services (such as mergers, restructurings, and financial engineering jobs of various types). Today you have to compete for business from your own clients. To offer competitive capital market services requires a large infrastructure for tapping markets across the globe, or specialization into well-defined niches where particular expertise (as in futures and options, for example) is unique. Corporate finance, on the other hand, does not require quite such a large infrastructure, but it does require easy access to CEOs and chief financial officers. Firms have to choose between being a large global player and a downsized, national, specialized firm.

Many firms, recognizing the same trend that Charlie did, have moved more of their revenues into securities trading and merchant banking investments, letting yesterday's client business go to competitors if it couldn't be won profitably. Morgan Stanley has moved quite far in this direction. For the four years ending in 1991, merchant banking investments and proprietary trading together represented more than 40% of the firm's total noninterest income. Morgan Stanley is still a leader in offering basic investment banking services to the blue chips, of course, but these have declined in importance to the firm as trading and investment income have grown. In 1986, investment banking contributed about half of the firm's total revenues; in 1990, about a third. Morgan Stanley also developed considerable off-balance-sheet activities—in 1990, it managed $30 billion of investments for others, administered $15 billion of funds in its custody, and managed a $2.25 billion leveraged investments fund.

Kohlberg, Kravis & Roberts, the LBO group that left Bear Stearns & Co. in 1976, no longer thinks of itself as an investment bank. Originally, it did deals on behalf of corporate clients, taking a fee and an equity participation for itself. Later, it changed and represented a group of institutional investors that wanted to put some money to work in high-yielding LBOs. They organized large investment funds, and invited pension funds and others to subscribe. KKR, as manager of the funds, became the principal in the transaction, not the agent for somebody else. Other investment bankers brought it ideas and offered services. KKR changed from being a manufacturer of financial services to a user of them. It receives an annual fee for managing the funds under investment, plus a generous share of any profits when the investments are sold. KKR was very successful in attracting money to manage and in completing large LBO deals. Some of these have since been sold for big profits; others are still pending (though many of these investments will be much less successful than the early ones). Many other Wall Street firms noticed how well KKR had done and attempted to copy them. Several, including large investment banks like Morgan Stanley and Goldman Sachs, set up LBO funds of their own. These firms, however, find it difficult to act in the market at the same time as a principal (fund manager) and as an agent (on behalf of a client) because conflicts of interest often occur. KKR acts only as principal.

The success of firms such as KKR was responsible for a migration of some of the best investment banking talent into boutiques, like the Blackstone Group formed by two former Lehman Brothers professionals, Peter G. Peterson and Steven Schwartzman. Or like Bruce Wasserstein and Joseph Perrella, who left First Boston because, in their view, it did too much trading, and did not have enough commitment to merchant banking, and set up their own mergers shop. (Ironically, after they left, First Boston needed to show that their M&A capability had not been diminished, so it greatly increased its exposure to bridge loans. Several of these failed, and the firm would probably have perished but for its wealthy parent, Credit Suisse). Wasserstein and Perrella were quite successful initially, but when the mergers market dried up in the United States in 1990–1992, it was forced to look for other sources of revenue—mainly trading—to make ends meet.

Boutique bankers say they want to practice old-fashioned investment banking, but of course that's impossible with negotiated commissions and today's cutthroat competition for new issue business. What they have done is to set up niche businesses that, because of relationships or special talents, can survive doing a modest amount of financial advisory or investment management business, which is subject to much less competition.

Golden Men

Goldman Sachs chose to become a large global player. It had been known since the 1970s as a firm devoted to serving all the financial needs of corporations and large institutions—it aimed to become the bankers to the world's most competent financial professionals. To do this, the firm had to develop outstanding professional competence in the entire range of financial products, and to market its services broadly and aggressively.

The firm had ideas about competition that were unusual for Wall Street in the 1970s and 1980s: Goldman Sachs people could compete successfully for any kind of investment banking business, no matter whose it was. If they were good enough and tried long enough, they would ultimately get it. Effective marketing could do as much for Goldman Sachs as it did for Procter & Gamble.

Goldman was the first investment bank to set up a high-level investment banking sales force whose job was to cultivate and maintain relationships with chief executives and top financial officers of prospective clients. This group did not execute the business that was arranged: execution was turned over to specialists. The Investment Banking Services (IBS) representatives, as Goldman Sachs called such salespeople, spent all of their time marketing. Their job was to get to know all of the companies on an assigned list of 200 to 300 in a particular region, find out what services were needed, and field a team of specialists to assist in soliciting the business identified and to execute the transaction once the assignment was won. The representatives were on the road several days a week and on the phone constantly. They were given "credit" for all revenues generated by the companies on their lists, and at the end of the year the "scorecard" recording the sum of these credits helped determine compensation and promotion. The others on the teams, the product specialists, were judged on the basis of how much income was earned on the deals carried out in their specialty unit, such as equity issues, leases, or mergers. Each group depended upon the other to help in landing the business, getting the job done, and building market share. Prima donnas who couldn't get along with sales reps or product specialists found themselves ignored and their production in decline.

In the 1980s, Goldman Sachs faced the same problem that Charlie did. Its terrific relationships with clients were not going to be enough. To maintain them, transactions would have to be pushed to the forefront, and product proficiency improved. And, trading skills in fixed income and equities would have to be extended to overseas markets in Europe and Japan. All of the IBS reps would have to be retrained to become more market-oriented, and means would have to be found for people in the trading room to talk directly at any time of day to prospective issuing clients—no longer would they go through the IBS rep, who might be out of touch when needed.

"Our relationships and marketing capability are our strength," said one partner. "What's hot changes, but the clients don't. They always need something. Our relationships with them will die out, though, unless we have excellent execution capability too. And that means getting the best people we can into the transactional jobs." New opportunities for countless young Goldman Sachs associates and vice presidents were the result. Capital markets transactions desks in both debt and equities were set up. So were new product research and development teams, and whole new departments in asset-backed securities, real estate, project finance, and leasing. Some businesses were too complex to be handled by generalists, so special industry groups were set up to attack the unique problems and opportunities in banking, insurance, oil and gas, media, and public utilities. The international scope of the firm was also extended greatly.

Success became contagious: if so-and-so can produce a breakthrough, you can too. The great majority of Goldman Sachs's present general partners were selected because of their successes during the 1980s.

Goldman Sachs rose during the decade to become the leader in more of the industry and product league table rankings than any other firm. Overall it ranked second in 1990 and 1991 in total U.S. and global underwritings, and first in global equities, global mergers and acquisitions, and global private placements. It has become a leading international firm by virtue of the business produced in and the local ranking of its offices in

London (more than 1,000 employees), Tokyo (more than 500 employees), and much smaller offices in Frankfurt, Zurich, Paris, Hong Kong, Singapore, Sydney, Montreal, and Toronto. In 1991, its pre-tax profits were reported in the press to be well ahead of the $886 million that the firm reported earning in 1990, a record year for Goldman Sachs though a terrible year for the industry as a whole. Partner's capital was $1.7 billion at the end of 1991, ranking it among the top handful of U.S. investment banks.

In 1991, Goldman Sachs had about 7,000 employees worldwide, about the same as Morgan Stanley, Salomon Brothers, and First Boston. About half of them were support staff, and about half of the remainder were professionals engaged in trading, securities sales, and research. About 500 were investment banking professionals. The firm was then led by two co-senior partners, Stephen Friedman and Robert Rubin, aged 54 and 53 respectively, and a Management Committee of ten other partners whose average age was 47. Almost all of the firm's partners have spent the majority of their careers at Goldman Sachs; many have worked nowhere else. As one partner put it, "We believe we can compete, no matter what the business of the day may be, no matter where the competition has to occur or who the competition is. But to compete successfully, we have to be able to operate effectively as a team. Without teamwork, we can't do it."

In a recent interview, John L. Weinberg, the firm's longtime chief executive who retired in 1989, explained why he continued to be optimistic about the firm's prospects:

> There are new and rapidly developing technologies in the world marketplace to make it possible to do better what we do in the securities business, raise capital and reduce risk. We have learned a lot about how to deal with volatility and risk in all businesses . . . Today most of the trading we do is integrally involved with hedging strategies and techniques. . . . The illusions we had in the 1980s are gone. Everybody looks at things pretty realistically now.
>
> If you don't do the job right, you get hit very quickly. If your products or services are overpriced or aren't good quality, the market will soon tell you.
>
> You can't kid the marketplace.[14]

Goldman Sachs didn't have to worry about the marketplace. It had adapted to it very well.

NEW MEN AND ALIENS

Goldman Sachs's vision of its future is perhaps clearest when it considers itself as a global wholesale financial-services provider. Salomon Brothers, after recovering from its Treasury auction scandals, will no doubt reaffirm that it belongs on the same track. So will Merrill Lynch, though its interests have to be balanced with the concerns of a global retail financial-services provider. Shearson Lehman Brothers and First Boston, both powerful wholesalers in the past, may have to operate for a while with clipped wings until their parents regain confidence in them. Lesser wholesalers, such as Kidder Peabody, Smith Barney, and Prudential Securities have similar problems.

However, there are some new competitors in the game that wish to establish themselves as serious players in investment banking. They plan to acquire market share by taking advantage of opportunities presented by deregulation and the self-inflicted wounds of many of the top investment bankers.

The Banks Are Back

They are back, but only a few have shown strong enough interest in the wholesale banking of the future to develop effective investment banking capabilities. For most large banks, investment banking is too difficult, too competitive, and too expensive to have high priority or to be targeted as a principal line of business. The banks are not as strong as they used to be, and most will have to choose between retail banking with interstate aspirations and converting their wholesale operations into investment banking businesses.

J.P. Morgan, however, has always been only a wholesale bank and for years has been planning a serious effort to gain leadership in investment banking transactions. Morgan was one of the first banks to press the Fed for a carve out of the Glass-Steagall Act that would allow underwriting of securities under Section 20. In 1989, the Fed allowed Morgan and a few other banks to underwrite corporate debt securities; this was extended to corporate equities in 1990. These changes gave Morgan the chance it had been waiting for—to add securities market expertise to its existing, but shrinking, wholesale-banking activities. Hence, Morgan took a fresh look at its strategic position and the evolving trends in the marketplace. According to its 1990 annual report:

> Our firm is unique in fusing the character of a trusted advisor with the capabilities of a global financial intermediary. It is the combination of these elements that differentiates us from competitors.

The implication is that other wholesale-oriented commercial banks lack the capabilities of a global financial intermediary, and its investment banking competitors lack standing as trusted advisers. Morgan's "uniqueness" may be wishful thinking, since many investment banks, including Morgan's cousin, Morgan Stanley, seem quite capable of attracting clients on the basis of their capital market and corporate finance advice-giving capabilities.

Still, Morgan's trading skills are excellent: its reputation, quality rating, and wholesale sector know-how are second to none in the banking industry, and the firm has been working steadily on the problem of moving its business into capital markets for more than ten years. It emphasizes its commitments to global swaps and derivatives markets, where there is a premium on capital strength, innovation, risk analysis, knowledge of local markets, and speed and precision in executing transactions. J.P. Morgan is a primary government bond dealer in all seven major industrial countries. Trading represented 34% of all revenues at J.P. Morgan in 1990, nearly as much as its lending operations (46% of total revenues).

The bank has also developed a credible mergers and acquisition advisory business (9% of total revenues in 1990). Morgan has global reach and clout—much more than any other U.S. bank or investment bank—which it believes will enable it to generate substantial investment-banking business in the future, both in and outside the United States.

Morgan has also cleaned up its balance sheet by writing down all its third world loans; it has selected a trader, Dennis Weatherstone, to head the bank, and has emphasized noninterest income to such an extent that it was 60% of total revenues in 1991, up from 47% in 1988. Trading profits were $1.3 billion, significantly more, incidentally, than Morgan Stanley's (trading assets represented about 50% of Morgan's balance sheet). Loans had declined to less than 29% of the bank's total assets. J.P. Morgan had $18 of assets for each dollar of capital (Morgan Stanley had $25). It also managed about $85 billion of assets for others and offered custodial and other operational services.

In 1991, J.P. Morgan handled a $1.3 million municipal bond issue for New York City, arranged a $5.5 billion loan syndication for Kuwait, managed a $1.5 billion zero-coupon bond offering for the French Treasury, underwrote a $425 million debt issue for the Mexican cement maker, Cemex, and co-managed a $250 million Eurobond issue for Nippon Telegraph & Telephone Co. Its quick success in underwriting U.S. corporate debt securities was reflected by its jumping to seventh place in the rankings in 1991 from nowhere only two years before.

The bank was considered very profitable, with net income over $1.1 billion in 1991 (Merrill Lynch with record net income in 1991 of $696 million earned more than any other investment bank). J.P. Morgan's 1991 return on equity was 20% (Morgan Stanley's was 16.7% in 1991). Its tier 1 capital ratio, 6.9% in December 1991, was very solid. At year end 1991, Morgan's market value was over $13.2 billion, more than twice its book value of capital (Morgan Stanley's market value was $5.2 billion, 2.2 times its book value). Morgan's banking subsidiary, Morgan Guaranty Trust Co., is the only big U.S. bank to retain triple-A ratings.

Its staff of 13,000, 18% fewer than at its peak in 1987, each generated approximately $85,000 of net income in 1991, almost 30% more than that contributed by the average Morgan Stanley employee (of whom there were about 7,000). It has operations in ten cities in North America and twenty-four cities in Europe, Latin America, and the Far East. One-third of its professional staff are non–U.S. nationals, and three of its top five executives, including Weatherstone, are foreign born.[15]

Bankers Trust is another bank with wholesale market ambitions. It was an early and successful challenger of the securities industry on commercial paper and, like Morgan, one of the first banks to set up Section 20 securities subsidiaries.

Bankers Trust has focused on corporate finance and trading in order to break its way into investment banking. Much of its corporate finance work has been tied to complex loan syndications for LBOs and restructurings. Trading activities center on government securities and foreign exchange, and account for about $1 billion of revenues. Noninterest income is about three-fourths of Bankers Trust's total, and nearly half of this in 1991 was from trading-related activity. Net income in 1991 was $667 million, a record for the bank. Return on equity was 23%. The stock market, however, doesn't value Bankers Trust shares as highly as it does J.P. Morgan's; the market is too aware of Bankers Trust's unmerchant-bank-like possession of numerous Latin American loans, as well as its heavy reliance on trading profits, which subjects its earnings to considerable volatility. Bankers price-to-book ratio was 1.9 at the end of 1991, though both were well ahead on the average for money center banks of less than 1.0. But analysts treat Bankers Trust very well for a money center bank and have repeatedly complimented chief executive Charlie Sanford (himself, like Dennis Weatherstone, a trader) for managing the bank's skillful transition from also-ran to market leader.

Sponsored Players

During the 1980s, a new kind of competitor emerged, an investment bank owned and controlled by a large industrial or financial corporation. Among these were the Shearson Lehman investment banking and brokerage conglomerate, which was acquired by American Express in two steps in 1979 and 1984; Dean Witter, a large retail brokerage, which was acquired by Sears Roebuck and Co. in 1981; Bache Halsey Stuart, another wire-house that Prudential Insurance absorbed in 1981; Donaldson, Lufkin & Jenrette, which was absorbed by Equitable Life in 1985; Kidder Peabody, which became part of General Electric Capital Corporation in 1986, and First Boston, which was absorbed into CS First Boston in 1989. These combinations were seen at the time as very powerful. The financial backing of such parents, the synergies that come from cross-selling products and services, and the highly sophisticated marketing, systems, and international capabilities now available to the otherwise crudely managed bankers, would greatly upgrade the quality and efficiency of the investment banks. Those not similarly married off would suffer rapid loss of market share. The superfirms were enough to make the earth tremble.

Except that it never happened. Not with any of them, and there are several reasons why not. To start with, investment banking businesses are very different from ordinary businesses; they rely on a loose, adaptive, market-oriented structure. They are of necessity highly oriented to the short term, and they thrive on volatility in the markets and inside their own firms. They integrate, somehow, the special disciplines of the trading pit with the pin-stripe environment of the financier. Firms constitute, as one young Goldman Sachs vice president once explained to me, "a group of individuals who think of themselves as independent businessmen who chose, more or less on a daily basis, to work with each other." Success is rewarded early and often by bonuses unthinkable in industrial companies. Titles mean less than in industry—there are, for example, nearly 200 managing directors and hundreds of principals and even more vice presidents at Morgan Stanley.

These differences make integration with parent companies (and thus the opportunity to benefit from synergies and other resources) next to impossible. Needless to say, the officers and employees of an acquiring company, in which success tends to be a product of time in grade, company loyalty, skill in handling company products and politics, willingness to take unwanted assignments, and uncomplaining acceptance of what one is paid, are often horrified at what they find after the marriage has been completed. Pay scales are completely out of whack (who at GE could expect to make $23 million for developing a proprietary trading product that might last a year and a half?), no one follows orders, control systems are worse than primitive, and nobody plans anything. Virtually everyone is under fifty and extremely self-confident, if not arrogant. To start with, then, there is massive cultural incompatibility.

Most acquirers know that, so they plan to leave the investment bank alone, to run its own affairs in its own screwed-up way. They expect, however, that little by little, appropriate integration will occur. What the acquirers did not expect was the trouble their new subsidiaries could get into. After all, the newly acquired firms were no longer playing with their own money.

They were playing with Mother's money, and were quite willing to risk it. Ultimately this did not please the Mothers very much, especially when they lost big, as almost all of them did, even during one of the most profitable decades ever for investment bankers. Once Mother sees things falling apart and steps in herself, the risk exposures drop, and the control and organizational systems are cleaned up, but then the profits seem to languish. The money-making machines don't work very well when they are subject to smothering maternal controls. It's a difficult balance to strike— daring and creativity versus discipline and control.

On the whole, the experience of the sponsored players during the 1980s was so poor that it is unlikely to be repeated for some time. Robert Winters, chief executive of The Prudential, gave policyholders the following explanation of the troubles of Prudential-Bache (renamed Prudential Securities, Inc.):

> We've taken a lot of criticism in the media about the firm's $259 million loss. . . . We got hurt less than some, but no one likes to see a loss of this magnitude. We've taken steps to ensure that it won't happen again.
>
> There has been a change in management at the top, and we've restructured or exited the businesses that were losing money.[15]

One factor that many point to as contributing to success in investment banking is the relatively small size of the organizations, which can make them entrepreneurial and adaptive. A firm with 7,000 employees, half of whom are clerical, will have professionals working in dozens of different specialty areas. Each of these areas is regarded as a small business unit in its own right, and must contribute its own entrepreneurial effort and adaption to changing markets. Professionals tend to stay in one field for fifteen or twenty years, and thus become real experts in what they are doing. The strong succeed, the weak are weeded out. None of the investment banks, however, is comfortable operating as a large organization of, say, 25,000 employees. Such large units have to be run like a real company, and that doesn't seem to encourage success. Surely, one lesson learned over the last decade or so, as competitive pressures have increased in all industries, is that size by itself is no blessing. Eventually economies of scale run out, and the point of diminishing returns is reached. If the objective of the organization is stability, then this point may not be reached for some time; if it is competitiveness, it may be reached relatively quickly. Acquisitions almost always raise the combined head count to levels well beyond the point of diminished returns.

It is by no means clear, after several years of experience, that large financial services groups like General Electric Capital Corporation, Sears Roebuck, or American Express gain any particular benefits from owning investment banks. In some years they can be very profitable, but in other years they can produce large losses and claims on the parent's capital. There are very few instances of synergies between parent and subsidiary, or examples of cases in which the parent's activities or connections have substantially increased the subsidiary's business. So far, the record only seems to show that acquisitions of U.S. investment banks by large noninvestment-banking organizations has resulted in more heartache than joy.

Many of the firms acquired by strong parent companies early in the 1980s had to call upon them for help in 1990. The parents learned that mistakes by securities affiliates could be very painful and could even, as in the case of American Express and Credit Suisse, threaten their own earnings, credit ratings, and stock prices.

Where Are All the Foreigners?

During 1990 and 1991, several investment banks (or their parents) were reported to be quietly searching for buyers. Most knew that the list of American insurance, finance companies, and other financial services industry buyers was very short. Few of those who stepped in during the early 1980s would do it again, if given the chance to turn the clock back. Large banks were precluded by regulation and didn't have the spare capital anyway. Manufacturers, long disdainful of the morals and values of Wall Street, had no interest. The only chance, the firms figured, was to find a rich foreigner, one wanting to establish a significant position in the U.S. market. A number of meetings were set up in Europe and Japan.

None of the pigeons took the bait, however. In part this was because the price tags, even discounted for market conditions, were still thought to be high, and the highly profitable part of the cycle seemed nearly over. Also, a great many of the most promising banks and securities firms (Deutsche Bank, Swiss Bank, Warburg, Industrial Bank of Japan, Nomura) had seen enough of bad loans and difficult market conditions to have put on the brakes. A year or two earlier the story might have been different, but then, of course, the firms would not have been for sale.

One senior executive of a large European bank told me that he had been shown eight or ten U.S. firms during the 1990–1991 period. "If we wanted to," he said, "we could probably have bought any of the American investment banks then, except perhaps a few of the biggest.

"We turned them all down, not because we were not interested in having a large presence in the U.S. capital market, but because we were afraid of what would happen to us if we did buy them. These firms use a lot of capital, they take much greater risks than we do, many of them are smarter and more devious than we are. They are impossible to manage. In fact, we were a bit afraid they would end up taking us over, through the back door. It is not difficult to imagine our U.S. investment-banking affiliate insisting on taking over our global capital market activity, then our swap books, and next all the treasury functions of the bank. We would be left managing the mortgage loans to European farmers and not much else.

"And how would we control those maniacs when they decided they had to be aggressive in the markets for one reason or another? Our ability to manage our risks would be out the window, our ratings might be downgraded, and our central bank would be having a cow.

"Maybe all this wouldn't happen, but enough of our board members think this way, so that we would never get the votes to acquire a firm of significant size."

As it turned out, none of the firms being shown were sold (although in 1991 Baring Brothers bought a minority interest in Dillon Read, a comparatively small firm, from Travellers). In the early 1990s, it did not appear that anyone wanted to get into the securities business through acquisition.

Market entry, then, will have to be the result of building one's own firm, or adapting an allied business to participate in today's financial services marketplace.

Asset Managers

One company that has successfully defied conventional wisdom about the size of the firm, acquisitions, and the capabilities of outsiders to master investment banking and expects to play a major role in wholesale finance in the 1990s is General Electric Capital Corporation (GECC), a wholly owned subsidiary of the General Electric Company. GECC was founded years ago to help finance sales of GE equipment to customers and dealers. It was a captive finance company, like Ford Motor Credit Company, General Motors Acceptance Corp., and Westinghouse Credit Co. Like most of these companies, GECC also sheltered its parent's income from taxes by incurring substantial borrowings and acquiring depreciation and investment tax credits. The opportunities for tax sheltering were such that GECC had to grow well beyond the size it needed to take care of GE equipment sales. It had to become a true finance company. Most of the other captives did the same, though on a smaller scale. GECC originally stuck to the wholesale side of the financing business, making loans to small and medium-sized companies that did not have access to Wall Street capital markets. It specialized in various types of leasing, accounts receivable financing, private placements, and real estate finance. Later, a series of hotshot GE managers on their way to the top (including Jack Welch in the late 1970s) introduced new and imaginative ways to make money. GECC insisted, however, on maintaining standards of credit management that would make GE's internal auditors proud.

By the 1990s, GECC's portfolio included substantial investments in the senior debt and other securities of LBOs, computer leasing, commercial real estate financing, credit cards, and mortgage insurance. Its $70 billion of assets were the principal part of General Electric Financial Services, a

$115 billion holding company with other units that included acquisitions in investment banking (Kidder Peabody) and insurance (Employers Reinsurance, the second-biggest insurer of other property and casualty companies). Like KKR, GECC operated in the market as a principal, not as an agent. Unlike KKR, GECC did not depend on outsiders to invest in its funds. GECC was a major user of global capital-market services, but it was playing entirely with its own money.

In 1990, the worst year in memory for both the banking and the investment banking industries, GECC increased its earnings contribution to GEFS by 20%, to $979 million, after write-offs of $839 million in its LBO and real estate portfolios. This was 90% of GEFS's net income of $1.1 billion and represented a return on total assets of 1.4% and on equity of 24%. GEFS contributed nearly 25% of General Electric's $4.3 billion in net income. It achieved these results without excessive leverage, at least by banking standards—its equity-to-assets ratio is 12.8%. It wrote off its problem loans promptly, and with its parent's help it maintained triple-A bond ratings from both rating agencies. By the end of the 1980s, GEFS emerged as one of America's largest issuers of corporate debt securities: it maintained more than $40 billion of commercial paper outstanding (which it distributed itself at rock-bottom rates) and about $17 billion of long-term debt. Securities repurchase agreements accounted for $33 billion, and marketable securities backed about 85% of its total liabilities. Though approaching the marketplace from a different direction, GEFS had become one of the most formidable nonbank financial services players in the United States.

GECC did not take deposits and therefore was not regulated as a bank. Most of its assets are financed by commercial paper, which is not insured by the FDIC. Since it is not restricted by liability insurance, GECC can enter any business it wants. However, "Banking in the traditional sense," said Gary C. Wendt, chief executive,

> is of no interest to us. We are not in business to service customers who merely want to borrow at the lowest rate. We're specialized providers of financing. Everybody's money may look the same, but when we lend ours out, it better come specially wrapped and have some unique benefit to the user.[16]

GECC has been successful because it has positioned itself as an investor in financial assets, not as a provider of services. It has attracted, evaluated, and protected its assets by liberal use of personnel from GE's manufacturing arms, savvy line people who know how businesses work and understand good management and what it takes to meet a payroll. A firm believer in adapting to change, GECC has looked for businesses where it could find a favorable angle. It was among the first lenders to the LBO sector, and its early loans have been extremely profitable, though the firm is now writing off some of its later ones. At present GECC is giving much emphasis to looking for suitable pockets of opportunity in Europe and the Far East. It has good credit analysts (because most of its exposures have not been to top credits and it has learned a lot over the years by working with weaker companies), good work-out people, and highly skilled managers who keep their cost of funds at a minimum.

GEFS has emerged as a hybrid company—it looks like a bank, but doesn't act like one. It sells financial services, but only on its own terms. It's run by manufacturing people, accountants, and control people, almost all of whom have been trained at General Electric's management education center. The company itself is huge, but it is divided up into numerous stand-alone business units that are dynamic, aggressive, and very competitive. Its return on assets has outperformed almost all banks over the last few years, yet about half of its total assets are loans, as compared to 29% for J.P. Morgan. Maybe it's a prototype for the wholesale bank of the future.

Whither Wholesalers?

In the past, banks, investment banks, insurance companies, captive finance companies, and large foreign banks doing business in the United States all had separate and easily recognized identities. Most firms provided a mix of wholesale and retail services that were separate and distinct from each other; there was little overlap of products and services.

Today the wholesale finance business has been changed beyond recognition. Deregulation, market globalization, and technological improvements allowed market forces unrestrained access to the industry. Competition at levels never seen before ensued. Financial services became a combative profession. The young, brave, and talented were promoted (just as they are in combat) over their wiser but more cautious seniors. Casualties occurred, both among those too dumb to move and those too brave to slow down. Firms have now regrouped around their more experienced leaders and selected more realistic objectives.

The new pattern that is visible through the mist is one of large overlaps of the natural (or preferred) service areas among different types of players. The fundamental business is no longer services and advice, but market making: buying and selling financial assets (ranging from stocks and bonds to securitized receivables or mortgages to entire companies) in the market and making a dealer's profit on the trades. Morgan Stanley must now compete with its former clients J.P. Morgan, Equitable Life, General Motors, General Electric, Industrial Bank of Japan, and Deutsche Bank for assets to trade. The increased intensity in the trading markets has made trading harder and riskier. Many potential competitors, including most of the commercial banks and a number of more specialized securities firms, gave up their seats at the table when the stakes increased.

Only a few remain. Winners among the survivors, they include only those firms that have adapted well to the new, trading-dominated, highly competitive environment. They are big and tough and they dominate their fields. Five investment banks (including a couple set back on their feet by well-meaning parents) now account for more than 50% of all underwriting and merger-related business in the United States. Two commercial banks have thrown away any aspirations for retail service business and converted themselves into investment banks. Two or three other commercial banks that could be players hang on the fringes losing valuable time. GEFS and other large captives that seem designed specially for the job are major competitors for financial assets.

So far, insurance companies and foreign banks have been only passive players in the U.S. market, a few trying to achieve through acquisitions what they could not build themselves. They all had other problems with the changes in the financial services environment in their own sectors, and were either afraid to move or didn't know how. There may be room for one or two other serious players, but probably not for long.

The U.S. wholesale market is now a global one. Debt and equity markets are highly integrated around the major financial centers of the world. A powerful player in one market has to protect its ability to compete effectively by becoming part of the world market system. Such a player can then begin to compete in wholesale markets in Europe and Japan, as these become more open and accessible. American firms that enter these markets find, however, that the players there are different from the ones they know at home.

PART II

THE RISING TIDE IN EUROPE

The 1980s were a busy time for Europeans. In Britain they began and ended with Mrs. Margaret Thatcher, whose career as prime minister (1979–1990) was not only one of the longest in history, but surely one of the most productive and controversial. Thatcher's Conservative administration discarded trade union-dominated economic policies, cut taxes sharply, abolished foreign exchange controls (which had been in place one way or another since 1914), broke the backs of the steel and coal mining unions, started a war with Argentina to defend a tiny, godforsaken island that just happened to be a Crown colony, allowed medium-range nuclear missiles aimed at the Soviet Union to be installed in Britain, shook up the City of London irrevocably with top-to-bottom financial reforms known as the "Big Bang," and sold $40 billion of government-owned companies to the private sector through privatization offerings. Thatcher herself fought continuously against too much European integration, lectured Ronald Reagan and George Bush on standing up to the Communists and to terrorists, and then went out swinging after an aborted effort to force every citizen, regardless of income, to pay his or her share of the cost of local government through a poll (or head) tax. Exhausted, the country was probably relieved to exchange her for a grayer, more cautious, and less-controversial prime minister, John Major, which it did in the fall of 1990. Major was comparatively unknown to the British electorate, and was hindered by Mrs. Thatcher's latter-day unpopularity. But he managed the Gulf War skillfully and recovered enough support to squeak through the closest general election in years in April 1992. Mrs. Thatcher will be remembered for many things, but probably the most enduring will be her resolute faith in free-market economics as the best way to create jobs and wealth in a modern society. There is much evidence to suggest that, on the whole, her policies worked and growth was greater than it might have been. The rest of Europe watched.

119

Mrs. Thatcher's time in office roughly corresponded to that of France's François Mitterrand (1981–199-) and Germany's Helmut Kohl (1982–199-). Mitterrand, a hero of the French Resistance in World War II and a lifetime socialist, replaced Valéry Giscard d'Estaing as president, perhaps more because the French had grown tired of Giscard's somewhat high-handed ways than because they had been drawn to socialism. Mitterrand's early economic policies were the direct opposite of Mrs. Thatcher's, including a manifesto for the nationalization of all major French industrial companies and those banks and insurance companies that were not already government-owned. The nationalization program began in 1982, and was handled rather sensibly, notwithstanding the fact that more that 50% of the market value of the Paris Bourse had to be exchanged for marketable government bonds. The program, however, was discontinued in 1986 when it became clear that the new, socialist economic policies were not working. Disappointing economic results caused the socialists to lose majority control of the French legislature to a centrist-Gaulist conservative coalition led by Prime Minister Jacques Chirac; an awkward period of his "cohabitation" with President Mitterrand in the principal offices of state then followed. During this period, Mitterrand was unable to prevent the legislature from passing a denationalization (i.e., privatization) program. The program, which provided for the sale of seventy large banks, insurance, and industrial corporations, began immediately. Within a year, twenty-two companies with a market capitalization of $17 billion were returned to the private sector. In the French presidential elections of 1988, Mitterrand was re-elected and was able to dislodge Chirac but not to command a majority for further nationalization efforts. Afterwards, French industrial policy became known as *ni-ni*, for neither privatization nor nationalization; in fact, Mitterrand's government continued to allow small amounts of privatization to proceed and, in general, stuck close to moderate, pragmatic policies. In 1991, Mitterrand tired of his prime minister, Michel Rocard, who had recently announced a program under which private companies could acquire up to 49.9% of state-owned companies if they injected new capital. The program would both generate proceeds to help balance the budget and alleviate the government's need to supply new capital to its industrial progeny. Edith Cresson, an outspoken, shoot-from-the-hip socialist who was a close colleague of Mitterrand's, was appointed to replace Rocard. She immediately took the opposite line on privatization, suggesting that powerful, state-owned companies representing one-third of the French GNP should constitute the country's main competitive entry into the European struggle for market share. Her proposal did not gain much support, however. It suffered not only from the realpolitik of sharp budgetary constraints, but also from the prospect of continuous conflict with the new EC competition commissioner, Sir Leon Brittan, a tough opponent of state aid to industry. Cresson quietly reversed herself, and case-by-case privatization continued. Cresson, however, proved to be a disaster as prime minister. After ten months in office, "she had broken all records for her unpopularity," according to the *Financial Times,* and she resigned in April 1992 after the socialists' "catastrophic defeats" in regional and local elections. Hoping to reverse the declining fortunes of the Socialist party, Mitterrand appointed 66-year-old Pierre Bérégovoy, a self-taught economist and long-serving finance minister to replace Cresson. Bérégovoy, a one-time metal worker of Ukrainian descent with a limited formal education, is known as an economic pragmatist. In France he is credited with reducing inflation and liberalizing financial markets and is popular in business circles.

In Germany, Helmut Kohl led an awkward coalition of Christian Democrats, Christian Socialists, and Free Democrats into office in 1982. Kohl, a right-of-center political pragmatist, had served for the preceding ten years as chairman of the Christian Democrats, Germany's most enduring political party; organized after the war by Konrad Adenauer, the CDU had governed alone or in coalition for twenty-one of the next thirty-three years. Unlike Thatcher and Mitterrand, Kohl came into office without a reform agenda. Indeed, before the collapse of communism, his public achievements were confined to serving as international spokesman for the growing German economy. Kohl was something of a German Lyndon Johnson, whose skills and interests were almost entirely tied to domestic politics. He nonetheless rose in importance as a leader in the European Economic Community (EC), especially on East-West matters. After the Berlin Wall came down, however, Kohl dropped everything to engineer the reunification of the two Germanies and to become its first freely elected chancellor in fifty years. This was a hard-core political job, requiring endless promises, compromises, and exaggerations, at which Kohl proved to be extremely capable. He operated on the theory that economic considerations had to be set aside in order to get the political job done as quickly as possible. Once it was, the economic repairs could be made.

As the new Germany of 80 million people became a reality, Kohl became the EC's leading spokesman on the future of Europe. He encouraged wishful thinking about a politically and economically unified greater-Europe encompassing not only the EC, but the other non-EC countries of Europe and those of Eastern Europe. He also favored a common European currency, one that would be managed by a single (presumably, German-led) central bank.

Kohl was well on his way to becoming Mr. Europe when the Persian Gulf War revealed Germany's schizophrenia when cast in any role other than an economic one, and revealed just how dependent it (and thus the rest of Europe) remained on the United States in the business of war and peace.

By the time the Berlin Wall fell, however, the three European leaders (and some others) had firmly set in place a remarkable economic transformation in Europe. They had recognized that, whatever their national politics, Europe as a whole was vulnerable to economic competition from

America and Japan, both of which, being more efficient because of their political unity, were able to sustain higher growth rates and thus to accumulate more financial and technological wealth than could the Europeans. Economically, Europe was operating at a disadvantage relative to its principal global competitors. And economic realities could not be ignored in politics.

The European leaders recognized that old systems of national economic planning and full-employment policies were part of their problem. They also recognized how constraining and underproductive it was to maintain a dozen or more separate economic entities, with separate and expensive sets of policies and regulations across one large marketplace. Even Mitterrand must have realized that to grow and prosper, their economies had to stand the test of competitive world standards, and long-standing industrial policies that were heavy on subsidies and government controls did not fit the new model. Being competitive meant that free-market forces had to be respected.

The initiative that came to be known as "1992" was a response to this need for greater competitiveness and higher growth in Europe. It began in 1985 with a European Economic Commission white paper entitled *Completing the Internal Market*, an impressive document drafted with considerable input from European industrialists representing several countries that lobbied hard for its acceptance. EC member countries, with Thatcher's successful examples fresh in their minds, began to consider the potential advantages of reshaping European economic policies to provide more freedom for market forces and more economic unity among countries. They began to see Europe's potential as an economic whole, which could be realized only at the cost of national policy concessions. The benefits of unity were seen to be greater than the costs of concessions, at least in all of the countries except the skeptical United Kingdom.

Momentum for these ideas accelerated. Removal of minor trade barriers led to the elimination of important barriers in financial services. New, commonly applied standards in banking and other financial services were adopted. A common currency was discussed, and even political union—long the most unthinkable of European notions—became discussable. The private sector sat up and took notice, and commenced a process of restructuring businesses to suit the new European order. Increasingly this restructuring occurred through takeovers and other aggressive, free-market methods. And then, as if on cue, the Soviet empire confessed its disillusionment with socialism and collapsed into economic rubble at the feet of the EC countries, looking to be revived as a capitalist society.

Throughout Eastern and Western Europe the recognition was spreading that to ensure growth and prosperity in the future a greater emphasis had to be placed on the private sector, free markets, and competition. The tide of capitalism was rising again in Europe.

4
RENAISSANCE

In the 1980s, inspired by the movement for European economic reform, the EC member countries took a fresh look at the 1958 Treaty of Rome. They decided that national restrictions on the free flow of commerce were killing growth and dissipating the principal advantages of membership in the Economic Community, and they resolved to forge a "single market" of 325 million Europeans, which would have a GNP approximately equal to that of the United States. This was what the 1958 treaty had originally tried to accomplish, but it had failed because of intra-European restrictions and administrative costs. These factors were contributing to stagnation and to the economic malaise that had come to be called "Euro-sclerosis" during the 1970s. The commission then set the goal of achieving a single, internal market by the end of 1992. This was approved by the European heads of state in 1985 and given legislative backing in 1986 in the Single European Act, which defines the internal market as "an area without internal frontiers in which the free movement of goods, services, persons and capital is ensured."

1992 AND ALL THAT

Paolo Cecchini, an economist from the University of Padua and a senior official of the European Economic Commission, was asked to prepare a study of the potential effects on EC growth of removing all of the internal impediments to economic activity, which included border costs, local preference buying, and regulations and quotas, or voluntary export restraints. The Cecchini Report was presented in 1988 and caused a stir: a true single market would add the equivalent of five percentage points of gross domestic product and add 1.75 million jobs in the EC over its first five years.[1]

123

The Single Market Idea

The idea, in short, was to allow more competition by removing barriers that reduced it. More competition meant freer markets for all the things that mattered—goods, services, persons, and capital. Freer markets meant more opportunity for growth and profits across what would become the world's largest, and potentially most important, economic region. All this was to be achieved not by harmonizing national regulations, an impossible and exceedingly expensive and counterproductive task, but simply by removing regulations altogether, or at least reducing them to a serviceable minimum.

In 1985, the commission identified 277 areas where regulatory removal or replacement on a European basis would have to occur before 1992. By the end of 1988, the halfway point in the implementation program, about 90% of the regulatory proposals had been submitted, and almost half of these had been adopted by the Council of Ministers. Not all of these recommendations, which appeared in the form of proposed directives of the commission, were easy to gain agreement on, as the economic interests of the various states were at times quite contrary. Nonetheless, the issues were tabled and fought over, and many workable though imperfect compromises were reached.

One of the most important areas affected by the drive toward the single market was financial services, an industry that accounted for about 3.5% of total employment in the EC in 1985 and about 7% of GDP. To a large extent, a common market already existed in Europe for goods, but this was not the case with respect to services, especially financial services, where substantial barriers existed between countries in banking, insurance, and securities transactions. These barriers blocked the free flow of capital and competition and helped increase the cost of capital to European corporations.

An early objective of the commission therefore was to provide for the dismantling of capital and investment barriers as soon as possible, so the necessary financial lubricant could begin to ease the many microeconomic adjustments that had to follow. In June 1988, the finance ministers agreed to remove all remaining controls on capital flows by mid-1990, including those of a short-term monetary nature not linked to commercial transactions (e.g., commercial paper and money market funds). Another important objective was to permit cross-border marketing of financial services and the free circulation of financial products. This was intended to bring down rapidly the costs of mortgages, consumer credit, insurance, and brokerage. Both objectives were achieved well before the 1992 targeted implementation date.

To bring about the new regime for financial services, however, the commission had to issue a series of directives setting forth the terms of governance for distinct sectors such as banking, securities, and insurance. Each of these required harmonization of essential standards for supervision and regulation of the institutions involved and for protection of depositors, investors, and consumers. Standards were to cover such things as solvency, "fitness and properness," disclosure of information to clients, and consumer protection. There also had to be mutual recognition as to how these standards were to be applied and enforced. In effect this involved an effort to replace existing national standards with new ones, though the new ones would be as simple and basic as possible.

The effort to achieve common regulatory standards and application in banking, which was the first of three areas of financial services for which directives were to be presented, was probably the easiest upon which to secure agreement. In part this was because the countries had long been members of the Bank for International Settlements, the Swiss-based club for central bankers that had been set up originally to deal with reparations payments after World War I. It was a useful forum for central bankers to discuss common problems, and as a result a significant degree of convergence of policies affecting the financial services sector emerged. The BIS had been concerned for some years about the widening gap between banking regulators over the standards for capital adequacy and solvency. As a result, it formed a committee chaired by Peter Cooke of the Bank of England to study the issue and make recommendations for all the countries to consider. Cooke's committee worked closely with the Federal Reserve and ultimately produced recommendations on risk-adjusted bank capital adequacy, which established minimum standards of capital-to-assets ratios. These recommendations, originally presented in draft form in 1986, were revised and accepted in 1988 by all the EC countries, plus Switzerland, Luxembourg, Japan, and the United States, for implementation in two stages between 1989 and 1992. This was an extraordinary achievement of financial diplomacy and cooperation, and of course it made the task of the authors of the EC Banking Directive considerably easier.

The Banking Directive embraced three important principles: first, a bank would only need a single license to conduct a full range of banking activities anywhere within the EC; second, banking services, based on the model for universal banking prevalent on the Continent (and recently permitted by financial services reform in the United Kingdom) were assumed to include all aspects of the securities business (except mutual funds); and third, responsibility for bank regulation and supervision would remain with the home country of incorporation, not the host country in which the bank is operating.

The securities and insurance directives proved more difficult to finalize. It was hard to reach consensus on regulation of the capital adequacy of nonbank securities firms, as well as on the treatment of investment funds, takeovers, new issues, secondary market activities, and conduct-of-business rules. The root of the difficulty was in the structural and traditional differences between German-style universal banks, in which all activities were conducted and regulated under one corporate roof, and the more modern U.K.-style financial services companies, in which different activities were contained within separate entities (or subsidiaries) and regulated accordingly, as was also the practice in the United States and Japan. Nonbank securities firms, a rarity on the Continent, were powerful players in the London and other international markets. These firms were not covered by the BIS capital adequacy agreement, which was seen as a competitive advantage for them. Many regulators were concerned that the regulatory advantage might result in irresponsible behavior by some firms, possibly causing risk to the whole European financial system. Again the BIS came to the rescue, working behind the scenes with the International Organization of Securities Commissions, and in June 1992, a draft Capital Adequacy Directive to be appended to the stalled Investment Services Directive appeared and was adopted. The framework of the capital adequacy provisions is to require a minimum amount of capital relative to the amount of business being done, the ability to boost capital by issuing subordinated debt up to 250% of equity, and to permit flexibility to accommodate underwriting and stock borrowing and repurchase agreements. These provisions, which will require capital increases for a number of firms, will substantially equalize the competitive conditions of banks operating under the BIS standards and of securities firms. The Insurance Directive has also proved sticky because of significant differences in industry practices among countries. Still, it was expected to be released, if not approved, before the required implementation date of December 31, 1992.

Onward to the EMU

Indeed, progress in hammering out the new policies and directives was so good that expectation levels began to rise and serious discussion was often heard about adoption of an Economic and Monetary Union (EMU). Such a union would involve a single European Currency Unit (ECU) and some sort of single Europeanwide program to regulate interest and exchange rates by a single European Monetary Institute (EMI). The EMI, if successful, would convert itself into a single European central bank by 1999. The idea of an EMU was not entirely new—a European Monetary System (EMS) for the minimization of intra-European exchange rate volatility had been in place for many years—but the EMU was very ambitious and, some thought, aggressive.

Britain under Thatcher was unwilling to participate in the EMS, for fear that its national economic sovereignty would be lost, and the monetary policies of a bunch of socialists or wild-eyed Teutonic fundamentalists imposed in its place. Though Thatcher finally gave in to the EMS, the much broader EMU is clearly centered around the willingness to give up independent national economic policies in order to obtain the benefits of Europeanwide policies. These, many thought, would favor the historically hard-currency, low-inflation countries (Germany, the Netherlands) and squeeze the softer, high-inflation countries (Britain, France, and Italy).

For an EMU to mean anything, control over the money supply (starting with the ability to create money) must be handed over to a body that has broad, regional objectives in mind. And beyond the money supply, ultimately, lies the area of common European taxation rate and loss of control of national fiscal policies. Displacing the cherished idea of economic sovereignty is difficult enough, but bringing tax rates (which vary widely across the EC) into line would be an enormous task that would take a long time to effect. No doubt, by the time these matters are resolved (if they ever are), the EC would be far down the road to political union, in which some sort of United States of Europe might be a reality. But this still seems a long way off.

Or so it seemed until the heads of state of the twelve EC nations convened at a summit meeting in Maastricht, Holland, to complete a treaty on December 11, 1991, which substantially revised the Treaty of Rome. The new treaty, subject to approval by the legislatures of each country, provided for substantial political and monetary accord among the member countries. Its political provisions cover common citizenship, foreign policy, a common defense organization, and close cooperation in home and judicial affairs. All of the countries but Britain went on to subscribe to a separate agreement on maintaining employment levels and the quality of life.

The monetary provisions of the treaty determined a schedule for EMU. By agreement of the EC members, it will occur in three phases. Phase I, which began at the beginning of 1991, did little more than authorize the gathering of data on the convergence of important economic indicators from each country, i.e., inflation rates, interest rates, and budget deficits. Phase II, which will begin in 1994, involves the creation of the EMI, which is to coordinate (not control) national monetary policies and to monitor the economic convergence data. Before the end of 1996, the commission will report on the readiness of the EC for Phase III, which may occur when a majority of the countries can pass four tests of convergence. If these conditions are met (early predictions are that nine out of twelve countries will be able to pass the convergence tests by then), full EMU would come into being and the EMI would be changed into the first European central bank. Britain was granted an "opt-out" clause, through which it may choose not to participate in Phase III until such time as its doing so has been approved by Parliament. Although the last of the arguments on EMU compromises have certainly not been heard, the Maastricht agreement provides for full monetary union under a single central bank by a date not later than January 1, 1999.

After Maastricht, which most observers regarded as a hurriedly cobbled together effort to provide for a substantial increase in the scope and potential role of a centralized EC, several countries decided that the terms of the treaty were such that they should be submitted to a national referendum. In the spring of 1992, the Irish approved the treaty, but the Danes rejected it. The Danish vote stunned much of Europe, and encouraged those who were unhappy with the proposals to speak up. The sudden rush toward political unity came to a halt, and more thoughtful discussion of what the effort was all about began to emerge. The possibility developed that some fundamental renegotiation of the treaty may be necessary. At the heart of the discussions was whether a single currency and a centralized monetary policy would produce economic benefits sufficient to outweigh the political disadvantages.

Martin Feldstein, a former chairman of the U.S. Council of Economic Advisors, weighed into the debate with a much discussed article in *The Economist* in June 1992, in which he expressed considerable doubt about the EMU. Feldstein argued that

> the creation of a single market for goods and services [which he enthusiastically endorses] does not require a monetary union. It is possible to have all the benefits of free trade without a common currency. Indeed a shift to a common currency could actually diminish trade within Europe. It is also likely to reduce economic well-being by raising future unemployment and increasing the cyclical volatility of activity within individual countries. And it would cause a higher rate of inflation than the current monetary arrangements.

Feldstein continued to argue that the impact on individual countries would be severe and that the proposed common currency lacked the "virtues of a store of value and unit of account that only experience can bring," experience that many of the older currencies already possess. He used the example of the economy of the state of Massachusetts, which was propelled into higher, then lower growth rates than the rest of the United States during the 1980s because it did not have its own "New England dollar" to manage in relation to the U.S. dollar.

Feldstein's article brought an immediate response from four prominent European economists, Paul de Grauwe, Daniel Gros, Alfred Steinherr, and Niels Thygesen, which was published in a subsequent edition of the magazine. The group offered a rebuttal of each of Feldstein's arguments, ending with the view that the EMS was already close to a de facto monetary union, that no substantial exchange rate realignments have occurred for more than five years, and that general capital mobility was achieved in 1990. The EMU, they argued, which will consolidate all of these successes, is full of "calculated risks, but so is the status quo, which was achieved only through the creation of the EMS." They believe that the risks are worth taking.

The ink was scarcely dry on the rebuttal from the European economists, when a huge crack emerged in the EMS. Burdened by the weight of its assistance programs for Eastern Germany, the Bundesbank had insisted on maintaining exceptionally high interest rates in Germany. Because of the EMS, these high rates were passed on to the other countries (which were obligated to maintain the value of their currencies in relation to the other currencies, including the Deutschemark) despite the fact that several were struggling to extract themselves from recessions. In September 1992, market forces ganged up on the pound, the lira, and the peseta and these currencies were forced outside their EMS bands. Pressure was growing too on the French franc and the Irish punt. The result was that the Deutschemark, because of Germany's exceptionally strict monetary policy—short-term rates were over 9%—was suddenly and sharply revalued relative to most of the other European currencies, something that was not supposed to happen under the convergence policies of the EMS. These events occurred just before the French referendum on the Maastricht treaty, and surely diminished enthusiasm for it, though it did squeak through.

In the end, the EMU is just a detail in relation to the larger view of a changed Europe. Whether it comes in on schedule is less important than the new, widely accepted movement toward greater economic cooperation and restructuring.

For the first time in its long history, Europe now seems to have a future of the sort that dreams can be made of—a vast, benign democratic entity that embraces a vibrant market economy from the Urals to the Atlantic. In such a dream, Europe, after a lapse of a hundred years, would again be the richest and most powerful region in the world; and the next century would be its to make, a renaissance equal in importance to that of the fifteenth century. Dreams such as these, sketched out for us by our long-term thinkers, Euro-optimists, and journalists, do seem to contain more than a glimmer of reality. But of course, Europeans have their reasons to remain skeptical about such grandiose possibilities. Most prefer to take it one step at a time.

European business and financial leaders, ever distrustful of false expectations raised by politicians, are especially cautious about the longer term. They know that politicians get carried away with the rhetoric of the day and underestimate the difficulties in bringing about such a monumental event as European political and/or economic union. They are well aware of the difficulties of making one Europe from a patchwork of different nationalities, languages, and cultures. They also know that during times of recession, voters look to their governments for help, and are reluctant to take on additional tax burdens for the benefit of those living in the poorer parts of Europe. These considerations illustrate the constant potential for backsliding that exists on the way to 1992 and the greater goals beyond. Still, most of the leaders agree that Europe has entered into an irreversible process of market integration, one in which most of the benefits will come from a newly deregulated, reinvigorated, and competitive private sector. That is something that almost everyone agrees would be a good thing, and something that is now, for the first time, achievable—as long as their governments do not mismanage the process.

THE FIRST EUROPEAN MERGER BOOM

Enthusiasm for these new European economic policies spread quickly into the private sector, where emphasis was given to cutting costs, increasing productivity, and improving profit performance. The 1992 initiatives further encouraged European corporations to invest in the infrastructure necessary to service a unified single market, and many companies began or accelerated programs of expansion through acquisition of other companies in Europe. Before long, even the cautious and cynical among European companies had to take note of their more aggressive competitors. The result was a period of unprecedented, continuing, and extraordinary growth in merger and acquisition transactions in Europe in the latter half of the 1980s, one that promises to continue through the 1990s.

This period coincided with one of great industrial restructuring in the United States. The U.S. merger boom of the 1980s, as we have seen, was driven primarily by relatively easy credit conditions, a relaxed regulatory environment, rising stock markets, aggressive entrepreneurs, and rapidly growing foreign direct investment in the United States by European and Japanese corporations. It also reflected attempts to redress market value misalignments and efforts by companies in newly globalized industries to improve their own competitive performance and to position themselves better in the principal markets for their products and services in the United States, Europe, and Asia. In this sense, the late 1980s reflected extraordinary corporate realignments on the part of companies from all three of the world's major economic regions.

The most active area for this sort of corporate restructuring was within the United States, where more than $1.2 trillion of disclosed merger and acquisition activity involving more than 8,000 transactions occurred between 1985 and 1990. During the earlier booms in the United States (1898–1904, the 1920s, and the 1960s), there had been some parallel merger activity in the United Kingdom, indicating a degree of international involvement and spillover, but there were no similar M&A transactions in continental Europe and Japan (neither of which had any history or experience with such market-driven transactions). The U.S. merger boom of the 1980s did, however, ignite a substantial global response, one that appears to be continuing in Europe in the early 1990s, well after the boom in the United States has subsided. In 1990, for example, the volume of completed mergers and acquisitions outside the United States was almost twice the volume inside its borders. Indeed, M&A transactions have become global in a very short period of time. In 1985, domestic U.S. transactions accounted for 85% of global M&A activity; by 1991, the U.S. share had declined to 20%.[2]

Cross-border transactions involving U.S. companies grew by a factor of about four during the 1985–1990 period (transactions declined by about a third in 1990, an off year for mergers everywhere). During this period, 87% (by volume) of these cross-border transactions represented sales of U.S. companies to non-U.S. buyers. This seems an extremely large percentage, one which appears to reflect a sort of lassitude or decline on the part of U.S. industry, otherwise known for its aggressive actions in M&A. However, most of the U.S. companies operating in Europe do so through subsidiaries or European companies acquired in earlier periods, so U.S. companies did not, generally speaking, have a great need for first-time, strategic-positioning acquisitions in Europe. On the other hand, the reverse was the case for many European companies which were substantially underrepresented in the United States until the 1980s, when direct investment grew from $70 billion to $275 billion.[3] European companies increasingly recognized that the United States was too large a market to cover effectively by exports only. They had to be closer to the market and to manufacture products in the country to avoid uncompetitive expenses associated with foreign exchange differences, higher European labor costs, and delivery and service delays. In any event, during the 1985–1990 period, many European companies found the rationale, the courage, and the funds to acquire companies in the United States, where they found many sellers willing to take their money.

Transactions entirely outside the United States grew the most rapidly of all during the 1985–1990 period—from $20 billion in 1985 to $200 billion in 1989, before turning down to $150 billion in 1990. Of these non-U.S. transactions, a cumulative total of more than $350 billion, or 60%, were intra-European deals. Intra-European transactions increased by a factor of nine from 1985 to 1989, before settling back a bit in 1990. So did the Europe/non-Europe deals, in which about three-fourths of the transactions by volume involved Europeans acting as buyers.

Accompanying these developments in European mergers and acquisitions, though somewhat overshadowed by them, was Europe's first experimentation with leveraged buyouts. For the most part, these transactions were smaller, and less fully leveraged than their American counterparts. European LBOs were almost always friendly transactions in which the original management of a company sought financing for its purchase from the owners. Thus European LBO transactions are called *management buyouts* (MBOs), or *buy-ins* (MBIs) in going-private cases. Sometimes, when the two types of transactions are combined, they are called *bimbos* (BI-MBOs).

Originating in the United Kingdom, the MBO derived much of its design and practice from early American LBOs. These involved original shareholders selling control of the company to financial investors that borrowed most of the money for the transaction (pledging the entire company to the lenders) and hired (or retained) management to run the company effectively and to maximize its cash flow. The debt would be repaid as soon as possible and then the shares would be resold to the market, or to another company, to realize the investors' profit. Some very large MBOs occurred in the United Kingdom, including the $3.7 billion transaction for Gateway PLC in 1989.

MBOs did not appear in significant volume on the Continent until 1986, after which, however, they became suddenly popular in France, Sweden, Italy, and Germany, where there had not been previously many ways for owners of companies to sell their businesses at market prices. The majority of MBOs in both the United Kingdom and on the Continent derive from a private sale of a family company or a division of a local public company. Other deals have been completed by overseas vendors, by MBIs, and by privatizations. A recent study by KPMG Peat Marwick McLintock notes that family company sales are an especially prominent source of MBOs in Germany (55% of all deals), Italy (48%), and France (45%).[4]

Total U.K. and continental European MBOs combined aggregated more than $50 billion for the five years ending in 1990. In the United States, where volume was about four times greater, LBOs comprised as much as 25.8% (1988), and as little as 7.3% (1990), of total M&A transaction values during the same period. MBOs comprised a much smaller percentage of all M&A transaction values in the United Kingdom (with a high of 14.0% in 1989) and in continental Europe as a whole (a high of 3.6% in 1988).

The U.K. market in MBOs declined sharply in 1990, in parallel with, but still less than, the U.S. market decline. Large public LBOs were virtually nonexistent in the United States during the year. The continental European market, however, declined only slightly during 1990, and finished the year with about the same aggregate financial volume of MBO transactions as in the United Kingdom. Deal-doers still seemed to believe that European M&A transactions would pick up sharply again once the recession had passed.

By all measures, European corporations had entered the M&A field much more aggressively than most observers expected, with total transaction volume growing far more rapidly than M&A volume anywhere else in the world. These data suggested that an M&A boom had taken hold in Europe—a boom that involves acquisitions within single European countries, between European countries, and between European and non-European companies. They also demonstrated that European expansion was occurring simultaneously on two fronts—both within Europe and in other regions of global importance to European corporations, mainly the United States.

However, global merger activity (by volume) in 1991 declined by more than a third from the 1990 level, which itself was significantly below the 1989 level.[5] Most of the decline occurred in the large M&A markets, the United States, and the United Kingdom. The volume of non-U.K. European transactions held up much better, largely because there were fewer entrepreneurial deals being attempted for which financing was scarce on the Continent, and the boom was still in fairly early stages. Continental corporations, banks, institutional investors, and regulators were still getting used to the idea of market forces influencing corporate actions. Many observers believe that with a bit more time, and somewhat better market conditions, the merger boom in Europe will resume; after all, there is a lot of restructuring yet to be done there.

Restructuring European Industry

The boom appears to be the result of several related factors. First, there has long been a need for industrial restructuring in Europe because of unwieldy government ownership, inefficient corporate combinations, large family-owned positions that precluded active trading markets in shares from developing, and the absence of opportunities to take over companies that were thought to be underperforming. Many large European companies had share prices that were well below what shareholders could have received if the company were broken up and sold off in pieces. Also, the globalization of several industries meant that European companies, like U.S. companies a decade before, either would have to become larger and more international, or find themselves the targets of takeover by their competitors. The need for restructuring became apparent with the early privatizations by Mrs. Thatcher and the general recognition that large-scale ownership changes would be necessary if European industry was to be brought up to global competitive standards.

Second, the special motivations associated with the 1992 single market initiatives forced competition-minded companies to think strategically within the context of the single market.

Third, financing for the transactions was fairly easy to come by, in large part because of the increasing liberalization of capital markets that was occurring in Europe at the time.

And finally, there was the transfer to Europe of much of the M&A know-how that had accumulated in the United States during the 1980s. A number of the U.S. M&A players set up shop in Europe in the late 1980s to participate as advisers or investors in the European boom. Many of these firms have been successful, as indicated by the fact that five of the top ten advisers on intra-European deals since 1985 have been U.S. investment banks.

Although it is difficult to predict how long the growth in European M&A volume will continue, particularly after the turndown in volume in 1990 and 1991, it appears that it still has a good way to go. Most European M&A activity during the period 1985–1990 involved U.K. corporations with long histories of securities market transactions. French and Italian corporations were the next most active M&A participants, followed by German corporations, which—despite the size of the German economy—accounted for less than 5% of the intra-European volume.

There are many differences among the structures of business enterprises within Europe. On the Continent many enterprises, including numerous very large ones, are not organized as publicly owned limited liability corporations as they are in the United States and the United Kingdom. A recent study by Booz, Allen Acquisition Services for the European Economic Commission showed, for example, that only 54% of the top 400 companies in the EC are publicly traded, versus 99% in the United States. Out of the top 100 domestic companies, 67 are publicly quoted in the United Kingdom, 56 in France, 45 in Germany, and less than a third in all other EC countries. Furthermore, the study reports, in the three largest EC economies, only a relatively minor share of the domestic GNP can actually be accessed through public takeovers. Nor do many of the continental European countries have a tradition of, or substantial experience with, market-driven domestic M&A activity. As a result, only a comparatively small percentage of enterprises in continental European countries have so far participated in such transactions.

Many of these enterprises recently have discovered better ways of managing their business and financial affairs through capital markets. More active and efficient stock markets have encouraged many closely held European companies to go public for the first time, creating a liquid market in their shares. Once public, companies become interested in the M&A market, either as buyers of other companies, or as sellers. As the M&A market becomes more active, and more potential participants become aware of alternatives in this market, then even more family or closely held businesses begin to consider selling out through the M&A market instead of selling to a bank or a competitor at a less-attractive price. Thus there exists a substantial potential for future M&A transactions, especially in continental Europe, which in terms of merger and acquisition activity is substantially underdeveloped compared to Anglo-Saxon countries. This potential has already begun to show itself in the rapid rates of growth in such transactions originating on the Continent.

Economic restructuring in Europe during the 1990s is likely to reflect the American experience in the 1980s, which was driven by intense international competition, liquid financial markets, and the aggressive strategies of the New Men. The American economic restructuring occurred at the corporate level, predominantly through M&A and self-recapitalization transactions. The conditions of competition in the U.S. domestic market help explain why the restructuring took this particular form: the market is open to corporations from all economic regions, enjoys a benign antitrust policy, is free of capital and other controls, involves only limited government subsidization, and is relatively transparent. The 1992 initiatives aim to create the same conditions in Europe; therefore the results should be similar.

Uncertainties as to how much latitude will be granted to European companies remain, especially in the murky area of antitrust policy. The European Economic Commission has issued a regulation on mergers, which gives it the power to investigate large transactions and to prohibit those that create or strengthen dominant EC-wide market positions. It is not authorized to interfere with transactions on other than competitive grounds. Individual countries, however, have antitrust policies based on domestic market considerations only, and these can be used to prohibit transactions on vague industrial policy grounds. Such policies sometimes come into conflict with the EC regulation, as do commission rulings related to state-owned companies that might be considered to be subsidized. So far these matters have been handled on an ad hoc basis, and almost everything has been allowed to go through, but the rules are far from clear and could be applied differently in the future.

The commission is also struggling with regulation of cross-border takeover practices, where two schools of thought are currently in conflict. One, the Anglo-Saxon school, seeks a level playing field, in which defensive practices that disregard shareholder interests would be prohibited, and a similar set of rules that would not discriminate against bidders would be in effect throughout the EC. The other school, the Germanic, would retain measures that allow management boards to use their best judgment unilaterally in matters related to takeovers. While this conflict awaits official resolution, barriers to cross-border takeovers appear to be eroding across the EC. The Anglo-Saxon view of economic Darwinism appears to be prevailing, even if it is not universally liked.

There is evidence that the American and European restructurings have indeed been on parallel courses, and that the industries most intensively involved in restructuring in Europe have been the same ones that experienced restructuring in the United States during the 1980s. A 1990 study published by INSEAD has shown an unusually high degree of correlation between American and European industries in both buying and selling companies involved with M&A transactions. In both regions most activity has occurred in those industries that have been globalized over the past several years, such as foods, oil and gas, chemicals, and financial services.[6]

Thus the underlying motivations for the greatly increased European merger activity appear to be heavily strategic: i.e., related to the search for long-term offensive and defensive goals for the post-1992 European market, as well the search for market share and first-mover advantages. In this context, M&A activity can deliver productive assets much more quickly and opportunistically than greenfield investments, although implementational problems can offset some of these benefits, especially when they involve cross-border managerial problems.

Many continental European countries have structural and/or regulatory barriers to takeover activity: control over voting rights, privileges granted to management to take actions without shareholder approval, and restrictions on shareholder access to information. These barriers are sufficient in some countries (especially Switzerland, Germany, and the Netherlands) to preclude most hostile takeover attempts. In general, these barriers are being dismantled, though gradually. Also, funds have been found to finance even hostile takeover moves by the New Men of Europe. During the past several years many such New Men have appeared, in the United Kingdom, in Italy, France, Switzerland, Belgium, Sweden, and other countries. As in the recent U.S. boom, these players act as extremely potent catalysts in the process of restructuring through the market for corporate control.

The Rise of the Barbarians

Hostile takeovers take some getting used to—nobody likes them at first. They are almost always thought of, initially anyway, as wild and unruly attacks on worthy corporations by unscrupulous, greed-driven raiders who intend to strip the company's assets, fire its employees, bank the profits, and then catch the next train out of town. This attitude is exemplified by the title of a 1990 best-selling book on the RJR-Nabisco LBO, *Barbarians at the Gates*. But perceptions of hostile takeovers are changing. Many academics, executives, and financial regulators now see takeovers as beneficial because of the challenges they bring to established corporate rule. Even some of the corporate rulers would agree with this; after all, they make hostile offers too. Even crusty old AT&T played the takeover game in its 1990 contested bid for NCR. The critical point seems to be when the hostile route is followed for the first time by a blue-chip, well-regarded establishment company. This happened in the United Kingdom as early as 1957, when an affiliate of Reynolds Metals (advised by S.G. Warburg) bid for British Aluminum, in a deal that made Warburg's reputation. In the United States, such legitimacy did not come about until 1974 when International Nickel (advised by Morgan Stanley) tendered for the shares of Electric Storage Battery. In both cases the bidders pointed to the poor record of the existing management and the relatively high price they were offering. Shareholders should have a choice, they said, and not be intimidated by management. Both deals succeeded and subsequent hostile deals were regarded mainly on economic grounds, not as unseemly attacks on a noble established order by low-grade corporate pirates.

Carlo de Benedetti, a flamboyant Italian entrepreneur (chairman of Olivetti), shocked the whole of Belgian society in 1987 with his surprise raid on Société Générale de Belgique, a giant holding company that owned most of everything in the country. The board had such tight control over the group that it never feared a takeover attempt, despite the fact that its share price was sadly depressed and Belgium had very few laws restricting takeover activity. De Benedetti did not succeed, though he did drive the company into the arms of a French-controlled group and send the stock price almost straight up. His efforts led to an increase in Société Générale's market capitalization from 143d to 47th in Europe for 1988, a fundamental financial restructuring and a total management change. De Benedetti claimed the following year that whenever he visited Brussels, banners would be unfurled from windows all over town saying, "Thank you, Carlo."

Sir James Goldsmith's aggressive attempt to acquire BAT Industries, one of Britain's top industrial corporations, through what would have become a junk bond-financed hostile-takeover bid valued at approximately $20 billion was ultimately unsuccessful, but it did alert the market to the previously unthinkable possibility of huge, U.S.-style takeover efforts being brought to bear on even Europe's most important companies.

An offer by Goldsmith or de Benedetti, however, was hardly the same as one from AT&T, especially in conservative quarters on the Continent. But it was a step in that direction, and it led to the frequent appearance in France and Italy of hostile deals, often sponsored by well-known companies. It was becoming clear that market forces, once channeled by a bona fide, fully financed offer, could succeed just as well in continental Europe as in the Anglo-Saxon countries. Except, of course, when legal antitakeover measures were part of the scene, or where corporate structures or management practices made opposed takeovers impossible. There were several cases in the early 1980s where established companies were able to rally support from officials and block a transaction on the dubious grounds that the public interest was not served by the deal. In the light of the new EC policies on open markets and free competition, such rulings have become quite rare.

Though the EC has not yet agreed to regulations governing takeover procedures, changes are already occurring. Until recently the British and continental European approaches to takeovers were quite different. In Britain any company wishing to acquire more than 29.9% of another company's shares had to bid for all of the shares. In France, by contrast, a shareholder (or combination of shareholders) acquiring one-third of a company's shares could take over the company after purchasing a total of only two-thirds of a company's shares, thereby leaving one-third out of the deal in minority shareholdings with limited rights. The Perrier case helped change all this. A group led by the Agnelli family of Italy attempted such a takeover of Perrier in 1991, but the move was opposed by Nestlé of Switzerland, allied with Banque Indosuez, which bid for all of the shares at a higher price. Nestlé also sued in French courts to block the Agnelli bid on the grounds that the Agnelli group had been formed specifically to block the Swiss group's bid before it was made. The courts ruled in favor of Nestlé, which went on to win the contest. Early in 1992, the Paris Stock Exchange announced a proposal to require public tender offers to be for 100% of a target company's stock. This proposal quickly received the endorsement of then economics minister Pierre Bérégovoy, who said, "I have pronounced myself in favor of 100% takeovers after seeing the problems resulting from current rules."[7]

Even formal takeover barriers such as authorized voting restrictions do not, of course, prevent a defender's board from finally bowing to market pressures and coming to agreement with a pursuer. Nor do they prevent a pursuer from initiating the game by going public with proposals for a friendly takeover at a fair price to shareholders that in turn are free to exert pressure on the defenders. Even in Switzerland, where shares owned by foreigners can be denied voting rights by unilateral management action, takeover prospects make Swiss board members nervous.

"How can this be?" I asked a senior Swiss banker friend who sits on several boards. "You have all the votes locked up."

"Yes, that is true," my friend replied, "but still there have been some offers. Gentlemen from the Swiss business establishment have not been inclined to do the sort of things at home that they might do abroad, for fear of public disapproval and not wanting to foul their own nests. So we get instead the likes of Tito Tettamanti and Werner Rey [controversial New Men of Switzerland] instead, and the conservative Swiss are reluctant to accept their proposals even when they are fairly priced. They have noticed, however, that Swiss stock prices are very low by world standards, reflecting limited liquidity and stringent voting restrictions. They also notice when someone offers a substantial premium over the market price for their shares. The Swiss, after all, are known to like money.

"Some investors believe the Swiss market will change and that share prices will not only rise to world levels but will become subject to takeovers. I don't know if these investors are right, but many institutional managers in London and New York think Switzerland may be a play. As a Swiss, I find that impossible to believe. As a banker, however, I know that replacing passive Swiss shareholders with aggressive international ones is not good for our peace of mind.

"What if," he continued, "someone like AT&T, or Siemens, or ICI—first-class companies which have made acquisitions before—announced through the press that it had talked to one of our large companies about a merger but had been rejected? And then the company said that it believed that such a rejection, though consistent with Swiss practice, was not in the best interests of shareholders, who should have the opportunity to decide for themselves what to do. If the company should go on to say that it would pay a premium of 30% or 40% more than the market price if the shareholders managed to persuade the board to rescind all voting restrictions, the market could very well support the proposal. The stock price would rise and pressure would be brought to bear on the board to find a way to deliver the premium to the shareholders."

"What would the board do then?" I asked.

"It's a tough question, because it would all be out in the open; the board could be criticized by its Swiss and international shareholders, by the Swiss government (which tries to conform its policies to EC practice), and by many foreign governments. We may be able to reject one or two of these despite the criticism, but sooner or later we will lose.

"And," he added, "don't forget Continental." The shareholders of Continental AG, the German tire company, unexpectedly voted in 1991 to abolish voting limitations after Pirelli proposed to merge the companies against Continental's wishes. "We and the Germans have similar rules. Although the effect of the vote was later overturned, the Continental case was a powerful precedent in the matter of shareholder voting. We, too, must be guided by it."

The Swiss have maintained restrictive practices on share ownership by foreigners. These are criticized periodically by the press and the foreign financial communities.

"If we know we will ultimately lose on this issue," my friend observed, "why not begin now to shape things as they must be in the future? This way, at least we might have some influence on the outcome."

Stirring Up the Banks

The 1992 initiative has given the European banks a lot to adapt to, more perhaps than any change they have faced since 1945. First, they have had to adapt to the BIS proposals for risk-adjusted bank capital adequacy. For many large banks, these are not too arduous, but for banks with a history of aggressive lending efforts in the third world, or in real estate markets, these new standards can be oppressive. Borderline banks will have to forgo growth strategies until they are able to strengthen their capital bases. Also, banks have to worry about the impact of future capital adequacy and accounting rules. High-yielding loans to weaker credits would require greater reserves in order to keep inside the capital adequacy lines. Tougher accounting standards would downgrade asset values, requiring even more capital.

Second, the banks have to face the removal of protective barriers that have insulated domestic banking from foreign competitors. With a common banking license, banks based in France can open retail branches in Spain or Italy, and German banks can open branches in France or the United Kingdom. Services can be offered in other countries without branches at all; they can sell credit cards and other services by mail or phone instead. The expected effect (already in evidence) is for competitors to flock to those EC countries where banking spreads are especially high such as Spain, Denmark, and France. This would ultimately bring the spreads down to EC norms. Similarly, banks in countries slow to adapt to electronic banking can expect to be challenged by banks from countries that are more advanced. For most banks, common licensing means more competition at home, pressure on spreads, and the need to upgrade technology. Declining spreads mean pressures on profits. Fewer profits mean the constraints of the capital adequacy tests may become more binding.

Third, banks will have to face competitive changes in the wholesale banking arena, mainly from the increasing appeal of the securities markets to their traditional customers. European capital markets have developed considerably over the past decade, thanks in large part to the volume of activity in the Eurobond and equity markets. Now, however, absent capital controls across Europe, there is widespread integration of domestic capital markets with the Euromarkets, and greater familiarity with the markets on the part of issuers. Not only are securities issues eating into the lucrative territory of bank loans, the banks themselves (acting as investment bankers under their universal banking umbrella) are fueling the movement. Capital market new issues by Europeans have increased substantially over the past several years, and markets have expanded to include many securitized products, such as asset-backed securities and commercial paper. Interest rate and currency swaps, and derivative products involving futures and options, have greatly increased the depth and range of capital market alternatives to traditional bank financing for larger corporations. Also, the industrial restructuring that is taking place will create a greater supply of common stock to be traded in the equity markets, bringing this sector of continental European finance up to world standards.

A differentiation between retail and wholesale banking similar to that taking place in the United States is also developing in Europe. This is not surprising in view of the substantial degree of world capital-market integration that now exists. The net effect of this development on European banks is to put great pressure on long-standing *hausbank* relationships. Traditional clients of large European banks are already receiving many offers of aggressive and innovative financing from foreign investment banks and other commercial banks, which they sometimes regard as too good not to take down. It is true of course that indigenous banks continue to maintain excellent relationships with wholesale banking clients and retain the largest market share in their own countries. But they admit that they are often forced to match an attractive offer from a foreign bank to retain their own client's business. To contend with this dilemma, the banks will have to become innovative, imaginative, and aggressive—traits that history has not required of them, and that few will find it easy to develop.

The industrial restructuring in Europe affects European banks in two major ways: their clients will restructure (and many will disappear in the process) and the more open, market-oriented attitude that a restructuring environment presents will accelerate the pace of change toward price-driven, opportunistic banking. The banks will also be affected by the movement toward EMU. On one hand, reduced volatility in intra-European interest and foreign exchange rates would squeeze the banks' substantial trading profits, and on the other, currency union would substantially increase the risks of having loan portfolios concentrated in single economic regions, as almost all of them now are. Accordingly, the European banking industry will itself substantially be restructured as banks seek ways to cope with these developments.

Many European bankers disagree with these conclusions, questioning the speed of change and its effect upon their relationships with clients which, they say, have held up very well so far. The facts are, however, that industrial restructuring is a reality, and so are the market forces that restructuring has released. Financial innovation and capital market activity are increasing for a very simple reason: they can lower the cost of funds to borrowers. Often the cost of market-supplied funds is lower than bank loans, and this is affecting the relationships that banks have with clients, especially the larger European corporations. American and British investment banks and large wholesale banks have been gaining market share by virtue of effective cross-border marketing and innovative, aggressively priced products. This may partly explain the more than 150 mergers, acquisitions, or cross-shareholdings involving European banks that took place in 1990 and 1991, more than 30 in Germany, France, and Italy alone.[8]

These are tumultuous times for European banks, especially for their senior managers—those in their fifties and sixties whose lifetime experience and training in banking have not equipped them to deal with the current realities.

NOT SO QUIET ON THE EASTERN FRONT

At the same time that the single market initiative was announced in Europe, Mikhail Gorbachev became the Secretary General of the Communist Party of the Soviet Union. Gorbachev had been a member of the Politburo since 1981, and was a protégé of Yuri Andropov, the former KGB head who succeeded Leonid Brezhnev in 1982 and died in 1984. Gorbachev certainly knew the Soviet economy was in bad shape when he came into office in 1985; just how bad he wasn't quite sure, because the statistics were so terrible.

Encircling them (as Russians always thought foreigners were doing) were the Americans, with the world's largest economy; the Europeans, who were seeking to unify themselves into a marketplace of equal size; and the Japanese, the world's most efficient economy, which still seemed to harbor dreams of a Southeast Asia Co-Prosperity Sphere. To the east, the Soviets saw a big surly China and to the south, in Iran and Afghanistan, were millions of Islamic fanatics. Also, the NATO countries had recently deployed hundreds of powerful medium-range nuclear missiles all around Europe, the Afghan War was costing a bundle, and those crazy Americans had come up with something from the comic books called a Strategic Defense Initiative, or *Star Wars*. The new American defense plan probably wouldn't work, but the Russians would have to try keep up with it anyway, even though they couldn't afford it and didn't have the technology.

The Soviet Union had 290 million people in 1990, and there were another 100 million in the satellite countries of Eastern Europe, where as poor as they were relative to their western neighbors, most were a lot better off than the Soviets. The eastern and western halves of Europe were about the same in total population, but the western half was at least four to five times more productive economically. The Americans and Japanese were even more productive. The only thing the Soviets had that the other Europeans didn't was a vast army equipped with nuclear weapons. And Gorbachev knew that it cost most of the Soviet annual budget to keep it going, not to mention the cost of upgrading its equipment.

"No wonder my two predecessors dropped dead," Gorbachev must have said to himself, "once they figured all this out. But where do we go from here?"

Perestroikan Economics

"We go west," was Gorbachev's answer. "Our only hope is to make them think they have defeated their old enemy, 'Godless communism.' Then they won't need to destroy us—either with bombs or through a high-tech arms race that would bankrupt us. Instead the West, and the Americans in particular, will take pity on us as repentant sinners. They will lend us money and help us learn how to be capitalists like them. Hey, if you can't beat 'em, join 'em."

And so it happened—the end of communism, the Soviet bloc, and even the Soviet Union and Gorbachev himself. All, amazingly, in just a few years from 1986 to 1991, without a shot being fired (at a Westerner). Seventy-five years of fierce ideological struggle ended, thankfully, with a whimper, not a bang.

It started with the Geneva summit in November 1985, Gorbachev's first meeting with Ronald Reagan, whom he charmed and who agreed to meet again to discuss arms reduction. On New Year's Day, 1986, Reagan appeared on Soviet TV and Gorbachev on U.S. TV, each expressing hope for world peace. Then there were more summits and meetings. Arms reduction talks began. The Afghan War ended in 1988. Gorbachev became a world media figure, appearing everywhere as the new lovable Russian who only wanted peace and good will. Reagan believed him. So did Thatcher. And Mitterrand. Kohl saw him as heaven sent, someone who could reduce the dreaded threat from the East, which might otherwise, for the third time in a century, turn the whole of the Federal Republic into a battlefield. Maybe, too, thought Kohl, this could cool things off enough to bring about German unification—that would really be something!

While Gorbachev was turning foes into friends, the reverse was happening inside the Soviet Union. His policies were shocking, even horrifying to all the communist *nomenklatura*. So he had to duck and weave to outsmart his opponents. Whatever policy he made could be changed next week. He consolidated power, placed his own people in key jobs, and continued to urge reforms without really changing much inside the economic system. Things did open up, however, and the scent of democracy got into the air. Eastern Europe and the Baltic States smelled the change first and bolted before the Russians were ready. This forced Gorbachev to accept domestic elections, more turmoil, and the return of populist Boris Yeltsin, whom he had previously purged from the politburo.

The pace of change accelerated—no one knew exactly where they were going, but they knew they were there going fast. The Berlin Wall fell on November 9, 1989, and German unification occurred a year later. By the end of 1990, all the former Eastern European satellites were free republics—weak, wobbly, and uncertain, but free. After this, Kremlin internal control deteriorated, which resulted in the breaking apart of the old (pre–Soviet Union) Russian empire led by the Ukraine, Byelorussia, Georgia, Moldavia, and Kazakhstan and the return of ethnic violence to Armenia and Azerbaijan. Serious fighting too had broken out in Yugoslavia, in Georgia, Romania, and along some of the frontiers separating the former satellite countries. Then came the bungled KGB coup attempt in August 1991, a temporary truce between Gorbachev and Yeltsin, and the beginning of a series of urgent cries for financial aid from the West.

But Gorbachev and his pragmatic "let's make a deal" approach to statesmanship couldn't hold on. Discontent was everywhere, and he had to take the blame. The economy was a mess. Inflation was out of control and shortages of food and other consumer goods were worsening. Marshall Goldman, an economist and sovietologist, observed that Gorbachev was faced with a dilemma. He wanted to move toward a market economy; for years he had known that this had to be done. But he was hesitant to subject the Soviet Union to the type of economic shock that such reforms would involve, reforms that should have been begun about the same time that perestroikan expectations began to build in the country. "He also concluded," noted Goldman, "that unless reined in, the reforms would ultimately shrink his powers and those of the Soviet Union over central economic control, thus reducing the Soviet Union to an ineffective economic entity."[9] Indecision thus may have been the real cause of Gorbachev's isolation and removal from power a few months later.

Most Western economists believe the Soviet economy imploded, collapsing from within. It was a totally unworkable system that could only be fixed by drastic reforms in several areas simultaneously. Any foot dragging or efforts to ease the pain it would cause the hapless public would only give reactionaries time to reject the reform efforts already put into place. A concerted, full-power attack on the old system had to occur for there to be any hope of change. Goldman spelled out what would be needed in a presentation in Moscow in June 1989. His proposal

> included provision for price reform, monetary reform, convertability of the ruble, abolition of the industrial ministries, privatization and breakup of state enterprises and of state collective farms, freedom of entry [to the market] for family farmers, private and cooperative stores and factories, as well as joint ventures, including some that could be owned 100% by foreigners. There would also be a series of safety net provisions to sustain the poorer members of society. Food subsidies should be reduced or eliminated. This combined with reduction in military expenditures would help bring the national budget into balance.[10]

These recommendations were harsh medicine indeed, especially for a society at the limit of its patience. Such a program might work in a smaller country like Poland, some of its critics said, but in a vast, poorly administered land with no living memory of a market system, little confidence existed that reforms could be brought about fairly or successfully. So Gorbachev the politician tried to avoid that which Gorbachev the economist knew must come. The result was one new plan after another, drafted by a series of economic advisers and never fully put to the test.

After the attempted coup, economic conditions deteriorated further and Russian President Boris Yeltsin, bright with the acclaim bestowed on him for his bold rescue of Gorbachev from the KGB, moved to consolidate most of the Soviet Union's economic power within the Russian Republic. On November 17, 1991, he announced that Russia was taking control of all Soviet resources within its borders, including almost all oil, gold, and diamond reserves, the country's main collateral for hard-currency borrowing. Yeltsin added that Russia would obligate itself to repay outstanding Soviet debts incurred before that date. The Ukraine, Byelorussia, and Kazakhstan joined in the Russian declaration, at least for the time being. All this was of great interest to the senior finance officials from the Group of Seven industrial countries, who had just arrived in Moscow for a meeting with Gorbachev's advisers.

Gorbachev made some additional efforts to recover his position, but soon it became clear that without the cooperation of the large republics, he was out of business. Finally, on December 8, 1991 (the day the Maastricht meetings began), Yeltsin and the leaders of the Ukraine and Byelorussia announced the formation of a new "Commonwealth of Independent States," open to all members of the former Soviet Union, and declared that "the U.S.S.R. as a subject of international law and geopolitical reality, is ceasing its existence." The CIS would abandon all efforts to reform the old regime; instead it would create a new one out of whole cloth. Each republic would be truly independent, though the CIS would provide a "coordinating body" to handle defense, foreign affairs, and the economy. Within a few days, other republics rallied to the new commonwealth, the capital of which was to be in the Byelorussian city of Minsk, and before Christmas, Gorbachev, bowing to reality, resigned his offices. The mighty Soviet Union, terror of the Western world for decades, had simply voted itself out of business.

The world rejoiced at the collapse of the place Ronald Reagan had called the "Evil Empire," and began happily to construct visions of a future free of the threat of war and massive arms budgets—until it began to figure up the costs of the transaction and its contingent liabilities.

Who's Gonna Pay for This Mess?

Perestroika, Russian for "restructuring," had not been a success. The monolith of the Soviet command economy was impervious to reform. A centrally controlled, closed, price-administered system enveloped the entire economy. Such a system could not coexist with a market economy; whichever was stronger would instantly make the other obsolete. Even in East Germany, the bloc's most advanced and efficient economy, the goods and services that were produced could not be sold competitively in an open market. Given a choice, no one (not even East Germans) would buy East German goods, which were of lesser quality and more expensive than Western goods.

Not only that, the command economies were so inefficient, so underinvested, and so lacking in leadership and training that the work force was next to useless. Workers from the world's worst economies are not in great demand, even when wages are low. And management was so bad, and central controls so rigorous and mindless, that most of the equipment in use was worn out and obsolete. In short, the economies of Eastern Europe were completely uncompetitive with the Western economics with which they desperately wished to be joined.

The Soviet Union in particular was revealed to be a primitive economic wasteland: crops rotted in the field or on the way to market, giant combines were hopelessly inefficient, there were no consumer goods, the ruble was considered worthless abroad and increasingly unacceptable as payment for goods and services traded between Russians. As the political reforms began, the economic chaos increased. The GNP decreased in 1990 and 1991 at a rate somewhere between 10% and 20% per year. Savings disappeared. The budget deficit for 1991 came in at six times the estimated figure. Hyperinflation (at 400% a year) broke out as the system broke down. "The only limit to the money supply in the Soviet Union today," said the head of the central bank's money supply department in September 1991, "is the capacity of the money presses."[11]

Meanwhile, oil production, the nation's main source of foreign exchange, was strangled by underinvestment and poor maintenance. Output plummeted—in 1990, the Soviet Union produced more than 11.6 million barrels of crude oil per day, an amount greater than the combined production of all of the Middle Eastern countries. In 1991, production declined sharply because of deteriorating oil field facilities and decisions to conserve oil for domestic use. The International Energy Agency estimated that production would drop further to about 9.5 million barrels per day by mid-1992, representing a total decline of about 20% since 1990.[12] Gold reserves were dwindling fast too. According to Grigory Yavlinsky, a young economist serving as deputy prime minister and head of a four-man interim committee that was managing the Soviet economy just before Gorbachev's ouster, "gold reserves have dropped by over two-thirds over the past year and now amount to just 240 tons. Another 110 tons have been 'pawned,' but we are unable to redeem it." Western estimates had long assumed reserves of between 1,500 and 3,000 tons.[13] Apparently, unbeknownst to Gorbachev and his economic policy makers, budget deficits were routinely erased by selling off gold reserves.

Yavlinsky was also the father of a plan to hire a group of Harvard economists to institute a program of economic shock therapy, like Marshall Goldman's, to transform the Soviet Union into a market economy as quickly as possible. Such reforms would then become the basis for securing Western financial and technical aid. He was also the author of an interrepublic economic treaty designed to provide a free-enterprise common market to replace the former Kremlin-run system and to form a "guarantee against the chaotic disintegration of the country." This plan was rejected when the new commonwealth was formed and economic management was turned over to a 36-year-old Yeltsin man, Yegor Gaidar, a protégé of Stanislav Shatalin, whose 500-day plan for Soviet economic reform in the early days of perestroika was never adopted.

Gaidar had a plan too. Yeltsin was ready for harsh measures if they would stabilize the economy. On January 1, 1992, prices were freed in Russia on all but a few basic goods, and they shot upward at a frightening rate. The idea was that the price increases would unclog the awful Russian distribution system, and goods would be attracted to the market. Gaidar's plan also required Russia to halt the runaway expansion of the money supply, cut back defense spending by 85% from 1991 levels, seize control of hard currency circulating in the market, and consolidate and reorganize the country's hardly existent banking system. The other republics agreed to go along with the effort to bring the economy under control, though everyone knew the measures would be extremely unpopular.

First, however, there would be a Russian-declared moratorium on principal repayments on foreign debt. Gaidar explained that this part of the new policy was necessary to conserve scarce foreign exchange and to prevent political crisis. Soon after, he declared the Soviet Bank for Foreign Economic Relations (*Vnesheconombank*) bankrupt. By mid-January, the moratorium had been extended to interest payments as well, and $84 billion of Soviet debt went into default. The biggest exposures were among the German banks, where a total of $20 billion was owed—though all but about $5 billion was counterguaranteed by the German government.

Then, in mid-January 1992, the ruble was devalued in order to return it to convertability into foreign currencies. Immediately the ratio of exchange fell to about 150 rubles per dollar, though at this level an average Russian's monthly wage was valued at about $3.50. At such exchange rates, imports would be virtually impossible but exports (if the Russians could make anything anyone else wanted) would be very attractively priced.

Following these measures, the next step was to ask for financial aid and food from the West. Most estimates of the minimum amount necessary exceeded what was likely to be available by ten or more times. The United States first offered $650 million, primarily in surplus food and medicine; this amount was generally thought to be a drop in the bucket, but it was just about all Bush could come up with in an election year in which Americans wanted help with their own economy.

After the early months of 1992, the world watched as the new Commonwealth of Independent States buckled down for the storms to come. If only they could get through the winter, some nervous observers noted, they might have a chance to see both an economic recovery and to preserve their democracy. Those who were more optimistic pointed out that the commonwealth had few options and reverting to the old economic system probably wasn't one of them. Yeltsin, after all was a communist official before he became a democrat, and he was capable, many thought, of being as tough as necessary to see the reforms through.

Yeltsin, however, was having a difficult time of it. The people were unhappy with the harsh living conditions that his reforms had brought. By the end of the winter, there was very little evidence that the higher prices had succeeded in attracting surplus food and other goods to Moscow. Meanwhile, Yeltsin was having troubles with his fellow CIS republics, and with the parliament of the Russian Republic, known as the Congress of People's Deputies, which wanted some changes in the reform plans to alleviate the suffering of the people. Yeltsin and Gaidar then presented the $24 billion aid package, patched together on short notice from Western governments and international lending agencies. Continuation of the reforms, they said, was crucial to receiving the grant. But the parliament wasn't satisfied—it wanted a victory of its own, so Yeltsin gave it Gaidar, who was removed from his post as finance minister on April 2, 1992. The move was generally thought to be a symbolic tactical maneuver by Yeltsin, rather than a reversal of the economic reform program. Gaidar was to retain his position of first deputy prime minister, and would continue to serve as de facto minister of finance. Bad news and controversy continued to plague the economy. The grain harvest was well below earlier estimates, forcing Yeltsin to send army units into the fields and to hustle up additional foreign credits for supplementary purchases. Inflation continued to soar; both internal and external trade was torpid, observers on the scene reported, because a surprising number of bottlenecks remained in the system, untouched so far by reforms. The head of the Russian union of industrialists (i.e., factory managers) complained that the rapid pace of reforms was bankrupting the country's large manufacturers, which had been denied badly needed interenterprise credits. The government promised an extra $3.8 billion of relief (equal to 20% of the current quarter's GNP) and postponed the freeing of energy prices for up to a year. Then the chairman of the fledgling central bank, Georgy Matyukhin, held responsible for the restraint of credit to industry (part of the effort to reduce the growth in the money supply), was sacked, reportedly because he was discovered to be a CIA agent intent on undermining the institution.[14] Despite these setbacks to reform, efforts were strengthened to consolidate support from the IMF and the principal Western countries. Plans were announced for attracting foreign capital investment and for privatizing as many as half of all major enterprises by 1995. On June 15, 1992, the day before Yeltsin left for a visit to Washington, Gaidar, in a surprise move, was appointed prime minister. Like Gorbachev, Yeltsin, under pressure, was playing one tune for his domestic audience and another for the international community.

Things were somewhat better in Poland, Czechoslovakia, and Hungary, which were trying to make independent economies out of satellites once fully dependent on the Soviet system. A vastly disproportionate share of the manufacturing output of these countries had routinely been shipped to the Soviet Union in exchange for oil and other materials. All of a sudden the former Soviets could not pay for the goods they imported, and demanded hard currency for their oil. This really squeezed these economies, but perhaps they benefited from having to scramble around in search of other ways to use their economic capabilities. Bulgaria and Romania were less affected by the squeeze, and had less opportunity to learn how to adjust, and in the post-Soviet economy they found themselves slowly sinking. Acute political problems were also a legacy of Soviet control in several of the Eastern European countries. In Poland, political fragmentation led to economic paralysis. In Czechoslovakia, differences between the Czechs and the Slovaks proved to be unreconcilable, and the country split up, much to the economic disadvantage of the four million Slovaks. Yugoslavia became involved in civil war, and ceased to exist as either a state or an economy.

So when you add it up, there were 390 million people in the former Soviet Union and eastern bloc who were, at the outset, good for nothing. Most could not make anything anyone wanted, many could not feed themselves, they had no savings (or wouldn't before long), and they were badly undereducated in economic life. They were stunned by what had happened to them, bitter at the jobs done by their governments, and envious of any of their number who seemed to be doing better than the rest. Nearly four hundred million people needed to be fed, retrained, motivated, and recycled into usefulness. Otherwise they would start walking westward, adding to the numbers of economic refugees swamping the social services systems of their neighbors in Western Europe. Already war refugees from Yugoslavia, and hardship cases from all over Eastern Europe were pouring into Germany, Switzerland, Italy, and Austria as "asylum seekers." Or, they would start fighting with each other, as they had already begun to do in Georgia and Armenia, perhaps ending up in civil war with the local guerilla groups using tactical nuclear weapons. Or maybe, some thought, they would revolt, bring down Yeltsin and the others, and impose a harsh, totalitarian regime again that would, presumably, revert to being at daggers-drawn with the West. None of these alternatives was appealing. The mess had to be cleaned up somehow, and former members of the Soviet bloc could not do so entirely by themselves; part of the burden of paying for it must fall on the West, especially Western Europe, its closest first-world neighbor.

Germany was the first to pay heavily for economic and political reforms in the former Soviet bloc. First, to accelerate unification, it had to bribe the Russians, offering $30 billion in aid and troop subsidies over a two-year period (1989–1991) to get their consent to the fast track. The Federal Republic also had to pay for the integration of East Germany; it had already spent more than $100 billion on economic reunification by early 1992, and this sum represented only a partial payment of the total bill. It will be years before subsidies and unemployment benefits are no longer needed in Eastern Germany on a large scale.

No one seemed very happy with the situation in Germany after the initial euphoria of unification had passed. The former eastern *länder* (states) immediately experienced an incredible economic depression, which they did not anticipate when they brought the wall down. Industrial production fell by 35% to 40% in the first year, and stayed there. Unemployment rose by the end of 1991 to almost 50% of the full-time work force. Before unification, East Germany had a labor force of nearly 10 million; by the middle of 1992, it had dropped to 6 million, of which 1.4 million (23%) are officially unemployed, and another 1 million are on short time.[15] One unemployed East Berliner I spoke to in 1991 said, "You know, we only wanted to reform our system in the German Democratic Republic, not to destroy it. We are now like economic prisoners of war." And across the city, in prosperous

West Berlin—where, as in the rest of Germany, citizens were having to pay
for unification through taxes, higher interest rates, job displacement, and
lower growth—a young woman walking down the stylish Kurfürsten-
damm wore a T-shirt inscribed with the slogan "I want my Wall back."

No matter how you look at it, the economic cost of integrating the two
Germanies is going to be high. Though the initial impact of converting
their savings into Deutschemarks at a favorable exchange rate meant that
many East Germans went on a spending spree, buying up TVs, appliances,
automobiles, consumer disposables, and even, reportedly, the services of
West German prostitutes. This happy first encounter with capitalism was
replaced by the grim reality of unemployment and hard times. West Ger-
man-funded public works projects and small retail businesses, which have
grown up in the void left by the Communists, have started to blossom,
and these have helped offset the plunging industrial economy, but the outlook remains bleak, even two years after unification.

By the end of 1991, there were some signs that the economic free-fall in
East Germany had bottomed out and recovery had begun. Optimists circulated forecasts of a 10% growth rate for 1992 for the East, but even if this
is achieved, East Germany's GNP at the beginning of 1993 will still be 25%
below what it was in 1989. And if a 7% to 10% growth rate can be sustained, according to Kurt Biedenkopf, the prime minister of Saxony (one
of the eastern *länder*), per capita GDP in the East will reach only 65% to
70% of the West's by the end of the decade. But he adds, "As long as
people see things steadily improving they will not worry so much about
being equal with the West."[16]

Though polls indicate that many easterners have returned to being optimistic about the future, many blame the politicians, especially Chancellor
Kohl, for their current predicament. They have taken to hurling eggs and
tomatoes at him when he comes to visit, which, understandably, he does
less often than before.

Meanwhile, in the former West Germany, the taxpayers foot the bill for
restructuring through higher interest charges on a great surge of government borrowings (derived from a budget deficit which by the end of 1992
touched 4.5% of GNP). The problems of unification are threatening to con-
taminate Germany with the American disease—runaway budgets, huge
deficits, and massive borrowing requirements. New public borrowing is
expected to jump in 1992 to about $110 billion (6% of GNP); total German
public-sector debt outstanding is forecasted to exceed 50% of GNP by 1994.
It was around 40% before unification.[17]

This level of borrowing pushed up inflation in Germany to more than
4.0% in 1991, and accordingly the independent-minded, inflation-hating
Bundesbank put the squeeze on the money supply, driving *real* rates to a
post-war high of more than 5%. In March 1992, the Bundesbank gave a

stern warning to the government that the situation was getting out of control, and that if spending (mostly on the East) was to continue as forecast, then taxes would have to be raised, for a second time since unification.[18] Not everyone in Western Germany is happy with this situation, and loud political grumbling has been heard. Kohl sternly lectures his countrymen on their responsibilities and their obligation to help their kinsmen in the East, and they grumble some more, though in their hearts they know he is right.

Eastern Germany, of course, differs from the rest of Eastern Europe because it has been adopted by a generous, rich uncle who is a member of Europe's most exclusive club, the EC. All the money flowing eastward, for investment and for subsidies, will ensure the recovery of the economy eventually. The other Eastern European countries are on their own. Their economies have fallen just as much as Eastern Germany's but their recoveries are much less certain. Shock therapy has been unavoidable, though its effects are unevenly distributed. One consequence has been a splitting into two groups: the high-potential countries (Hungary, Poland, Czechoslovakia), and the others (Bulgaria, Romania, and Yugoslavia). A study published by the World Bank in September 1991 illustrated the dimensions of the economic problems in these countries. The high-potential countries are predicted to recover the GNP per capita they enjoyed in 1989 by 1996 or 1997; for the others it will be much later.[19] But even these less fortunate countries have at the outset an economic advantage—the ability to depreciate their currencies to such an extent that wage rates are very cheap and new investment is thus attracted.

They also face a common political problem—their agricultural surplus (the one thing they can export right now) cannot be sold inside the EEC (the most logical place to send it) because of the Common Agricultural Policy, which would assess a tariff of 100% of its value, at least, under existing agreements, for the next five years. Perhaps necessity will be the mother of change in this long out-of-date policy, which nothing else so far has been able to budge.[20]

Economists surveyed the wreckage of the Soviet bloc and by mid-1991 had begun to produce some useful studies that have helped illuminate its future prospects. One study by Collins and Roderick of the Washington-based Institute for International Economics measured how much foreign capital would be needed to raise the amount of productive capital investment per worker to the same level as in the West within ten years. The answer is about *$1.5 trillion per year*. The study also estimated how much capital the region could be expected to attract. The answer is between $30 and $90 billion a year (most of which will go to East Germany), or a maximum of 0.6% of the annual requirement. Less than one percent of what they need is likely to be available. The World Bank announced its own study, which calculated that Eastern Europe, excluding the former Soviet Union, would need $20 billion per year until the year 2000 in order to have any economic growth at all. It added that because private investors were wary, most of this money would have to come from the official (i.e., the governmental) lending sector (which, of course, didn't have it). Michel Camdessus, the managing director of the IMF, announced in April 1992 that it estimated that the fifteen republics of the former Soviet Union would also need more than $100 billion in aid over the next four years if the transition to market economies in those countries was to be prevented from collapsing. Of this, the IMF and its sister organization, the World Bank, would lend $37 to $45 billion.

A study by Richard Blackhurst, director of economic research at the GATT, points out the similarities between the Eastern European countries today and the four "tigers" of Southeast Asia (Hong Kong, Taiwan, South Korea, and Singapore) twenty years ago. The prospects for growth through increased world trade, he says, are promising. Blackhurst also points out that migration of the Eastern Europeans may not be the nightmare others have predicted, not because they won't migrate (they will) but because the absorption capacity of Western Europe and other parts of the world may be much greater than originally thought. He compares the beneficial American experience with immigration from 1840 to 1920 in coming to this conclusion.[21] But despite trade and resettlement, the cost of reabsorbing Eastern Europe into the Western world is going to be extremely high.

The Germans will not be alone in paying for the redemption of 390 million communists, though they may think so for a while. Other countries will contribute, mainly through international aid and development organizations. Food aid and credits will be forthcoming. There will also be some direct loans and grants, but considering the budgetary state of almost all of the OECD countries, nothing like what is being asked for. The 390 million themselves will pay the price in a lower standard of living, and this will not be shared evenly among them.

Various deals will be proposed as the Russians and the other republics sell off such things as the Kurile Islands to the Japanese, nuclear weapons to NATO, high-technology defense industry factories, and banking and commercial licenses and mineral exploration rights to foreigners. They have a lot to sell, and no doubt there will be a large demand once matters settle down a bit and some of the first-round reforms occur such as legalizing private property. But the last, best hope is for the countries to build a competitive private sector that can pull them out of their slump. Western corporations are needed to make direct investments, but until the economies are rebuilt these can be expected only in modest amounts. So the answer has to lie in creating the private sector de novo through the transfer of assets from the public sector. Privatization, and on a vast scale.

The Hard Road of Privatization

In July 1990, the world was encouraged to believe that the economic reunification of the two Germanies would go as smoothly as the political, and that the quick conversion of East Germany into a truly Westernized society would be the pattern for the rest of the newly liberated countries in the East. The locomotive for the restructuring of East Germany would be privatization programs that would turn the formidable state-owned industrial base into one that was owned by private citizens from noncommunist Germany and the rest of the world. Market capitalism would replace autocratic communism in a comparatively painless transition, at least in Germany.

It has not worked out like that at all, at least not yet. The results to date of East German privatization, though in some respects encouraging, are on balance disappointing. There are several reasons for this.

First, the economic mess left behind by the communists was far worse than anyone thought possible. All of the early data, such as those from the CIA and the World Bank that showed the GNP per capita of East Germany to be on a par with Sweden, have been proven to be completely wrong. Capital stock was obsolete and badly undermaintained. "We were ill informed, and greatly underestimated the enormity of the transition," said Hilmar Kopper, chief executive of the Deutsche Bank.

In East Germany more than half the plant and machinery was over ten years old. One economist, Anne Kreuger of Duke University, estimated that the true value of the capital assets in the country (book value minus modernization costs) was zero. And the devastation of industrial pollution has been far greater than anyone had imagined, probably making the whole worth far less than zero after cleanup costs are added. According to the Statistical Office of the Federal Republic of Germany, the productivity of East German workers in 1991 was 28% of that of their West German counterparts. And East Germany was thought to be several times more productive than the worst of the Soviet bloc countries.

Second, there was no infrastructure for a capitalistic system. This has been resolved for the most part by the absorption of the eastern *länder* into the Federal Republic, but initially there were substantial issues to resolve concerning the identity of original pre-communist or pre–World War II ownership of East German property, and responsibility for pollution cleanup, product liabilities, and for compensating discharged workers. In most of the other eastern countries, the legal rights of owners of private property have not yet been established, and no operative legal system yet exists through which disputes and claims can be processed. There is no banking system (not one we would recognize, anyway) for short-term business credit or loans for financing equipment. There remain in most countries disputes as to who pays for cleanup costs and severance allowances. And there continue to be great obstacles to making any sizable cuts in the work force of the businesses that one might buy.

Third, the economies are completely misaligned with the West's, according to a report from the Kiel Institute of World Economics. East Germany had twice as much of its total capital investment in heavy industry as did West Germany, and somewhat less than half as much in retailing and services. At least half of the existing plant in the East would be surplus and unneeded, even if it were efficient.[22]

And finally, the open-market policies of the West are killing what's left of the industrial base in the eastern *länder*. The West exports goods to the East, where they are in great demand. The East cannot yet manufacture much of anything that the West will buy. The rest of the eastern countries at least have a currency they can depreciate until somebody will buy something, but the East Germans are stuck with the still-hard Deutschemark, which they cannot depreciate. But wage rates in Germany, according to a 1991 trade union agreement, must be the same by 1994 in the underproductive East as in the superproductive West, where wages are already 138% of U.S. rates. (In Poland, by comparison, wage rates are only 6% of those in the United States; in the Commonwealth of Independent States they are less than 1%.) If this wage agreement is actually carried out, it can only guarantee exceptionally high unemployment in the eastern *länder* for years to come.[23]

So all eyes are on the privatizers and their mission in the East. They are expected to replace ancient, inefficient businesses with highly entrepreneurial ones that respond to the incentives of the free market. But there have been a great many problems in getting the privatization effort off the ground.

Some initial greenfield investments have been made, and some old factories have been taken over and converted to modern manufacturing, an example being the Volkswagen absorption of the pathetic Trabant auto works in East Germany. These plant investments are important because, among other reasons, they allow investors to learn more about worker retraining, but only small amounts of capital have been committed to such projects so far.

Expectations are highest in the area of selling off old communist conglomerates, or kombinats, into as many viable pieces as possible. In Germany the government agency handling such privatization efforts is the *Treuhandanstalt*, or Treuhand for short. It has a massive job, needing to find a home for, or otherwise liquidate, all of the economic properties of East Germany, originally more than 12,000 so-called companies altogether. On one hand the Treuhand is driven by the need to sell off properties as quickly as possible (so as to end the subsidies and loan guarantees it must make to keep hundreds of nonviable East German companies alive); on the other hand it is reluctant to liquidate companies, lose jobs, and throw employees on the welfare rolls. Political considerations so far have led to favoring jobs over speed, making some economists worry that a large part of the former East German industrial base may be perpetuated inside West German borders, where it will live on efficiency-killing subsidies for years. The Treuhand is unavoidably political. It is made up of former East German government officials (who are very resistant to the idea of liquidations) and headed by a Thatcher-like West German former state government official, Brigitte Breuel. Her predecessor, West German industrialist Detlev Rohwedder, was murdered by terrorists in April 1991. Since reunification, the Treuhand had disposed of about 8,000 companies by mid-1992, though only about 300 have been sold to non-Germans. It has closed less than 1,000 companies but during 1992 it began a major program of worker layoffs. Its operating budget for 1991 was $22 billion, of which $12.5 billion was borrowed from the German government. Total debt was estimated to reach $150 billion by 1994.[24]

To buy a Treuhand company, investors have to search one out from a catalogue that offers almost no business or financial information. They then have to arrange and pay for an investigation—there are no audited financial statements. If they want to bid for the company, they must state a price and submit a business plan that includes an "estimated opening balance sheet." If there are no other bidders, and the business plan is acceptable to the Treuhand, the sale may be made. Management buyouts are also possible if the management group can attract financing. If there are several bidders, all submissions are made to the Treuhand, and a winner is announced in due course. The winner, however, may not be the high bidder. If the business plan or other features of one bid seems better than the others, it can be accepted without explanation. There is no way to ensure or enforce that promises made in a business plan will be kept; therefore the business plan can be whatever you want it to be. Accordingly, it is useless as a means to determine the winner of an auction. Indeed, these practices can only encourage arbitrary behavior on the part of the Treuhand, which can lead to uneconomic solutions and open the door to corruption.

Despite these awkward procedures, the Treuhand has at least managed to sell off a hundred or so large companies to other companies, and several hundred to entrepreneurial groups, who may be able to improve them. Indeed, there is plenty of evidence that the Treuhand is getting better at moving companies out, though not necessarily at killing off those that can't be sold. One independent survey reported that 70% of the companies still on the Treuhand's books were not commercially viable. The process would work better if it could be depoliticized, but that is absolutely impossible at a time when all of Germany expects the government to handle the tasks of the Treuhand in the best interests of the whole country. Of course, there is rare agreement on what those best interests are.

The privatization experience of the rest of Eastern Europe is far less advanced. In Poland, Czechoslovakia, and Hungary, where foreign investment lags well behind that attracted by East Germany, there have been some privatizations although in Poland and Hungary the programs are behind schedule. In the other countries, there is much less to work with, and very little has been done.

Despite a year of aggressive economic reforms, involving some progress and many setbacks, Poland had privatized only five companies by the end of 1991. The original plan was to privatize half the state-owned sector by 1993, and to transform the private sector into one resembling that of a Western European country by 1995. Even the few companies that have been privatized have not received an infusion of Western capital and know-how, but have simply been told to soldier on alone, comforted possibly by the knowledge that their shares are now owned by the Polish public instead of the state. In 1991, privatizations of Polish industry raised about $260 million (about a third of what had been budgeted). For 1992, a budget of $860 million was established, though privatizations in important industries (defense, auto and aircraft manufacturing, tobacco, and pharmaceuticals) requiring government approval were excluded. Some of these companies are quite likely to fail in the future, in which case privatization, already a bitter political issue, may be substantially cut back. Many fundamental matters of economic and social policy for the new country must be decided before the Polish privatization efforts can advance much further. The idea of socialism has not died in Poland, and real private ownership of existing tangible properties is hard for many people to swallow. In any event, essential legal and financial systems have to be put into place, new banking and tax systems established, and trade and foreign direct investment policies have to be devised. These things take time, but they can be completed more quickly when the country has agreed on the central issues involved. Such agreement is difficult to achieve in a country with twenty-nine different political parties sitting in its parliament.

In Czechoslovakia a more ambitious, ingenious program was undertaken in January 1992. Called "coupon privatization," the program consisted of selling coupons at a nominal fee to all citizens over eighteen. The coupons could be exchanged at auctions to occur between May and October 1992 for shares of newly formed companies representing about 40% of the economy with another round of auctions planned for 1993. Shares so received could be deposited in one or more of 450 private investment funds, which would accumulate blocks of shares of the various companies and manage their portfolios by trading the shares in the market. One such fund, calling itself Harvard Capital and Consulting (its founder is a recent Harvard undergraduate) used an aggressive marketing campaign, backed by Czech television commercials and a network of 22,000 commission agents soliciting coupons, and claimed to have signed up about 30% of all coupon holders for its fund. Harvard Capital's marketing effort was assisted by promises that their investors would receive a tenfold return after one year. The fund managers presumably would seek to acquire control of the companies being auctioned, and cause them to be managed efficiently. The $9.3 billion received from the sale of coupons was retained by the government, not invested in the companies, most of which suffer from the same competitive problems as East German firms and are likely to fail unless they receive foreign financial and management support. Still, in one quick stroke in May 1992, Czechoslovakia provided for the privatization of more than 1,200 state-owned corporations. The program was very popular with the public, which regarded it as a kind of high-stakes lottery. Many Czechs, however, expressed skepticism over who would end up with the coupons (crooks and former communist officials, many thought), and how the exercise, without any new money or know-how going into the companies, would actually help the economy and preserve jobs.[25] The future of the privatization program, however, was cast into doubt by the split-up of the country, which was announced in June 1992.

Blood in the Water

Western bankers have descended on the privatization scene like a school of sharks scenting blood in the water. They have not come to lend money (too risky), but to give advice on restructuring companies and the process of valuing and selling them, to find attractive long-term investments, and to help reorganize the banking systems. Their fees are paid out of the proceeds of sales or by hard-currency grants from the World Bank, the European Bank for Reconstruction and Development, and other development assistance organizations.

Most of the banks know very little about the constantly changing economic environment in which their clients must operate, but at least they have some idea about what a successful privatization looks like when it is done right.

These efforts are necessary and useful, though so far only in a very limited way. Privatization by selling off the assets of the old Soviet-style economies will not produce much net revenue for the sellers or provide much free-market revitalization for the economies. The real economic benefit for these countries has to come from job-creating de novo investments in high-demand industry sectors. Initially these will be in the retailing and service sectors; then gradually they should spread to the manufacturing areas where knowledgeable companies from Western Europe, the United States, or Japan can set up plants with modern equipment and management methods. These companies will look for opportunities to take advantage of low wage and foreign exchange rates. Unless things change, they won't find such opportunities in Eastern Germany, but they may very well find them in Hungary, Poland, and Czechoslovakia, if internal politics don't kill off investment incentives.

The most urgent need that banks can help address is rebuilding the financial systems in the former Soviet bloc. These must be completely changed in order to provide a rational basis for the utilization of currency (in some countries the local currency, e.g., the ruble, is difficult to exchange even for local goods and services), a basis for collecting and safe-guarding deposits in which the public can have confidence, an efficient payments mechanism, and a simple but effective basis for granting loans for working capital and equipment purchases. If only A.P. Gianini were alive today—it is his kind of post-earthquake banking that is needed. Rush-ing to set up stock markets and futures exchanges before a basic banking system is in effect is a foolish waste of time and effort. Shares of nonviable companies that trade for a while in the gold-rush market environment of the moment are not likely to do much for the economy; whereas offering working capital to money-starved new businesses so they can grow is very likely to help.

It is unlikely that Western banks will extend significant commercial cred-its to the Eastern countries (except possibly to the former East Germany). European banks (especially German banks) already have problems with a substantial portfolio of pre-1989 loans. Most banks will prefer to wait for a clearer picture of the political system to emerge, especially with respect to the identity of obligors, past and present, and until a proper legal and financial infrastructure exist, and some reliable forms of hard currency income are available, before extending much in the way of credit lines. Banks today are more cautious than when they loaned hundreds of billions of dollars to third world borrowers in the 1970s.

Governments should look to the example of South Korea in the 1970s as a role model for infrastructure building, government planning, and prag-matic law making, which resulted in a powerful industrial society assem-bled on the base of very little. They should also recall Mexico in the late 1980s for examples of success in privatization, deregulation, and re-access-ing foreign capital markets. These countries, and no doubt others too, were able to make substantial economic progress by opening their stifled and overregulated systems to the free-market forces.

Already the lure of taking part in the great Eastern European economic recovery has prompted several well-known bankers to quit their jobs and set out for the Klondike. Ronald Freeman, a senior managing director of Salomon Brothers, joined the European Bank for Reconstruction and Development to head the bank's merchant banking operations. Another Salomon managing director, Jay Higgens, joined forces with former World Bank Treasurer Donald Roth to raise $250 million from financial institutions for investment in the new region. A Goldman Sachs vice president, Wolfgang Sietz, left the firm to set up his own company specializing in investment banking services in Berlin, Prague, and Budapest. Investment guru Dean LeBaron, who heads Batterymarch Financial Management, has organized several trips for large U.S. pension funds to the former Soviet Union to look over its long-term investment potential. He has been shown formerly top-secret, high-tech defense plants that the Russians are apparently willing to sell to the highest bidder. Certainly these men believe that there are terrific opportunities in Eastern Europe for those who can find them. Their advice seems to be: "Go east, young man."

Other, less entrepreneurial bankers will have to work out for themselves what approach to take in dealing, or not dealing, with Eastern Europe. Such considerations inevitably will take them back to basics—the essential structure of their respective banking businesses and how adaptable they are to the many claims for their attention. Not all will decide to play in the East, but it is as clear as it can be that the services of Western banks in Eastern Europe are desperately needed. Services of all types are called for, but especially those that have been adapted from efficient Western operations to accommodate needs in local markets, as well as new ideas for deposit gathering and credit granting. There will also be rewards for those who can overcome numerous barriers and obstacles to the efficient sale of companies and find ways to trade financial assets within their systems. For many bankers, the Eastern front will be the new frontier of the 1990s and the years beyond.

5
UNIVERSAL STRATEGIES

As Europe faces up to an era of major regulatory reform, extensive industrial restructuring, and absorption of one of the largest and most mangled economic systems ever, it can take comfort in its universal banking system. That system has become the standard for all of Europe, and perhaps in time, will for the United States and Japan as well.

Universal banks, in broad terms, offer all forms of financial services under one corporate structure. They derive from an early Italian idea of *mixed banking*, in which a bank would not only make loans, but would also purchase securities from its customers for resale (and vote them on the customer's behalf as appropriate).[1] They are designed to be large, stable institutions that one can rely upon in bad times, a lender of last resort. Their stability derives in part from their structure—the ability to transfer funds and capital from one sector of the business (e.g., industrial holdings) to shore up another sector (commercial banking) if necessary—and in part from the dominance of their national corporate banking systems, in which rates and fees can be expected to provide a sufficient income to cover the costs of ensuring capital availability in the future. They also enjoy close ties to their principal clients, and may take up board seats or own shares in their clients' companies.

Universal banks come in all sizes, but the ones that count are the big ones. In all of the countries that follow the orthodox universal banking model—Germany, Switzerland, the Netherlands, Sweden, Austria, Belgium, Luxembourg—a small number of large and powerful banks have emerged that dominate the commercial and industrial scene in their respective countries. Such banks, though owned by the public, have quasi-governmental standing. They are able to effect corporate policies when necessary and are influential advisers on legislation and public economic policies. They are cornerstones of the establishment.

UNIVERSAL DIFFERENCES

Universal banking in Europe has various forms, each quite different from the others. Nevertheless, the German universal bank has become the standard against which non-Europeans appear to judge all universal banks. In Germany, banks are free to engage in securities and insurance businesses under the umbrella of their regulated banking activities. They may also own significant shareholdings of industrial corporations, which in practice provides some of them with directorships and a degree of influence over their customers unusual in most other countries. They are called universal banks because they can do almost anything they want, providing that the banking entity itself meets the nominally strict regulatory standards of the banking supervisory authorities.

In the German form, universal banking has evolved to conform to the fact that the German economy has had to be totally rebuilt twice during this century; the result has been an industrial system made up predominantly of privately owned firms that maintain extremely close ties to their main banks, or hausbanks. Privately owned firms are freer to do as they like than publicly owned ones because they do not have to disclose their results to the public and do not have to consider the interests of public shareholders when making transactions—for example, when transferring assets between different companies within a group.

Over the years, a number of the family groups sold shares to the public and, to cement their relationships, some of the larger banks bought positions in their clients' firms. In other instances, firms faltered and banks exchanged overdue notes for shares. In time, the larger banks accumulated some significant holdings in German industry, and often occupied seats on the supervisory board, or board of nonexecutive directors, of the companies. The supervisory board is chartered in German law to appoint members of the firm's management board, or board of executive directors.

Especially during the early postwar period, a time of rapid growth, industrial companies were constantly in need of capital, and capital markets were weak to nonexistent. By maintaining close ties to their banks, which included full disclosure of their operating results, the companies were able to turn to the banks for money when they needed it. As insiders, the banks were often willing to provide it. The amount of borrowing permitted by the banks might also be higher than in other countries where banks maintained more arm's-length relationships. In this context, the German system resembles the Japanese practice of cross-shareholdings among members of a keiretsu, or post-zaibatsu family groupings of companies.

In all universal banks across Europe a common theme emerges. This is the close, almost paternalistic, virtually exclusive relationship between client and bank. There are certain mutual benefits and obligations in such relationships.

Hausbanks

The hausbank has duties that its clients expect it to perform. It must be willing to extend funds when they are needed, even if the creditworthiness of the company is in doubt. If the company gets into trouble, the bank is expected to assist it in restructuring and debt rescheduling. The client can also expect the bank to support management, both in general and at the supervisory board level, especially when a senior bank executive is a member of the board and the bank is a shareholder. In the case of closely held companies, long-standing personal relationships between proprietors and senior bank officials have forged bonds that in time become institutionalized and are carried on by their successors. When the proprietor needs money, he can borrow against his shares in the company, or sell shares to the bank directly, even though these are not publicly traded; the banker knows the company well enough to value the shares himself.

On the other hand, the client also has duties to the bank. It must manage the business sensibly and well; it must consult with the bank and keep it fully informed of its plans; it must use the money borrowed from the bank for reasonable purposes, which the bank must agree to; it must pay the fees and rates that the bank charges without complaint; and it must remain loyal to the bank, giving it first call on all of its principal business. In practice there is a delicate balance between the hausbank and the client; they are mutually supportive but their relationship is based on maintaining mutual confidence, which, if lost, usually can be re-established only by replacing the individuals involved. Banks have been known to arrange the firing of chief executives of client companies in whom they have lost confidence. On balance, the greater power seems to be with the banks, except for the largest multinational industrial groups.

In Germany, and to a lesser extent in Austria and Sweden, the large universal banks have accumulated substantial shareholdings in their largest clients, i.e., those which over the years have needed new capital the most. Now that other capital market opportunities have appeared, the banks appear to have de-emphasized the practice of share accumulation, and have been reducing their shareholdings. Nonetheless, there is still a high concentration of minority shareholdings in the largest industrial companies in the hands of a small number of large banks.

In the rest of Europe, universal banking has developed differently, with little interest in shareholdings and more in spreading activities throughout the Continent and other parts of the world.

Swiss Myths

To many non-Europeans the mention of Swiss banks conjures up visions of secret accounts, money laundering, and cold-eyed little gnomes guarding Alpine vaults. Much of this is a false image. What makes the Swiss interesting to others is the extent to which the country's role in world finance exceeds its economic importance and position in world trade.

The Swiss universal banks are similar to the German ones, but different in two important respects. First, because large Swiss companies are comparatively few and most are publicly owned, their connections with the large banks are not as close or exclusive; for example, the Swiss bankers do not take substantial shareholdings in their clients. Second, for a very long time a large part of Swiss bank business has come from international funds management and overseas lending, so domestic corporate banking is less important overall to the banks. For generations neutral Switzerland has provided a safe, trustworthy haven for foreign capital. Recognizing the value of foreign deposits, the Swiss enacted a variety of laws that added to the strength and the confidentiality of the banking industry. In time, more money flowed into Switzerland than reasonably could be invested there, so the Swiss became adept at international lending and investing. At the end of 1989, foreign assets represented 29% of total assets for Swiss banks (or more than 50% if fiduciary funds were included) as compared with 16% for German banks, 12.8% for Japanese banks, and less than 10% for American banks.[2]

The Swiss regard their country as "overbanked," with 625 active institutions in 1990 servicing a population of 6.5 million. The four largest banks (the three large universal banks plus Swiss Volksbank), however, account for about 48% of the nearly $800 billion of banking assets. Cantonal banks account for about 20%, and 142 foreign banks for 10% of total assets. There are also regional and savings banks, specialized trade and securities banks, credit cooperatives, finance companies, and private banks.

The large universal banks are in three basic businesses: domestic banking in Switzerland (retail, wholesale, and mortgage banking), which accounts for about 40% of their assets; international banking (wholesale and investment banking outside of Switzerland), which accounts for the rest of their assets; and private banking and funds management of approximately $750 billion (mostly foreign), which does not appear on their balance sheets.

Banking in Switzerland is quite profitable for the universals. Together, the three largest reported net income (after losses, depreciation, and provisions) of about $1.3 billion for 1991. This level of earnings, which is after transfers to "hidden reserves," is low in terms of return on equity relative to other European banks. This, however, is because of stringent capital adequacy rules in Switzerland. Profits were derived in roughly equal parts from interest income, commissions on funds managed, and trading, custodial, and other income. Approximately 64% of total income is from noninterest sources. It is probable that about half the total profits of the big three universal banks come from Swiss business, the other half from private banking and funds management.

The operations of Swiss banks outside the country have not been very profitable, especially in recent years, during which all of the big Swiss banks have suffered mishaps. Credit Suisse had to bail out First Boston, Union Bank of Switzerland (UBS) lost large amounts sorting out U.K. stockbroker Phillips & Drew, and Swiss Bank Corporation was caught up in underwriting losses in Germany and bad loans in the United Kingdom.

Though Swiss universal banks are permitted to own nonbanking assets, UBS and Swiss Bank Corporation have stuck closely to banking-related activities. Credit Suisse, however, has drifted into some other businesses and formed a holding company to separate its banking and nonbanking activities.

Now calling itself CS Holdings, a "worldwide financial services group based in Switzerland," Credit Suisse separately incorporated its investments in a bank (Credit Suisse); an investment bank (CS First Boston); a private bank (Leu Holdings Ltd.); a 45% investment in a major Swiss electric power company (Electrowatt Ltd.); and life insurance investments (CS Life). The idea was to exclude the electric power company and other nonbanking investments from the capital adequacy requirements of Swiss banking laws. But the Swiss Banking Commission rejected the idea; its decision was supported by the Swiss Federal Court, which ruled that under the law governing universal banks, all of the holding company properties had to be considered part of the bank, sustaining the German concept of complete integration. This meant that all the assets had to be covered by the bank capital requirements, so no real benefits from setting up the holding company were realized. CS Holdings (after absorbing substantial losses in rescuing First Boston in 1990) found itself having to raise additional capital from the market.

The big Swiss banks have been quite advanced in seeing themselves on one hand as domestic, universal institutions protected by their own laws and banking practices, and on the other as European-based international wholesale bankers and money managers. They are highly international in their outlook and activities, and are intimately involved in the globalization of all financial markets—a process that will require them to improve their international trading and investment banking skills. They are looking for ways to combine their abilities in trading and foreign exchange with their strong balance sheets to secure a prominent role in the international wholesale market of the future. CS Holdings has acquired a controlling interest in First Boston Corporation and in Credit Suisse First Boston. Swiss Bank Corporation has acquired a prominent U.S. derivative securities firm, O'Connor Associates and, like Union Bank of Switzerland, has been active in the Eurobond and international equities markets for a decade or more.

All three banks have securities subsidiaries in the United States that are grandfathered under the Glass-Steagall Act, and seats on the New York, London, and Tokyo stock exchanges.

The Swiss international banking community also includes its Geneva-and Lugano-based private banks, which are specialists in wealth management for overseas clients. Swiss bank secrecy laws have traditionally been helpful in building up the huge accumulation of foreign assets that are managed in Switzerland. The total of such assets is estimated at approximately $1.5 trillion (of which half are managed by the three large banks). These funds provide the Swiss with enormous placing power that enables them to compete in the global new issues markets. The Swiss worry that an inevitable erosion of bank secrecy laws in Switzerland, as the country conforms its laws and regulations to those of its EC neighbors, will cause some of these funds to leave the country. But the amounts under management are large, the service is good and reliable, and the debt ratings of the banks are among the best in the world. The secrecy veil is still pretty effective and money in Switzerland is still thought to be safe from seizure or corruption, so most of the Swiss clients will probably stay where they are. No other tax haven offers a similar list of qualifications. Indeed, during the first month of the war in the Persian Gulf, approximately $10 billion in new accounts were opened in Switzerland. Several billion dollars of new deposits reportedly came into Switzerland with the unification of Germany, and additional funds made their way over the Alps when the Soviet Union fell apart.

Private banking in Switzerland is currently centered on twenty-two smaller, older, and usually privately owned institutions that have maintained a specialized business of managing investments for overseas clients for many years. Quiet, discreet, and efficient, these banks are now attempting to attract institutional clients by offering Swiss global investment management skills to predominantly domestic-oriented pension funds and other clients in the United States, Japan, and other parts of Europe.

Switzerland also prides itself on a growing capital market, which is used by Swiss and non-Swiss alike. Bond issues denominated in Swiss francs are periodically sold by Japanese, U.S., and European companies, and in recent years the big three banks have allowed significant deregulation of underwriting practices to make more room for non-Swiss firms. Stock exchange commissions also became negotiable in early 1990. The all-electronic Swiss Options and Financial Futures Exchange has been very successful, and before long the Swiss hope to create a similarly efficient national stock market from the several regional exchanges that exist at present.

But Swiss universal banking is not without its problems. High interest rates (accompanying un-Swiss inflation rates of about 6%) in 1990 and 1991 have pushed local mortgage and other lending rates to their regulatory ceilings. Some banks are feeling the pressure of interest rate returns falling below funding costs, and a deterioration in the market value of their portfolios (not unlike the U.S. S&L problem). There is some concern too that closer alignment with the EC will result in greater levels of foreign competition in Switzerland, though the borders have been open to foreigners for many years. Bank consolidations have been occurring for the past several years and now appear to be accelerating. More than seventy bank acquisitions have occurred since 1975, about a third of which involved smaller banks being absorbed by larger Swiss universal, cantonal, or regional banks.[3] The banking industry has been somewhat destabilized by these developments and the prospect of a more competitive environment both at home and abroad. Because of these factors, Moody's Investor Services downgraded Credit Suisse's cherished AAA rating to AA-1 in January 1992 and Swiss Bank Corporation's a few months later, creating a shock that rattled the whole country. Credit Suisse, the smallest of the big three, was the most heavily exposed to the much riskier securities industry, but all the banks were facing unfavorable economic changes in their business. However, no one seriously believed that the Swiss government and banking authorities would allow these changes to so erode the Swiss banks' reputation for safety, stability, and quality as to deprive them of their ability to attract foreign money.

Latin Variations

In France, the large state-owned banks are universal banks too, but with a few important differences. They compete vigorously with each other, and as most of the large industrial companies either are still predominantly state-owned (or were until recently), the clients resist exclusive relationships with any single bank. There are also some large *banques d'affaires* that, through elaborate holding company structures, own substantial industrial investments, often involving de facto controlling positions with which they engage in a lot of wheeling and dealing. Paribas and Indosuez are the largest of these groups in France, and Société Générale de Belgique and Group Brussels-Lambert are the largest in Belgium.

The Italians have an extremely complex, state-controlled, fractionalized banking system that, according to a 1991 Salomon Brothers' report, is undercapitalized and overbanked, but underbranched. There are more than 1,000 commercial banks in Italy. They are divided confusingly into six categories: 1) six large, "public law" banks, which are organized as foundations, or public corporations to act in the public interest; these banks, which include the Istituto Bancario San Paolo di Torino, and Banca Nazionale del Lavoro, in aggregate account for about 25% of Italian banking assets. The government recently permitted them to convert to joint-stock companies and to sell a minority of their shares to the public; 2) three "banks of national interest" controlled by the state-owned holding company IRI; these banks, which account for about 15% of total banking assets, include Banca Commerciale Italiana, Credito Italiano, and Banco di Roma; 3) a large number (110) of "private banks," which include Deutsche Bank's Banca d'America e d'Italia, and several active publicly traded banks; 4) 75 savings banks (Casse di Resparmio); 5) 113 cooperative banks; and 6) 728 rural and artisan banks. The principal merchant bank in Italy, with a finger in every pie, is Mediobanca, which used to be controlled by the banks of national interest.[4]

In keeping with the times and sentiments throughout the rest of Europe, Italian banking is undergoing rationalization from two directions at once: through mergers (several of which have been completed in the last three years) and through privatization of the state-owned banks, a process that has been slow to get under way but has finally begun. The changes are creating opportunities for foreign banks interested in retail banking, and increased activity in the securities markets has captured the attention of a number of foreign investment banks.

All but one Italian bank, the Istituto Bancario San Paolo di Torino, are concentrating on their domestic prospects and ignoring activities outside Italy. San Paolo, Italy's most profitable and best managed bank, is going against the tide, trying to build a network of alliances and associations across Europe (and one with Salomon Brothers) so it can have at least a small stake in post-1992 European banking developments. In April 1992, San Paolo increased its capital by offering $1.2 billion of new shares to the public, thus becoming Italy's largest, as well as its most efficient, bank. Though permitted to sell up to 49% of their shares to the public under a 1990 banking reform, the other large Italian banks have yet not stepped up to do so.

Britain after the Blitz

The several financial services reforms in Britain in 1986, which were known as Big Bang in the City of London, permitted commercial and investment banking to be combined for the first time. Prior to Big Bang, investment banking did not really exist in Britain—instead there were *brokers* and *jobbers* (i.e., market-makers in securities) who were members of the stock exchange, and *merchant banks*, which acted as underwriters of securities, but were not members of the exchange. The British system that was replaced by Big Bang went back to the early nineteenth century, in which the different players were kept separate from each other as a way of ensuring markets that were both fair and not too competitive. The new system emulated American investment banking (in which brokers and jobbers could be combined, and could underwrite securities), but to ensure fair and safe markets, investment banks would have to be separately incorporated, separately capitalized, and separately regulated.

Most of the large clearing banks and merchant banks set up substantial securities affiliates, but all of these suffered from the competitive conditions that followed Big Bang and the weak trading markets that followed the 1987 stock market crash. As a result a number of bank-supported players have left the equity and debt markets altogether. (These events are described in more detail in Chapter 6).

In the United Kingdom, as in the United States and Japan, a sacred principle of bank regulation is the separation of banking from commerce and industry, so British universals cannot stray outside the financial services field. Otherwise they now possess all of the powers that universal banks have in Germany and the other European countries. Barclays and National Westminster Bank have made substantial efforts to establish themselves in the securities business in the United Kingdom, though other large clearing banks have not. These two banks, as well as Lloyds Bank, are also actively involved in insurance. Large merchant banks such as S.G. Warburg and Kleinwort Benson have attempted to create full-service investment banks in the American style, concentrating their activities on trading, corporate finance, and money management. Somewhat out of step with the rest of the City, Midland Bank has instead tried to escape its financial doldrums (it has been the worst-performing U.K. clearing bank for some time) by merging with HSBC Holdings, the parent of Hongkong Shanghai Banking Corporation, in an exchange of shares valued at about $5 billion. Combined, the new bank will be Britain's largest in terms of assets, but only 52% of these will be European; the rest will be divided between Asia (30%) and America (16%).

Throughout Europe universal banking has emerged as the common pattern for all countries. And among European universal banks, one bank stands out.

DEUTSCHE BANK ÜBER ALLES

German banking is not quite what it seems. Many non-Germans believe that the whole system is dominated by three or four giant, highly profitable banks. Most German bankers, on the other hand, believe the country is horribly overbanked and business is tough and competitive. There is truth in both viewpoints. At the end of 1989, there were 4,271 banks in (West) Germany, and nearly 40,000 branches, one of the highest branch concentrations per capita in Europe. These banks fell into two categories: 4,203 universal banks and 68 *spezialinstitute*, or banks with charters that limited them to special functions such as mortgage lending, postal savings, and offering government-sponsored credit. The universals include 322 commercial banks, and 3,821 savings institutions and credit cooperatives of various types (which have their own central banks). The savings institutions in the aggregate account for more than 80% of all the branches, but only a third of the assets in the system. The commercial banks include 169 regional banks, 86 private banks, 60 foreign banks, and 6 *grossbanken*, or large national banks.[5]

The grossbanken among them had over 3,000 branches and accounted for about 35% of the assets in the banking system before reunification. This may seem a high level of concentration to American observers (though the top six U.S. banks, after the recent mergers, now account for about 25% of total U.S. banking assets), but it is not as compared with other European countries. The top five banks in the United Kingdom, for example, represent 73% of total assets, the top five in France, 63%, and in Spain, 51%.[6]

The grossbanken, however, are extremely influential in Germany because of their client relationships, shareholdings in the clients, and representation on their supervisory boards.[7] Based on a report in 1979 by the German Monopolkommission, the three largest universal banks (and a few large insurance companies) held "significant shareholdings" (i.e., aggregating 25% or more of the outstanding shares) in 13 of the 100 largest German industrial companies. By comparison, 19 of the largest 100 companies were more than 25% owned by individuals and families, and 15 by other industrial companies among the largest 100. Only 19 of the top 100 companies were more than 50% owned by the public, and 8 were government controlled.

Many non-Germans appear to believe that the German banks own German industry. This view overstates the situation, but is partly correct. Alfred Herrhausen, the late chairman of the Deutsche Bank, commented in 1987 that the ten largest German universal banks owned stakes of 10% or more in (only) 86 companies in 1986, down from 129 in 1976. Of these they held stakes of 25% or more in (only) 31 companies in 1986, down from 60 in 1976.[8]

Though perhaps less extensive than generally thought, these ownership positions in industrial corporations have been very controversial in Germany, where antitrust considerations have been raised along with the issue of the need to separate banking from industry to ensure the safety and soundness of the banks. In the case of the former, the German Monopolkommission, after an extensive investigation, proposed in 1980 that bank ownership of corporations be limited to 5% to 10% of outstanding shares; a later proposal recommended raising this limit to 25%, but neither was put into law. The banks have argued successfully that though a potential for monopolistic behavior may exist, there is no evidence that the banks have taken advantage of the potential. Indeed, they claim that their ownership positions are for investment purposes only, and are sufficiently diverse so that they could not restrain trade in one sector without hurting other bank investments in the sector. Seeing the handwriting on the wall, however, the banks have voluntarily reduced most of their holdings to below 25%. The issue has become moot for the time being, but it is likely to be raised again at the EEC level as harmonization of financial policies continues.

With respect to the issue of bank safety, German banking regulators do not seem to be concerned that a large industrial bankruptcy could bring down such powerful and well-diversified banks as the grossbanken, which carry the investments on their books at cost—a very low figure in most cases relative to market values. Indeed regulators seem to believe that the industrial shareholdings of banks help stabilize the economy by reducing the risk of bankruptcy, both through their ability to assist in restructuring and because they can exert a conservative, restraining influence on those who may need it.

German banks in general are commonly represented on corporate supervisory boards, in part because they are businesslike, well informed, and aware of details of company operations that other nonexecutive board members, such as labor unionists and government officials, are not. In a 1974 study, the Monopolkommission reported that about 1,300 firms included bankers on their supervisory boards, of which about half were publicly owned companies. Of these, 320 companies had selected directors from among the grossbanken, with most of the rest coming from large regional banks and private banking firms. Herrhausen offered a picture of the composition of the supervisory boards of the top 100 German industrial companies in 1986: of 1,466 total board members, 717 were labor representatives, 368 were industrialists from other companies, 69 were politicians or government employees, and 165 were bankers, who often served as president of the board.[9] Many senior bankers, particularly at the top three banks, were sitting on quite a few boards—this has become a major activity of top German bankers. These directors are all paid about the same by their banks—a relatively modest salary—but they are allowed to retain their director's fees and to own shares in the companies on whose boards they sit. Insider trading has never been illegal in Germany, and no doubt many bank directors have profited on what they have learned sitting around the boardroom table over the years.

It is worth remembering that bankers in the United States were extensively represented on the boards of their clients until only recently. Up to about 1920, most of American industry was closely held by individuals and families (as in Germany today), and bankers sat on the boards of companies they loaned money to in order to watch the store. Partners of J.P. Morgan & Co. sat on the boards of 20 of the 100 largest companies in the United States in 1919; and a recent study has associated their presence in the boardroom with an approximately 30% rise in the common stock equity value of companies concerned.[10]

After 1920, when many more companies came to be publicly owned, American bankers were often asked to join the boards to represent the public shareholders and to add respectability to companies that were not well known at the time. The chief executive of a large commercial bank would quite naturally expect to serve on half a dozen or more boards as a demonstration of prestige and position. Even as late as 1975, partners of Goldman Sachs were represented on the boards of about 80 public companies. At that time, 55% of the largest 1,000 U.S. industrial corporations had a commercial banker and 37% had an investment banker on their board of directors. Today, only 29% of the boards of the largest 1,000 companies include a commercial banker, and only 23% an investment banker. Board representation by bankers in the United States has declined with increased competition in financial services (companies do not want to be tied to a single banker by virtue of board representation) and the rise of lawsuits aimed at board members.[11]

The remarkable achievements of German industry have caused many observers to praise the banking system that spawned them. The banking system is strong, protective, generous, and stable, they say. It is not weak, speculative, short-sighted, and greedy, as many banks in the United States appear to be to Europeans. A few major banks have the power to control Germany's most important management appointments, investment selection, and strategic decisions, and they exercise their power benignly and well. Large companies become dependent on the banks for money, yes, but also for influence. The system has worked, and German industry has flourished.

A study published in 1991 by Jeremy Edwards of Cambridge University and Klaus Fischer of the University of Bonn, however, questions whether the German banks deserve all the credit they get. Their study of German lending and bankruptcy practices reveals that banks are not nearly as willing to lend, or as quick to rescue faltering clients as most people think. The whole system is much more loosely constructed than is commonly supposed, though it is also clear that association between the major banks and their clients is closer than in most other countries.[12]

It was also true that in Germany capital market development that might lure the companies into impure habits was discouraged. The banking system was not market-oriented at all. German universal banks had great relationships with their German clients, but they did not produce skills and services that could be exported.

"Financial market efficiency in Germany has been among the lowest in Europe," claims Alfred Steinherr, a leading academic observer of universal banks, "which is why Germany has been the largest net importer of financial services in the world." Steinherr questions whether there is an inverse correlation between market efficiency and industrial productivity. Maybe, he suggests, such a correlation exists if the system is largely closed to competition from outside, as the banking-industry relationship in Germany has been, but once the system is opened up the relationship should change. Once the major companies are exposed to capital market development and the deregulation of intra-European banking activities, they are going to want some of the benefits for themselves. And where would that leave the grossbanken?[13]

The Grossest Banken

The largest of the grossbanken is Deutsche Bank A.G., the flagship of the Deutsche Bank Group, which reported $297 billion of assets at the end of 1991, the seventh-ranking bank in the world, employing 71,000 worldwide. The bank was founded in Berlin in the 1860s by a group of wealthy businessmen wanting to challenge London as the principal European financial center (a goal it has not yet achieved). It turned its attention first to developing domestic business and became the largest bank in Germany by far in the years before World War I. It was also the largest bank immediately after World War II, and still is though it was broken up by the allied powers after the war.

In 1957, the Allies allowed the bank to be reformed under the leadership of the legendary Herman J. Abs, a close adviser of Chancellor Konrad Adenauer. The Deutsche Bank soon became one of the main engines of the postwar economic recovery called the "German Miracle."[14] Since then, its ties with industry and government have always been close, and the "spokesman" of the management board, or chief executive, has long been regarded as a virtual shadow minister of finance.

In 1991, Deutsche Bank had a risk-adjusted BIS tier 1 equity capital ratio of 5.6% and total capital of 10.7%, well above required levels. It reported pre-tax operating profits from interest, commissions, and insurance of $3.2 billion and trading income of $372 million. Other income, largely from dividends, amounted to $781 million. Net income in 1991, after write-downs and provisions of $812 million (compared to $1.25 billion for 1990), was $940 million, a return of only 0.32% on assets and 8.3% on book value. Solid, maybe, but not particularly profitable. Not much of a growth stock either, as analysts' forecasts of earnings per share through 1992 showed a five-year compounded growth rate of zero, though 1991 net earnings were 16.5% greater than 1990's. Still, in September 1991, the bank's stock traded at 27 times earnings, and 1.7 times its equity book value of $9.5 billion.

There were at least two reasons for Deutsche Bank's high market valuation. The bank owns substantial industrial holdings in the form of minority interests in German corporations, many acquired at very low cost during the two postwar rebuildings of German industry. In September 1991, the market value of these holdings (after estimated capital gains taxes) was estimated by Goldman Sachs to be $8.3 billion. If you subtract this value from the market capitalization of Deutsche Bank's common stock ($17.5 billion in September 1991), the remainder is the value attributed by the market to the banking business. After this adjustment, it appears that the market was really valuing the banking business at 13.1 times earnings and no more than its book value. These are much more reasonable levels.

The second reason for the stock valuation is the market leadership position of the bank—its raw power, or charisma—which is considerable. It is not only the largest German bank by far (Dresdner Bank was second with 1990 assets of $173 billion and market value in September 1991 of $7.8 billion), but also the one with the most industrial holdings and board seats. Deutsche is also the bank with the clearest sense of mission—it wants to remain the most powerful bank in Germany (after the consolidation of East Germany), a very powerful bank in all the rest of Europe (west and east), and a powerful bank in the emerging global wholesale banking and securities market. Its mission has been backed up by sensible strategic moves.

It was quick to realize that insurance was an interesting business and to decide to build its own insurance products and distribution force, aimed mainly at the German market. This integration of banking and insurance under one roof caused other banking groups to follow Deutsche Bank's lead. They also followed Deutsche into international capital markets in the 1970s, and into London-based Euromarket headquarters in the 1980s. Deutsche's Euromarket presence has always been substantial, though conservative. Also, Deutsche upgraded its grandfathered U.S. investment-banking subsidiary, Deutsche Capital Corporation, to become a primary market dealer in U.S. Treasury securities and the leading securities market competitor in the United States among international banks.

Anticipating changes and opportunities in the European banking industry following the 1992 initiatives, Alfred Herrhausen, Deutsche Bank's chairman at the time, believed the bank had to be more active in expanding throughout Europe. In 1986, benefiting from Bank of America's troubles, it purchased the Banca d'America e d'Italia for $630 million; since then it has made other, smaller European banking investments in Spain, Portugal, and Austria. In 1989, Deutsche acquired Morgan Grenfell & Co. for $1.5 billion in order to buy into the Anglo-Saxon world of mergers and acquisitions which was beginning to penetrate Europe. Herrhausen, a frequent and highly visible spokesman on German economic affairs, was murdered by terrorists soon after the Morgan Grenfell deal was announced. Herrhausen's successor, Hilmar Kopper, is less known for strategic vision than for his practical approach to solving problems. So far he has had plenty of opportunity to practice his specialty.

Deutsche Bank was quick to purchase about half of the branches and outlets of the former East German Deutsche Kreditbank in 1990 and to beef these up with more than 1,000 experienced Deutsche Bank personnel. Though the bank remains extremely cautious about the creditworthiness of the region (the bank's eastern German loans totaled only about $1 billion in 1991), it has reached out for retail deposits, opened new branches, installed new technology, and started to make money. Bravely commenting on the progress toward unifying the banking system, Kopper said in July 1991, "We will soon see the light at the end of the East German tunnel, which will allow the country to develop into an engine of economic growth in Europe."[15] Deutsche also seeks to assist its industrial clients in selecting and financing new investments in the eastern *länder* and throughout Eastern Europe.

Further, Deutsche Bank is deeply immersed in the general problem of refloating the former Soviet Union, preferably after first being paid on loans already outstanding. This will be a long and thankless job, one that starts with the Russians rapidly falling into arrears on debt payments while the prospects for repayment deteriorate further. Though Boris Yeltsin has declared that the newly reconstituted Russian Republic, together with some of the other republics, would take on the obligations of the former Soviet Union, it is not at all clear that they will have the means to do so for quite some time. Kopper urged the Group of Seven industrial nations to grant $5 billion in credits to the Soviet Union, through the BIS, to prevent a default by Moscow on more than $50 billion of private sector borrowings. But, he added, "We have to have someone in the Soviet Union who can arrange this and with whom we can negotiate."[16] The Group of Seven did not come forward, and the Soviet Union did not last. By the end of 1991, all debt payments had ceased and discussion turned to various forms of foreign aid.

Deutsche Bank's role in the financial recovery of the former Soviet Union and the rest of Eastern Europe is an important and difficult one. As the largest bank in Europe's wealthiest nation, one with extremely close ties to German industries eager to participate in the rebuilding of the economies in the East, Deutsche is highly visible and controversial. As the senior executive of the bank, Kopper cannot avoid a great deal of public attention and exposure, which can be extremely dangerous in Germany. He must maneuver carefully among several objectives, many of which have conflicting components. One objective is to play the dominant role in Eastern European (and East German) economic restructuring without building up large bank exposures to these extremely risky credits. This is especially difficult when you become, however reluctantly, a sort of agent for German economic policy (under pressure to pump bank money into the region), and the "best friend" of the Russians, the Ukrainians, the Poles, the Czechs, and the other hard-pressed clients. To handle these roles without risking too much of the bank's own money will certainly be a great challenge.

At a more mundane, but equally important, level is the question of how to avoid letting the problems of the eastern front distract attention from opportunities in the West. Deutsche must protect its thin profitability and fat market shares from increasing competition for corporate and wholesale banking in Germany, where Deutschemark-denominated commercial paper has recently been introduced, aggressive foreign investment bankers have been allowed to operate, and capital market use is increasing, especially in the area of stock issues and initial public offerings. How to project the bank's solid but sober presence into the other European markets for wholesale banking and capital market services is another challenge.

To respond to these competitive pressures, Deutsche Bank inevitably must modify the bank's traditional Prussian character and adopt some of the more responsive and flexible practices of American and other international banks, which enable them to attract new business and maintain relationships. Such changes are easier described than made. However, most observers of the German banking scene believe that they will be made, sooner or later. There will also be great changes in other long-standing ways of doing business, including adapting a more publicly aware profile with respect to insider trading (not yet illegal in Germany, but very controversial there and much deplored by Kopper), and behind-closed-door practices in general. For all its strengths, the German financial marketplace—largely a market for old-fashioned commercial banking services dominated by well-placed insiders—is thought of as dull, uninnovative, rigid, and expensive by non-German clients. Will otherwise loyal German clients begin to see it that way too after a few more years of heavy competition? None of these adaptations will be easy, or managed quickly.

Other German Strategies

All eyes in European banking follow Deutsche Bank closely. It sets the trends and requires the others (principally the four other large banks that are publicly traded: Dresdner, Commerzbank, Bayerische Vereinsbank, and Bayerische Hypo-Bank; and the Westdeutsche Landesbank, which is not) to follow suit. Dresdner Bank has revealed that Allianz, the German insurance giant, now has a 22% stake in the bank. Dresdner also followed Deutsche into East Germany and bought up the other half of Deutsche Kreditbank. It has also announced a 10% stock swap with Banque Nationale de Paris (BNP), France's largest commercial bank, as a way of spreading its activities across Europe.

Commerzbank, Westdeutsche Landesbank, and the other German banks have been more cautious in the East, and less effective in the West. Commerzbank has recently chosen to exit alliances rather than enter into them. It has disbanded Europartners, a long-standing, but not especially successful joint venture with Crédit Lyonnais, Banco di Roma, and Banco Hispano Americano. It also walked out on a proposed 10% cross-shareholding with Crédit Lyonnais, supposedly because agreement could not be reached on the terms of the exchange.

Most German regional and savings banks will not be distressed by the disintermediation, securitization, or other goings-on in the wholesale markets. They will continue to stick to what they know and have always done, offering basic banking services to the retail public and to smaller German companies. No doubt they will find, however, as different marketing approaches succeed, and new banking products are introduced—especially increased use of electronic transfers and credit cards (in which Germany lags behind the rest of Europe)—that their firm grip on their loyal customers may begin to weaken.

Citibank has had exceptional success with a retail finance company, Kundenskredit Bank (called KKB Bank) which it acquired several years ago. KKB offers a variety of high-grade, low-cost financial products to blue-collar workers through different marketing methods. It has been very profitable and captured a significant market share. (Citicorp is about to repackage KKB under a Citibank brand name, possibly undoing what it has built so far.) Under the 1992 banking rules, any banker with a new idea is free to try it out in Germany or elsewhere within the EC. Most German banks have yet to adapt to this new reality.

There is also a relatively small number of private banks in Germany that manage funds for wealthy clients and handle securities transactions, a few discrete mergers, and other financial deals. These banks, like their Swiss counterparts, are well connected, very low profile, and knowledgeable. But they are not especially international in their operations. The largest is Sal. Oppenheim, which retiring Bundesbank president Karl-Otto Poehl joined in 1991. Others include Trinkhaus & Burkhardt, 70% owned by Midland Bank of the United Kingdom; Merck Finck, 100% owned by Barclays Bank; and Schroeder, Münchmeyer Hengst, which is controlled by Lloyds Bank. Clearly the British banks have found an answer to their strategic problems in Germany in the private banks.

There are about sixty foreign banks with branches or subsidiaries in Germany. Most lose money, but claim to be on the scene for the long term. Morgan Guaranty Trust, the leading foreign branch banker, makes a respectable profit but has to work very hard to do so. U.S. automobile companies, oddly enough, do very well in Germany through their consumer finance subsidiaries. The other foreigners appear to concentrate on marketing to home-country companies, servicemen, and tourists.

The banking business is especially tough for foreigners in Germany for two reasons: the clients, both retail and industrial, really are loyal to their traditional banks, and the deposit-taking and lending services the foreigners offer usually lack substantial value-added as compared to German banking services. Recently, however, the major wholesale and investment banks have had more success. Efforts to open the Frankfurt capital market and turn it into a world financial center have created opportunities for presenting innovative and high value-added products to large (and some medium-sized) companies and wealthy individuals. Some investment bankers believe the camel's nose has got under the tent, but it will take time to tell.

ENTANGLING ALLIANCES

Of all financial institutions, large universal banks have the most difficult task in sorting out their strategic plans for the post-1992 competitive environment in Europe. On one hand, great opportunities to expand one's franchise into neighboring territories now exist; on the other hand, the same opportunity exists for competitors of various sorts to invade one's own territory. A sort of financial-industry civil war lies ahead, in which one must launch effective and timely offenses into promising strategic territories, while at the same time defending the high ground at home from both countrymen and foreigners. The most powerful weapons in these skirmishes will be new products and services, new marketing and distribution methods, and the cultivation of new, nontraditional clients. Like all other battlefields, this one will be bloody, dirty, and confusing. Many initiatives will be required, most of which will be expensive and risky. Everything will seemingly be happening at once, with the final outcomes highly uncertain.

"These are extremely dangerous times for us," one continental banker told me recently. "We have lived our entire lives doing routine work for good pay. We had no fear of invasion nor any desire to invade others. The banker's life was, as always, dull but happy.

"Now we face great changes with no preparation. One false step, or even a true step taken at the wrong time, could be the end for us. We are faced with having to make decisions we would prefer not to make at all, and we are ill equipped to make them. However, we cannot do nothing; we must do something—but what?"

Strategic Stakes

Many European banks felt like this. Indeed, they felt worse because they also had to deal with meeting capital adequacy standards, a recession that was pushing up bad loans all over the place, and the question of what, if anything, to do about business opportunities in the United States and Japan, two clearly important markets that had been too little regarded in the past.

There were several alternatives: one could merge with another bank in a grandiose, American-style stock-for-stock transaction that would create a new (local) banking colossus out of two or more existing banks. The Dutch have especially liked this approach, as evidenced by the merger of the two largest banks in the country (Amro and Algemene Bank), which triggered the merger between the next two largest (NMB and PostBank, which in turn has been merged with insurance giant Nationale Nederlanden, and is now reported to be about to acquire neighboring Banque Brussel Lambert). Or, one could acquire a somewhat smaller bank for its access to new territory, clients, or products. Deutsche Bank did this in Italy, and National Westminster Bank in Spain.

Perhaps just a controlling interest would be better and would involve less money. Credit Suisse controls just over half of Bank Leu, but that appears to be enough. Or a joint venture with another party to pursue specific opportunities together, to combine forces, and to save money. Europartners, the four-bank venture, was an example of this type of combination, but it was unwound by Commerzbank after a long run that was not deemed successful. "After all," the saying goes, "would you put your best man and your last dollar into a joint venture with two or three other guys who wouldn't either?" If not, how competitive could you expect the venture to be?

Maybe, instead, one should conserve one's resources for defending the home turf, and buy a small minority interest in a bank somewhere else so as to participate in international strategic developments, but only on a portfolio basis. An example would be the plans of BNP and Dresdner Bank to swap 10% of each other's stock. Or, one could just license out certain products and services to other banks and pick up a little royalty income. There are many kinds of linkages between firms, any of which could be called "strategic" in the sense that they have been forged as a result of adaptation to the new European banking environment.

Long a proponent of cross-shareholdings with "partners" in other markets, Crédit Lyonnais early in 1991 agreed to a 10% stock swap with Commerzbank and a loose-knit plan to share the costs of foreign expansion. However, it was not long before Commerzbank began to doubt the wisdom of the idea. It found Crédit Lyonnais somewhat arrogant and hard to keep up with. Its chairman, Jean-Yves Haberer, for example, refused to agree not to expand further on German territory. "We do not want to be the German arm of a French bank," a senior Commerzbank officer is reported to have said, no doubt revealing the true thoughts of his colleagues. The deal collapsed at midyear.

An interesting study by Carlos García-Pont and Donald Lessard at MIT reviewed 722 strategic linkages between pairs of European banks from 1980 through 1991, of which about 60% involved control positions through outright mergers, acquisitions, or majority equity purchases. Most of the linking transactions were small, but about half involved the 200 largest European banks, from which 90 paired relations involving 108 banks among the top 200 were found.

Of the 722 linkages studied, 85% involved banks from Italy, France, Germany, and Spain (in that order in terms of size). Linkages involving Italian banks were entirely in-country 45% of the time, whereas only 29% of those involving French banks were in-country. A substantial majority of the large bank linkages involved cross-border alliances.[17] Typical of such linkages was one involving minority equity cross-holdings between Banco de Santander (Spain) and the Royal Bank of Scotland, in which the objective of the alliance was identified as being "to allow the development of both groups throughout Europe to proceed more rapidly than either one could achieve on its own." The two would try "to develop new customers in Europe," they said, "and to improve cross-border marketing" by working closely together. Each bank could also tell its stockholders it had completed a strategic alliance that would take care of the need to do something about Europe, and then return to getting on with its regular business.

Many of these alliances, if experience is any guide, are doomed to fail. Although the high intensity of alliance making indicates special circumstances in Europe during the past several years, there is a long history of banking alliances going wrong. The most likely to succeed are the transactions that involve the transfer of control to a larger, more international entity. The "buyer" can simply cut and slash to bring the new prize into line, which is often necessary to recover the considerable premium over market value paid to acquire the "seller."

"Mergers of equals," as discussed in Chapter 2, are a misnomer—resolute leadership (not equality) has to be established early in a merger transaction and consolidation efforts have to proceed quickly and ruthlessly. There has yet to be a cross-border merger of equals (perhaps Midland and Hongkong Shanghai will be the first)—so far all of them have involved banks in the same country or region, usually for defensive purposes. Such proximity creates the opportunity to reduce redundant overhead, a step that is often very much needed, though few have been able to carry it through aggressively. Once done, however, the two banks soon become inseparable.

Joint ventures have the worst record, especially during the 1970s when dozens of consortium banks were formed, usually to compete in the Eurocurrency market. Soon these banks found themselves competing with their own parents, squabbling with partners, and struggling for resources and to retain key personnel. Today, none of the consortium banks remains in business as such—all have been disbanded or acquired by one of the partners. Even highly focused joint undertakings, such as Paribas and S.G. Warburg cooperating to acquire and manage the U.S. investment banking firm A.G. Becker in the 1970s, were not successful. The two venturing firms, no matter who they are, have different objectives, standards, and styles, and these usually change over time, throwing the partners out of step with one another. Often these ventures are the creatures of senior individuals of the two banks who forge the alliance to satisfy a need to accomplish a strategic objective or because of close personal ties. The venture thus is sustained mainly by the personal interests of its sponsors, who usually retire a few years later.

Finally, minority cross-shareholdings appear to do very little for anyone. Dividend income to be received is generally offset by dividends paid. Neither party has any real influence on the other, especially after a few years have passed. If the Royal Bank of Scotland is disappointed by Banco de Santander's lack of efficiency in producing new Spanish and other European clients for it, or in putting to work some of its special products designed for the U.K. market, there is nothing it can do except unwind the deal and look for some other way to Europeanize itself. While the linkage exists, relations with other European banks will be certainly no better than arm's-length. The Royal Bank of Scotland has given up its ability to cruise about opportunistically, though presumably, this was not something it wished to do at the time. The best that can be said of linkages like this one is that, unless they are highly focused with limited and obtainable objectives, they serve only as a learning experience. Perhaps, too, they give cautious banks an alternative to becoming involved in riskier and more expensive projects.

The Allure of Allfinanz

The large universal banks have an embarrassment of freedoms—that is, freedom to enter just about any business they like, certainly any financial business. In addition to the strategic decision making that must be undertaken, these banks also have to decide which functional product areas to emphasize. Most of the universals are well endowed with retail banking capability in their home countries, and with some experience and skill in dealing in foreign loans and securities and foreign exchange. Most, however, have limited experience in insurance, a $320 billion per year retail-based industry on the brink of changes equally as dramatic as those affecting the banking and securities industries.

A marriage of banking and insurance business within the context of a wide-open, newly deregulated single market in Europe has attracted much support, especially in Germany and France. The notion has been christened *Allfinanz* in Germany, and *Bancassurance* in France.

Allfinanz generates synergy, some say, by combining insurance companies with surplus capital and banks in need of capital fortification. It also makes efficient use of bank branches to sell a variety of insurance products, it helps reduce insurance company distribution costs by reducing dependence on high-cost traditional sales forces, and it makes more sophisticated banking and investment services available to insurance customers.

Though the banking and insurance industries are separated by regulation in the United States and Japan, the British, French, and Germans have experimented extensively with their combination. In Britain the most successful new financial enterprise to be formed in many years was Hambros Life, a company sponsored by Hambros Bank in 1971 to unbundle life insurance and investment of savings and repackage them into unit trusts. In 1985, Hambros Life was acquired by BAT Industries for more than $1 billion and its name was changed to Allied Dunbar. In 1988, Lloyds Bank acquired 60% of Abbey Life, which was floated on the London Stock Exchange in 1985 by ITT Corporation. Now called Lloyds Abbey Life, this insurance operation contributes about 20% of Lloyds's income, and expectations are for it to increase to about 30% over the next few years. Other large clearing banks have since entered the insurance business in the United Kingdom, just as various insurers have introduced more investment management and real estate-related products.

Deutsche Bank surveyed the life insurance market in Germany (premiums of $85 billion in 1989, Europe's largest) and decided to launch its own business, Lebensversicherungs-AG der Deutschen Bank in 1989. Within two years it sold 93,000 insurance policies valued at $3.3 billion entirely through its own branches and domestic subsidiaries. In July 1992, it also invested in a 30% interest in Gerling, Germany's largest privately owned insurance company. Not to be outdone, Allianz, Germany's largest insurance company, announced in 1991 that it had acquired a 22% interest in Dresdner Bank, through which similar insurance products would be sold. (The German Cartel Office subsequently ordered the stake to be reduced to 19%, a decision both firms have protested.) Allianz also sells insurance through branches of Bayerische Hypotheken und Weschel Bank, Germany's sixth-largest bank. Another German experiment in Allfinanz was less successful—the Bank für Gemeinwirtschaft, suffering from bad loan problems, brought in Aachener und Münchener Beteiligungs to take up a 50% interest in the bank, which then nearly went under, causing A&M countless difficulties.

The biggest Dutch insurer, Nationale-Nederlanden NV (Nat-Ned) raised the stakes by merging in March 1991 with the second-largest Dutch bank, NMB Postbank (itself a recent merger), to gain access to the bank's 5.5 million customers. The move upset its stockholders, who thought banking would degrade Nat-Ned's price-earnings ratio, and its brokers, who thought they would be cut out by direct sales through the bank's branches. Nevertheless, the transaction was completed under a new holding company called Internationale Nederlanden.

Several varieties of banking-insurance combinations have been attempted in France, mainly under arrangements in which insurance products are brokered through banks—a practice sometimes known as *rent-a-branch*. Some of the bigger players, like the government-owned Union des Assurances de Paris, have preferred to take minority stakes in a portfolio of various banking groups (such as Paribas and Indosuez) and in smaller nsurance companies throughout Europe, hoping thereby to be backing more than one horse in the race and to do insurance business in some form with all of them.

It may be too early, however, for the Europeans to congratulate themselves on the brilliance of Allfinanz. So far the greatest benefits have come to those insurance companies that have found bank branches a convenient and cheap way to sell a commodity-like product. To make any significant money from insurance, however, the banks need to contribute more to the process than renting out little insurance corners in their branches. They need to enter the product design and risk-taking processes themselves, which insurance companies naturally do not wish to give up to them.

One careful observer of Allfinanz in Germany, Joachim Süchting of the University of Bochum, has serious doubts as to whether there is any value-added in combining banking and insurance. The two businesses are quite different, he says. Banking has a very short-term outlook, while insurance is very long-term-oriented. Retail banking is perceived as an everyday, walk-in, soft-sell service business. The other is seen as an unwanted cost or a service the customer hopes never to use—a service that is complicated, hard to understand, full of fine print, and pushed aggressively. The sales skills, funds management, and actuarial talents needed to succeed in insurance are inapplicable to banking. And with insurance industry competition heating up, as national rules are amended to form the single market in insurance, profits will be under pressure and surpluses (i.e., net capital positions) less sure. Under these conditions, insurance companies and their regulators will be hard pressed to allow surplus capital to be used to support banking operations.

Peter Grant, a former vice chairman of Lazard Brothers in London, and now chairman of Sun Life Corporation, feels that banks and insurance companies are "far from being natural partners." Inevitably they will "cannibalize" each other's products and markets—"creating business by devouring its source." By this he means that when a bank sells an insurance product instead of an investment product of its own, it ends up selling the lesser valued product for less money, ultimately killing off its own product. He says both should "stick by and large to their own proper lines of business."[18]

Time will tell.

Universal Applications

It is clear that universal banking represents a formidable assemblage of resources, services, and market power. Citicorp and other American banks are envious, and indeed have sought to amend U.S. regulations to permit European-style universal banking to become the American practice. The universals, they say, combine the best of retail banking franchises with flexibility in delivering products and services at the wholesale level. A recent study at New York University by Ingo Walter and Anthony Saunders has concluded that "economies of super-scale" can be expected in an American form of universal bank that would result in lower costs and more efficient markets.

The 1992 banking directive has made it clear that universal banking will be the standard for Europe. In the United States, legislative reform was not possible in 1991, but the Federal Reserve allowed banks to participate in securities markets through Section 20 subsidiaries. Only in Japan is universal banking being held up, but even there it is only a matter of a few years before changes are adopted to conform Japanese banking practice with the world standard.

But are universal banks really competitive? And, if they are not, how long will they be able to represent the world standard?

In countries where universal banks are dominant, capital market development has lagged. The most advanced capital markets, having developed greatly over the past decade, are now the lowest cost providers of wholesale financial services, and access to these markets is no longer precluded by borders or other constraints. The spreading efficiency of capital markets has resulted in the introduction of commercial paper, money market funds, various forms of securitization, and other innovative products to markets that used to exclude them. Before long, capital market integration will be a reality that users of wholesale banking services throughout the world will appreciate. Similar innovations in retail banking are occurring as well, and the common banking passport in Europe after 1992 will help to spread them.

Large universal banks are like battleships—powerful but not very maneuverable. In financial innovation, maneuverability and specialization are needed. Bureaucracy and institutional rigidity are counterproductive. The next several years will provide us with ringside seats in a great competitive struggle, not only between universal banks and specialized investment and retail services banks, but also between players mounted on strategic alliances and others taking completely different approaches.

6
ALTERNATIVE APPROACHES

Though the large continental universal banks are Europe's most prominent financial institutions, they are not the only ones to have emerged as powerful players during the 1980s. Two particular types of banking institutions have shown an ability to develop local market share and to extend their business abroad: the French banques d'affaires and the British merchant banks. However, in each case only one or two have been strong enough to compete effectively outside their own country, where the emphasis so far has been centered on wholesale and investment banking activities.

LES AFFAIRES FRANÇAISES

The French do things their own way. Their banking system appears to outsiders to be complex, confusing, and laced with insiders and politics. Within just a few years, the French have nationalized their banks, then partially denationalized some of them, leaving the rest waiting to know their fate. The largest French bank is an agricultural co-op. Then come three large deposit banks that operate nationally. There are also numerous savings banks and credit unions that funnel into something called the Caisse des Dépôts et Consignations, a government-controlled trust dating back to 1816, which now manages assets of $300 billion in a broad range of investments. There are also two large banques d'affaires with substantial nonbanking investments, then a group of smaller, fairly specialized banks. Except for the smaller, private banks, all of the chief executives are appointed by the government, often from among the best and brightest graduates of the elite Ecole Nationale d'Administration. These appointments are frequently changed without much explanation.

During the periods of heavy government intervention and controls, the principal banks were subject to lending ceilings, which discouraged innovation and competition, and forced a lot of financial services business into the hands of small, nonbank suppliers. Banking regulators often have the idea that unapproved innovation by banks, being inherently an effort to circumvent official policy, is undesirable and to be discouraged. This attitude led the big banks to stand still while the nonbank sector, particularly the finance company part, innovated and expanded.

The securities sector was highly traditional and unimaginative until Mitterrand's nationalizations in the early 1980s. Since then things have been very exciting on the Paris exchange—privatizations returned, then disappeared again, then reappeared in a different form. But most important, after Big Bang the whole marketplace was reformed in a process the French inappropriately call the "Small Bang," which got under way in 1988.

Indeed, the Small Bang had a much bigger effect on the French securities market than the Big Bang did in London. The reforms allowed undercapitalized French firms to take in outside investors (including foreigners) for the first time, required the full negotiation of commission rates in 1990, changed trading procedures to improve market transparency, offered good technical backup, and substantially increased market surveillance and regulatory enforcement. Brokers were also allowed to make markets in securities and to trade for their own accounts. The effect of these changes was to send all but 4 of the original 58 member firms (new members were permitted to join in January 1992) out to find partners, and 13 became majority owned by foreign firms. Non-French firms, mainly from the United States, the United Kingdom, and Japan, now handle about 30% of the volume of trading in French equities on the Bourse. The market is now thought to be modern and efficient for smaller-sized trades, but it still lacks liquidity for large block trades, which tend to be executed on London's SEAQ International screen-traded system. During 1991, as much as 20% of all the trading in France's fifty largest companies was handled on SEAQ, a situation that has plunged the French into a frantic effort to develop a competitive block-trading system for the Bourse.[1] Further reforms in the nonbank sector include the formation of a futures and options exchange, the Matif, which has grown up to become the Europe's largest market for futures and options, rivalling London's International Financial Futures Exchange (LIFFE) and Futures and Options Exchange (FOX). The large insurance companies and banks have also experimented extensively with bancassurance. Deregulation of the securities markets in France, however, has been rough on the brokers. Intense competition and low trading volume resulted in collective losses for the industry of over $100 million in both 1990 and 1991.[2]

As elsewhere in Europe, large corporate borrowers in France now have a wide selection of financing alternatives available to them, many in the capital markets. French government-controlled industrial borrowers have ong been extremely active in the Eurobond markets, and, as any banker French or otherwise) will tell you, these companies care only about the owest rate and the cleverest new idea. Wholesale banking in France is lowing into the securities markets, a trend that is expected to accelerate rapidly when more of the larger companies are privatized.

Investment banking activities in France are dominated by a small number of banques d'affaires, principally Bank Indosuez, Paribas (short for Compagnie Financière de Paris et de Pays-Bas), and Lazard Frères. The first two of these own substantial holdings of shares, and sometimes control, industrial companies in France, often making them captive clients of the bank.

France, some say, is a country run by engineers. The French love of technology is not restricted to industry. The nonbanking sector of the French financial services industry has been quick to exploit new opportunities for distribution of financial products through electronic means. Among these are Europe's most advanced electronic funds transfer system, which works like a public utility—anyone can get on it for a modest fee. A variety of credit card and deposit-taking products have begun to drain business away from the traditional banks. Over the past few years, since the abolition of credit controls in 1987, the banks have been free to fight back in the electronic medium, which has improved consumer services and lowered costs, but also lowered banking spreads from about 6% in 1985 to less than 4% in 1991.

Retail branch banking, though regarded as completely safe from foreign competition—at least for now—has been under attack in France from nonbank players offering high-tech, innovative services. Perhaps the most successful of these is the Compagnie Bancaire, a wholly owned subsidiary of Paribas. Its remarkable story, and that of its accommodating parent, is typically French.

A Nonbank Célèbre

Compagnie Bancaire is wholly involved in nonbank financial services concentrating in real estate (leasing, financing, and development), business equipment finance, and consumer credit. It operates through a highly decentralized system of customer-oriented joint ventures with many different distribution channels. It has a life insurance division that sells through banks, through a mail-order house, and through its own consumer finance arm. It has an asset management subsidiary that sells products through coupons, telemarketing, and television and radio. It offers mortgages, credit cards tied to money market funds, and various forms of leasing arrangements. It is creative, quick-moving, and profitable. During the past few years its operations expanded into the United Kingdom,

Spain, Italy, Belgium, and the Netherlands. In 1990, net operating profits were $300 million in a market hit by high interest rates, increasing credit losses and tough competition. The following year profits were off about 30% because of poor (recession-related) results in U.K. mortgages and equipment leases, and souring French mortgages.

Compagnie Bancaire was formed in 1946 by a young financial technocrat named Jacques de Fouchier to serve the smaller companies that the big banks ignored. Later it focused on consumer financial services. It devised imaginative financial products and then arranged for them to be distributed by others. Compagnie Bancaire financed these sales by issuing securities in the capital markets, not by taking deposits. It became a financial services processing factory for which capital was the raw material. To ensure the firm's access to capital, Fouchier invited Paribas to acquire a 48% interest in 1969. It was a very successful investment for Paribas, so much so that in the 1970s Fouchier took over as chief executive of Paribas. He then recruited André Lévy-Lang, a young man born in Egypt to Turkish parents, to join the firm. Lévy-Lang, who graduated first in his class from the celebrated Ecole Polytechnique and served for a while with the French atomic energy commission and with Schlumberger, proved to be a man of remarkable ability, and in 1983 he took over as head of Compagnie Bancaire. It continued to grow by introducing new nonbanking financial services that were well received in the market.

Today many French bankers believe that stodgy, old-fashioned branch banking is dead. One need never visit a branch, they say.

"One day you will get a surprise in your mail," one successful consultant said recently, "or a phone call, inviting you to participate in a new personal credit plan, designed for well-off individuals such as yourself.

"This new program, called, let's say, the 'red-white-and-blue' plan (after the colors of our French flag), will be offered as an all-purpose, high-technology personal finance service. It will function as a money market fund, paying top rates, but it will also offer a credit card with a large borrowing line, access to automatic teller machines anywhere in the country, discount brokerage and insurance services, and other services for the well-to-do not yet offered as a package in France."

"But," I asked, "won't the conservative Frenchman prefer to stick with his traditional bank, and see this as a blatant—probably American—effort to steal his business away?"

"Perhaps, but the French are curious, and quite willing to try new things. It is quite stylish to do so. But if the value is truly there, he will stay with it, just as happened in America."

"If the government will only stay out of the way (and you never know about that in France), the French consumer will respond quickly to bona fide innovation in banking and finance. The French, in that sense, may be more American than the Americans."

Affaires Dangereuses

Paribas was on the list to be nationalized following the Mitterrand election in 1981. The bank was then headed by Pierre Moussa, a pure-capitalist type who had succeeded Fouchier. Moussa fought the nationalization effort but failed in the end. He and a deputy, Gérard Eskenazi, did succeed at the last minute, however, in selling off most of Paribas's non-French (mainly Swiss) holdings to a Belgian-Swiss joint venture called Pargesa. Moussa's actions infuriated the Mitterrand government, which passed its feelings along to the French Treasury, then headed by Jean-Yves Habérer. Moussa was arrested for plotting against the government, acquitted, and then drifted off to form an investment business of his own. Habérer, ready to retire from the Treasury, was tapped to replace him as chief executive of Paribas. Eskenazi, in the light of Habérer's appointment, also resigned from Paribas, but stayed on at Pargesa to run the former Paribas assets in Switzerland.

In 1986, Jacques Chirac became prime minister during the time of "co-habitation," and Paribas was returned to the private sector through a share offering. Chirac chose a friend, career Paribas employee Michel François-Poncet, to replace Habérer (who was sent to head Crédit Lyonnaise) and urged him to restore Paribas's greatness as a banque d'affaires.

Francois-Poncet inherited a profitable, well-run bank with substantial investments in an industrial portfolio worth about $9 billion. It was a time when banques d'affaires had rediscovered their stock market prowess and the glories of growth through conglomeration, chiefly through takeover battles. Paribas's chief rival, Compagnie de Suez, had been especially visible in this area in 1988 when it swept up Société Générale de Belgique (SGB), a $2 billion Belgian holding company that had come into the hands of Italian financier Carlo de Benedetti, and a year later when it bought control of Groupe Victoire, a $5 billion French insurer.

Compelled to keep up with the headlines, François-Poncet launched in 1990 an ill-considered $4.7 billion hostile bid for Navigation Mixte, a Marseille-based conglomerate involved in insurance, transportation, and food processing. Mixte was headed by Marc Fournier, a 63-year-old takeover veteran. Fournier immediately allied with his main bank, Crédit Lyonnais (headed by Habérer), and as a defensive tactic aggressively bought shares in Paribas. The two finally reached a standoff in which Paribas owned 40% of Mixte and Mixte owned 12.7% of Paribas. At this point, Paribas could not get more shares without having to pay a ridiculous price, and Fouchier was still accumulating, so Paribas surrendered. Then Gérard Eskenazi approached his former colleague, François-Poncet, and made a proposal—he would return to France to join the Paribas board and then negotiate a peace with Fournier on Paribas's behalf. The Paribas board, however, included Jean Peyrelevade, who was then chairman of state-owned Union des Assurance de Paris (UAP), a former member of the socialist cabinet of 1981, and a former chief executive of Banque Indosuez, the principal company in the Suez group. Peyrelevade strenuously opposed Eskenazi for political reasons, and the idea was rejected. Various other intrigues then followed and Pargesa's other shareholders turned on Eskenazi, leaving him out in the cold. Then, 78-year-old Fouchier made a timely reappearance on the scene and proposed a two-tiered reorganization in which François-Poncet would be retained (for a while) as chairman but his old protégé, Lévy-Lang, would be promoted to chief operating officer.

While this was being considered, new stock buying in Paribas broke out, prompted this time by Michel Albert, a Paribas board member who was chairman of Assurance Generale de France (AGF), another large state-owned insurance company. He increased AGF's holdings to 9%. Apparently, Albert was either jealous of the rising influence of Peyrelevade and UAP, or he wanted to raise AGF's profile at Paribas in order to do insurance business with it, or both. Finally, an elegant all-parties truce was made, Fouchier's management succession plan was accepted, and Paribas and Mixte began a program for unwinding their investments in each other. Then, Paribas announced a plan to swap its 7% stake in Group Brussels-Lambert, Belgium's second-largest banking group, with Pargesa for Paribas's former Swiss holdings (enabling it to reconstitute Banque Paribas Suisse, with François-Poncet replacing Eskenazi as president). A year later, Lévy-Lang became Paribas's chairman and chief executive.[3]

At the end of 1990, Paribas had $144.5 billion in assets, plus $56 billion in assets managed for others in its Paribas Asset Management Group. It operated in fifty countries, with 26,000 employees. Net income of $440 million was reported for 1990, down from about $600 million in 1989. However, most of the 1990 income was from nonrecurring asset sales; only $70 million was from operating earnings. The botched Navigation Mixte deal cost Paribas nearly $1 billion in pre-tax income; the investment portfolio also had to provide $160 million in additional reserves. Lévy-Lang noted that 1990 had been "a difficult year for Paribas," but, apparently already feeling the effects of economic slowdown in Europe, added that "1991 evidently will not be easy either, the principal problem being the rise in credit risks in the banking sector, a situation we share with many other banks."[4] In early 1992, Standard & Poor's downgraded Paribas's long-term debt rating from AA to AA-.

Still, Paribas was strong and healthy. It stands, as Lévy-Lang said, "on four elephant legs": Paribas itself (the banque d'affaires), the industrial portfolio, a 500-branch retail bank (Crédit du Nord), and Compagnie Bancaire. It would take a very heavy blow to knock this elephant over. And although the elephant has shown that it can exhibit fancy, if not always graceful, footwork, under Lévy-Lang it is not expected to feel much urgency to do so.[5] Paribas continues to exert itself in investment banking, especially in Eurobond new issues, bond trading and swaps, and a rapidly growing quantity of European mergers and acquisitions, where its large industrial holdings provide substantial captive business. The pressure to pull off a great takeover coup has almost completely faded in the wake of the Navigation Mixte disaster. French observers expect Paribas to follow a quieter and more technical approach to banking for a while, based on internal growth and new product development, joint ventures, new forms of distribution, and greater effort to take the Paribas show abroad.

Paribas's one and only rival as a banque d'affaires, Compagnie de Suez, named for the canal it financed in the last century, has been a poor role model. Under Renaud de la Genière, chief executive until he died in October 1990, Suez's objective was to increase in size to "European scale." Pursuant to his two white-knight acquisitions of control of SGB and Groupe Victoire, de la Genière issued large amounts of new shares. He was also forced into selling off a 34% stake in Victoire to UAP, France's largest insurer and Victoire's chief competitor, a transaction that created many complications.

There were other problems too—SGB was faltering under the weight of its unprofitable industrial holdings, making it a very expensive sick investment for the group. Banque Indosuez, the flagship of the group, and Créditsuez, its very profitable consumer finance arm, both complained that the capital they wanted to expand their businesses and to protect their market shares in the post-1992 period was being eaten up by the industrial portfolio.

De la Genière was replaced by Gérard Worms, who immediately began to off-load money-losing investments, reduce the size of the group to more manageable proportions, and produce some cash for more urgent investments. In his first year in office he sold over $1 billion of assets, though many observers felt a lot more still needed to be sold. Like Lévy-Lang, his counterpart at Paribas, Worms had come into his job unexpectedly; he was a mild-mannered career employee being given the reins of a dynamic, aggressive enterprise that was devoted to the old-fashioned strategy of growth through conquest. Like Lévy-Lang he too saw that the times were changing. Consolidation, internal development, and attention to profit were the formula for success that both would now follow.

L'Banque Industrie

Replacing Compagnie de Suez in 1990 as the most headlined French bank was Crédit Lyonnais, which had embarked on an especially aggressive, all-encompassing European expansion program. The strategy was formulated by the bank's chief executive, Jean-Yves Habérer, whose aim was to make his bank one of four financial cornerstones of the new Europe that will dominate the activities of the Continent for years to come. These banks, according to Habérer, were Deutsche Bank, Barclays, San Paolo di Torino, and Crédit Lyonnais (the leading banks from the leading countries). They would, he believed, have the capital strength, the domestic market share, and the intra-European networks to repel all threats and to intimidate others—they were the ones that would become the grand financial oligarchs of the next century.

To secure the lasting loyalty of clients, however, Habérer believed it was necessary to go one step further—the bank had to own them. It had to have such a strong voice in the decision-making channels of its clients that it could direct what actions were taken. This is a form of universal banking more German than the German, where the banks do not direct their clients' actions, except perhaps when rescuing them from bankruptcy. Habérer called this type of real-man universal bank a *banque industrie*.

Habérer, approaching sixty, is a special creation of the French. Graduating first in his class at the elite Ecole Nationale d'Administration, he joined the French Treasury as an *Inspecteur Général des Finances*. This is an appointment for only the brightest of the bright, which entitled Habérer to the lifelong admiration and fawning of just about everyone with whom he came into contact. He rose to the top quickly, becoming the head of the French Treasury while in his forties. He is described as arrogant, brilliant, intimidating, admired and feared by all, and virtually friendless. His time as head man at Paribas was preparation for his present role as the true and final creator of a great European bank, France's contribution to the future of European finance.

Habérer knew, when he began the rapid expansion plan, that it was a long way from where he was to where he wanted to be. Crédit Lyonnais was not one of Europe's great banks. To become one, it would have to expand on several fronts simultaneously. It would have to increase its ownership of meaningful industrial holdings and its loans to the industrial sector. Under Habérer, shareholdings increased by 50% (to about the same size as Paribas's portfolio) and loans soared by about 80%. Next, it would have to increase its intra-European alliances and networks. Several acquisitions and purchases of strategic stakes followed; it bought banks in Britain, Belgium, Spain, and Italy and opened a branch in Germany. By the end of 1991, Crédit Lyonnais was perhaps the best-connected of any European bank.[6]

The strategy contained a not-so-secret weapon, its relationship with the Mitterrand government. Habérer, a superb politician himself and apparently long a friend of the socialists, maneuvered himself into the useful position of being the government's favorite banker. The government owned all of the voting stock of the bank (though some nonvoting shares were held by the public) and could exercise its power at will, as Habérer knew very well, having been suddenly dumped as head of Paribas when Chirac became prime minister. So it made sense to be on the same wavelength with the Treasury and the rest of the government. Habérer had defined and offered to execute a master plan for ensuring that at least one French bank was at the top when the post-1992 financial regime settled in, after which major changes would be rare. He wanted the government to back his acquisition and growth policy knowing there would be disappointments, loan losses, and other mishaps along the way. In other words, he wanted to ride the government's horse "hell for leather," regardless of normal banking cautions, in order to enter the next century with a large and powerful financial machine intact. The strategy would be expensive—capital infusions would be necessary (Crédit Lyonnais received four under Habérer)—but as the bank increased its holdings in formerly government-owned companies, it would in fact be buying back with one hand what the French government was privatizing with the other. Such symmetry must have brought tears of joy to the eyes of the civil service.

An example of Habérer's strategy was a plan (later examined by the EEC competition commission) for Crédit Lyonnais to pay $400 million for a 10% interest in Usinor Sacilor, a state-owned steel maker. The investment would be financed by Crédit Lyonnais through a shareholder rights issue, to which the government would subscribe by giving the bank another 10% interest in Usinor Sacilor; the bank would then own 20% of the steel company and have its capital increased by $400 million without any real cash having changed hands. One of the other large government-owned banks, Banque Nationale de Paris (BNP), is to make a similar investment in Air France, which is also owned by the government. In mid-1992, Crédit Lyonnais announced it would acquire a minority stake (reportedly a 10% interest for $280 million) in Aérospatiale, the debt-laden government aircraft maker. Needless to say, the privatized banks can't do things like this.

Nor can they afford to risk the losses to shareholders of massive write-offs from such aggressive lending and expansion policies as Crédit Lyonnais's, which in 1991 involved several lending fiascos (including a soured $1 billion loan to controversial Italian financier Giancarlo Parretti to acquire MGM/UA Communications) and loan loss provisions triple those of its main French competitors. The bank's increasing exposure to risky loans (Maxwell, Olympia & York) resulted in the downgrading of its bond rating (from Aa1 to Aa2) by Moody's Investor Services, despite the government's (Aaa rating) continuing ownership.[7]

Given an unlimited commitment of government resources, Habérer's strategy would no doubt succeed, and Crédit Lyonnais would emerge as one of the great European banks, though the battle would hardly be fairly won. There are several weaknesses in the strategy, however, which together diminish the probability of victory. First, France's partners in the single European market may object to such blatant tampering with free competition and refuse to permit it to continue. Second, Habérer, who has not addressed the problems of how to expand rapidly without buying excessive quantities of low-grade paper, may make such an awful mess of the loan portfolio that the government will blow the whistle. After all, this is what really hurt the American banks in the 1970s and 1980s, and the French know it. Third, Habérer and his strategy are on everyone's casualty list for the infighting that surely will follow the next presidential election in 1995—time is short to accomplish all he hopes for. And, finally, Habérer has neglected the investment banking and capital markets side of the business. Indeed, even companies in which the bank has holdings, assuming they are sufficiently creditworthy, will prefer to use the capital markets for their financing requirements rather than borrow from banks. Thus, Crédit Lyonnais could finish the 1990s with lots of impotent industrial holdings in companies using the capital markets, lots of alliances with foreign banks whose major clients are also using the markets, and tons of bad loans acquired as the bank amassed gigantic size that is of no use.

Habérer knows these things, but he shrugs them all off, quoting a proverb, "No one is a prophet in his own country. Indeed, I'd say, no one is a prophet in his own profession."[8]

The French banks are experimenting on all fronts at once—in retail financial services, where technology and innovation are encouraged, at least by nonbank competitors; in wholesale banking through extensive capital market activities, which have been eased by structural deregulation and reform that has increased competition and lowered costs on the Paris Bourse; and in finance company operations, through which portfolios of investments in nonbanking assets are traded actively. Some banking groups are expanding into Europe through the traditional means of branch openings, others through alliances and strategic holdings. Still others are expanding through acquisitions. France, unlike any other country in Europe, is capable of blurring distinctions between the public and private sectors, on occasion ruthlessly combining the best of both to great advantage.

The French combination of innovation, wide-ranging experimentation, and highly talented, ambitious leaders backed with vigorous government support is formidable. Certainly, French bankers have the potential to field a very competitive team for the European banking championships in the years ahead.

This view is shared by a senior Italian banker, Alfonso Jozzo, chief of international banking at Italy's Istituto Bancario San Paolo di Torino (one of Habérer's cornerstones). He feels that the French enthusiasm for technology and change, their willingness to take great risks at the government's expense, and their go-it-alone attitude make them the most adaptive, powerful, and opportunistic country in Europe.

"Everyone thinks the Germans will rule the European economy after 1992," Jozzo said. He explained that in thinking this everyone overlooks the problems that the Germans have in adapting to new situations, in introducing innovation and new ideas in the service sectors, and, of course, the many difficulties and great expense of sponsoring the economic recovery of the East. "They also overlook the French, who may possess just the qualities needed to come to the top over the next few years," he added. "No one is expecting this, so maybe it will happen."[9]

RULING BRITANNIA

On October 1, 1991, Sir David Scholey, then fifty-six, relinquished the position of chief executive of S.G. Warburg Group, which he had held for the past ten years, though he would continue as chairman of the Group. He was succeeded as CEO by an old Etonian, the Rt. Hon. The Earl Cairns, fifty-two, who, as Simon (Viscount) Garmoyle (before inheriting his late father's title), had joined the firm twelve years before to head corporate finance. Before that Lord Cairns had been a popular and respected stock-broker, who understood financial markets long before most merchant bankers knew that it was important to do so.

In Britain, a powerful executive chairman (i.e., full time) in reality retains most of the powers of an American chief executive officer, and a British CEO is more like a chief operating officer, or day-to-day manager of the firm. The change in leadership at Warburg, therefore, was not substantial, but the press made much of the event and in most cases praised Scholey. "Probably the most successful merchant banker of his generation," said the *Sunday Times*. Scholey steered Warburg, according to the *Times*, "not only into a major position in corporate finance but also through Big Bang. His house is one of only three that can say they got the securities industry right." However, added the *Financial Times*, "he has had the misfortune to be tipped as next Governor of the Bank of England [the present governor, Robin Leigh-Pemberton, had said he would retire when his term expired in June 1993], but favorites rarely end up with the Bank job." Scholey's move, therefore, the paper continued, "may say more about his ambitions than his chances."

Still, Scholey was the City's leading light. A fast-tracker from a good public school and Christ Church, Oxford, he joined Warburg in 1964 from a small merchant bank, Guiness Mahon, and was made a director in 1967. He was chosen in the late 1970s by Sir Siegmund Warburg as heir apparent and was nurtured by the old man to succeed him, which he didn't really do until Warburg died at eighty in 1982. By then he had developed all the qualities to lead the firm effectively. He was a top deal-man, a tireless busi-ness-getter, a shrewd politician, a clear-headed strategist, and a resource-ful network builder. He was, of course, Sir Siegmund's loyal and obedient servant, but also his student and beneficiary. He was appointed to the Court of Governors of the Bank of England (i.e., its board of directors) in 1981, served on various public commissions and was knighted in 1987, one of only a very few merchant bankers to receive such a distinction from the government of Margaret Thatcher.

A German Envelopment

Like most London merchant banks, Warburg's origins are foreign but, unlike the others, its are very recent. The firm that became the leading British merchant bank was established in 1946 by two German Jewish emigres, Warburg and Henry Grunfeld. Warburg, a banker from the family firm of M.M. Warburg of Hamburg, had fled Nazi Germany in 1936 and set up a small trading business in London. Grunfeld, an industrialist, came later. The undisputed leader of the two was Siegmund Warburg, then thirty-six—an autocratic, driven banker of the old German school, who believed in meticulous control, high standards, strict confidentiality, unquestioning loyalty to both the firm and its clients, and handwriting tests to determine the character of all job applicants. Every meeting and telephone conversation with a client was documented with a written note. Every incoming piece of correspondence was circulated among all of the directors. Everyone knew everything, but of course only one person was in charge. "Warburg," according to Peter J.R. Spira, a former vice chairman of the firm who began his career in the 1950s, "provided the vision, the genius, and the contacts but he could not have succeeded without Grunfeld, who had the sharpest brain in the City of London (and possibly still has). At the age of 86, Grunfeld still is in his office daily."

Warburg's strategy was clear from the beginning: he would make the bank over into a quintessential British institution by hiring the brightest sons of the establishment, training them, and turning them loose on the City to demonstrate their capabilities with innovative, tireless service to clients. Then he would promote them, compensate them generously, and send them out to recruit others like them. He and Grunfeld would orchestrate things from the shadows, although in his own case, his role was well illuminated. Though Warburg's considerable international connections were often employed advantageously, the bank was incorporated in Britain, headquartered in Britain, and was in all ways British, not German or European. Despite this emphasis, Warburg himself made no effort to conceal his German origins and characteristics. He believed that combining German rigor and determination with British establishment connections provided a mix that stood out in the crowded field of merchant banking and could be seen as a comparative advantage.[10]

Warburg's big break came in 1957, when the bank represented an affiliate of Reynolds Metals in an unsolicited takeover of British Aluminium, Britain's first hostile deal. Reynolds was a blue-chip company, but it was American and there was great opposition to the deal initially. Warburg, however, successfully made the case that Reynolds's price was fair and that

British Aluminum's managerial record was poor. He raised the issue of shareholders' interests and ultimately won both the financial and the public relations battles. Afterward, his firm was sought out by others seeking to make acquisitions, and its offices, then at 30 Gresham Street, soon became a well-known and respected address in the City.

Eurobonds and International Adventures

The 1960s in Britain, however, were times of little growth, high taxes, stiff foreign exchange controls, and limited merchant-banking opportunities. Warburg began to look abroad for business. He found it in the growing market for Eurodollars, or dollar deposits in European banks or branches of U.S. banks. Several European bond issuers had launched dollar issues in the United States, as they had done before the war, but U.S. demand for the issues was not strong. Underwriters like Kuhn, Loeb & Co., which had been active with European issuers for a long time, began to look to European investors to take the securities. Warburg had been a partner of Kuhn Loeb (a Kuhn Loeb partner had simultaneously been a partner of Warburg's, an early strategic alliance that was later disbanded) and suggested that his firm put together the first European issue of non-European currency bonds sold within Europe. Warburg understood that the banks and other holders of Eurodollars needed good-quality paper in which to invest. They needed securities that were denominated in dollars but that, unlike U.S. securities, were free of withholding taxes and were in bearer form (which did not require the purchasers to reveal themselves to tax authorities anywhere). The result was the first Eurobond offering, a $15 million issue for the Italian State Highway Agency, Autostrade. The issue was a success, and the Eurobond market was born. The rapid development of the Eurobond market gave Warburg a chance to cash in some of its international chips and to develop a wide network of business associations in Europe, Japan, and the United States.

Siegmund Warburg's last brainstorm, however, proved to be something of a disaster. This involved a complex, mutual minority shareholding arrangement with Paribas, and a joint majority investment in the Chicago-based investment bank A.G. Becker & Co. The arrangement, launched in 1974, was hailed as a model for the financial world of the future—it combined the capital-raising and investing strengths of the two firms in Europe and America while preserving everyone's independence. The concept was not dissimilar to some of the strategic alliance investments being launched today in Europe. In reality, the deal was bulled through by Warburg and Fouchier and produced far more strife and conflict than it did business. The joint investment in A.G. Becker failed when Becker did, an occurrence the strategic alliance was unable to prevent. The arrangement lasted for several years, not really coming to an end until Warburg's death, after which Paribas bought out the firm's interest in Becker. Paribas then took over running the American firm, and, after losses estimated at about $200 million, sold what was left to Merrill Lynch in 1984. Throughout this period the alliance was a disappointment and a distraction, which kept both firms from developing their international market positions more effectively.

Surviving Big Bang

Scholey's biggest challenge, which faced him very soon after he took over as head of the firm, was dealing with Big Bang. In 1983, the Thatcher government and the Stock Exchange entered into an agreement that involved certain concessions by the Exchange in return for withdrawal of an antitrust suit that had been lodged against the Exchange by the previous government. To many observers at the time, the concessions seemed mild. The most important of them was the shift to variable commission rates (from fixed minimum commissions) after three years. Such a move was similar to the abolition of fixed commission rates by the New York Stock Exchange in 1975. For the London Exchange, however, the agreement would abolish the financial system used by the City of London for more than a century. As soon as this became understood, the press christened the event "Big Bang," either in recognition of the explosive force of the changes that were coming, or to refer in astrophysical terms to the beginning of a new universe.

Under the old system, the City was a rabbit warren of different service providers, each protected from its neighbors in the interests of fair play and a good living for all. Merchant banks, for example, were not permitted to be members of the Exchange. Nor were commercial banks or insurance companies. The Stock Exchange consisted of brokers and jobbers. Brokers executed purchases and sales of securities strictly as agents, for a standard commission. Jobbers were market makers; they were forbidden to deal with anyone except other jobbers and brokers—they could not trade with ultimate investors, who were required to do their business with brokers only. High fixed-commission rates kept the system going, but when customers became free to negotiate rates, they would drop precipitously. When this happened, all who studied the situation knew, there would be insufficient income to continue to support the old system of separated functions. Brokers and jobbers, and even merchant banks, would have to be free to combine. It became clear that three years' notice would scarcely be enough to prepare for the momentous changes that lay ahead.

The Stock Exchange changes were accompanied by a re-regulation of the securities market (passed ten days after Big Bang, which put teeth into enforcement and clarified [in time] the duties and obligations of all market participants). The duties and minimum capitalization of market makers both for government bonds, or gilt-edged securities, and for stocks, were set forth by the Bank of England and new rules and penalties for crimes against the marketplace were established under a new Financial Services Act.

Few brokers had any capital—it had all been paid out over the years— and jobbers had to develop distribution of their own. This resulted in a wave of mergers between Stock Exchange member firms, ultimately involving all three major jobbers and nineteen of the top twenty brokers.

In August 1984, Scholey dazzled the City with the announcement of a four-way merger (to be effective three years later, after October 27, 1986— the day when Big Bang would officially occur, through which Warburg would combine with one of the two leading jobbers, Akroyd & Smithers, one of the largest brokers, Rowe & Pitman, and "the government broker" (in gilt-edged securities), Mullens & Co. The Warburg plan was to take the initiative in changing with the times by assembling the strongest across-the-board team possible, in an effort to become a British equivalent of Goldman Sachs or Morgan Stanley. The merger was valued at about $450 million, the largest transaction of its type ever done in Britain. The deal was especially courageous in light of Warburg's recent experience in combining forces with Paribas and Becker. Scholey would spend years working to integrate all the separate companies and businesses into one smooth-functioning organization. Scholey could not afford a mistake; he had bet the whole firm on the decision to move quickly and grab the best.

Taking the High Ground

Unlike almost all of the other Big Bang acquisitions, the Warburg combinations were successful, and the firm has emerged as the unquestioned leader of the post-Bang City. Some of its success can be attributed to its having assembled and developed the best talent. Some too can be credited to Scholey's organizational approach, which involved dividing the firm into three separate but equal units: S.G. Warburg & Co. (banking and corporate finance), S.G. Warburg Securities (securities sales and trading), and Mercury Asset Management Group, a 75%-owned investment advisory company with $60 billion of assets under management at the end of 1991. Its corporate finance arm continually ranks at or near the top in mergers and acquisitions in both the United Kingdom and in Europe. Its new issues business is also highly successful, not only in terms of domestic U.K. business, but also in terms of Eurobond transactions, where Warburg, alone among U.K. banks, usually ranks in the top ten. Its securities and investment management arms are equally well regarded. Its three legs are all strong and profitable, are market leaders, and are oriented toward global markets. This is something no other firm in Britain can claim today. The group employs a total of about 5,000 people, of whom about 40% reside outside the United Kingdom, mainly in continental Europe, Australia/New Zealand, North America, and Japan (in that order in terms of number). Group net income for the year ended in March 1990 was $195 million, providing a return on shareholder's equity of 17.7%. Nineteen ninety was a record year, which was not exceeded in 1991, when pre-tax profits declined 30% because of difficult market conditions in the United Kingdom. Try as it might, Warburg was unable to squeeze as much profit out of its marketplace (the United Kingdom and Europe) as the big American investment banks did out of theirs. By the end of their fiscal years for 1991, at least three of the largest U.S. investment banks reported net income three to four times that of Warburg's approximately $130 million.

Warburg sees itself today principally as a European wholesale and private banking house. It has bought brokerage firms in Germany and France, bought out its partners in a Swiss investment-banking joint venture, and set up offices in Italy and Spain. Its board of directors is the most multinational of any merchant or investment bank, including executive directors from Holland and Denmark and prominent nonexecutives from Germany, Holland, Canada, and the United States. Its U.S. and Japanese presences, however, do not offer significant local competition, though they are members of the New York and Tokyo stock exchanges, respectively.

The Changing Competitive Scene in Britain

Britain has long believed in active, efficient capital markets. It has encouraged its commercial enterprises to become incorporated and to sell shares to the public. This practice has not been followed to anywhere near the same extent in continental European countries, where family-controlled companies, or partnerships, dominate the private sector. In France, for example, about 900 companies were listed on the Paris Bourse in 1988, and those comprised a market capitalization equal to about 29% of GNP, a proportion that was approximately the same as in Germany, Italy, and Spain. In the United Kingdom, the market capitalization of listed companies was then equal to 88% of GNP. In the United States, which has a large number of small listed companies, the proportion was about 50%.[11]

Since Big Bang, Britain's financial markets have become much more efficient and competitive. Trading in equities has risen about 3.5 times (though much of this increase is due to trading in international equities), and in gilts, trading volume is roughly double the 1986 level. The cost of executing orders (exclusive of a 0.5% stamp tax that was 1.0% in 1986) has declined from about 1% of principal amount to about 0.8% for large institutional orders. Commissions on block trades have virtually disappeared, but investors must pay the dealer spread. The quality and depth of market making has improved considerably under the SEAQ system, which closely resembles the U.S. electronic over-the-counter market called NASDAQ.

Before Big Bang there were only a handful of market makers; there are now 25 market makers in equities and 19 in gilts, though the totals reflect a decrease of 7–8 firms since October 1986.

The increased trading activity, however, was not enough to offset post–Big Bang trading losses on the part of the major U.K. brokers and dealers. The market segments specializing in U.K. securities were not growing, indeed the gilt-edged market was shrinking as the U.K. Treasury redeemed, rather than issued, debt. After the crash of 1987, trading volume in British stocks dropped off, and all the firms that had piled into the market after Big Bang had to fight hard for business, slashing commissions in the process. There was too much capacity in the industry, many said. In the face of continuing losses some of the capacity was gradually withdrawn. Nearly all of the several U.S. banks that had bought U.K. brokers shut the businesses down or substantially curtailed them. All of the large U.K. banks, except Barclays, which had carved out a strong market position with its Barclays de Zoute Wedd (BZW) subsidiary, pulled either out of gilts, or stocks, or both. So did several of the other merchant banks, preferring to rely as they had before on the merchant bankers' traditional vocation of living by their wits, rather than on their capital. In the process, three of the four largest banks (NatWest, Lloyds, and Midland) withdrew from serious competition in the capital markets, and all of the merchant banks but Warburg and Kleinwort Benson headed for niches. Some began to look around the rest of Europe for things to do, but most lacked the European infrastructure and only had their wits to offer, which was often not enough.

Institutional investors were the biggest beneficiaries from the changes as more-liquid markets improved their ability to manage portfolios well, even though the net decrease in execution costs was somewhat smaller than anticipated. Corporations have benefited too, with more efficient and imaginative new-issue markets in London, though often these are not competitive with rates offered in the Eurobond and Euro-equity markets.

The overall result has been an increase in capital market usage, new market technology, greatly enhanced competition, various new forms of securitization (e.g., sterling-denominated commercial paper, mortgaged-backed securities), and drawing into London transactions in international equity and other securities. As of the end of 1990, approximately 50% of all stock trading volume in London involved trades in non-U.K. securities, mostly other European equities. Similarly, as much as 50% of large order trading volume in French and German shares is now transacted in London, usually with international investors.[12]

The biggest losers from the U.K. market-reform effort were the British and foreign banks that rushed in to make strategic acquisitions of securities firms. Vast sums of money were poured into the market—$6 billion on acquisitions, technology, overhead, and trading losses combined, according to one estimate. The money first created overcapacity and then price wars.[13] The biggest trading losses were experienced by those newcomers who were unfamiliar with market making or who tried too hard to reach for market share.

By the early 1990s, the capital markets and corporate finance battlefields in the United Kingdom had been left to a small number of survivors from the old regime, plus four or five powerful American investment banks. These American firms, which employed 1,000 to 1,500 employees each in London alone, captured much of the business given up by the retreating British. Most of these firms needed to make very few adjustments to accommodate Big Bang—they had functioned as broker-dealers handling large blocks of securities at negotiated commission rates for the past fifteen years and had fought through their own wars of attrition. They already did business with British institutions in U.S., European, and Japanese shares, and adding British shares to list was not difficult. None of the firms felt they were obligated to make markets in all British shares, so they picked and chose to preserve profitability. They also were well acquainted with British industrial corporations, for which they had handled transactions in the United States and in the Eurobond markets. Many of these clients welcomed their aggressive marketing attentions and new ideas. Before long, U.S. investment banks, staffing their ranks with bright young Brits from all the right places, began to carve out leading market share positions in the merger market and in some areas of financing for British corporations.

Siegmund Warburg, after all, pulled off a miracle. He set up an old-fashioned German Jewish bank in 1946, and forty-five years later it had become the leading merchant bank in Britain, headed by a knight and a belted earl. This was achieved without any significant acquisitions before Big Bang, all through internal development. It is an impressive lesson in how to penetrate a market from the inside out, rather than by conquest. The lesson has not been lost on the Americans, who have been following Sir Siegmund's advice for nearly a decade now, and have been encouraged by the results so far. They ask, "If Warburg can do it, why can't we?"

MEMORABLE MISTAKES

There were a number of other strategic initiatives undertaken by banks in Europe during the 1980s that were very successful for a while, but in the end were failures. After a few years (at most) of glory, these firms ultimately had to be restructured in painful ways. Perhaps the strategies were at fault, perhaps the implementation. But certain mistakes are memorable—they stand out as hazards to be avoided in the future.

Morgan the Bully

Morgan Grenfell & Co. is the direct lineal descendant of a banking firm established in London in 1838 by George Peabody, a wealthy Baltimore cotton merchant who moved to England and devoted himself as much to philanthropic affairs as to business. In 1854, Peabody was looking for someone to run the firm and invited Junius S. Morgan, an American banker from Hartford, to become his partner. Morgan took over the firm when Peabody retired in 1864 and renamed it J.S. Morgan & Co. Morgan's son Pierpont worked for a while in the firm, but later returned to New York and set up his own bank, which initially functioned as the New York correspondent of J.S. Morgan. The two Morgans specialized in placing American railroad securities with wealthy European investors and developed generalized investment-banking businesses. The senior Morgan, however, was best known for financing European governments, especially those in political difficulties. He died in 1890, and the *New York Tribune* commented that "probably no other foreign banker was so well and widely known and liked, or exerted so great an influence in the United States as he did."[14]

J.P. Morgan inherited his father's holding in J.S. Morgan but was too busy to run it himself. So he sent his son Jack to do so, and Jack worked closely with one of the firm's salaried partners, Edward ("Teddy") Grenfell, a well-connected British financier, for the next fifteen years. In 1905, Teddy Grenfell became senior partner when Jack Morgan returned to New York to manage J.P. Morgan & Co., and the firm became Morgan Grenfell & Co. It retained close ties with J.P. Morgan, and together the two firms arranged a substantial amount of financing for the British government during World War I. After the Glass-Steagall Act of 1933, J.P. Morgan was divided into commercial and investment banking units, which ultimately became known as Morgan Guaranty Trust Company and Morgan Stanley & Co., respectively.

By the 1970s, Morgan Grenfell was a leading London merchant bank, one still recognized as having inherited the Morgan clout and client list. It was more than a bit sleepy, however; its bankers lived the genteel life of the City, in which few firms called on clients of other firms, and most rarely called on their own clients. If the clients wanted you, they asked for an appointment. In 1974, the firm selected Bill Mackworth-Young, an ex-stockbroker, to succeed the old-regime, Morgan Guaranty-trained Sir John Stevens as chairman and chief executive and to liven things up a little. In 1975, Christopher Reeves, an ex-Army man who had worked for a while with Sir Kenneth Keith, a well-known British entrepreneur and chairman of rival merchant bank Hill Samuel, became head of the banking division. Reeves had worked at Hill Samuel with some of the country's emerging financial New Men, who were all interested in expanding their empires as quickly as possible.

Reeves wanted to get the jump on the next batch of mergers and acquisitions, which he believed these players would precipitate. He set up several M&A teams in the firm, headed by young corporate finance directors whose job was to promote the firm by promoting deals, regardless of whose client had to be called on to do so. After some early successes, Reeves's reputation shone; in something of a palace coup he replaced Mackworth-Young as chief executive in December 1979. Reeves was then forty-two, and the average age of the board was forty-four. Both were incredibly young by City standards. The "young turks" were widely thought to have displaced the "old guard"—the Reeves team were hard-driving, ambitious professionals, not old-fashioned "talented amateurs" from good families. They weren't titled, or rich, or even well connected. But they were hungry.

Reeves had been right in positioning the firm for a rise in merger activity. In the years 1972–1976, Morgan Grenfell advised on mergers worth in the aggregate about $2 billion. In 1986 alone, the firm was engaged in transactions valued at more than $25 billion. The merger boom of the 1980s was shorter-lived in the United Kingdom than in the United States, but steeper. It began in about 1983 and peaked in 1986 at a volume of about $40 billion, about ten times the 1983 level. Morgan Grenfell commanded the lion's share of this business, participating in more than half the peak year volume. Morgan ranked first in the London M&A league tables year after year. Its 120-man mergers group was reportedly producing almost half the profits of the whole 2,000-man firm. In 1985, Morgan Grenfell's profits were double those of the year before.[15]

Morgan's success was based on three principles: it was aggressive in marketing takeover ideas to equally aggressive if somewhat "racy" New Men who were looking for hostile takeover possibilities; the firm was thorough and professional in bringing to bear legal, accounting, and financial ideas that were tightly constructed and difficult to defend against; and it was tough in negotiating deals on its clients' behalf, occasionally riding roughshod over niceties like the Takeover Panel (London's then nonbinding, self-regulatory body that officiated acquisition transactions). Soon Reeves's team of mergers specialists headed by George Magan, Graham Walsh, Guy Dawson, and Roger Seelig began to be known as the City's "public school bully boys." They took pride in working with the most hostile of the new entrepreneurs (such as Owen Green of BTR, Ernest Saunders of Guinness, and Jeffrey Sterling of P&O Lines). They also represented unpopular clients, such as Allianz, the German insurance giant, when it attempted a hostile bid for Eagle Star Insurance. Reeves was not a deal man himself, but he was a great believer in delegating authority and in backing his winners. He told them that merchant banking was based on innovation and that they "must not believe that rules are written in tablets of stone." Seelig boasted that they "didn't just read the rules," which many of their competitors were just starting to do, they "changed the rules."

The merger men became headliners, being almost always in the limelight. Roger Seelig was probably the most flamboyant in dress and manner (one British friend of mine called him "flash Harry"), but they all belonged to a new cult of supremely confident, well-paid, fast-rising City superstars.

Their often controversial activities, successes, and arrogant style attracted far more clients than it repelled. Their merger prowess, however, made Morgan Grenfell cocky and overbearing.

Bill Mackworth-Young died unexpectedly in 1984, and Reeves succeeded him. Distracted by the continuing torrent of increasingly profitable deals, Reeves and the rest of top management took their eyes off the main event in the City during that time: the coming of Big Bang in October 1986.

The firm needed to address the issue of how it would position itself in the coming drastic changes. As a merchant bank, Morgan Grenfell was neither a broker or a dealer, nor a member of the stock exchange, nor a market maker in government securities. The basic choice facing the firm was to develop a first-rate securities business, probably by buying one of the leading brokers for a lot of money, or to go it alone as a corporate finance house. The bully boys favored the latter course, arguing that the securities business was very risky and consumed capital better used to underwrite mergers. It hesitated, but other major firms didn't. First Warburg, then Barclays Bank, then N.M. Rothschild, Hill Samuel, Kleinwort Benson, and several large foreign banks made important moves.

Several other merchant banks hung back, preferring to remain small, fringe players in the new marketplace, but Morgan Grenfell, the merger king, could hardly be expected to be relegated to the fringes. The result of its indecision was to limit the field of available partners. Finally it picked up what it could—a fourth-rate jobber, Pinchin, Denny & Co., and a fourth-rate government securities broker, Pember & Boyle.

The changes in Morgan Grenfell's business came rapidly and represented a confluence of several developments. First, in early 1986, there was the Guinness scandal, resulting from Morgan Grenfell's representation of Ernest Saunders, the aggressive chairman of Guinness plc, who had entered the competition for Distiller's Group (a major brewer and Scotch whiskey maker) when a much smaller supermarket company, Argyll, tried to take it over. The battle was a vicious one, in which a number of unpleasant moves were made by each side. Each potential acquirer was offering its own stock in exchange for Distiller shares, so each company's share price was crucial in determining which bid would be successful. Seelig was advising Saunders and urged that Guinness get its friends to buy stock in the company to support the price. Various people did buy (including Robert Maxwell), but Morgan Grenfell bought the most, often taking the friendly purchases on its own books. The firm bought about $250 million of Guinness stock this way, an amount greater than its entire capital at the time, for which it was later chastised by the Bank of England and required to raise additional capital. Guinness finally won with a bid valuing the company at about $3.5 billion.

The scandal derived from the fact that in addition to the independent purchases of Morgan Grenfell and its friends, Guinness had also arranged for illegal, concerted purchases by other friends (the "fan club" as it was called) of several hundred millions of dollars of stock against which Guinness would offer an under-the-table indemnification against losses. Among other investors, Seelig induced Wall Street arbitrageur Ivan Boesky to invest more than $140 million in Guinness stock and to short Argyll.

Meanwhile, Morgan Grenfell was embarrassed by the arrest of its chief securities trader, Geoffrey Collier, for insider trading within weeks of the new post–Big Bang trading rules taking effect. Collier had been hired from another firm and kept a trading account there, which he used for illegal trades after Big Bang began. The other firm discovered the trades and turned Collier in. The U.K. Department of Trade and Industry (DTI) is the enforcement body for securities violations. It maintains a reciprocal arrangement for the exchange of insider trading information with the SEC, and accordingly passed the Collier information on. Soon it received some information in return—Ivan Boesky had admitted involvement in the Guinness price-rigging scheme. The DTI immediately raided the offices of Guinness and Morgan Grenfell, and the scandal was soon out. Saunders, Seelig, and several others were arrested. The Bank of England believed that Morgan Grenfell's senior management had been lax and forced the resignation of Christopher Reeves and Graham Walsh. Magan and others from the merger squads resigned and went to work elsewhere. Sir Peter Carey, a former civil servant, was appointed chairman, and he began a search for a new chief executive from outside the firm. Saunders was later sentenced to five years in jail, and at the end of 1991, Seelig's trial (in which Seelig, now broke, was defending himself) was still in progress. In early 1992, the judge in Seelig's case dismissed charges against him, on the grounds that having become a nervous wreck, Seelig was no longer capable of defending himself properly.

The Big Bang was rough on marginal securities firms; what profits were to be made had to come from trading in large blocks and the introduction of innovative new products and investment ideas. The weaker firms were ill equipped for this and Morgan's new broker-dealer, discouraged by Collier's abuses and lacking talent and resources, sank quickly into losses from which it was not to recover. The difficulties of such firms were only exacerbated by the market crash of October 1987.

Peter Carey recruited John Craven, a well-respected City veteran (formerly of Warburg and Credit Suisse White Weld, which became Credit Suisse First Boston in 1978), to become chief executive in April 1987. Craven knew that the powerful and successful U.K. merchant banks of the future would have to be able to compete successfully with the large American investment banks, which had fully integrated corporate finance and securities brokering and were dealing on a global basis. He also knew that Morgan Grenfell was unable to aspire to be a powerful and successful integrated U.K. merchant bank. The Guinness scandal had required that the aggressive group of "entrepreneurs" doing mergers at the firm be disbanded; and in any event, U.K. M&A dropped off very sharply after the October 1987 crash. Morgan's principal profit source, though still functioning, was reduced to a fraction of what it had been. The firm was forced to face reality after the arrest of Collier and the discovery that the two weak acquisitions it had made could not compete successfully. The securities businesses were hemorrhaging, and something had to be done: the government securities dealership was closed, and Morgan's involvement in the now highly competitive Eurobond market was abandoned. Equities, however, were retained in the hope that Morgan might find a better broker to buy. After the 1987 crash, that hope too was abandoned, and equities were closed out the following year. Morgan Grenfell, once the mightiest of merchant banks, was now entirely out of the securities business, able only to offer specialized corporate advisory services and investment management. Now it too was just a niche player.

But at least it was a successful niche player. Under Craven, the firm was stripped down to its essentials, and with new and younger people having replaced senior management, Morgan's profits recovered. In 1989, Craven's success attracted the attention of Banque Indosuez, which made an offer. Craven parried, rejecting the offer but agreed to talk. Meanwhile the Deutsche Bank, already a 5% friendly shareholder in Morgan, was drawn in, and finally bid nearly $1.5 billion for the firm (approximately twice book value). The bid was quickly accepted. Craven became the first non-German member of the management board of the Deutsche Bank; the firm continues to conduct its business in London with a high level of autonomy and functions as Deutsche's global merger and acquisition specialists.

The lessons here are these: when old management goes to sleep or rests on its laurels, it is bound to be displaced from within (if not from without), but the new folks need to be protected from believing too much in their own early success, or they might bankrupt the firm. The Morgan Grenfell case is analogous to that of Drexel Burnham, except that it didn't get into quite as much trouble. But the damages incurred under the bully boys were such that Morgan was unable to regain the high ground in London and to emerge as one of the few integrated and independent firms. Happily, however, it was still worth quite a lot to the Deutsche Bank.

A Sweet, Then Sour Joint Venture

In the early days of the Eurobond market, Swiss banks were prohibited by Swiss regulations from participating directly as underwriters. But as most of the Eurobonds being offered, especially those issued by large, blue-chip American companies, were sold to foreign and domestic clients of the banks, they were important players in the Euromarket. They would purchase the bonds at the price at which the issuing companies sold them to underwriters, usually a discount of 2% to 2.5%, and then place them in their customers' accounts at the official offering price of 100%. Although institutional investors usually managed to buy the deals from other underwriters at a much lower price, one that represented a sharing of the large underwriting discount with large "wholesale" customers, the Swiss banks were not required to share; they could pocket the whole thing. Their clients didn't mind, as they had no other source of bearer bonds in top-quality companies and they were not about to move their funds to a country with less bank secrecy protection.

For many years Credit Suisse had enjoyed close relations with White Weld & Co., a prominent U.S. investment banker active in bringing underwritings to the Euromarket. In 1974, it created a joint venture with White Weld, called Credit Suisse White Weld (CSWW), to specialize in the underwriting of Eurobonds and the placing of these bonds in Switzerland. The venture came to be headed by John Craven (the same man later called in to rescue Morgan Grenfell). Though other American firms were active in the Eurobond market at the time, none had such direct access to the gnomes of Zurich who managed the large portfolios there. The joint venture prospered and expanded into other areas, and it was largely left alone by its parents.

One of the parents, however, was doing poorly in the tough market environment in New York that followed Mayday (negotiated commissions) in 1975. Its success in Eurobonds was not sufficient to save White Weld from intense competition in domestic investment banking in the United States. The firm nearly went bust and had to be absorbed by Merrill Lynch. Credit Suisse thought Merrill was too big and bulky to share the delicate relationship of its joint venture, and arranged to buy back the White Weld interest in CSWW in July 1978 and to resell it to First Boston. This transaction was complex because First Boston was at the time in serious trouble itself and badly needed a capital infusion. Credit Suisse decided to have the joint venture, now renamed Credit Suisse First Boston (CSFB), acquire a 40% interest in First Boston; First Boston would in turn take over the approximately 40% interest in CSFB that previously had been White Weld's. Craven opposed the First Boston arrangement, arguing both that the firm was financially weak and that it would be difficult to control. He was prophetic, but ignored. Craven then resigned, and Michael von Clemm, who had promoted First Boston as a replacement for White Weld, became chief executive of CSFB.

No doubt the main decision maker in the selection of First Boston was Rainer Gut, the new chief executive of Credit Suisse. He had taken over after a major Swiss banking scandal (the "Chiasso affair") required the resignation of his predecessor and the selection of somebody completely untainted by the turmoil in Credit Suisse's domestic operations at the time. Before returning to Switzerland to join Credit Suisse, Gut had been a senior executive of the New York investment bank, Lazard Frères, and he was therefore considered very cosmopolitan and very much oriented to the securities markets.

Once it was set up, Gut was willing to let CSFB run itself, with occasional help on a deal here and there. CSFB went on to enjoy a run of many years as the top Eurobond new issues house. It was bold and creative—but also brassy, disorganized, and often riven with internal strive. It fought often with First Boston over the division of fees, turf, and credit for deals done. In 1982, Jack Hennessey, a senior First Boston official, was sent from New York to try to manage the place. It was full of prima donnas, and Hennessey's task was not easy, but he held it together during the next several years of high visibility and profitability.

Meanwhile, First Boston, a prestigious investment bank organized after the passage of the Glass-Steagall Act in 1933, had discovered a money lode—mergers and acquisitions. It had become a market leader in the field a short time after the appointment of Bruce Wasserstein and Joseph Perrella as department co-heads. They were aggressive, innovative, tough, and in great demand, especially by the New Men of the American merger boom of the 1980s. They became the superstars of the mergers game, and soon their department accounted for the largest segment of First Boston's income. Like the bully boys of Morgan Grenfell, they wanted more power at the firm than they had, and they wanted more of the firm's capital to be made available to invest in the (at that time) highly profitable bridge loans that financed hostile takeover deals. First Boston's chairman Peter Buchanan, an old-fashioned syndicate man, demurred but promised a firmwide review of the issue. The review was held and in late 1987 Buchanan told Wasserstein and Perrella that the firm intended to spread its capital, as it had before, among all of its divisions, even though some areas like trading had recently lost substantial amounts of money and clearly were having problems. First Boston had to be a full-line firm, he said.

Wasserstein and Perrella objected to this conclusion, and quit to form their own firm, which quickly became very successful in attracting merger deals that might have otherwise gone to First Boston. Fearing that it might lose important business and clients if the merger market sensed it had lost its competitive capability, First Boston pulled out all the stops to demonstrate that it was still a powerful and aggressive firm. The firm substantially increased its inventory of high-risk bridge loans and junk bonds that it floated to fund out the bridge loans.

The relationship between First Boston and CSFB, however, was deteriorating rapidly: the high profits of the earlier years, when merger fees were dominant, seemed to be fading away; trading results were not improving; Buchanan seemed to be losing control of First Boston, as evidenced by Wasserstein and Perrella's departure; and First Boston was unwilling to listen to criticism or advice from CSFB, which it regarded more as a subsidiary than as the firm's largest stockholder.

The stresses and difficulties of the existing ownership structure were too great to bear. It had to be changed, and after lengthy reviews in New York and Zurich, it was. Late in 1988, Credit Suisse restructured its holding in CSFB, and CSFB's in First Boston, to effectively take control of both firms. A new holding company, CS First Boston, was formed to own 100% of First Boston (which would go private as a result), CSFB, and a new company called CS First Boston Pacific. The ownership arrangements were complex—Credit Suisse held 44.5% (the maximum the U.S. Federal Reserve would allow at the time), Suliman S. Olayan, a wealthy Arab who was to be a "temporary investor" until an appropriate partner from the Far East could be found, held 31%, and management of the respective operating companies owned the rest.

Buchanan left and Hennessey replaced him as chief executive of CS First Boston. Hennessey then began a fruitless search for a large Japanese shareholder to replace Olayan. Archibald Cox, Jr., (son of the Watergate prosecutor) was brought out of retirement to head First Boston Corporation under Hennessey, who would concentrate on leading the whole group. Cox had been Morgan Stanley's top man in Europe for a decade and knew Hennessey and the Credit Suisse executives well. His mission was to deal with First Boston's problems in the trading areas and its considerable exposure to bridge loans.

By the end of 1989, after the ill-fated United Air Lines attempted LBO signaled the end of the junk-bond-financed LBO period, First Boston was left holding more than $1.2 billion in bridge loans for deeply troubled LBOs. The market for junk bonds and similar paper had dropped like a stone. First Boston, which would not follow the Wasserstein-Perrella strategy when its authors were employees of the firm, but which had done so after they left, now found out that the firm's original reluctance was justified after all.

In November 1990, First Boston announced that Credit Suisse would pump $300 million in additional equity into CS First Boston, and purchase more than $400 million in troubled loans from First Boston, which would record losses for the year of about $500 million. To assist the rescue, the Federal Reserve agreed to allow Credit Suisse to increase its ownership in CS First Boston from 44.5% to about 60%, giving the Swiss absolute control over the firm.

Shortly afterward, Credit Suisse announced that its earnings for 1990 would be lower by about a third, and that it would undertake to raise new capital. In January 1992, Moody's downgraded Credit Suisse's long-term bond ratings from Aaa to Aa-1.

The most important lesson in the story is that the ultimate owners of joint ventures have to be able to exert control over their creations. Credit Suisse had controlling power over CSFB, which it exercised rarely, but nonetheless used to keep CSFB in line when it needed to. It knew very well that CSFB could not be governed as a Swiss bureaucratic institution but had to be free to be creative, excitable, and sometimes embarrassing. Yet by retaining the power to appoint CSFB's chief executives, and controlling how much capital CSFB could have and how it was used, it was able to retain the power it needed over the venture. However, the structure of the venture was peculiar: CSFB, though owned by Credit Suisse and First Boston, itself owned a large minority position in First Boston. In theory, Credit Suisse could exert its influence on First Boston through CSFB, but First Boston was a lot bigger, more aggressive, and more profitable than CSFB. First Boston was thus unwilling to take orders from CSFB, a fact that CSFB and Credit Suisse often resented. Under this type of structure, any kind of satisfactory fee-sharing agreement would be difficult, and the exercising of a restraining influence (when it was needed) would be impossible.

Craven had been right in fearing First Boston's unwillingness to be controlled by a foreign partner, regardless of the structure through which the controlling interest was held. American investment banks are risk takers by nature; they are more volatile and accident-prone than any banks in Switzerland or London. When governed by the star system, the firms glorify and overreward their most talented employees, who threaten to leave the firm unless they are allowed to do as they wish. Such practices do not leave much room for effective long-term managerial actions.

It is difficult for firms like Credit Suisse to know how to handle such people in a way that is acceptable to traditional banking colleagues. It is especially difficult when the matter is a crucial one, carrying all of the bank's strategic aspirations for business outside of its home country.

Still, Credit Suisse had been involved in the CSWW venture since 1974, and with CSFB since 1978. It had plenty of time to study the American investment banking culture and to recognize that it could not continue to be a controlling shareholder in a large U.S. and a large U.K. investment bank without adapting its own culture to conform to the new, highly competitive investment-banking style of management and operation. Having only a few senior executives in the entire organization who understood this new style was not enough to involve Credit Suisse in a meaningful way in the affairs and activities of its affiliates. Its failure to adapt cost the firm its ability to exercise control in a way that would be beneficial to the venture and to the parent equally.

An Arrow to the Heart

In February 1991, the chairman of National Westminster Bank, Lord Alexander, announced at a press conference that he had lost patience with the lousy operating results of the bank's investment banking subsidiary, County NatWest, and if the unit didn't get its act together within the next two years, he would close it down. This kind of tough talk was very new to the City of London, and the statement got everyone's attention, including Howard MacDonald's. MacDonald, a crusty Scot with no banking experience, had joined County NatWest from Dome Petroleum in Canada (where he had been chief executive) and had been charged to help turn the firm around. MacDonald didn't like to read such things in the papers; he was doing his best, but his biggest problem, he told everyone he saw, was dealing every day with the small-minded "High Street bank manager" mentality that impregnated NatWest.

But Alexander could afford to talk tough. He had been brought in to clean up NatWest in the aftermath of one of the most painful scandals in the long history of the City of London, the "Blue Arrow affair." The event had cost the bank the premature resignation of its chairman, Lord Boardman, the resignation of several top-ranking officers, and many embarrassing days in court for its current chief executive officer, Thomas Frost.

Blue Arrow was the name of an aggressive employment agency that was a County NatWest client. In early 1987, it decided to make a $1.3 billion hostile raid on an American competitor, MAI, Inc., a company much larger than Blue Arrow. The offer was successful because Blue Arrow offered a very high price in cash for MAI—the money was to come from a $1.4 billion stock issue to be placed by County NatWest. The issue was the largest stock offering of its type ever done, and it reflected a very large ratio of new money to pre-offering capitalization. The issue, amazingly, appeared to go well and seemed to be a coup for County NatWest, at the time a second-rate investment bank trying hard to make itself first-rate.

The trouble was, the market wasn't as dumb as it seemed. Only about 50% of the stock offering was actually taken up by investors—the rest was left with the underwriters. To support the issue, County NatWest bought stock itself, in the end owning 9.5% of the company, a fact it did not report as it was required by law to do. The Blue Arrow stock price, already sagging as a result of the unsold shares, was flattened by the market crash of October 19, 1987. By the end of the year, County NatWest had to report a loss of $80 million on its Blue Arrow position and another $150 million of other losses, generally trading losses attributable to the crash. NatWest in turn had to report its profits off by 30% for the year due to these losses and additions to loan loss reserves.[16]

The debacle led to further investigations, and it was revealed that County NatWest's parent was involved in the finagling and financing of the Blue Arrow shares; so was Blue Arrow's broker, Phillips & Drew, and its parent, Union Bank of Switzerland. County NatWest's chairman and its chief executive both left the bank early in 1988, but their departures did not contain the scandal. Various resignations and criminal indictments followed (the cases came to trial late in 1991, and the defendants were found guilty and were given suspended sentences in February 1992). The trial had raised additional questions about NatWest's CEO, Tom Frost, and he too resigned in March 1992.

Meanwhile, County NatWest, which had missed out on the attractive acquisitions of brokers during the pre–Big Bang period, saw an opportunity to recover ground when a first-rate broker, Wood Mackenzie, came on the market. Wood Mackenzie originally had been acquired by Hill Samuel, which in turn became engaged in merger talks with Union Bank of Switzerland. These talks were unsuccessful, but ultimately they resulted in the sale of Hill Samuel to Trustee Savings Bank, a large U.K. financial institution that had no knowledge of the City and wanted to acquire some. TSB, however, did not want Wood Mackenzie, so it was offered to County NatWest, which jumped at the opportunity. This event occurred about the time the Blue Arrow affair was made public.

Wood Mackenzie was an up-and-coming research-oriented broker originally from Edinburgh, which had been run for many years by a strong-minded, self-confident, fast-talking character named John Chiene. This deal was not Chiene's choice—he had already sold his shares when the firm was acquired by Hill Samuel. Chiene was not happy reporting to someone else, especially someone who knew little of the brokering business. This problem was aggravated by the dreadful market conditions that followed the crash of October 1987. He and Howard MacDonald did not last long together.

The trading and brokerage businesses were losing money in buckets in 1988 and 1989. County NatWest withdrew from some of the toughest sectors, the U.K. and the U.S. government securities markets, and settled in to make the most of things under difficult circumstances. In 1990, it lost $95 million more, its fifth consecutive year of losses, prompting Lord Alexander's remarks.

MacDonald was then in his mid-sixties and looking for a successor. His was a job that few experienced City people wanted, so he looked outside the usual circle and found John Drury, an Australian former oil trader with no experience in corporate finance. Drury was told to cut costs and get the brokerage business running right again. Then came Alexander's intemperate remark, and MacDonald was soon gone. Drury replaced him as chief executive, but NatWest installed Sir Geoffrey Littler, a former senior civil servant at the Treasury with no banking or securities experience, as chairman. Under Littler and Drury, County NatWest has turned around. Through the end of 1991 it was operating in the black, though barely so, with an increased share of the brokerage market and a revamped corporate finance marketing effort in place. "Winning business," however, said *The Economist*, "would be easier in partnership with National Westminster."

None of the four large clearing banks found the transition into the securities business to be easy. The one with the greatest success, Barclays Bank, quickly realized it needed an experienced hand at the tiller, a helmsman that top management of the bank could rely on, cooperate with, and take advice from. For this job, it hired away the top securities markets man at Kleinwort Benson, Sir Martin Jacomb, a soft-spoken, urbane former barrister who was well respected in the City. Jacomb was the principal architect of Barclays de Zoute Wedd, an amalgam of the Barclays pre-Bang investment bank, a top broker, and one of the top two jobbers. BZW has certainly had its profit problems and other troubles, but it has held together and emerged five years after Big Bang as perhaps second only to Warburg in British investment banking.

At the time of Big Bang, NatWest was slightly bigger and more profitable than Barclays. It was the leading clearing bank in a country in which the top four clearing banks controlled over half the entire banking market. Before becoming governor of the Bank of England, Robin Leigh-Pemberton was NatWest's chairman. The bank was strong, very profitable, influential, and almost totally focused on traditional forms of branch banking, at which it was very good. It was a cautious wholesale lender, which made the usual mistakes but not to the same extent as other U.S. and U.K. banks. It did not understand or enjoy investment banking, and it left this activity to the County NatWest minor leaguers to look after. The bank did not understand the importance of the events that would substantially free up securities markets in Britain, and ultimately in all of Europe—markets that would become the preferred financings ground of all of the bank's major wholesale customers. Accordingly, its preparation for Big Bang was minimal; it only got into the securities business seriously when Wood Mackenzie came on the market unexpectedly. Even then, and after the Blue Arrow affair, NatWest didn't know what to do with County NatWest. It made no effort to take the distressed and floundering firm inside the NatWest organization so their respective problems could be worked out. It never looked for or found a Martin Jacomb or a John Craven to lead County NatWest, nor ever managed to sort out the tangled mess that represents the organizational interface between investment banking and wholesale lending activities. Five years after Big Bang, none of these problems have been resolved. Until they are, it appears doubtful that NatWest's own future as a major player in the European and global banking environments of the 1990s can be assured. Even Lord Alexander now says that "leading banks must have an investment banking arm."[17] But the arm, to be useful at all, must be firmly attached to the rest of the body.

The markets for financial services in Europe are in the midst of change so profound that it will inevitably alter the entire industry. The most important of these changes is economic. The policy decisions that have released these forces are irreversible, at least over the next decade or so. Europe has struggled to make these policy changes—to move economic policy toward the free market and away from government controls—in order to improve its economic growth and increase prosperity. The appeal of the free market has been so great that it has led nearly 400 million people living in Eastern Europe and the former Soviet Union to abandon their own system in the hope of participating in the economic benefits of the new Europe.

The free-market approach in banking, already crystallized in the 1992 banking directive, will introduce increasingly harsh competitive conditions into Europe. Banks there will encounter many of the problems that have plagued banks and S&Ls in the United States. The issues facing them include disintermediation, securitization, the decreasing importance of branch banking, the requirements for new technology-based banking products, the flight of wholesale banking customers to the capital markets, the need to increase capital exposures to the securities markets in trading positions, and the need to integrate capital market activities around the world in order to produce the best rates for one's clients. At the same time European banks will see a deterioration in the client-bank relationship. Large companies with plentiful opportunities will be less inclined to cling to hausbank relationships, and even loyal depositors will use money market funds to an increasing degree.

Market forces linked to these changing conditions have already caused the introduction of low-cost commercial paper in Britain and Germany. Securities markets in general are in much greater use than they were a few years ago. Stock markets in Europe (despite sagging prices in 1992) are active as they have never been before, encouraging greater amounts of merger and acquisition activity, privatizations, and initial public offerings. Foreign bankers and investment bankers have set up aggressive marketing programs to reach areas of the European heartland that have never seen such possibilities before. The quandary facing European universal bankers recalls the old song about returning American G.I.s after World War I: "How do you keep 'em down on the farm, once they've seen Paree?"

The draining of business away from the banks cannot be ignored—otherwise the banks will just melt away. In the effort to replace it they may follow the course of commercial banks and S&Ls in the United States, i.e., if you can't lend more to your old customers, find new ones to lend to. The trouble is, the clients that want to borrow from the banks are the ones that can't borrow from the markets. A powerful need to replace the run-off can stampede banks into lesser-quality loans and an inevitable encounter with loan losses and increased provisions. Once banks are caught in this downward spiralling path of lost business, reduced margins, good loans having to be replaced with bad ones, subsequent loan losses, and further profit erosion, their capital adequacy comes under pressure. All of these things happened to large American banks during the 1980s, includ-ing eight banks that had triple-A ratings at the beginning of the period.

The European tradition of universal banking has worn well; of the tiny handful of banks in the world today that still retain triple-A ratings, almost all are universals. But these banks, with their large market share, may have the most to lose as the floodwaters of increased competition and disinter-mediation rise and carry away their clients. To respond to the challenge, especially from new rivals offering securities market products, the big uni-versals must change. They are not organizations that are well adapted to change.

Few organizations are naturally equipped to adjust to so many important changes at once. Most of the banking industry in Europe, whether built on the German, Swiss, French, or British models, is solid, slow-moving, and bureaucratic, with little knowledge of the new and different lines of busi-ness they are now required to perform. Most do not have skills and ser-vices that export well. Most also fear acquisitions, judging them either impossible to manage themselves, or too risky to leave in the hands of the acquired managers. Yet those that adapt to the new environment promptly, as Warburg did in Britain before Big Bang, are the ones that will be the most successful.

These changes will force many European banks (like those in the United States) to look at banking as a collection of specialized activities, from which they may have to select those things that they are best able to com-pete at. Banks in Europe also have the option of participating in insurance and investment management businesses, but these too are changing rap-idly as the powerful forces of competition are allowed to enter the market-place. There are no safe and easy businesses left. Banking, whatever else it is, is no longer dull.

PART III

JAPAN COMES BACK TO EARTH

As the 1990s began, Japan was recovering from one of the world's greatest speculative episodes, a decade of exceptionally easy money when prices of financial assets skyrocketed. The upward journey had been dizzying. Japan had broken into the small club of financial superpowers, a wonderful soul-filling redemption for those many Japanese who had worked so hard in the great postwar economic recovery.

It felt good to receive the recognition that was due, many Japanese thought, but at the same time it was uncomfortable. International relations, long of great importance to the country, were filled with unending conflict and disagreement over economic issues. These tensions were spilling over into the world political arena, where inflammatory antiforeign commentary had become commonplace, and this made many conservative Japanese uneasy.

"These foreigners," many Japanese thought, "are always complaining, always telling us that we do not compete fairly, that we have to change to accommodate them. We know this is not so; our success is a result of our hard work and competitiveness. They do not work as hard as we do, nor do they try hard to sell products in Japan. Their criticisms are unfair, and do not reflect an understanding of our situation at all. It is time for us to resist their criticism and insults. We have been successful in our economic endeavors, and they should respect us. But instead, it's complain, complain, complain. . . . This is no way to treat an economic superpower!"

Politicians and the media, of course, have fanned the flames, urging the Japanese to stand up against pressure and intimidation by foreigners, especially by the United States. Polls asking Japanese what they thought of Americans showed that increasing numbers of Japanese were disdainful of them.

Deeper anxieties were involved, however. Japanese were irritated at the way Washington pushed them around on economic issues; it seemed that

217

U.S. officials never restrained the urge to tell their Japanese political coun-terparts in public how to manage their domestic affairs, yet refused to acknowledge any criticisms of their country. Still, all Japanese knew that the relationship with the United States, though perhaps not as important and beneficial to them as in the past, was still one on which they were dependent and could not easily change. Many Japanese found this situa-tion a bit humbling, but most preferred it to any practicable alternative.

Not having any other major responsibilities, Japan has become what the Japanese themselves call a nation of "economic animals," who have no other duties in the world except to concentrate on their own economic development. This condition unavoidably attracts criticism from the United States and European governments when they think the animals are too aggressive or hard to handle. It also means that the United States, and everyone else, ignores the Japanese when crucial decisions affecting the world as a whole are made.

However pragmatic this trade-off may have been at the beginning of the postwar period, it now irritates the Japanese to be taken for granted—to have economic power but no strategic influence. They were upset over the nonrole of Japan in the Persian Gulf crisis of 1990–1991, during which a prominent Japanese journalist, Yoichi Funabashi, noted in *Foreign Affairs* that "an economic superpower found itself merely an automated teller machine—one that needed a kick before dispensing the cash." Japanese were angered and humiliated by the criticism they received for being slow to come up with their $13 billion contribution to the war effort—an amount that was simply expected, not appreciated—and the ridicule that sur-rounded their sending a few minesweepers to Kuwait to help out after the war was over.

Equally, Japan has been a nonplayer in the many international deliber-ations on the collapse and rebuilding of the former Soviet Union and its satellites. The most important worldwide economic undertaking of the twenty-first century will take place, many Japanese think, without Japan having any part to play except to be shaken down by everyone for financial contributions. Just like economic animals, not like a superpower.

"The post-war Japanese way of life seems to have reached a dead end," wrote Kazuo Ogura, a Japanese Foreign Ministry official, in the *New York Times* on the occasion of the fiftieth anniversary of Pearl Harbor. He went on:

> We are plunging into an era in which the esteem of the international community cannot be won by holding aloft our war-renouncing con-stitution, accommodating international demands and internationaliz-ing the economy. Efforts in such areas served to give us our present peace and prosperity, but now they are inadequate.

What the new era will offer instead is not at all clear. Ogura suggests:

> What prevents Japan from developing a stronger political voice is the absence of a clear vision of what ideals the Japanese as a people want to uphold.

He added that having seen the collapse of a fanatical "code of previously held ethics, the Japanese have shied away from projecting their beliefs and ideals internationally," and indeed, "even now, they still appear to be apprehensive of even expressing one."

This viewpoint leaves us wondering whether the Japanese aren't actually facing a new dilemma. On one hand, they can continue along the postwar road to increased international integration, little by little dismantling traditional Japanese ways. This road leads to greater political and economic responsibility and involves carrying the full burdens of a superpower; it also leads to greater growth and prosperity, as Japan quietly adjusts to a world of increased trading and financial reciprocity. To travel this road, however, requires them to pay the price of foregoing some of their Japanese identity. This is something not many Japanese over the age of forty—those running the country today—are happy about. How the next generation will feel about this issue is not yet clear, though as a result of education and exposure, they ought to be more relaxed about it.

The other road the country might take requires a Japan-first attitude and little more in the way of international accommodation than absolutely has to be provided. This is the road of the proud samurai, which many Japanese can relate to, and it would mean using Japan's economic resources mainly to ensure Japan's interests in the world. This road, however, is really the road of the economic animals. It inevitably leads to the end of Japan's role as a superpower, as well as to isolation and international sanctions and reprisals. It would be a repetition of the mistaken ideology of the thirties in economic form.

In any case, it's too late to take the latter road. Japanese citizens have enjoyed too much prosperity and freedom to revert to the old ways. In fact, Japanese complain that too many of the old ways still remain, and their prosperity and freedom now are not what they should be. Prices are outrageous, especially for land and real estate, as well as for rice and ordinary consumer goods. Too much of their hard-earned pay is dissipated by high prices; it still takes forever to be able to save up to buy a house. And when they can buy one, it is tiny and located nearly two hours away from where they work. "If we're so rich," many Japanese ask, "why do we live so poorly?"

Also, the stock market, a source of easy money for most Japanese white-collar workers for the past two decades, inexplicably plunged more than

40% in early 1990, and continued to fall over the whole of the next year. With the plunge (as in the case of the 1929 crash in the United States) came scandals: politicians on the take, large investors getting reimbursed for their market losses from commissions charged to ordinary investors, banks and brokers lending to mobsters so they could speculate in the stock market. Things were falling apart in Japan, many thought, because the economic animals were in control, and no one would, or could, do anything about it. Prime Minister Toshiki Kaifu claimed to be trying, and for his troubles he was yanked from his job by the invisible political puppet-masters of the Liberal Democratic Party. His successor Kiichi Miyazawa seems to have been set out with equally short strings.

The 1990s began as restless and uneasy times in Japan, one of the world's richest and most envied countries—the "miracle economy" of the 1960s and 1970s, and a certified economic superpower in the 1980s. It was now a country, however, about which many new questions were being asked by Japanese and non-Japanese alike: Can Japan keep it up? Is the country really an economic superpower, or is it just a place where they specialize in manufacturing, have a lot of corruption, and recently experienced a great speculative boom? Without enormous capital surpluses, which now seem to have dried up, how can the Japanese maintain their seemingly dominant position in the world of finance? How long are the Japanese themselves going to put up with the economic animals? And when will the general public finally revolt against high prices and rigged markets?

In the 1990s, Japan will have little choice but to fit itself into the world economy so that it is not (to use a Japanese expression) always "the nail that sticks up, and gets hit." It will have to make adjustments to accommodate foreign requirements that it integrate its economy further into the economies of North America and the new Europe on a cooperative and nonthreatening basis. Most of these adjustments will be inside Japan, where reforms of agricultural, distribution, and contracting practices will open the doors to the fresher air of free-market economics. Otherwise Japan will almost certainly be exposed to exclusion and harassment, which will cause it to fall behind the other regions in economic growth and world influence.

Much of this adaptation and integration will have to occur in the financial field, where there are many dissimilarities and misalignments with the United States and Europe following a decade of extensive market integration and financial deregulation in those regions. In fact Japan has already begun this adaptation. As the differences with the United States and Europe have narrowed, Japanese financial institutions have lost some of their comparative advantages of the past few years, such as having regulatory protection, high assured profits, and large amounts of low-cost capital to throw around. The more convergence there is with the highly competitive, free financial markets in the West, the greater the competitive pressures on the Japanese banks and securities firms.

Meeting these competitive pressures will be a great challenge, but it is one that most Japan-watchers believe the Japanese will be able to manage. Rising to the challenge will involve huge changes in the financial services industry, and the reward will not be financial dominance, but merely a respected place on the level playing field. This reward may seem small in relation to the effort required, but it is unquestionably greater than what Japan would receive if it took the isolationist road.

7
THE RISING OF THE SUN

The war in the Pacific ended on September 2, 1945, with the signing of the peace treaty on board the *USS Missouri* in Tokyo Bay. The Emperor had broadcast his surrender message to his stunned but submissive subjects a few weeks before; in it he noted that despite their best efforts, the "war situation has developed not necessarily to Japan's advantage."

It most certainly had not. Military casualties numbered 2.3 million, and civilian casualties from intense fire bombing and nuclear attack exceeded 500,000, nearly ten times Britain's civilian losses in the Blitz. More than 3 million homes had been destroyed. There was no foreign trade, no functioning economy at all. One-third of Japan's productive capacity had been destroyed. More than one-fourth of the national wealth had been wiped out; this was five times the loss from the great Tokyo earthquake in 1923, and it represented ten years of economic effort. National income per capita had dropped to 58% of the prewar level, which was then only about on a par with Italy, Poland, and the Soviet Union.

The Greater East Asian Co-Prosperity Sphere was no more. Japan had lost all of its overseas possessions and colonies. The size of the nation's territory was suddenly halved. Assets abroad exceeding $20 billion in value were lost or forfeited, and, what was worse, 6.5 million Japanese had to be repatriated from China, Korea, Southeast Asia, and elsewhere. The return of all of these people to a devastated, jobless, foodless Japan—swelling the population by nearly 10% when the country could least afford it—added to everyone's misery. Homelessness, disease, runaway inflation, hoarding, and ruthless black-market profiteering capped it.[1]

EMPIRE ECONOMICS

Yet the Japanese, emerging less than a hundred years before from their misty, isolated islands in the Pacific into vigorous trade with the West, had many friends initially. Forced to conclude a treaty of trade and friendship with the United States by the menace of the Black Ships of Commodore Perry in 1854, Japan went on to sign similar treaties with Britain and France. In 1868, under the pressure of change from such dramatic events, samurai from the western part of Japan overthrew the nobles who had ruled the country on behalf of the Emperor for 250 years. The new leaders restored the authority of the Emperor Meiji and proceeded to modernize Japan as fast as possible.

Prewar Imports

The ensuing transformation of Japanese society and the Japanese economy was possible only because of the assistance the new nation received from the principal powers of the day, particularly Britain, France, and Germany.

The samurai spirit was irrepressible. The Japanese believed that they were capable of anything the Europeans were, especially in Asia. If the Europeans were allowed to have colonies in China, for example, why shouldn't the Japanese, who had great need of the natural resources, be entitled to similar arrangements? War with China in 1894–1895 was perhaps inevitable in Japanese eyes. The Europeans didn't mind too much. Britain furnished Japan with warships, and Germany helped train her army in modern fighting methods. Skirmishes with Russia over Chinese territory around Port Arthur led to the Russo-Japanese War of 1904–1905, which ended in a clear victory for the Japanese, the first major defeat of a European power by an Asian nation.

The Japanese also received advice on how to organize their economy from the foreigners. The original Japanese banking system set up by the Meiji government in 1872 was modeled, unwisely, after the American system of that period, in which there was no central bank. This system failed to do the job for which it was intended; the Japanese, unlike their role models, realized its flaws and quickly changed to a different system. A new law was passed in 1882 providing for a strong Ministry of Finance and a central bank, the Bank of Japan, which according to its own history,

> was of epochal importance not only in the consolidation of the currency and banking system, and the establishment of a credit system, but also in laying the foundation for the modernization of the Japanese economy and the growth of modern industries.[2]

One of the overlooked secrets of Japan's extraordinarily rapid rise from an isolated, feudal society to one of great economic power lies in the early establishment of a strong, centralized banking and credit system that from the start was used as a potent instrument of national policy. The original encouragement of savings (from a low base), the marshaling of these funds for economic expansion, the arrangement of foreign credits, and the ruthless allocation of capital to areas of greatest need were among the vital achievements of the Meiji financial system.

Perhaps one of the many Japanese student-visitors who flooded the capitals of Europe in the late 1800s in search of the best features of foreign societies to bring back home picked up a copy of *Lombard Street*, Walter Bagehot's little book on the English capital markets of the 1870s. If so, only a substantially edited version would have been allowed off the boat. The Japanese could surely appreciate the need for a staging yard for capital, certainly a scarce resource in their country. But they had no capacity for adopting the free-market activities that such a capital market required. They adopted the aspects of Western economic theory they needed and could relate to, but free-market thinking would have to wait another hundred years or so, until Japan's rigid and authoritarian society would, at last, be ready for it.

The Russo-Japanese War left huge debts to be repaid. Some of these had been borrowed quite easily through large bond issues in New York and London. Accordingly, Japan went through a period of balance of payments deficits and adopted a tight monetary policy at home to correct them. When World War I came in 1914, Japan received an economic windfall. It supplied both sides in the war with material and munitions, and its exports soared. It became a creditor nation briefly, only to experience the great earthquake of 1923, which required additional borrowing from abroad in large amounts.

The Great Depression that began in 1930 was as hard on the Japanese as it was on the industrialized nations. The loss of trade with Europe and the United States was especially damaging. Dangerous levels of unemployment and economic distress induced the country's leaders to look to the resource-rich countries that were Japan's neighbors. In particular, China, a land rich in iron ore and oil and offering large potential markets for Japanese products seemed to be the place for a colony, one fashioned in the European style.

The Manchurian "incident" occurred in 1931, setting loose the militarists who would dominate Japanese politics until the end of World War II. The government issued large amounts of debt to supply the fast-growing need for military equipment, creating high inflation that had to be suppressed by foreign exchange and price controls imposed by the still-powerful Ministry of Finance and the Bank of Japan. The economy straightened out, and by 1935 virtually full employment was achieved. In 1936, an attempted military coup put the entire country on a war footing. In 1941, the Japanese attacked Pearl Harbor and the Pacific War began, to be ended four years later after the dropping of atomic bombs on Hiroshima and Nagasaki. Then the country had to be rebuilt.

Learning to Love Leverage

The rapid recovery of the Japanese industrial and financial system from the devastation, suffering, and demoralization of the war was made possible, as in Germany, by a benign and helpful conqueror, as well as a society of skilled and educated survivors whose motivation for recovery was enormous.

The Japanese case had two additional features: the MacArthur occupation, and the resurrection of Japan's prewar financial system. This system utilized the maximum amount of financial leverage possible in pursuit of its growth and development objectives. No system anywhere else has worked so well or is more deserving of being copied, though at the same time few are more difficult to copy.

The Japanese approach to leverage was as simple in concept as it was difficult to visualize in execution. All money and credit originated in, and was subject to, the meticulous control of the Ministry of Finance. Funds were allocated only to those carefully researched industrial areas that were best able to use them. Banks were the vehicle for distributing the funds. To do this job efficiently, the banks maximized their loans-to-deposits ratio. To guard against mistakes or having "financial accidents," the banks were subject to extremely tight and careful regulation.

Companies relied upon their own relationships with banks, suppliers, agents, and customers to maximize their borrowings, which were, however, approved only if they were for the right purposes. Companies could finance only new facilities and inventories. Nothing was available for unauthorized investments or for speculation. Foreign capital controls were airtight too. The system leaked, of course—as all systems do—but only a little.

In the end, Japan attracted an enormous amount of capital, talent, and other resources from all sorts of domestic and foreign sources, utilizing extraordinary amounts of leverage in doing so. It was able to get away with such high levels of debt exposure, as so many other countries during the same period were not, because of the intricate, finely meshed web of mutually supporting safety nets that its centrally controlled, highly organized society had erected to protect the lives and prospects of its most promising enterprises. The entire nation became a team of organizers, promoters, specialists, and uncomplaining workers, all striving to achieve the common good.

MACARTHUR'S PROCONSULATE

The American occupation of Japan lasted until 1952, and General Douglas MacArthur was its only head. His power over the Japanese was nearly total, and they regarded him as the Emperor's virtual successor.

MacArthur did not dabble in details. He was a Ronald Reagan sort of leader—big on basic concepts, confident in his ability to apply them, inflexible once a decision had been made. His commanding presence, extensive experience in Asia, age and high rank (he had been a general for thirty years), and public reputation made him appear infallible. MacArthur's orders for the occupation from President Truman were very general, including such vague notions as "to remove obstacles to the development of a peaceful democratic society, and foster a free economy adequate for peaceful existence."[3]

MacArthur made several major decisions early. The Emperor would be treated as having been above the fray. He would not be tried as a war criminal or deposed. War criminals would be sought out, however, and a small number (including Prime Minister Hideki Tojo) brought to trial and convicted right away. Japan could have its own government, but it would have to do what it was told. The political left would be suppressed subtly, not allowed to agitate or take over any important elected posts. Japan would be expected to rebuild itself—not much in the way of aid would be offered—but the United States would not obstruct the process. The prewar concentrations of wealth that were inevitably, as in Germany, overwhelmed by and made subservient to the political forces of the day would be broken up.

MacArthur's staff included many administrative experts, scholars, lawyers, and others sent from the Democratic Truman administration. In this group were many who preferred to see Japan reshaped along social democratic lines, but they worked for section heads who were mainly Army generals selected by MacArthur and extremely loyal to him. Nevertheless, there were enough of these "left-leaning civilians" to leave their mark on the occupation.

Before long, the war crimes trials ended and a satisfactory government headed by former foreign minister, Shigeru Yoshida, was put in place. The main issues then facing the occupation were the economic ones related to reconstruction and the breakup of monopolistic control, and the political ones involved with ensuring that the system did not stray from the prescribed right-center path. Before long, however, MacArthur's staff became divided over these issues. The New Dealers strongly favored (and apparently received support in Washington for) land reform, labor unions, and strict antitrust and banking and securities laws. They were hoping to construct a utopia of enlightened government in Japan, modeled closely after Roosevelt-era policies, without regard to whether these policies could be applied in such a dissimilar society as Japan's.

The hard liners, on the other hand, were suspicious of communism in any real or suspected form and preferred to side with the rich and powerful, if sometimes shady, figures who emerged in the postwar political structure.

The Yoshida government, banding together for strength and mutual protection as few governments have done since, "endured the unendurable" with endless backroom compromises and trade-offs, and an inexhaustible capacity to "re-discuss" with their American masters questions that had already been decided. For the second time in a century a new political and economic pattern for modern Japan emerged, again from proceedings that were usually kept secret from both Americans and Japanese.

Fixing the Tickets

Politically, a very effective compromise was worked out. The new constitution forced on the Japanese by MacArthur in 1947 retained the old bicameral parliamentary system, called the Diet (like Bismarck's parliament, on which it was partially modeled). The Japanese system follows the British system in naming the head of the majority political party as prime minister. The majority party at the time was the Liberal Party, which merged with the Democratic Party in 1955 and obscured any ideological differences between the two. As pragmatic centrists, the new Liberal Democratic Party (LDP) embraced all wings of the moderate political spectrum; only radicals were outside.

There are, of course, parties within the great umbrella party, known as factions. The factions independently rally around one influential member, who tries to generate enough political and financial support for his faction members to gain a plurality of seats in the lower house of the Diet. If he can do this, he will have the greatest claim on the party leadership, and thus automatically become prime minister. The powers of the prime minister are such that numerous spoils of office are available to reward and assist supporters down the line. These usually take the form of financial payments and postings. Such rewards attract further support for the faction until, for any of a variety of political reasons, the faction leader has to step down, and other factions have a crack at the top.

Such a system requires substantial financial contributions from supporters in order to function. Therefore there were few restrictions on corporate or individual "gifts" to politicians, sometimes called *cannonballs* by the Japanese press, and the system of competing factions has become increasingly dependent on them.

This dependence on political contributions has meant, among other things, that the interests of the contributors have to be taken into account in the consensus-building process by which Japan is really governed. From the beginning, businessmen were deeply involved in the entire rebuilding process, and their interest in every area of economic policy was extensive. Businessmen's access to high-ranking political figures in Japan has thus been comparatively easy since Yoshida's day.

To keep things working smoothly, the government had to have a means for reconciling the many conflicting interests, particularly economic ones, that such open access always revealed. To aid the ever-skillful politicians, whose meetings and negotiations often took place in Tokyo's ancient geisha houses, the government relied heavily upon its exclusive civil service (also modeled after the British one). The civil service established priorities based on the national interest, to which all were expected to bow. If you wanted money for textiles when textiles were part of the national economic plan, you and other textile men might get some. But if you were asking for something not in the plan, you would hear a familiar sucking in of air over the teeth, and be told it was "very difficult," and to come back later, perhaps with a request in a different area.

The system worked well: capital was allocated where it could best be used, and the process was completely Japanese and familiar to all. Everyone who needed to be taken care of, was. Under such a system, the radicals never had a chance, and indeed until only recently the LDP had continuously controlled an absolute majority of seats in both houses of the Diet.

How much of this was visible to MacArthur's people during the occupation is hard to know. The system, now highly refined and sophisticated, was certainly at its crudest stage before 1952. Still, political money had to be raised, no doubt from those who had money at the time—the black market operators, the gangsters, speculators, and other questionable characters. It must have been clear that the financial support for the Yoshida faction was not coming from millions of housewives and schoolchildren contributing a penny a week. An establishment of increasingly powerful individuals, made up of politicians, old regime officeholders and functionaries, and business leaders became increasingly visible behind the scenes of the party.

Nevertheless, the party had to get people to vote for it. Many Japanese would do so simply because it was moderate, and the conservative, mainstream Japanese had had enough of extremists. The swollen urban population was somewhat untrustworthy—this group, hungry and dissatisfied, would agitate for labor unions and for other rights and social benefits that the government couldn't afford either economically or politically. About 30% of the national population, however, was then rural—farmers mostly. Voting districts were arranged to provide much more leverage for country folks than for city dwellers. As a block, the farmers' support at the polls made the LDP invincible.

MacArthur's land reform program, which passed in 1947, virtually expropriated all farm landholdings of absentee landlords above 2.5 acres, and returned them to the farmers who worked the land. This was an enormous windfall for most of the farmers, many of whom became very rich when land prices in increasingly prosperous Japan soared out of sight. The LDP took credit for the bounty, and blamed the unfortunate confiscation of property from the rich on MacArthur.

Next came subsidies for the rice farmers. In 1945, the government wanted to increase rice production quickly in order to feed the hungry. The farmers were offered good prices by the government, which in turn sold the rice at a lower price in order to make it affordable for the urban masses. The farmers no doubt found this to be a reasonable system, and came to depend upon it. They turned the subsidy into a right with which the LDP was not prepared to interfere. The price of rice is still set annually after a series of negotiations between the government and the growers association. The subsidies (still considerable) have been reduced as the agricultural community has become less important to the LDP and as foreign disapproval of the practice has mounted; but when the party's fortunes suffer, the result is still usually a firming up of rice prices.[4] Nonetheless, foreign pressure, especially from the United States, to reduce rice subsidies and to allow imports is making some headway.

Thus the main elements of the postwar political equilibrium were that the powerful paid and the farmers voted. The system has survived until now without significant change. Despite the LDP's poor showing in the polls in recent years, the Lockheed and Recruit scandals, Takeshita and his two little-known successors, and the mysterious process of selection of the current prime minister, Kiichi Miyazawa, significant reform of the old ways worked out by Yoshida and his colleagues appears unlikely.

Nor is it likely that the general, if here today to comment, would decry his work. Instead, he could point to one of the world's most stable democracies and note with satisfaction that it did not show a trace of communism during the difficult cold war period. Today Japan is a powerful ally, loyal to all the political positions of the United States in Asia and elsewhere, and a fine example of how a democratic, free-market economic system can flourish in Asia.

Fortifying Finance

The Ministry of Finance reorganized the banking system in the late 1940s, and has not changed it much since then. It provided for several different kinds of banks and bank-like institutions, each confined to its own place in the great economic anthill: the giant postal saving system, government-owned development and reconstruction banks (specializing in infrastructure), an export credit bank, agricultural cooperative banks, credit-cooperative banks, trust banks (for holding institutional savings and pension funds), long-term credit banks to finance capital equipment for industry, large urban commercial banks, and, finally, small (mainly rural) commercial banks.

The Ministry of Finance was also responsible for the insurance industry and for securities and commodities markets, both of which had been reasonably active before the war and only needed dusting off. The ministry, however, being responsible for everything financial, had to referee the overlapping interests and secular battles between the various types of financial institutions. Therefore whenever it decided to change someone's mandate, it would do so only after considering the effect such a change would have on the other institutions in the system. In an environment in which access to high officials is easily obtained, and in which a minor regulatory issue of importance only to a few can be rapidly politicized, clashes within the Ministry of Finance were not infrequent, and sometimes could be resolved only by refusing to allow any changes at all. The notion that every bank had a single, rightful place in the system made it hard to alter anything.

MacArthur, however, had imported a New Deal obsession: banks should not participate in the securities business, for fear that conditions similar to those that brought on the Crash of 1929 might be repeated. Banks, given such power, would surely abuse it, and the architects of Japanese reform wanted to use regulation to curtail all potential abuses of power. The Japanese securities industry had been a pygmy in comparison with the banks in the prewar period, though like securities markets in other countries, it had enjoyed a "golden age" from about 1927 through the mid-1930s. Its function, as seen by a Ministry of Finance official, was to draw into the system's net any private wealth or savings that had so far escaped it. In practice, securities firms underwrote corporate bonds and share issues and provided a market for those who wished to speculate in such securities.

In 1947, the occupation authorities insisted on the passage of a securities act, modeled after legislation passed by the Roosevelt administration in 1933 and 1934. A Securities and Exchange Law was passed containing Article 65, which permanently separated banking from securities activities, as had been done in by Glass-Steagall in the United States. At the time no one in Japan had any idea that the securities industry would become so powerful, and that banks would one day lobby hard to be able to enter the business.

By the end of 1947, most of the work of establishing a financial system that could extract the last drop of financial effectiveness out of any money put in to it had been completed. The Americans, however, were nervous about Japan's lack of economic progress so far (it had had virtually no help from the outside) and increasingly anxious about an outbreak of communism in the cities. They had also grown more tolerant of the Japanese, whom the authorities had come to respect, and they decided to come forward with some financial aid. Conditions improved somewhat, but it wasn't until the outbreak of the Korean War in 1950, and the U.S. decision to supply its forces there from Japan, that the recovery well and truly began. By then Japan had most of the elements of its amazing leverage machine in place, and was able to benefit enormously from the recovery.

Creating Keiretsu

Less than five weeks after the Japanese surrender, two Army trucks drove up to the headquarters of Mitsui & Co., Ltd., and removed forty-two large crates filled with securities valued at ¥1.2 billion (about $300 million at prewar exchange rates). Mitsui was one of the big four zaibatsu, or large industrial holding companies, that had dominated industry and finance before the war. It was now to be destroyed.

If the New Dealers on MacArthur's staff had a single most important objective, it was the abolition of the great zaibatsu, which had monopoly powers that made them convenient instruments of any government in power and deterred competition to such an extent that free-market economic conditions could never develop. American experience with the great trusts in the nineteenth century, and their breakup in the early part of the twentieth, was the source of their conviction. If Japan was to be like America (which many earnestly hoped it would be), the zaibatsu would have to go.

Mitsui was indeed powerful; it was probably the world's largest private business, even after the manifold losses caused by the war. Mitsui was a family-held company that had been in business under the same name for 300 years, making it perhaps the world's oldest company. The family, whose holdings in the company in 1945 were estimated to be worth—even then—in excess of $600 million, owned the controlling holding company outright. The holding company in turn controlled twenty large subsidiaries, including a major heavy industry and shipbuilding company, a major chemical company, a major bank, a major trading company, a major insurance company, and other large corporations in all sectors of the economy. All together the twenty subsidiaries controlled an additional 300 companies, branching out all over the Japanese domestic, colonial, and international economies. The enterprise was said to employ about a million workers in Japan and another million outside the country, mainly in China and Korea.

The four biggest of the ten or so zaibatsu (Mitsui, Mitsubishi, Sumitomo, and Yasuda) controlled assets estimated at the end of the war to be $30 billion. Much of this was thought by the occupation authorities to be from excess war profits, government indemnities being paid even after the surrender, and black market profiteering in scarce materials and food hoarded during the war's closing months. Mitsui, the largest zaibatsu, was a special target.[5]

Getting rid of the zaibatsu was a complex task, however, especially for American officials who did not read or speak the language. But Mac-Arthur's people were impatient and told Yoshida that they wanted to speed up the process. Yoshida dealt with the problem in a typical Japanese way. He gathered representatives of the big four together and asked for their ideas; he also talked it over with other politically influential persons (including some who were involved with the zaibatsu before the war or married into their families). He stressed the need for a quick, unanimously acceptable solution that would give the Americans what they asked for, if not necessarily what they wanted.

The first step, accepted by the occupation authorities, was for the government to purchase the holding company shares in each zaibatsu from the families for non-negotiable government bonds. The government would then, over time, divide the companies into acceptable nonmonopolistic units and sell the shares in these companies to the public. This part took some time to work out, during which the occupation administration became impatient again (or perhaps had to answer an urgent inquiry from Washington). Suddenly, in early 1947, the Anti-Monopoly Law was handed down, presented to the Diet, and passed.

This law meant business. Holding companies were outlawed; the zaibatsu were to be divided up immediately—Mitsui into 170 companies—and the shares sold as soon as possible. No more than 100 former zaibatsu employees could work in any of the new companies. The ancient, invaluable zaibatsu trade names could not be used. It looked as if the objectives of the occupation had been achieved in one swift, sharp stroke.

Things don't actually work like that in Japan, however, as the Americans on the scene must have known after two years' experience in "changing things."

Nevertheless, the U.S. reformers ticked the matter off as a job well done, reported the end of the zaibatsu to Washington, and started looking into their own long-awaited, postwar employment opportunities. They took their eyes off the ball; meanwhile the Japanese went along, saying nothing.

When the shares were sold on the market, each zaibatsu made great efforts to keep large concentrations intact within the former zaibatsu circle of companies, institutions, and individuals. Companies bought shares in each other, only a few percent each to be sure, but in aggregate a large amount. (Today, the shares of Mitsui & Co., the trading company which is the most direct successor to the old zaibatsu, are still 30% or 40% owned by other Mitsui Group companies.)

The new companies, as before, arranged for most of their business to be done with each other, compared notes, offered support to other group members, held high-level meetings together, and cooperated as if they were still a unified whole. The restriction on the number of employees able to work for any of the companies was circumvented in various ways. Many were not employees, but "advisers," or "consultants." Children of former employees showed up for work. When the occupation ended, the law was changed to allow mergers and the reuse of the zaibatsu names. By the mid-1950s, the zaibatsu had reconstituted themselves into "groups" with many of the characteristics of their prewar predecessors. These semiformal groupings are today called keiretsu.[6] They include not only the prewar groupings, but also numerous postwar affiliations. Today, they tend to be formed around leading banks, which have continued to encourage cross-shareholding. Indeed, the powerful Industrial Bank of Japan has attracted so many keiretsu affiliations that only about 25% of its shares are free to trade in the market, the rest having been taken up by keiretsu members.

During the 1950s and the 1960s, the former zaibatsu companies were Japan's most powerful commercial organizations, accounting, if anything, for a higher percentage of trade and finance than before the war. They had extensive business backgrounds, experience in acquiring foreign raw materials and in importing technology, association with foreign banks and investors, and comprehensive manufacturing skills all in one village, if not under one roof.

In the prewar years 1931–1936, the Japanese economy had grown at an average of 4.5%; from 1947 through 1971, Japan's annual growth averaged more than 10%.[7] Unlike the prewar economy, the postwar economy was not based on munitions and domestic consumption. It was a direct beneficiary of increased world trade, open markets, and the stable economic conditions of the Pax Americana.

ECONOMIC SOFTWARE

Three features of the system the Japanese devised for maximizing their economic performance after the war stand out today. First, there was total agreement within the country as to the common objective of the national effort: to rebuild the country, to feed and clothe the people, and to erase the shame of defeat through sacrifice and effort so that future generations both in Japan and abroad would respect Japan's present generation.

Looked at in practical terms, this objective meant that all efforts had to be directed at economic growth. There could be no diversions into such worthy, but for the time being inappropriate, goals as improving the quality of life, cleaning up the environment, or achieving equality between different members of the society. Growth was not to mean growth in return on shareholders' investments, though that was not unimportant in the long run, but immediate, short-run growth in the volume of sales and in the quantity of goods produced. Only such growth would produce employment and the opportunity to escape from poverty.

The second distinctive feature of the Japanese recovery was that the institutional foundations necessary to provide the economic growth were already in place. The banking system, tight as a drum, would recycle domestic savings to industry. Its objective was to maximize loans, mainly those to industry and commerce. Up through the mid-1950s, city banks (i.e., urban commercial banks) borrowed as much as 25% of their total capital available for lending from the Bank of Japan, and loans reached as much as 125% of their deposits. The banks themselves had little equity, and such high levels of leverage would have been considered extremely risky by banking authorities in the United States or Europe. But for all practical purposes, the banks were totally controlled subsidiaries of the Bank of Japan and the Ministry of Finance. These regulators knew the details of every loan as well as the daily cash flow and loan loss positions of the banks. The Ministry of Finance determined what sort of loans would be made and to what sort of borrowers, using strict, but effective, hands-on regulatory practices (summarized by one observer as "prohibiting everything except that which is permitted"). There was no getting around the system; it worked the way it was supposed to.[8]

The larger corporations, especially those that survived the reorganization of the zaibatsu (which accounted for perhaps 50% of early postwar Japan's sales and growth potential) were also set to go. These corporations specialized in manufacturing finished products. To maximize their effectiveness, they were encircled by a ring of smaller component manufacturing companies, which would scurry around madly to deliver large orders when times were good, and cut back drastically when they weren't.

Industrial Policies and Safety Nets

The banks loaned huge sums to manufacturers for factory expansion, the overarching goal of the system. These loans, many of which came from specialized long-term credit banks such as the Industrial Bank of Japan, were for the most part secured by mortgages or pledges of capital assets. Not many restrictions were placed on a company seeking more funds for expansion of its production facilities.

If, for example, Toyo Rayon, a prominent Mitsui Group company, wanted to expand capacity an additional 20%, that was fine with the banks. All the company had to do was to call and ask for, say, $50 million to manufacture a new nylon line.

"No problem, when do you want the money?" The banks were already familiar with the company's business, existing facilities, group affiliations, and capacity to repay the loan.

The manufacturers would then start to recruit and train additional workers to meet the new schedule. Some of the subcontractors would also be called.

Nowhere in the process, however, did anyone ask, "Who's going to buy all that nylon?" Or, "How long can you continue to increase output before you start affecting the selling price?" Or, "What kind of return are we going to get on this additional commitment to nylon? Would we be better off making something else?" No Japanese would have questioned this logic, even if doubts had occurred to them, for fear of being seen as out-rageously lacking in company spirit. Only a Westerner, a technical adviser perhaps, might have asked inconvenient questions.

The outsider would most likely be told, "Well, selling the nylon is up to the trading companies," (and the company's sales forces, which worked with the trading companies). "They will not let us down. Maybe we will have to shape it into a different kind of product? Or, sell some more in Brazil, or in Seattle, or blend it into something else to sell it to a new market? For car seats, maybe, or fishing line.

"But we must sell it. It is our duty to our company and to Japan. We can always cut the price, too, if necessary. As long as we break even, we're still ahead because of the jobs we have created and the new markets we have developed."

"But what if something goes wrong?" the outsider might ask, "you are so highly leveraged that your whole company, big as it is, may collapse. Then what about the jobs and the glory of Japan?"

"Nothing will go wrong. We will succeed because we must!"

"Yeah, but what if something terrible happens that you guys had no way of expecting, an earthquake for instance? What then?"

"Earthquakes are matters of fate and it is useless to dwell on the possibility. But, since you persist, what would happen is that our friends and sister companies in our keiretsu, the Mitsui Group, would assist us. Our loyal and dedicated main bank, our long-term credit bank, and our trust bank and insurance companies would all advance emergency funds. Our trading company would help by buying large quantities of our inventories and accounts receivable and in offering more generous supplier credits on the purchase of raw materials. Our Mitsui Group sister companies in industry would place large orders for simple products.

"The senior managers of our company would, of course, have to resign to take responsibility for the unexpected but unfortunate event, even if it was an earthquake, and they would be replaced by first-rate managers from other companies in our group. A tough review of our business and product strategy would take place, and if necessary, drastic changes that would not otherwise be permitted would be made.

"The Bank of Japan would be notified of our temporary problem, and it might instruct other banks, if necessary, to help too. The Bank of Japan would advance special emergency funds to the banks if necessary. Our existing bank loans might be rescheduled, repayments stretched out. It might take several years to work out of all the problems, but the main thing would be to preserve the company, its jobs, and its markets, and to restore conditions to normal as soon as possible.

"And if all this still didn't work, the company would be required to merge with another company selected by government authorities.

"Because of these arrangements, which give us security from short-term business anxieties, we are able to go forward with a highly positive attitude. We know we can risk everything on behalf of our company and its employees, because our friends will support us if a mistake is made. The main thing is to produce growth in the volume of manufactured goods. That is our mission. There is no other."

Invisible except when needed, and needed only rarely, the Japanese safety net was an intricate and effective device. It could only work, however, if the human skills and intelligence for using it—the software—were as good as its construction. This software was Japan's third distinctive feature, perhaps its most important one. It led to the appearance of a unified government-business-labor effort to generate efficient economic growth, which came to be called *Japan, Inc.* during the early 1970s.

Without an effective system for commanding and controlling this highly specialized and synchronized economy, the whole thing would have collapsed.

Not all of the companies in Japan could make nylon, for example. Neither could they all fall back on the same prewar technologies and products, for fear of competition from imports of superior products made elsewhere. With no money, how could they get the best technology? Where would the trained people needed to operate the equipment come from? And how should the great Japanese dilemma of trying to build a large manufacturing base without local raw materials be handled?

Oddly enough, in many ways, the elaborate system that the Japanese evolved after 1945 was similar to the one developed by the Soviet Union. Everything was specialized. The factory made the products, somebody else sold them, somebody else used them. Financial and other resources were provided centrally. The initial emphasis was on rebuilding infrastructure and manufacturing capability, not on supplying an impoverished population with consumer goods.

But the software in Japan was very different. The Ministry of International Trade and Industry (MITI) did most of the economic planning. It started with Japan's physical limitations, its lack of natural resources. These limitations meant that Japan's economic progress would be constrained by its balance of payments. To manufacture products, imports of basic materials, including petroleum, were necessary. To import these materials, the country had to generate foreign exchange. To do that, the country had to export products. Without exports there would not be enough growth to meet national objectives.

To export, Japan would first need to decide what to export, and then how. MITI helped organize a council of business and government leaders, who drew up a list of potential items for manufacture, which could be manufactured competitively with Western countries and for which there were markets overseas.

"But for the time being, we should stick to, say, low- to medium-priced textiles," they reasoned. "We can manufacture good-quality products in this field, and we can make such a large quantity, aiming at worldwide demand, that we can cut the unit selling price below the competition's. This should enable us to increase our share of the world market and to generate substantial foreign exchange revenues.

"The plan, however, will have to be updated every year or so, because the foreigners may meet our competition or otherwise prevent it through tariffs or quotas. As we are successful in one of our target areas, we must expect resistance and complaints from those countries whose markets are being upset by our goods. Since the United States is the world's largest market for everything we should expect resistance there first. The Americans, of course, are devoted to the principles of free trade and to the economic recovery of Japan, so maybe they will let us use their markets without difficulty for a while.

"In any case, our objective is not to dominate the low-labor cost, low-technology markets, not for long. To upgrade our economy and our standard of living, we must move up the technology curve into other sectors.

"Some of our industries may become obsolete as this process of shifting product emphasis continues. They must be prepared to adapt themselves continuously to new technologies or else retire from business.

"To finance foreign trade, we should invite a few of the most prominent foreign banks into Japan. They can open branches here, make foreign exchange loans to our companies for importing raw materials, and discount their foreign currency receivables. Their parent banks can also make foreign exchange loans in their own countries to the subsidiaries of our companies operating there.

"We will need to borrow heavily from these banks, so we must explain to them our system for protecting companies in trouble and be sure that never, under any circumstances, does a Japanese company default on a foreign currency obligation, even if it has to default on or reschedule its loans to Japanese banks. This way, the foreigners will believe that the Japanese government is quietly behind all foreign loans, and therefore they will increase them, despite their concerns about our low coverage ratios. As we succeed in our recovery efforts they will wish to lend us even more money, gradually lowering its cost through competition."

The Japan, Inc. software turned out to be as remarkable as the rest of its economic machine. With it, the ministries concerned were able to drive the Japanese economy through a period of exceptionally high growth for more than twenty years, restoring its war-devastated standard of living after only one generation. Through the allocation of national energies and resources, mainly capital resources, they fed and starved individual industries as necessary to keep up an optimal mix of technology, products, and revenues. In the process, they rescued some firms from mistakes or scandals, and were embarrassed by others that polluted the countryside and poisoned the people with toxic effluents. In time, money and effort had to be made available to address the health and social problems of rapid growth, and some of the singular focus of a unified national economic policy began to be lost.

The rapid development of the Japanese economy was praised and encouraged. In America, there was much popular support for the hard-working Japanese and their struggle to rebuild their lives and their country. By the 1960s, Americans had become fascinated with Japan, much as they had been with China during the 1980s. Joint ventures, technology licensing, and various other business associations followed.

Reaching the Top

By the early 1970s, however, Japan found itself engaged in a long-term struggle with its Western allies, especially the United States, over its one-sided trade practices, as the disputed product areas moved up the technology curve from cheap textiles to steel to consumer electronics to autos to sophisticated semiconductors, and perhaps next, to high-speed computers. Gradually the "little brother" relationship came to an end. Japan was no longer a developing economy, it was a developed one. It was the economic equivalent of a powerful, menacing, and determined young heavyweight boxer emerging from adolescence.

The postwar recovery period came to something of an unplanned end when the United States abandoned the gold standard in 1971 (an event still known in Japan as the *Nixon shokku*), and forced the world into an era of floating exchange rates, which would in time push the worth of the yen to more than twice the fixed, and substantially subsidized, value (¥360 per $1) it had enjoyed from 1947 to 1971. From then on, Japan was on its own. Its currency would float in the market like everybody else's, and not be pegged to an unrealistic exchange rate that actually lowered the price of Japanese exports.

The oil price rise in 1973 (known in Japan as the *oil shokku*) threw Japanese industry into panic. More than 90% of Japan's oil was imported; to pay for it at the cartel's new prices, Japan would have to rev up its export machine again. As it did so, it began to increase its trade surpluses with the West, especially the United States.

In the late 1970s, the international community seemed to decide that the Japanese had had enough help and that they would have to fit into the world trade and financial system like any other developed country. Surplus countries had an obligation to reduce exports and increase imports, just as deficit countries had the reverse obligations. Naturally, few countries actually did much to meet these obligations because the domestic political fallout would have been too great.

They did, of course, talk about the situation, increasingly at international economic summit meetings. The Japanese were always outnumbered and outgunned at these meetings, and its prime ministers developed the habit of promising things they had no means to deliver. The disputes continued, and indeed, intensified. Most concerned Japan's enormous trade surplus. The world perceived Japan as having run its export machinery at full capacity, and its imports at minimum, despite the objections of its trading partners.

During the 1980s, relations reached a state of maximum tension. The Japanese growth rate, which had slowed to an average of 5.3% in the decade following the oil shock of 1973, had declined further to less than 4% for the period 1980–1987, and almost half of that was provided by growth in exports. The domestic economy was only growing at about 2%, which by Japanese standards was virtually the same as a recession. Japan was seen to be dumping exports into the United States in order to keep its domestic economy afloat.

In the late 1980s, the Japanese government changed the thrust of its economic policies: domestic growth would be favored over exports, and the money supply would be increased to encourage this growth. Further efforts to liberalize imports were made, but because of the rising yen, market forces began to take over, and even fussy Japanese consumers were drawn to the low prices of good-quality foreign goods. Japan also continued to liberalize its capital markets through deregulation and encouragement of foreign participation in such institutions as the Tokyo Stock Exchange. The policies worked. The trade surplus with the United States began to decline in 1986.

There was also a substantial increase in Japan's export of capital for both portfolio investments and direct manufacturing investments abroad. In 1980, the Japanese net capital account showed an inflow of $2.3 billion; in 1983, it was an outflow of $18 billion, and in 1986, the outflow had reached $113 billion. It peaked at $147 billion in 1989, after which it began to decline sharply. By the end of 1991, the long-term capital account had completely reversed direction and showed a historically high surplus (inflow) of $37 billion, much of which was the result of high foreign portfolio investment in Japan during the year. Much of this investment, aimed at picking up bargains in the blown-out stock market, was later regretted.

Needless to say, the outpouring of funds during the peak period 1983–1989 attracted the attention of financiers everywhere. The Japanese in the 1980s, like the Arabs a decade before, had become the world's richest and most active cross-border investors. And like the Arabs, their surplus disappeared after a few years. With banks under pressure, and the economy slowing, Prime Minister Miyazawa explained in April 1992 that Japan's ability to solve the world's economic problems was limited. "Japan will have to take a break from being the world's sugar daddy," he said.[9]

Many Westerners still believe in Japan, Inc., but in reality it has long been retired, to be called back only in the event of a national emergency. Economic goals, as expressed by the government and the politicians, are now less clear. The government has substantially backed away from its role as an authoritative national economic planner. For the first time, efforts are being made to bring the economic animals under some kind of control. And general economic policies aimed at international convergence are being followed. The distress in the financial system that was revealed in 1990 and 1991 following the collapse of the stock and real estate markets has aided the reform process.

All this, however, is happening more gradually than many people would like. The Japanese often appear to be maddeningly indifferent to what the other industrialized countries regard as their responsibilities, and equally uninterested in the contributions of other countries to a healthy and peaceful world. Perhaps this behavior reflects parochialism, or a kind of global political immaturity. If so, it is bound to change as Japan begins to feel the chill of being left out of important new economic developments in the world. Change and convergence, however, are bound to involve a price, payable no doubt (as in all the other democracies of the developed world) in some form of decreased economic efficiency.

8

THE SUPERNOVA FADES

Japan suddenly emerged as a financial superpower during the 1980s. It was producing huge amounts of liquidity, through reduced domestic expenditures, easy money, foreign earnings, and a savings rate that continued to be among the highest in the world. The difference between the increase in the money supply and the inflation rate in any country is called *excess liquidity*. In Japan, excess liquidity was −3% of GNP in 1980 and 0.2% in 1981, but thereafter it grew rapidly. The government had intervened, changing its monetary policies, abruptly and significantly. After the Plaza Accord in 1985, at which the financial authorities of the leading countries agreed to halt the growing value of the U.S. dollar (still buoyed by Reaganomics) and to shift resources to bolster the major European currencies and the yen, the Japanese government pumped up the domestic economy with heavy spending and slashed the Bank of Japan discount rate to 2.5%. As a result, money coursed through the economy.

From 1982 to 1985, excess liquidity averaged about 2.0%, but in 1986 and again in 1987 it exceeded 5.5%. It fell back to an average of 3.6% in 1989 and 1990, after the Bank of Japan began to tighten the ropes again; then it sharply reversed direction, plunging to −2.6% in 1991.[1] The 1980s, in other words, began and ended with a substantial rise and fall in excess liquidity.

In most countries, excess liquidity goes right into consumption and runaway inflation is the result. That was not the case in Japan during this period—a great deal of it was redirected into investments in securities and real estate. As a result, the inflationary effect of the excess liquidity appeared mainly in the market for financial assets, not for goods and services.

THE "BUBBLE ECONOMY"

The engines for this increased investment activity in financial assets, which the now-sober Japanese refer to as the *babaru keizai*, or "bubble economy," were three: corporations, financial institutions, and households. Unusual circumstances impelled each of these sectors to increase its investments in stocks and real estate; thus Japan experienced one of the greatest speculative periods in the history of financial markets. And because of the recent global integration of markets, Japanese investment power found its way into markets abroad.

In the stock market, incredible levels of activity occurred during the 1980s. The Japan Nikkei Stock Average index rose from 6,569 at the end of 1979 to 38,916 at the end of 1989, a nearly sixfold increase reflecting a compounded growth rate of 18% per annum. During this period, even amidst the great Reagan bull market, the era of yuppies and American greed, the Dow Jones Industrial Average only increased threefold.

At the end of 1989, the market capitalization of all equity markets in the United States was $3.5 trillion, reflecting an average price/earnings ratio of 14.1; in Japan, the market capitalization was $4.4 trillion, reflecting an average p/e of 70.6. The Japanese market overtook the United States' in 1987, though in 1980 the Tokyo market capitalization had been only 26% of that of the U.S. markets.

The volume of stock trading in Tokyo, expressed in dollars, also increased sharply, from $50 billion in 1984 to $2.3 trillion in 1989, an amount greater than the value of all shares traded in the United States during that year. This development was a surprise to many observers who were aware that at least 50% of Japanese shares, being tied up in cross-holdings, never traded at all. Thus the volume totals were made up only from that portion of companies' shares that did trade. These did so at a pace that was more than twice what it was in the United States at the time.

The real estate markets were experiencing similar price rises during this period. A Tokyo Stock Exchange real-estate price index more than tripled from 1984 to 1986, and then grew another 43% by the end of 1989. In 1986, the price of land in Tokyo was 150 times the price in New York City. The unit cost of land for the country as a whole was about 40 times as high. The cash yield on these investments was virtually nothing. At one stage, the wags had it, the land covered by the Imperial Palace in Tokyo (about the size of Central Park in New York) was worth more than all the land in the state of California, and the real estate in all of Japan (which has about the same area as the state of California) was worth more than all the real estate in the United States.[2] The Japanese, at least, seemed to believe it.

The Japanese also developed a frenzied interest in golf club memberships, for which an extremely active secondary market existed. Purchases of such memberships enabled you to own a bit of the green you were hitting on and to bypass any sort of social inspection as to your suitability to join the club. Golf courses represented great opportunities for land speculation; it was also prestigious for an ordinary businessman to show that he could pay a lot of money for a membership, as much as $2 million at the market's peak. There was so much interest in golf memberships that a whole new industry of brokerages emerged. If you didn't want to buy a membership itself, you could buy instead the Nikkei Golf Membership Index, which rose at an annual rate of more than 10% during 1989 and 1990 and peaked in March 1990 after increasing 50% in just eight months.[3]

At the heart of the great speculative period were the financial institutions and corporations. In the first place, banks began to lend large sums to finance investments in real estate and stocks, especially to large corporate clients. By the end of 1990, banks were carrying $375 billion of property loans on their books, more than twice the amount of five years before.[4]

Second, Japanese institutions were in the process of setting up modern pension funds, which had recently been made mandatory. Trust banks and insurance companies were eligible to manage corporate pension funds for their clients. As most of these funds were new and underfunded, corporations were still providing substantial sums of money for investment. Such investment trust funds increased ninefold from 1980 to 1988, when they represented $400 billion (after which their growth rate slowed considerably).

Some corporations asked if additional sums could be managed for them in a separate, tax-advantaged investment account called a *tokkin*. Corporations could use tokkins to invest surplus funds, which were considerable, and to take advantage of the rising markets generally. Tokkins also enabled them to make some market investments outside of their keiretsu holdings, which were publicly known, semiofficial, and thus difficult to sell. Tokkins more than tripled from the beginning of 1986 to the end of 1988, when they reached $240 billion. This pool of funds found its way into the stock market, adding to the already considerable supply of liquidity pushing share prices up. With the pickup in domestic economic growth in 1988 and an increase in corporate demand for working and investment capital, companies began to withdraw funds from tokkins and their influence started to decline.

Deleveraging with Zaitech

Some Japanese corporations began to realize than they could make more money investing in financial assets than they could in their manufacturing businesses, where profits were not growing very fast in the early 1980s. First they began to borrow money from banks for simple financial speculation. After a while, this process became more sophisticated: they issued securities with a low cash payout, and invested the proceeds in other securities that were appreciating in value. Their transactions were leveraged as much as possible—for instance by issuing convertible debentures with a coupon of, say, 4% to invest in real estate or in a portfolio of stocks, warrants, or options that would have the potential to appreciate severalfold in a year or two.

Such "high-tech" financial transactions are called *zaitech* in Japan. Many old-timers thought zaitech was sinfully speculative—but plenty of companies did it anyway. It became a very fashionable thing to do; lists were made of the most active zaitech companies and their stocks became market favorites. Their high stock prices and p/e ratios were justified on the grounds that the prices included the rising market value of the zaitech portfolios.

In 1984–1989, the heyday of zaitech, Japanese companies issued a total of about $720 billion of securities (including about $150 billion of stock purchase warrants), of which more than 80% represented equity securities. The Japanese total new-equity financing during the period was more than three times the volume of equity new issues in the United States, which was an economy nearly twice as large as Japan's with its own bull market going on.

Of the Japanese issues, just less than half ($294 billion) were sold in domestic capital markets, mostly in the form of convertible debentures (a bond issue that can be converted into a fixed number of common shares at the investor's option) and new share issues. The rest ($330 billion) were issued in the Eurobond markets, mostly in the form of low-coupon bonds with stock purchase warrants attached (a form of security similar to a convertible debenture, except that the conversion feature can be detached and sold separately). Japanese investors did not usually compute the dilution in earnings per share following the issuance of a convertible debenture to allow for the new shares that would someday be outstanding, so the share prices rarely declined when the issues were first made. This was quite advantageous for the issuers, and quite disadvantageous for the investors, which is why so many convertible bonds and bonds-with-warrants were issued.

The banks liked zaitech deals too, though they had only a small role in underwriting them. They could act as guarantors of the prompt payment of interest and principal on the bonds being issued. They could also buy the warrants to replace stock in a keiretsu holding, liberate profits from the portfolio, and reinvest them on a more leveraged basis. They could buy the straight debt bonds at a big discount, e.g., 30% or 40%, once the warrants were detached. The bonds could then be repackaged with an interest rate swap, and thus converted into a floating-rate asset to be funded in the London deposit market and held as a profitable international banking asset. Zaitech seemed to offer something for everyone, which no doubt explained its popularity.

One consequence of the financial surpluses and of zaitech was the rapid reduction in the amounts of borrowing that Japanese companies had traditionally relied upon to grow. Ratios of long-term debt-to-total (book value) capitalization, i.e., long-term debt plus equity, began to decline for all Tokyo Stock Exchange-listed companies—from more than 50% in 1980 to 39.6% at year-end 1990. In 1990, only 42% of corporate debt outstanding, or 17% of total capitalization, was provided by bank loans. Bank borrowings were being displaced by bond issues, which would be redeemed by conversion into common stock in the future. And what bank loans were made often supported zaitech operations or investment in the lending bank's own certificates of deposit, which the borrower maintained at virtually no cost for relationship purposes.

The decline in leverage was much more significant if market prices were substituted for book values in the calculation. A useful study published by the National Bureau of Economic Research in 1989 showed that Japanese debt-to-equity (at market prices) ratios were half those of U.S. companies.[5] But even these ratios did not tell the full story—though many companies were using surplus cash flow to repay debt, others were engaging in zaitech, increasing their debts in order to invest in other securities.

The real test of leverage therefore had to change; now what mattered was the ratio of *net* interest payable to total operating income (interest received minus interest paid divided by operating income). According to Tokyo Stock Exchange data, all listed manufacturing companies in aggregate showed a decline in their net interest ratio from 30% in 1980 to *minus* 5.3% in 1990; such levels show that Japanese companies have, for all practical purposes, become totally deleveraged.[6] Put another way, they would have no debt at all if they sold their zaitech holdings to repay it. This, of course, is a very big change from the heady, overleveraged days of the miracle economy.

After the Fall

During the latter part of 1989, inflation in Japan (mainly as expressed in the prices of financial assets) began to rise at a rate that alarmed Japanese monetary authorities. The consumer price index was already increasing more than 3% per annum—a rate quite high for Japan—even though wholesale price rises lagged well behind. Interest rates were nudged upward in response, with the discount rate double its previous level at the end of the four rises during 1989. The Ministry of Finance was also watching the international scene closely; inflation and interest rates were rising in Germany, but of greater danger to that economy was the prospect of peace breaking out—or reunification. Soon after the fall of the Berlin Wall, German rates jumped sharply upward, in anticipation of the inflationary effect of absorbing East Germany into the economy of West Germany. Real interest rates in Germany lurched to 5% in December 1989. Japan had an outbreak of sympathetic illness: its interest rates shot up, and its real rates of interest also reached 5% by mid-1990, up from 2% a year earlier.[7] The drastic moves to tighten money supply forced adjustments in the prices of financial assets, mainly stocks.

As in the case of the October 19, 1987, crash of the U.S. stock market, which responded to a powerful rise in interest rates during the summer, the Japanese market also adjusted from an all-time high Nikkei index of 38,916. And it kept adjusting. In March of 1990, it attempted to rally, but the recovery was very short-lived. The slide continued, passing through 22,000 on the Nikkei index in December 1991, and through 15,000 in August 1992 (representing a 61% drop from the late 1989 high). Even at this level, however, Japanese stocks were still trading at 33 times earnings (before adjustments) and offering a dividend yield of only a bit more than 1%. Many market observers believed that the market was likely to go down further. Compared to U.S. and European stock prices, Japanese stocks still seemed highly valued. If it had not been for brave contrarian foreign investors who bought $45 billion of Japanese shares at an average Nikkei level of about 25,000 (and who had theoretically therefore already lost about $18 billion by August 1992), the market would have reached even lower prices.

The market drop differed from the U.S. crash of 1987 because it did not happen in one day, and because the international markets did not all plunge downward simultaneously. Most of the rest of the world thought the Japanese market was overvalued anyway, and a correction was overdue. It was nothing to get too upset about.

Unless, of course, the market continued to fall and the Japanese economy plunged into a depression because of bankruptcies, bank failures, and a series of policy mistakes on the part of the government. That is what happened in the United States in the 1929–1933 period; the Dow Jones Industrial Average fell more than 80% before the turnaround began, five years after the market's peak. An 80% decline in the Nikkei from the December 1989 level would put it at about 8,000.

A great many Japanese investors had bought into the market on margin. Individual investors owned 20.4% of the stock market as of December 1990. During the 1980s, Japanese individuals (otherwise known for their thrifty and conservative habits) loaded up with debt to the extent of 20% of their disposable income (Americans are at 19% in this comparison, which excludes mortgage debt), much of it incurred for speculative purposes.[8] Individual bankruptcies doubled in 1991 over the previous year. Total consumer credit outstanding exceeded $500 billion, three times higher than in 1980, and much of it was in trouble. Many had to sell their holdings to cover margin calls. Companies in trouble with margin loans, of which there were many, were forced to sell their stock portfolios, especially tokkin funds.

Some of the largest investors were not only out of pocket, they were angry at their brokers for putting them into the market and assuring them of profits. They asked for reimbursement, and as was later revealed when the matter became one of a series of financial scandals that rocked Japan in the summer and fall of 1991, they received under-the-table payments aggregating $1.5 billion from the Big Four (and a few other) brokers. These payments were made very selectively, to the firms' best customers—for instance, Hitachi, Toyota, and Matsushita, certain government pension funds, and the family of LDP "godfather" Shin Kanemaru. The government tax office discovered the abuses and forced disclosure of the names of the recipients. The public was outraged, perhaps more because it was not allowed to share in the reimbursements, rather than that they had happened in the first place.

Some zaitech players were caught in a terrible squeeze by the falling market, and had to report large losses. Zaitech had been attractive to weaker businesses that were fighting hard just to stay even, and many had overdone it. The investments all went down, but the debts remained. Many such companies, as well as real estate developers and large speculators, ended up among the exploding Japanese bankruptcy statistics, which showed liabilities of about $30 billion for the first half of 1991, six times that of the full year 1989, and the largest amount ever. Full-year bankruptcy estimates for 1991 exceeded $50 billion; most of these bankruptcies are related to loans secured by stock market or real estate investments.[9]

The real estate market was never especially liquid, even during the market heyday. After the stock market drop, it was almost completely illiquid. Properties could be shuffled off the books of an investor, onto the books of a subsidiary or affilated company, but actual building sales were rare. The stock market was not much better. After the first few months of the decline, the volume of trading had fallen to one-quarter of its pre-crash level. Most institutional investors holding large positions sat tight, aware that their holdings would surely panic the market if offered for sale. But their unrealized losses mounted. The pressure caused by these losses even did the unthinkable: it threatened the realm of keiretsu holdings.

During the summer of 1991, Dai-Ichi Mutual Life, one of the major insurance companies, announced that it was selling some of its long-term holdings in three large Tokyo banks, a move that greatly surprised the market. Dai-Ichi said it could use the money more efficiently elsewhere in its business, but most observers saw the action as a major blow to the keiretsu system, forced by market conditions. Together Japan's top-five life insurance companies (including Dai-Ichi Mutual) lost a total of about $82 billion, or 60% of their unrealized profits, in the fiscal year ended in March 1992, and all of them moved to reduce dividends to policyholders.

These events demonstrated that the market drop had put pressure on previously secure areas of Japanese business. As this pressure built, some companies were forced to sell off relationship shares. A huge overhang of potential sell orders frightened the market to even lower prices.

Bank shares were especially vulnerable to forced selling, because so many companies own shares in their keiretsu bank. These companies would occasionally borrow from the banks, pledging their bank shares as collateral. Japanese banks are very traditional about this, and insist on the collateral (usually 1.4 times the amount of the loan), even though they may not need it. During the zaitech era, many companies hocked their low-yielding bank stock in order to invest in other securities such as warrants. With the crash, the price of the bank stock would drop below the level of the loan, forcing the bank, under its rules, to demand more collateral. The investments that the zaitech player had made were also underwater, of course, and could not be sold without taking big losses. So the bank would sell out the collateral—at any price—and the bank's share price would drop further, thereby repeating the cycle.[10]

The crisis fed on itself during most of the period 1990 through 1992. Publicly traded companies known to be deep into zaitech saw their share prices drop even further. Some also saw their stock prices fall well below the exercise prices of their outstanding warrants and convertible bonds, which they had fully expected to be repaid by the conversion of these securities into common stock. If the conversions did not occur when the bonds matured, then the companies would have to pay them off. More than $170 billion of such warrants and convertibles maturing in 1992 and 1993 were trading below their conversion prices in April 1992. Japan was rapidly becoming a country of very big numbers.

The sinking financial economy also had major effects on the real economy of Japan, the industrial core. Consumers, frightened by plunging stock and real estate prices, and the deteriorating value of pension funds, cut spending back sharply. Industrial production fell by nearly 9% in the 12 months ending May 1992, the biggest drop since the oil shock was felt in 1974. GNP growth dropped to 2%, and unemployment approached 3%, signifying a veritable recession in Japan. Imports, after a prolonged rise, dropped by 5%, and exports, following the traditional Japanese response to a slump, shot up by 8%, accounting for about half of the country's entire GNP growth for the period. With this, Japan's trade surplus surged—estimates for 1992 put it at $100 billion, a record—inviting another heavy dose of trade friction from Europe, the United States, and, for the first time, from its South East Asian trading partners.[11]

Staggering the Banks

The market collapse had an especially severe effect on the banks. Many, it turned out, had been trading in the shares of their keiretsu holdings in order to realize some of the unrealized gains as a way to supplement their income from banking operations. They would sell old keiretsu shares to record the profit, then buy back new shares or warrants in the same company to maintain their position. According to a September 1991 Salomon Brothers study, this practice, which had become prevalent in 1987, resulted in a substantial overstatement of the banking profits of the major Japanese banks. For the year ended March 1989, for example, all large Japanese banks reported net profits of about $10 billion; however, if net gains from the sale of securities were excluded, the resulting banking-only profits would be $4.6 billion, a decline in profits of about 55%. A year later, after the market drop, the result was much worse; reported net profits were $9 billion, and after the profits from securities sales were excluded, the net figure was about $2 billion, a 78% decline. Put another way, the banks used their stock portfolios as huge loan loss reserves to cushion bad earnings performance.

The banks, of course, turned out to be overexposed to loans tied to the stock market and to real estate, which also plunged 30% to 40% in value over an eighteen-month period beginning in January 1990. They also financed golf club memberships, which fell by 50% during the same period. With companies, now deleveraged, no longer needing to borrow for ordinary business purposes, the banks loaned them money for speculative purposes instead. "After all," the banks said, "these loans are collateralized by the assets they are financing. They're basically safe." Perhaps they ought to have added, "as long as the market doesn't plunge by 25% or more. After that, the collateral may not be worth much." But they might also have added, "it would help if the valuation of the collateral were reasonable in the first place."

After the market drop, the banks saw a substantial increase in problem loans to regular small business and individual customers, something that was quite unprecedented. These exposures were crippling to the numerous small credit cooperatives, or *shinkin banks,* institutions roughly comparable to American S&Ls. Few of these banks are expected to survive the crisis on their own—the Ministry of Finance will have to rescue them or parcel them out to other banks.[12]

The big banks suffered too, but it was not easy to find out how badly: Japanese banks are not required to disclose nonperforming loans until a year or more after first failing to collect interest. The *Nihon Keizai Shinbun,* Japan's main financial daily newspaper, made some estimates, however, in October 1991. The paper estimated that interest was not being paid on $11.5 billion of loans held by the fifteen or so large city banks, and on another $11.5 billion of loans to three long-term credit banks, the Industrial Bank of Japan, the Long-Term Credit Bank, and Nippon Credit Bank. It also estimated that the exposures of the long-term banks to bankrupt or

rescheduling companies was almost $20 billion, or eleven times their oper-
ating profits for the year and 38% of their combined unrealized gains from
shareholdings. The long-term banks, having little customer business away
from their dwindling transactions with large corporations, were the most
affected by the need to replace traditional business with market-oriented
loans. These exposure estimates were prepared on the basis of loan difficulties that the paper already knew about; they did not include any problem loans that had not yet surfaced in the fall of 1991.

David Atkinson, a Salomon Brothers analyst in Tokyo, estimated at the
same time as the *Nihon Keizai* that total nonperforming loans of all the large
Japanese banks would be somewhere between $150 billion and $300 billion, or 7% to 14% of total loans by the end of March 1992, necessitating
large write-offs.[13] The banks would then have to finance the write-offs by
selling shares from their portfolios, which would depress the market further, which would cause more loans to lose their collateral value, and so
forth.

In April 1992, *The Economist* also revealed a confidential study made at
the end of 1991 by the Bank of Japan, which apparently found about $220
billion of bad loans in the banking system. Of these, $75 billion was carried
by the four long-term credit banks alone. Another $220 billion was also
expected to be on the books of nonbank financial companies (leasing, consumer, and housing finance), which would have to turn to the banks if
their loans became uncollectible. All together, the study suggested, 10% of
all Japanese bank and nonbank loans were probably in trouble.

Yoh Kurokawa, president of Industrial Bank of Japan, offered a realistic
assessment in the summer of 1991: "We will not be able to do a rights issue
[of common stock to replace devalued capital] this year so we will have to
keep to our 'no-increase-in-loan-assets' policy, regardless of events inside
or outside Japan."[14] He added that he did not expect total bank asset
growth to exceed 2% in 1991, about the same as in 1990.

Kurokawa acknowledged the increasing exposure of Japanese banks to
troubled real estate and other loans in Japan, and to real estate loans in the
United States and Britain—factors that would force the bank to be more
conscious of profits and loan quality, rather than growth, in the future—
but he pointed out that Japanese banks are less exposed to real estate and
nonperforming loans than U.S. banks are. "Japanese banks are not full of
lemons," he said.

At least not as far as we know. Japanese banks entered the post-crash
asset devaluation phase of their recent cycle about two years after the U.S.
and the U.K. banks did. It is often impossible to tell whether a loan that is
current today will turn into a nonperformer tomorrow. Lending is coming
to be as tricky a business for the Japanese as it is for everyone else. Certainly the magnitude of the changes in the stock market and real estate

sectors, and the exposure of the banks to them, was greater in Japan than in other countries, so the possibility is strong that the difficulties the Japanese banks are facing at home in terms of loan quality deterioration may still be in early stages of development. Their position is comparable in some ways to that of U.S. banks with portfolios of highly leveraged loans after the LBO boom broke in late 1989.

Because of the large banks' "weakening long-term profitability and changing risk profiles," Moody's downgraded the bond ratings of ten Japanese banks during 1990, though most are still in the Aa category. No Japanese bank has a triple-A rating today, though almost all of the large banks did in 1985. The agencies are concerned about the sharp deterioration in asset quality, adverse profitability trends, and the continuing effects of financial market deregulation in Japan. Their ratings, however, still reflect a strong element of confidence that the Ministry of Finance will keep its banks from defaulting on overseas obligations.[15]

No matter how you look at it, the Japanese banks, like their American counterparts, have been hit by a tidal wave of bad debts from which it will take years to recover. Their experience is certainly similar in nature and in size to the domestic credit problems that the U.S. banks discovered in the early 1990s. The question that has not yet been satisfactorily answered is, of course, where was the Ministry of Finance, the formidable all-controlling guardian of bank safety and soundness, when all this speculative lending was going on? Maybe the banks had become too powerful to be restrained; maybe the Ministry of Finance worried that the banks had to replace lending business lost to the big corporations and did not want them doing it in third world countries; maybe it preferred loans backed by collateral to unsecured loans. The system also offered rewards for those willing to tolerate higher levels of speculation in stocks and real estate than usual; perhaps political realities had tipped the balance. Maybe the Ministry, like the banks themselves, believed that after nearly ten years of growth in values of financial assets, the growth would continue indefinitely. Most likely, in their haste to put assets on their books that reflected a superpower rate of growth, they got the valuations of their collateral wrong. Just like the American banks in the 1970s.

The market drop also hurt the capital positions of the Japanese banks. Japan had signed the BIS bank capital adequacy agreement, requiring its banks to meet the tier 1 and total capital-to-assets ratios that the Europeans and the Americans had accepted. The Ministry of Finance had argued, however, that Japan was different from the other countries, and special consideration should be given to its banks. Japanese banks, it asserted, appeared to be undercapitalized by Western standards, but because of exceptionally close supervision by the Ministry of Finance, and tight restrictions on what banks could do, they were safer than they appeared.

Furthermore, Japanese banks owned shares in the profusion of companies that were linked to them by keiretsu ties or otherwise. These shares were carried on the books of the banks at cost; in reality they were worth a substantial amount more. The unrealized gains from these holdings actually would make up any capital shortfall that Westerners might detect. After some discussion, the BIS agreed to allow the Japanese to count the after-tax value (45%) of their unrealized gains from listed shares as part of their total capital.

Salomon Brothers research showed that for a composite of six large commercial banks the September 1989 book value, adjusted for 45% of the unrealized gains in the securities portfolios of the banks, would be 3.7 times the historical book value. That's a lot of unrealized gains! The study also showed, however, that six months later, after the market fall, the adjusted ratio declined to 2.4 times historical book value. This represented a sudden drop in BIS capital of about 35%, and it created a serious problem for the banks. As the market continued to fall, the amount of lost capital also increased. In April 1992, the ratio of unrealized gains to book value had declined to 1.5. At a Nikkei index of 17,000, three of the top ten Japanese banks (Sakura, Bank of Tokyo, and Tokai) would report total capital below the 8.0% level required by the BIS by January 1, 1993. At 15,000, seven banks would be below 8.0%. At 11,000, nine out of the ten would have no hidden reserves at all, and total capital would be in the area of 5% for these banks.

The problem is made worse by the fact that unrealized gains have been taken to absorb loan losses in the past. As these gains disappear, the ability to write off the loan losses "off the books" also disappears, forcing these losses back onto the books. The more losses that are taken, the more the size of the remaining stock portfolio is reduced, and the lost capital cannot be replaced by selling new issues of shares when market conditions are adverse.[16] This condition places a high premium on internal profitability and on reducing the amount of capital required in the business by adopting no-asset-growth policies, as Industrial Bank of Japan has done. These are the type of constraints that large U.S. money-center banks felt during much of the 1980s; they create a situation that forces banks to look for higher margin loans at higher risks, develop alternative sources of income, or arrange large, cost-cutting mergers.

INNOCENTS ABROAD

During the 1980s, the Japanese became highly visible abroad. Their mounting exports required that they set up large sales and support facilities outside Japan. As the United States was the largest market for their products, much of this investment was in the United States, where in time it attracted other investments on the part of Japanese trading companies and banks. Then, as Japanese economic policy began to favor overseas manufacturing, the Japanese began to make increasing amounts of greenfield investments to construct small plants and assembly facilities. Gradually these grew into full-scale factories aiming to service much of the American market from within the United States, rather than rely on exports from Japan. These investments attracted Japanese equipment suppliers, who wanted to follow their clients abroad.

A Binge of Foreign Investments

Total foreign direct investment in the United States doubled during the five-year period 1982–1987, from $700 billion to about $1.4 trillion. This, of course, was the time of the growing twin deficits of the Reagan administration, during which imports were sucked into the United States at an unprecedented rate, and money to pay for them was sucked out. These funds, augmented in Japan's case by major efforts at financial deregulation, which released a substantial surplus of domestic savings to seek higher-yielding investments abroad, found their way back into the United States. Once returned, about 80% of the money went into portfolio investments and banking assets, and 20% into direct investments in factories, warehouses, and companies. Nearly half of the portfolio investments were by central banks of friendly governments, and the rest were spread among private sector investors all over the world. The Japanese were responsible for a substantial portion of the increase in portfolio investment in the United States during the period up to 1988, but they were not alone. Americans became nervous at so much money being invested in the United States on an opportunistic basis—hot money that could leave as fast as it arrived, wrecking the markets in the process. In time, the United States learned not to be afraid of this hot money overhang, which in reality only represented a small percentage of all U.S. portfolio investments, but it took several years.

Japan became a massive capital exporter in the mid-1980s. Its long-term capital outflow peaked in 1989, when $147 billion was invested overseas. Of this amount, about $112 billion reflected net securities investments, and $35 billion was for direct investments. After 1989, however, things changed radically in Japan—the trade surplus was declining, the domestic economy began to absorb funds, and net portfolio investment dropped to $35 billion, though direct investments increased. By 1990, the net capital outflow had dropped by two-thirds to $44 billion; by the end of 1991, the outflow had disappeared altogether—the capital account showed an inflow of $37 billion. Almost all of the shift had occurred in the portfolio investment accounts. From being a massive overseas investor in 1988, Japan had become a significant importer of capital three years later.

Japanese overseas direct investment reached $48 billion in 1990, before declining the following year. Approximately 45% of these investments were made in the United States, about a third in manufacturing facilities, a bit more in finance and real estate. At the end of 1990, total Japanese direct investment in the United States exceeded $83 billion, as compared to $256 billion from European countries. Japan's rate of growth in U.S. direct investment, however, was the greatest of any region (through 1990), and its total of such investments was the second-largest of any single country. The Netherlands had fallen to third place, but the United Kingdom with $108 billion of direct investments was well ahead. Though Japan's purchase of U.S. properties has now fallen off considerably, its five-year spending spree of more than $80 billion startled the Americans and gave rise to concerns that too much of the country was being bought up by the Japanese.

Samurai Takeovers

These concerns are not well founded. Japanese direct investments are very small in proportion to the total value of plants, factories, and real estate in the United States; Japan represents 20% of all foreign direct investment in the United States and less than 10% of foreign-owned manufacturing investments. Foreign investments as a whole represent less than 5% of all U.S. investments and about 7% of GNP.[17]

The Japanese investment surge included substantial acquisitions of real estate and banking assets. By 1992, the real estate market in the United States had slumped almost as much as the market in Tokyo, and investors wanted to get their money out, not put more in. The Japanese banks operating in the United States had their share of problems with loan losses, and indeed were attempting to extract capital and borrowed funds to return to Japan. These banks had been successful in competing for business in the United States by offering cheaper loans than their U.S. competitors; now they didn't want the business, and were endeavoring to adjust to their problems at home by sharply curtailing asset growth, especially overseas. When cheap-rate lenders run out of money, they cease to be competitive.

The banks made substantial investments in their U.S. operations, often by acquiring U.S. banks or branches, especially in California. Few of these investments, which have involved purchase prices in the area of two to three times book value, have been successful financially. Today, most of the banking assets they acquired would be lucky to be valued at one-times book value.

Manufacturing companies, however, may have made the greatest mistakes. Initially cautious and unwilling to risk much, Japanese manufacturers confined themselves to small, experimental transactions. None of these would have much impact on the acquiring companies. Gradually, however, some companies tried out larger deals. Before long, it became fashionable for Japanese companies to be seen making large deals in the United States, even though acquisitions in general were alien to Japanese business practices and dealing in the intense, warlike merger marketplace in the United States, where high fees had to be paid for advice from investment bankers and lawyers, was completely unfamiliar to most of these companies.[18]

The result was a number of what must be called questionable (if not downright foolish) investments by Japanese in the United States. In 1987, Bridgestone wanted an important position in the U.S. tire market, and worked out an arrangement with Firestone to pay $1.25 billion for a 75% stake in Firestone's tire business. But then, Pirelli, working with Michelin, made a tender offer for Firestone at $58 a share. Bridgestone decided to compete—it could have offered something sensible like $65, but instead it decided to take the deal out of play with an offer of $80 per share, or $2.6 billion. This was more than $500 million more than might have been necessary. Then Bridgestone poured more money into Firestone to improve it. The investment may have had wonderful strategic logic, but in the short to medium term it has been an economic disaster. The first year after the acquisition, consolidated (i.e., Bridgestone plus Firestone) net profits were about $350 million; the next year, however, the consolidated company lost more than $200 million. Bridgestone's chairman announced that he was moving to Akron to put things right, but losses increased. Losses at Firestone were about $500 million for 1991, but were expected to be held to about $200 million if the U.S. economy improved significantly in the second half of 1992, which seemed unlikely. Bridgestone's own profits were of course affected by these losses, falling to less than 15% of their pre-acquisition level. Fixing the problems at Firestone will be enormously difficult for Bridgestone; Firestone has 53,000 employees spread over forty plants, and Bridgestone's English-speaking engineers and manufacturing experts are too few in number and too unfamiliar with American companies to be much help.

It may be too early to tell, but Sony's 1989 investment of $7 billion in entertainment "software" (Columbia Pictures and CBS records) could be a similar disaster. The movie business, for which hugely expensive contract buyouts and payouts were required, was left in the hands of Hollywood producers Peter Gruber and Jon Peters. The two were told that Sony, which knew nothing about movies or the bizarre management practices of the movie industry, would not interfere with their decisions. Money was spent freely, and the results were certainly questionable. Peters left after a year, saying he was "unable to adjust to corporate life." Most observers wonder how long the payback period for such a large investment in such a volatile industry, in which the owner has given a proxy to old-style Hollywood managers, can be. Some doubt the payback will ever come.

Sony's actions have been mirrored by its rival Matsushita, which acquired MCA a year later for a somewhat less inflated price. And in late 1991, Toshiba and C. Itoh, a large Japanese trading company, spent a more modest $1 billion to buy a 12% interest in a new venture that acquired Time Warner's film, cable, and pay television business. Toshiba's motivation for the investment appears to be the same as that of its two competitors, though it and C. Itoh are far less exposed. Sony and Matsushita were intent on controlling entire studios in order to get the industry expertise they needed and to benefit from the ill-defined synergies between electronic hardware and entertainment software that they claim they must have to succeed in the future. Time will tell, but according to David Sanger of the *New York Times*, "The accepted wisdom in Tokyo, echoed in Los Angeles, is that both Sony and Matsushita are being milked for cash by their Hollywood partners. That may say volumes about why Toshiba proceeded so cautiously."[19]

If the Japanese have indeed had some sort of comparative advantage over U.S. and European firms in cost of capital during the 1980s, it is difficult to see how they have benefited from it. To some extent easy money has been wasted on overpriced purchases with low returns on investments and indefinite payback periods. Few manufacturing companies took advantage of opportunities to make unquestionably strategic investments, as Honda did in building the third-largest U.S. automobile business. Most held back, and only played with small, token foreign investments. Many simply paid down their debts with their surplus cash and passed on the opportunity. Much of the financial advantage available to companies with high stock prices was diverted to zaitech, where it performed no lasting good. Now the period of advantage is over, and what have Japanese companies got to show for it?

It would have been better to have used this financial advantage to fund the cost of shifting a significant percentage of Japan's manufacturing capacity from Japan to overseas locations. In 1987, only 4% to 5% of the manufacturing capacity of Japanese companies was cited outside the country, as compared to about 25% for the United States and something near that for European manufacturers.[20] In 1991, the Japanese percentage had risen only slightly, leaving the country still a relatively high-cost producer (especially in terms of other currencies) and making it vulnerable to the international protectionistic sentiments that arise periodically.

The explanations for this appear to lie in the fear that most Japanese manufacturers have of contaminating their unique Japanese corporate cultures through acquisitions, in their realistic awareness of the difficulty of managing a foreign company well, and in the shortage of qualified Japanese for senior management or engineering jobs abroad, especially in the United States. Money was not the problem, at least during the zaitech years. Though there are notable exceptions such as Honda, most Japanese corporations have enormous difficulty in moving large parts of their manufacturing operations abroad. They are stuck where they are, for better or for worse.

Dumping Money and Roundtripping

During the 1980s, Japanese banks and brokerages were exceptionally active overseas. The banks sharply increased the amount of foreign assets on their books, funded overseas subsidiaries in the United States, throughout Europe, and in parts of Southeast Asia. Several banks, including Dai-Ichi Kangyo, Fuji, Mitsubishi, Sanwa, and Bank of Tokyo acquired banks, branches, or financial companies in the United States to increase their market positions more quickly. Sumitomo and Industrial Bank of Japan invested in minority positions in U.S. securities firms. Most of the major banks also invested in merchant banking operations in Europe to aid them in penetrating the Eurosecurities market. The principal Japanese banks visualized the world outside Japan as a vast new market, one that would be pregnant with opportunities for them as a result of the internationalization of the yen and the global integration of financial markets generally. Overseas loans of Japanese banks grew from $69 billion in 1980 to $1.06 trillion in 1990, a fifteenfold increase during the decade.

At first, in the 1970s, the Japanese banks found the easiest way to increase foreign lending was to participate in international syndications arranged by foreign banks. This introduced them to the practice of making large syndicated loans to third world borrowers, something they came to regret by the 1980s, though at the time Japanese banks were very aggressive in soliciting such loans. The Japanese banks had very little exposure to the credits other banks were full of, so they were eager to take these new credits on, often at quite low spreads over the London Inter-Bank Offered Rate (LIBOR), the rate they had to pay to acquire dollar deposits. Japanese lending activities appeared uneconomical to many international observers, causing Timothy Bevan, then the chairman of Barclays Bank, to accuse them of "dumping money."

By the early 1980s, however, Japanese were acquiring deposits in the Middle East and in Singapore and Hong Kong, and they were using the international bond and swap markets to substantially lower their costs of funds. Meanwhile, credit exposures were causing problems for banks in the United States and elsewhere, and before long Japanese loans could be made at rates at least 0.5% lower than comparable U.S. bank loans, while maintaining the same profit margin for both banks. In these circumstances, the Japanese began rapidly to increase their share of market for international loans, and for domestic loans as well.

As syndicated lending fell off with the dramatic rise in Eurobond activity in the early 1980s, the banks had to look for other sources of loans. They found them in domestic loans in the United States and a few other markets. In the United States, market access was open, regulatory obstacles few, and prospective clients were always happy to meet someone who would offer lower than average rates. U.S. banks were much less competitive in low-margin, plain vanilla corporate loans, which most eschewed. Japanese banks found themselves with the whole of corporate (and municipal) America to lend to, in the form of commercial paper backup lines, working capital and term loans, and foreign exchange facilities. Before long their principal competition for this type of business was from other foreign banks, especially other Japanese ones. By the end of 1990, foreign banks accounted for approximately 40% of all commercial and industrial loans made by large commercial banks in the United States from offshore and onshore sources; about half of this total was from Japanese banks.

The banks, however, still had relatively limited loan-making authority in their U.S. branches. Final approval of credit exposures and loan terms had to come from Tokyo, which often necessitated long delays while Tokyo got up to speed and decided what to do. Accordingly, most banks picked the sort of loans that Tokyo wanted and went after them until they ran out of money or the business became too competitive. Gradually, Tokyo learned about real estate loans, leasing, LBOs, bridge loans, work-outs, and other sophisticated, less creditworthy lending operations. They were more eager to break in new types of loans than to experiment with visibly lower-grade credits.

Despite their moving up the sophistication curve, both in terms of asset creation and funding techniques, Japanese banks experienced, along with most foreign banks in the United States, a steady decline in profit margins. Competition was now pretty intense, and loan loss reserves unavoidably were building up.

Japanese banks, unlike their U.S. counterparts, are not free to do whatever they want outside their home country. Japanese bank regulations (i.e., administrative guidance) cross the border, so the heavy baggage of Article 65 and the protection of the special interests of particular types of banks cross too. This means that to open a new foreign office, or an investment banking affiliate, or to act as a lead manager of a Eurobond, the bank has to get the nod from the banking bureau of the Ministry of Finance. However, international markets like the Eurocurrency markets are open and free, and do not at all resemble the regulatory framework that Japanese banks must follow. The structure of the banking industry and competitive conditions abroad are very different for the Japanese—there are no long-term credit banks, or trust banks, or credit cooperatives, and so forth. Nor are there the usual separations of commercial banking and investment banking. As a concession to reality, however, the Ministry of Finance approved small merchant banking affiliates of the commercial banks in London to underwrite new issues, and most of the major securities firms have set up commercial banks in European cities to make loans; yet neither has been especially effective in the business of the other.

While the banks were struggling to gain investment banking experience, the securities firms were benefiting from the huge increase in capital market activity, which was the result of zaitech and of Japanese investors having plenty of ready cash.

In the early 1980s, Japanese insurance companies were eager to acquire dollar bond investments, and many Eurobond issues were substantially subscribed in Japan. Then the Eurobond market introduced *zero-coupon bonds* (in which all interest is accrued to be paid at the final maturity). These were very popular in Japan because the tax authorities did not impute interest income annually, as the United States and most other advanced countries did. Thus Japanese investors could make an investment in a top international company that would pay at maturity four or five times the original investment. A guaranteed capital gain with no taxes to be paid was hard to beat. The Japanese individual investor did not know the market for international zero-coupon bonds, so he took what he was offered. Japanese securities firms would offer to underwrite, say, half of a large issue at a very aggressive rate by Euromarket standards. The firm would buy the issue, then repackage it into smaller units for resale at retail rates in Japan. Thus the brokers could offer issuers cutthroat rates and still make a lot of money in Japan, which of course they did.

After a flood of these issues, the Ministry of Finance gave out some administrative guidance that required brokers to limit themselves to taking down a third of any future zero-coupon deals. They were not restricted, however, from buying zero-coupon bonds of old issues in the secondary markets. The Japanese securities firms developed so much placing power through their institutional and retail business in foreign securities that soon they were invited into every deal. Before long they began to insist on lead managing Euromarket underwritings, especially those issued by Japanese companies. Soon European and American underwriters were displaced as lead managers. After this, in the mid-1980s, the great boom period of Japanese new issues began as Japanese companies started their zaitech efforts.

Zaitech was such an enormous business for the Japanese brokers that they became the leaders of the whole Eurobond market, with Nomura leading the league tables in 1988–1991 and the other Japanese securities firms all ranking within the market's top ten. As Euromarket transactions, however, these bonds were not what they seemed—they were really domestic issues in disguise.

Most of the zaitech issues were made by comparatively unknown Japanese companies, though a number of large, well-known companies participated too. Most of the investors for these issues, approximately 80%, were Japanese. The rest were opportunistic Europeans who piggy-backed on issues that always seemed to go up, and sold them as soon as they did. The most popular form of issue was the straight, unsecured bond packaged as a unit with detachable equity warrants. The warrants were a relatively new thing in Japan at the time, and they became extremely popular with Japanese investors looking for higher levels of leverage in stock purchasing than the margin rules permitted. The brokers liked the warrants, too, because the investors didn't really know how to price them, and they could make large profits in trading them.

Many of these deals could not have been done in the domestic bond markets in Japan, where interest rates and issuing expenses were higher, market practices substantially limited the sale of unsecured bonds, and warrants were unknown before 1987. Also, issuers in Japan had to file a lengthy registration statement and wait for several weeks before the securities could be sold. So the Japanese avoided their own market by issuing securities in London that would immediately be resold in Japan. This practice, unusual for a cash-rich country, is called *roundtripping.*

The less-competitive, less-open Japanese market was losing business to another market, and would continue to do so indefinitely unless changes were made. The United States experienced a similar shifting of market economics to Europe in the early 1980s, but adjusted U.S. new-issues regulations (under SEC Rule 415) to allow for shelf registration and quick market access, which soon leveled things off. In Japan, some steps have been taken to offer a similar form of shelf registration that would simplify the use of the Tokyo market. Nonetheless, all through 1991, Japanese roundtripping continued as companies endeavored to squeeze the last bits of benefit out of the Euromarket. Ultimately, Japanese roundtripping can be reduced only by deregulating new issues further, to follow international standards. This is a curious form of deregulation, one that is imposed from abroad as a country conforms to new, internationally convergent forms of financial regulation. It can be resisted or ignored for a while, but sooner or later the home country will find itself behind the times and doing no business. When this happens, most countries try to correct the situation by changing their domestic regulations. If such changes are not made, the countries providing the markets may decide to limit their availability and allow access only to issuers from countries that contribute their share to global financial orderliness. This is the sort of thing the U.S. government continually brings up.

Retrenching

During the second half of the 1980s, Japanese banks increased the dollar value of their international assets by 200%. At the end of 1990, according to the BIS, Japan's share of total international bank assets reached 35.5%, more than three times that of the next-largest country, the United States. International bank assets include foreign loans in all currencies to both residents and nonresidents. In 1991, Japan's international bank assets did not increase at all.

The banks were being pulled in several different directions at once. They had to respond to changes in the banking market at home; a burgeoning demand for zaitech and real estate facilities was halted by the market crash. The deleveraging of corporations, the rise of interest rates in Japan, and the opportunities to increase foreign lending in a market from which many U.S. and European banks were retreating drew the Japanese banks into more aggressive lending activities outside Japan. After the market crash, however, domestic loan demand grew at the same time creditworthiness declined. Bankruptcies increased sharply, the scandals revealed fraudulent loans that were nearly worthless, and the market drop wiped out much of the banks' capital, requiring them to cut bank asset growth generally and to concentrate (like banks elsewhere) on rebuilding profitability. Overseas loans had also begun to reveal extensive exposure to weak real estate and corporate sectors, and write-offs began to increase. All these factors forced the Japanese to retrench.

Some observers, especially foreign bankers living in Tokyo, believe that this period of austerity is temporary, and as soon as prices recover, the Japanese banks will plunge headlong once again into major asset-growth programs. Most Japanese bankers are more conservative about the future of their lending activities. They believe they will have to shift their focus from lending to fee-based activities, trading, and underwriting new issues. Until recently, they were only permitted by the Ministry of Finance to engage in trading and underwriting in the Euromarket.

Some Japanese banks appear to be anticipating these changes by building up their overseas capabilities in investment banking, trading, and finance company activities. Industrial Bank of Japan owns a U.S. government bond house and a merchant banking operation and is moderately active in the Eurobond market. Sumitomo Bank owns a 12.5% interest in Goldman Sachs and has set up a U.S. finance and leasing company in the United States. Dai-Ichi Kangyo Bank acquired the CIT leasing business from Manufacturer's Hanover Trust and has since expanded activities in trading and derivative securities. Endeavors such as these are still relatively small compared to the assets and revenue flow of the banks as a whole. Despite their size, however, they have represented excellent opportunities for these large banks to develop the techniques and skills that they will need as deregulation advances further.

The brokers too have been retrenching their international activities in response to new developments. Japanese Euro-issues were cut back as zai-tech transactions faded away and the stock market lost its special no-lose luster. Without a large capital surplus to invest in foreign securities, Japanese brokers had little to impress European and American clients with. Business fell off in all sectors after 1990 except the sale of Japanese shares to bottom-fishing foreign investors, and here the Japanese brokers had to compete with U.S. and European firms that could trade the shares either in Europe, the United States, or Japan. These firms, being more trading-oriented than the Japanese, were often able to offer better terms or ideas, and therefore increased their penetration into the brokers' share of the international market in Japanese stocks.

Meanwhile the Japanese penetration of U.S. and European securities markets remained minimal, and for the most part unprofitable. Most U.S. branches of Japanese securities firms have suffered periodic heavy losses. Nomura made the greatest effort to penetrate the United States, hiring Max Chapman, former chief executive of Kidder Peabody, to run its American operations. Under Chapman (and a Nomura co-manager), the firm raised its profile and activity levels in asset-backed securities, futures and options, and other instruments. It also participated in a number of U.S. underwriting transactions, sometimes as lead manager, but was not considered a major player in the investment banking sector. It made little effort in mergers and acquisitions because Nomura had invested $100 million in a 25% interest in Wasserstein Perrella, a New York-based M&A boutique. Wasserstein Perrella, however, did not do many Japanese deals, and soon its Tokyo representative resigned to return to New York and resume practicing law.

The Wall Street profit squeeze of 1990 affected the Japanese firms too. Several firms laid off numerous employees, all Americans, contrary to the job security expectations they were quick to encourage when hiring. When the markets returned to profitability in 1991, most of the Japanese firms remained conservative and cautious. In July 1991, Michael Berman, a top Nomura official in charge of government securities, resigned his post, apparently frustrated by the "rigid, risk-averse management style of Nomura's headquarters."

WHITHER THE COST OF CAPITAL ADVANTAGE?

For the last several years, conventional wisdom has held that Japanese companies have an advantage in cost of capital over American and European companies, and that this advantage enabled them to invest more in plant and equipment and other improvements than their competitors could afford. If Japanese capital costs were, say, 4%, and American costs 8%, all investment projects expected to return between 4% and 8% could be undertaken economically by the Japanese but not by the Americans.

Competitive efficiency, of course, is determined by many factors other than cost of capital. But Japan clearly had a competitive advantage in its younger and more modern manufacturing equipment, which was about 3 years old on average as compared to 6 in the United States. It was able to secure this advantage, economists say, principally because of the lower capital cost in Japan. So economists put a lot of energy and effort into studying the difference between capital costs in Japan and the United States.

The investigation began by exploring the actual costs of borrowing money and issuing equity securities. Here, a great many differences between Japanese and the American practices emerged, which significantly obscured the comparison. Among these are substantial differences in accounting practices (which on balance understate the profits of a Japanese company, relative to an American company, by between 25% and 40%), tax rates, real interest rates, and significant differences in the composition of comparable companies. Nonetheless, one could observe that the nominal cost of borrowing in Japan—a low-inflation country—has been less than the nominal cost of borrowing in the United States for several years. One could also observe the high prices of Japanese stocks, many of which traded at prices in 1989 that were 70 to 100 times their reported earnings (i.e., their earnings as reported in Japan, unadjusted for accounting differences). At such levels, Japan seemed to have a significant advantage.

The theory of cost of capital is a slippery thing. Academics, accountants, and corporate financiers disagree, with each other and with their peers, on the correct method for calculating cost of capital. It is supposed to be a combination of debt cost and equity cost blended on the basis of the debt-equity ratio of the company.

The debt cost is fairly simple to compute, but there are some variables that complicate the task. Properly done, the marginal interest cost for one more dollar of borrowing ought to be adjusted for taxes, inflation, maturity, and other factors. When we get through, however, we hope to have an after-tax, real cost of debt for maturities equal to the life of the project. At the end of 1991, this rate for an A-rated American company investing in a ten-year project of normal risk levels was about 3.5%. This assumes a nominal borrowing rate of 9.0%, which becomes 5.4% after a 40% tax rate, and then 2.4% after deducting the 3% inflation rate for 1991. For Japan, the net real interest rate at the end of 1991 was 0.7%, after a nominal borrowing rate of 8%, a 50% tax rate, and inflation of 3.3%.[21] On this basis, Japanese borrowing cost is cheaper, assuming Japanese companies are financed mainly with debt, which in 1991 was not the case.

But the cost of capital must also take the cost of equity capital into account. The total cost of capital, therefore, reflects the ratio of borrowed money to total capital—percentages that have changed rapidly in recent years for both U.S. and Japanese firms, with the former increasing leverage and the latter reducing it.

Calculating the cost of equity capital, however, is quite difficult. You can calculate it on the basis of the internal rate of return on the firm's retained earnings, or the historical return on book value equity. Or, you can do it by determining the marginal cost of raising one more dollar of equity by selling new stock to the market, in which case the market price of the company's stock is important. On this basis you want to know the return on the market value of the firm's net worth, or earnings divided by market value. This is the reciprocal of the company's price-earnings ratio. An American company with an average p/e of 17 would then have a cost of equity capital of 1/17, or 5.9%. A Japanese company with a high, pre-1990 p/e of 70 obviously would show a much lower cost of capital, i.e., 1.4%. But before you can make this comparison, you have to adjust the Japanese company's earnings data to U.S. accounting principles. According to a number of analysts of Japanese securities, including the late Paul Aaron of Daiwa Securities, who wrote extensively on the subject, there are several such adjustments, and when these are made, the Japanese p/e ratio is reduced by about 50%. A 70 p/e thus becomes a 36 p/e, reflecting a cost of capital of 2.8%.

But, if on top of the accounting adjustment, you correct for the 60% reduction in market value since 1990, the result is a p/e of 14.4, and a cost of equity capital of 6.9%, higher actually than the American average p/e (17) in 1991 with its equity cost of 5.9%. However, Japanese companies have become substantially deleveraged in recent years, and the capital in their business is now almost all equity; thus they are running on a richer mixture of equity and debt than Americans are. On balance, that should give the U.S. companies a slight edge in cost-of-capital terms relative to Japan's more unleveraged companies.

Economist Jeffrey Frankel of the University of California has been studying Japanese cost of capital since the mid-1980s. In a detailed survey published in the spring of 1991, he concluded that certain institutional factors and the speculative bubble that characterized Japanese financial asset prices during most of the 1980s probably did result in a somewhat lower cost of capital for Japanese companies, as compared to their American counterparts. He did not conclude that capital cost less in Japan because its markets were more efficient. On the contrary, by continuing the keiretsu system and other market control practices, corporations and institutions unwittingly were subsidizing the cost of capital for all corporations, a condition that appears to have ended with the market drop after January 1990.

Indeed, Frankel makes the point that the more the Japanese investors learn about how capital markets work in free-market environments, and the more deregulation opens up Japanese markets to foreign practices, the more the Japanese practices will evolve toward Anglo-Saxon norms. As this occurs, any cost-of-capital difference will decline.[22]

A study by Harvard Business School professors Timothy Luehrman and Carl Kester concluded that even for the 1980s, the real after-tax cost of capital was roughly the same for firms of comparable risk. DRI/McGraw-Hill has published numbers showing a U.S. cost of capital for the first six months of 1991 of 5.92% against a Japanese cost of 6.09%. Several others, including Isao Yamamoto of Nomura Research Institute and Steve Nagourney of Shearson Lehman Brothers, have concluded that the cost of capital in the two countries is now about the same. Jay Woodworth of Bankers Trust believes that capital cost differentials have been arbitraged away by global market integration.

The conventional wisdom on the subject of U.S. and Japanese cost of capital has thus shifted from seeing an advantage for Japan to seeing the two countries as roughly equal. Also, no one thinks that Japan can move backward along this road; it can only continue to move in the direction of further market integration with the developed countries of Europe and America.[23]

As long as markets trade on approximately comparable bases—without, for example, subsidies, capital restrictions, or substantially different speculative energy—market forces should soon wear away major rate differences for similar companies financing similar risks. The approximately 40% overpricing of the Japanese equity market in the period 1985–1989 was probably created by irregular market conditions and practices such as abnormal amounts of excess liquidity, the mispricing of convertible debentures and warrants, and the traditional (but perhaps fading) practice of maintaining keiretsu holdings, which substantially reduced the supply of many stocks available to be purchased. But the market prices have since been adjusted. Now that Japan's market is in reasonable alignment with those of the United States and Europe, it seems likely that the Japanese will adjust the remainder of their unique financial practices to follow global practices more closely.

As the sun rises on Japan in the 1990s, it does not illuminate a financial superpower. The bubble economy, inflated by speculation, market manipulation, questionable transactions, and high-velocity zaitech, finally burst. The stupendous valuations given to Japanese share prices and real estate were no more. As the Japanese markets were corrected, the world's largest banks suffered seriously troubled loans and rediscovered their long-forgotten humility. The brokers were shamed and forced to try to make a living in a normal market environment for a change, something they have found difficult to do, despite the continued existence of fixed commission rates. The great financial surpluses of the 1980s were replaced in 1991 with the first financial deficit in many years. The Japanese were among the world's hottest investors when their pockets were full of money, but not otherwise. Japan's cost of capital, no longer much lower than anyone else's, offered little help. Japan had come back to earth.

9

DISCARDING THE
THIRD WORLD REMNANTS

The 1980s in Japan were comparable in some respects to the 1920s in the United States. Both were periods of rapidly rising prosperity and international influence for countries that had not had much of either, countries that were unworldly and unsophisticated. In both periods, regulation was inadequate and scandals were plentiful. Speculation in all forms of financial assets replaced traditionally cautious attitudes about saving and investing. Instant millionaires were a dime a dozen. A surge of New Men appeared on the scene with the money-can-buy-anything swagger that goes with this breed in any age. The common investor was drawn into financial markets that were openly and cynically manipulated by rich professionals while the government looked on, seeing nothing. In both instances there was a price to be paid for the excesses.

The United States paid with a stock market crash of about 30%, followed by a period of tight money and mistaken policies that ultimately produced four more years of sinking stock prices and nearly a decade of economic hard times. It also saddled itself with a massive new regulatory regime for banking and financial markets unlike anything seen before. The lasting legacy of the 1920s, however, was the final casting off of a third-world financial mentality in favor of safe banks, fair markets, and full disclosure to the public of material information. Politics were changed too: the New Deal carved out a bigger role for government in economic affairs. The smoke-filled rooms were gradually aired out and a freer, more democratic—if sometimes less efficient—form of electoral politics was ushered in.

In Japan, the price of the excessive 1980s has not yet been fully counted. Its market crashed and banks and brokers have suffered as a result, perhaps more than even close observers thought possible. The secondary effects, however, are still to be seen. They are bound to be powerful and long-lasting, as much in Japan's financial and political practices needs fix-

269

ing. Japan's third-world mentality must be set aside if it hopes to expand its role and influence in the world.

THE EMPEROR'S NEW CLOTHES

The 1990s began in Japan shortly after the opening of a new era—the reign of a new Emperor, Akihito, who succeeded his father Hirohito on January 7, 1989. The new era is called *Heisei* (the achievement of peace), and it determines dates in Japan. The first year of Heisei, for example, is 1989; the third year, Heisei 3, is 1991. Emperor Akihito is younger, less formal, and much more modern than his father, whose 62-year reign spanned the war years and the difficult postwar recovery. He was of a different time entirely. His successor, though an Emperor without an empire, must wear the robes of a modern Japan well into the new era of the twenty-first century.

Japan is one of the world's most homogeneous and oldest societies. Its culture, itself a form of religion, is deeply inculcated among its members, who relate to each other as if all were members of the same family.

The Japanese are interested in and curious about foreign ways and practices, but are not much guided by them at home; in general, they are confused by and distrustful of foreigners. All Japanese who live in Japan are judged by their peers and superiors on their Japanese-ness, and those who have spent too much time abroad or in learning foreign languages are suspected of having lost something important.

Indeed, the Japanese make much of their uniqueness, which is often frustrating to outsiders. When foreigners complain, the typical reply is that "things are different in Japan, and we hope you will understand and accept that and not try to force us to make impossible changes." Japanese foreign policy for the past forty-five years has essentially been based on the task of getting foreigners to accept this. For the most part it has worked, even during periods of *shokku*, or shocks, which require some kind of accommodation to world events, but not fundamental change.

The new era will certainly be different. The great task of the Heisei era will be to bring Japan into harmonious alignment with the rest of the world, bearing its share of world economic and political responsibilities. Japan cannot succeed in this task without also transforming itself into a more open and diverse society. The economic animals will have to be tamed, or at least housebroken. If the country fails in this, it may again find itself isolated from commercial and other arrangements with Europe and America, and be much the loser for it. Japan, as it well knows, is a small island country dependent on the outside world for almost all of its raw materials. It is also dependent on access to the commercial markets of other countries, chiefly the United States. Without this access, it would certainly be no economic superpower.

The Japanese understand two kinds of "truth"—*tatemae,* or the spoken truth, and *honne,* the never-mentioned reality. Tatemae can be thought of as the party line, for instance, "We are different and can never change." It usually contains one or more untruths. Honne is what everybody knows is true, but never acknowledges, for instance, "If we don't accommodate the foreigners' wishes, we will be cut off from trade and investment, but probably not yet." One of the principal uses of tatemae is for speaking to foreigners and the press. One of the purposes of honne is for achieving consensus on internal Japanese matters, without destroying relationships. In the world of tatemae everything can be explained; in the other world, nothing ever is.

Tatemae holds that financial market activities in Japan are well regulated and up to date, utilize sophisticated practices, and on the whole are equal to financial markets elsewhere in the world. Honne knows that the markets are manipulated periodically, that politicians receive a substantial part of their financial support from market gains, and that basic trading practices are primitive and unsupervised in comparison to foreign markets. It also knows that the large brokers are less prestigious but more powerful than the large bankers, because they have more favors to bestow, and that the Ministry of Finance must bow to pressure from politicians not to rock the boat.

Tatemae also explains that scandals occur from time to time in Japan as anywhere else, but that these are isolated events deserving punishment rather than symptoms of a faulty system. Honne knows that the system is at fault; scandals come about only when corruption is revealed to the press, otherwise it is business as usual. Honne also knows that these things are not discussed because there is no benefit in criticizing that which one cannot change.

Taking Care of Business

Nomura Securities was founded by Tokushichi Nomura II, a young commodities dealer who opened up a small "securities shop" in Osaka in 1904. Securities markets had existed on a limited scale in Japan for a long time as a sort of high-risk affiliate of the rice and commodities markets. Securities trading was considered to be not much different from gambling, a popular diversion of middle- and lower-class Japanese. It was controlled by what Nomura called "low-life personalities," though he himself rose above the reputation of his profession and was ultimately elected to the House of Peers, the Japanese equivalent of the British House of Lords.

There were no securities laws to speak of, and the stock market was a rough place driven by rumors, tips, and manipulation. For someone who was determined and courageous, who had access to the right information, and who could see the benefit of making others rich during a period of great changes, the securities business in Japan from 1904 to 1940 was a great place to be. Tokushichi Nomura was such a person, and he prospered greatly during the zaibatsu period, accumulating a fortune of more than $60 million by 1907. He invested it in a small zaibatsu of his own, which was broken up after his death and the end of the war in 1945.

The firm was reconstituted in 1946 under the leadership of Tsunao Okumura, a prewar employee. Okumura, a onetime playboy, was now extremely effective at wooing politicians and government officials. He was part of a small cabal of business leaders who provided campaign financing during the early days of the LDP; this put him very close to all of the important postwar leaders of the country. Okumura was replaced as president of Nomura in 1959 by Minoru Segawa, a smart, tough, hard-driving sales manager who was "cold, stoic and feared by all." Segawa was chief executive until 1968, by which time Nomura had emerged as Japan's largest and most powerful brokerage. Kiichiro Kitaura replaced Segawa, serving until 1978. He expanded Nomura's research, investment trust, and international affiliations and increased its lead over rivals Nikko Securities, Daiwa Securities, and Yamaichi Securities.[1]

These Big Four today completely dominate the Japanese securities business. Each has brokerage offices all over Japan filled with customers men who maintain daily contact with business people interested in placing small orders for themselves or their companies. Securities are even sold door to door by "other salesmen," i.e., women (usually housewives) who work their neighborhoods like Avon ladies. The brokers also act as distributors of government securities and a limited amount of corporate bonds, and they sell and manage large *investment trusts,* or mutual funds.

By 1980, after several years of rising stock market profits, Nomura had adopted a much higher profile than at any time since the war. And under the leadership of Setsuya Tabuchi, Nomura had begun to achieve the recognition and prestige it had long sought. It had a dozen foreign offices, managed Eurobonds and domestic new issues, and had easy access to senior officials of governments and multinational corporations that were seeking financing. As the biggest Japanese brokerage firm, it received just about everyone of importance who visited Tokyo.

Nomura was very profitable, reporting net income for 1980 of $179 million (down 12% from its then all-time high earnings in 1979). These profits came mainly from brokerage commissions (58% of noninterest revenues), which were not negotiable but which did allow institutional investors some discount for large orders. Underwriting fees (23% of noninterest revenues) were also fixed, as were the amounts of securities allocated to the major firms during government bond and other underwritings. Banks, separated from investment banking because of Article 65, could not complete with the securities firms in Japan, nor could foreign firms. During 1980 Nomura's own stock reached a high of ¥429 per share, which capitalized the firm at about $3.2 billion, twice its book value.

The Big Four were not required to take trading risks, and they maintained comparatively small securities inventories. Nomura's income from trading was only 17% of noninterest revenues in 1980. Minimal trading inventories made the firm extremely well capitalized—its equity to total assets ratio was a remarkable 46%.

About 60% of all trading on the Tokyo Stock Exchange in 1980 was done by individuals, mainly stock market speculators. They cared little for research, wanting only to know which stocks Nomura and the others were pushing on a given day. Corporate clients were indifferent to Nomura's corporate finance skills; they only wanted to do whatever the previous company had done, at the same or better terms. There was never much competition for underwriting because the business was awarded according to keiretsu relationships. Here Nomura identified itself closely with the old Mitsui Group, but tried to be close to other groups as well. To retain those relationships, the securities firms—even the Big Four—had to "bow deeply" and do whatever their clients wanted.

Nomura's offices in New York, London, Hong Kong, and other places handled brokerage in Japanese shares for foreign clients, underwrote new issues for Japanese clients in the Euromarkets (and occasionally in New York), and devoted themselves to *takecare,* or entertaining visiting Japanese clients. This usually meant meeting them at the airport, arranging business discussions at the office, taking them to dinner at a local Japanese restaurant, and then drinking and playing mahjong with them until the wee hours. Takecare missions often occurred four or five nights in a week and also involved golf on Saturdays. As a result, Nomura's relationships with its clients were rock solid, but the clients got little in the way of imaginative financial ideas out of it.

The 1980s catapulted Nomura to incredible heights. Yoshihisa Tabuchi, a tough-minded veteran of the sales force, replaced Setsuya Tabuchi (no relation) in 1985. Like his predecessors, he maintained close ties to the LDP and its principal figures, shady and otherwise—there was little choice if the relationships were to be maintained—and with all other constituencies served by Nomura. Stock tips and new issue allocations were passed around to favored friends, but even without these, the surging market was enough to make many of Nomura's clients rich. Protected by Article 65 and fixed commissions, Nomura passed Toyota Motors as Japan's most profitable company in 1987 and was ranked as Japan's ninth-largest corporation by market value. Its consolidated net income was $1.8 billion for the year ended in March 1990 (ten times its profits for 1980). Nomura's net worth at that time was $12.3 billion and the market value of its shares (at ¥3,840 per share) reached $54 billion during the year (seventeen times its 1980 highest value). It then employed 16,000 people worldwide in 146 domestic offices and 52 offices or subsidiaries abroad. The firm continued to be very strongly capitalized in 1990, with an equity-to-assets ratio of more than 30. Brokerage commissions still comprised the bulk of its noninterest revenues (54%), where a trade valued at $40,000 in Japan would cost $376 in commissions (as compared to $188 on the New York Stock Exchange). Nomura also received about 30% of its noninterest revenues from underwriting fees.

By comparison, the largest commercial bank in Japan at the time, Dai-Ichi Kangyo Bank, reported net income of $654 million, net worth of $13.7 billion, and market value of $30 billion. The largest U.S. securities firm, Merrill Lynch, once Nomura's mentor, reported net income for 1990 of $191 million, net worth of $3.2 billion, and a high market value for the year of $2.9 billion, a mere 5.3% of Nomura's. Merrill, still the largest U.S. retail brokerage, had an equity to assets ratio of 4.7. Only 39% of its noninterest revenues came from brokerage.

Nomura basked in its position and loved being referred to as the "world's largest and most profitable investment banking firm." All lists of the great powers in investment banking for the next century included Nomura's name, and sometimes one or more of the other Japanese brokers.

Kickbacks and Market Rigging

In the summer of 1991, a Japanese newspaper published an account of payments being made by the Big Four to reimburse some of their major clients for losses incurred during the market drop of 1990. Several clients were unhappy because they had lost so much money. Nomura and the other brokers felt that they would have to make good on at least some of these losses to retain their clients' loyalty. After all, they reasoned, "We put them into these stocks in the first place—soliciting their business pretty aggressively—and if our competitors offer to reimburse them, and we don't, we'll be dead meat with important clients when the market recovers."

These "compensation" payments were not against the law; indeed, there are very few laws regulating the securities markets in Japan. Regulations are imposed as needed by the Ministry of Finance through its informal practice of administrative guidance. The Ministry may permit or prohibit activities as it sees fit; apparently it knew of these payments and did nothing to stop them. The Big Four made the payments by creating mispriced trades that guaranteed profits for the customer, a practice considered outright market rigging in other countries, and prohibited by law. There were also reports that the Big Four had rigged other trades in listed stocks and other securities, including U.S. Treasuries, in order to make money for favored clients.

Disclosure of the compensation payments and other suspicious transactions created a stir, especially since most of the brokers' clients had received nothing but losses. The securities firms initially denied the charge, then admitted that a small amount of compensation had been paid. The chase after the "real story" was soon on.

By mid-summer it was Tokyo's hottest item. Reporters were covering it from all angles and digging up new disclosures as fast as possible. Reluctantly the Big Four admitted that the compensation payments were bigger than originally indicated; indeed, they totaled nearly $1.5 billion, and were paid to 200 big clients of the firms, including company tokkins, institutions, and some individuals. The scale of the compensation and market rigging operation was staggering, even to U.S. observers who had been accustomed to large-number scandals since the S&L and insider trading revelations. The fact that the almighty Ministry of Finance, guardian regulator of financial markets in Japan, had turned a blind eye to the matter was equally shocking.

The press was soon onto other possible market manipulations, like the sudden appearance of a newspaper story in September 1991 announcing that Meiji Milk Products Company had discovered a drug that was "100% effective" in curing AIDS. Though the drug was untested and years away from the market, the company's stock price shot up from ¥777 to ¥1,200 per share. It so happened that a large number of Meiji stock purchase warrants were about to expire, worthless because their exercise price was ¥790. The happy result for Meiji was that the warrants were exercised, and the company saved about $50 million that it would have had to pay to retire bonds tied to those warrants.[2]

Then it came out that Nomura and Nikko had each paid $120 million to Susumu Ishii, the boss of a major *yazuka* (organized-crime family), before his death in September 1991. Ishii had apparently sold worthless golf club memberships to the two firms and used the money to buy shares in Tokyu Corporation, a railway and construction company, which Nomura subsequently promoted aggressively. Ishii acquired about 30 million shares, the stock went up, and he sold out at least some of his position for a suitably large, riskless, profit.[3]

The story set the media aflame and led to several hearings before an outraged Diet. A number of Nomura's top executives resigned, including Setsuya Tabuchi, then chairman, and chief executive Yoshihisa Tabuchi. The latter took a parting shot at Finance Minister Ryutaro Hashimoto, who he claimed knew about the compensation payments all along. Nikko's president, Takuya Iwasaki, also resigned when his firm's continuing involvement with the gangster became known. Finance Minister Hashimoto, trying to calm the situation, admitted that his ministry could have done better and cut his own salary by 10%, but by November he too was gone.

Setsuya Tabuchi explained that the resignations were to take responsibility for the scandals, adding the tatemae that they were the result of "innumerable discussions about Japan's position in the world and the drastically changing role of our nation's stock market." He went on, however, to suggest at least part of the honne: "The bubble economy hasn't only been a problem for Japan's securities companies. The difficulty is that there is a mismatch between the rules in Japan and the rules in the rest of the world."[4]

Tabuchi might have added that scandals like these are a product of Japan's long-standing tradition of slavish service to big customers, and of its postwar tradition of using brokers to pass favors back and forth between those on the inside, such as politicians and businessmen, and those with money who are on the outside, such as speculators, gamblers, and gangsters.

About the same time that Tabuchi was in the spotlight and the Ministry of Finance was promising tighter regulation, another now-famous stock market scandal was taking place. Daiwa Securities, Japan's second-largest brokerage, had some clients that had accumulated large losses in their stock portfolios following the market collapse. A reporting date was approaching and the clients did not want to book the losses. So Daiwa offered to park their stocks with other clients by arranging a sale of the shares at a greatly inflated price, about equal to the first clients' cost, together with guaranteed repurchase agreements at a somewhat higher price to compensate the obliging parkees. Such schemes are called *tobashi*, or "flying about" to avoid being caught by the accountants. The practice is well known in Tokyo, and it is understood to be widely used by favored customers. It is illegal in the United States.

One of the tobashi trades that Daiwa arranged was with Tokyu Department Stores, a large retailing company related to the Tokyu Corporation. Tokyu Department Stores, through Daiwa, bought a portfolio worth about $225 million for approximately $675 million, to disguise $450 million of losses for its owner. Daiwa agreed to repurchase the portfolio from Tokyu at a profit, but the market declined further and the portfolio's original owner was not able to repurchase it from Daiwa. Daiwa then told Tokyu it had a problem and couldn't pay the full price. A dispute ensued and finally Tokyu took Daiwa to court—hitherto an unthinkable action in a country where everything is settled behind closed doors, but Tokyu was desperate, and probably very angry.

Daiwa admitted to the offense and to several others like it. In the end, a Japanese solution was achieved; Tokyu and Daiwa worked out a settlement, and Masahiro Dozen, Daiwa's president, resigned to take responsibility for the event at a news conference broadcast on television.[5]

One senior Japanese executive, the president of a major corporation, explained that the scandals were part of the Japanese system, a combination of old feudal ways and modern efforts to distribute influence a little more broadly to prevent serious abuses of power:

> Deals are discreetly negotiated, intermediaries always get a share, wheels are always greased a little, and big people always get more than little people, but these things have to be contained within certain limits. . . . This helps democracy, as it provides a way for those committed to democracy to succeed in a country without democratic traditions. . . . [Small scandals] are a price you have to pay to get democracy moving in this country; to bring power and authority to the political establishment.[6]

Though many Japanese may have shrugged them off, once the scandals became public knowledge, they had to be publicly redressed. Those involved had to be punished, despite the fact that—except for the explicit market rigging charges, which had not been proved—no laws had been broken. Indeed, there were no laws. Nor were there prescribed penalties for such abuses. Penalties were assessed on the basis of what would satisfy the media, which was after all the principal institution bringing forward the charges.

After some efforts to impose lesser penalties, the Ministry of Finance finally required Nomura, in addition to the various resignations, to close 87 of its 153 branch offices, shut down its research department, and discontinue trading for its own account, all for a period of one month, which cost it quite a lot of lost business. The penalties were deemed appropriate, though they were neither required nor necessarily legal. They were not contested, of course.

"This kind of behavior is indicative of the lack of rule of law in brokering," said Bob Grieg, an American lawyer in Tokyo. "The system as it currently operates is very obviously beneficial to the privileged players and is difficult, if not impossible, for the less privileged or foreign players."[7]

Setsuya Tabuchi was right about one thing—the securities companies were not the only ones involved in the scandals. The bursting of the bubble economy brought many other improprieties to light. Golf course membership scandals came next, including one called, improbably, the Great Gatsby Golf Club, which was found by the Tokyo District Court to have sold 30,000 memberships after promising to limit the total to 1,800. At the Ibaraki Country Club, 48,000 memberships were issued instead of 2,800, and the fairways were getting crowded. Membership sales were so hot that

190 golf club brokerages had sprung up during the 1980s, many of them having ties to gangsters. Memberships found their way into the hands of politicians, who also received contributions from the land developers and others trying to promote more clubs.

Lending to the "Bubble Lady"

But the biggest scandals were saved for some of the biggest banks, which were found to have made or accepted nearly $5 billion in fraudulent loans.

Undoubtedly the most astonishing story was that of an uneducated, 61-year-old-woman, Nui Onoue, the owner of a restaurant in a seedy part of Osaka, who was able to borrow $2.5 billion to purchase a portfolio of stocks. Onoue was a creature of the late 1980s, whom the tabloids dubbed "the bubble lady." She had come to Osaka penniless as a young woman, worked as a hostess in bars, and found a well-to-do businessman to sponsor her in the restaurant business. She described herself as the "hidden child of a big shot," which still has special meaning in Japan and apparently was sufficient to explain herself to her bankers. She was also a fervent member of a peculiar Buddhist sect, dressed in special robes, and claimed to receive her stock tips directly from the gods. Onoue was a well-known eccentric in Japan at the time and appeared on television, flashing stock certificates and praying for divine intervention to make her stocks go up.

Where she got her money from in the first place is not clear, and many in Japan suspect her of being a front for the mob (perhaps the greatest beneficiaries of the bubble economy). She bought negotiable deposits from the Industrial Bank of Japan and then borrowed against them to invest in stocks; at one point these borrowings exceeded $730 million. With this kind of a stake she was showered with the attentions of her brokers and bankers. Everyone wanted a customer like Onoue, who invested passionately and heavily and who, apparently, was usually right. She parlayed her winnings into more CDs and more stocks, becoming the largest individual stockholder of Industrial Bank of Japan, Dai-Ichi Kangyo Bank, and Nippon Telephone. Her holdings were thought to be worth $3 billion, ranking her as one of the twenty-five wealthiest people in the world.

The market crash was bad news for people like Onoue, who had to produce mountains of cash to cover their collapsing portfolio. She did this by conspiring with Tomomi Maekawa, a branch manager of the Toyo Shinkin Bank (a local cooperative savings bank), to get the big banks to temporarily lend her $2.5 billion against thirteen certificates of deposit of Toyo Shinkin. These CDs, which totaled an amount equal to the entire deposits of the bank, were nothing but clumsy, handwritten forgeries. Yet some of the large banks, including the Industrial Bank of Japan, made loans against the forged collateral. The scheme was recycled every month or so to conceal the losses in the portfolio, but ultimately, Onoue and Maekawa were caught. The bubble lady pleaded guilty to fraud charges in Osaka in January 1992, but about $2 billion of her debt is thought to be unrecoverable. The discovery brought down the Toyo Shinkin Bank, which was taken over by Sanwa Bank after an all-parties restructuring effort brokered by the Ministry of Finance.[8]

This was the largest scam in Japan's history, but soon similar loan frauds were reported at Fuji Bank, Tokai Bank, and Kyowa Saitama Bank, all major city banks. According to James Sterngold of the New York Times, who covered the story from Tokyo,

> The amounts are so large, and the lenders who claim to have been taken in are of such sophistication, that experts wonder if there are as yet unidentified figures involved and whether the banks might have intended the odd activities to conceal questionable loans to influential people.[9]

Industrial Bank of Japan, aristocrat of Japanese banks and lender of long-term capital to the bluest-chip companies, was embarrassed by the loans. This sort of business was completely out of character for it. But, as indicated earlier, during the period of zaitech and deleveraging, IBJ's clients were less interested in borrowing long-term capital. So the bank had moved into more active areas such as financing securities and real estate transactions. IBJ's president, Yoh Kurosawa, a tall, urbane, pin-striped Japanese who had lived for a few years in Germany, knew Onoue. She had become an important customer in 1989, and the bank's Osaka managers had urged him to pay a traditional ten-minute courtesy call on her at the restaurant, which he did, to his later regret.

Kurosawa was subjected to grilling by the Diet and the media for days, and in the end, his predecessor, Kaneo Nakamura, then IBJ's chairman, took responsibility and resigned from the bank. Nakamura, a Harvard Business School graduate and industrial restructuring expert, had only recently stepped up to the chairman's office, an honorary position with little power. Nakamura took the bullet without complaint so Kurosawa could continue to run the bank.

Taizo Hashida, chairman of the Fuji Bank, which had been involved in a suspiciously similar $2-billion bogus deposit scheme, also resigned, as did a variety of less-senior officers from other banks that were less extensively taken. Hashida's resignation was the seventh of a top official of a bank or brokerage firm in a year.

Samurai Regulators

In Japan's samurai tradition, self-annihilation is a purifying event. So today, when things go wrong, the man at the top offers to take responsibility and to commit a kind of symbolic, corporate hara-kiri by turning in his resignation. After the noble deed is done, life goes on with others filling the place of the departed official. Nothing else changes very much.

Rules are rarely written down; they are left up to administrators to decide on the spot, based on discussion with the principals in the matter and with administrative supervisors. Decisions are never overturned, but different decisions can be made in subsequent cases. Explanations beyond a certain very general tatemae are neither offered nor requested. Everything is done through discussion, with the more difficult matters taking a very long time to resolve—unless the matter becomes public, which invariably it will, because it always seems to be in someone's interest to leak what is being discussed. "There are no secrets in Japan," the Japanese claim. For these reasons, perhaps, the Ministry of Finance, unlike the Securities and Exchange Commission in the United States, has no market monitoring and enforcement staff. The Tokyo Stock Exchange has only twenty-seven employees conducting market surveillance.

This form of governance has direct roots in Japan's not-so-distant feudal past, from which it also derives a strong authoritarian character. The big and powerful in Japan make the rules—they are different from everyone else. The samurai makes a virtue out of determination to succeed in his mission by whatever means, but also of unquestioned obedience to superiors. Duty and loyalty to others is very important, especially to one's family, clan, or company. Most Japanese, even today, live by these precepts. Everyone knows what they are and how judgments of each other's behavior should be made.

The current scandals, and the increasing mismatch between Japanese rules and the rules of the rest of the world, point to the need for reform of Japanese financial regulation along Western lines; for example, through regulatory organizations like the U.S. SEC or the Bank of England. Indeed, the Japanese press has clamored for the creation of such an agency, arguing that the whole string of scandals only proved the Ministry of Finance was too lax in regulating the banking and securities industries. Responding to the pressure, Prime Minister Kaifu asked an existing blue-ribbon commission (previously appointed to streamline the Japanese bureaucracy) to recommend a procedure for creating a new stock-market watchdog agency.

The commission was headed by Eiji Suzuki, chairman of Mitsubishi Kasei Corporation, and included eight other members from the business, academic, and labor communities. The commission delivered its report to the prime minister in September 1991, recommending major reforms, including the creation of a new enforcement agency, negotiated commission rates to increase competition, and new efforts to get organized crime out of the markets. The recommendations sounded good, and indeed a new watchdog agency was created in the spring of 1992. However, the watchdog was widely considered to have no teeth—the new agency with a staff of only 200 was to report to the old Ministry of Finance and was not to be given enforcement powers. The finance ministry had lobbied the commission vigorously and brought all its power to bear on the issue. In the end the ministry won the battle; there would not be real reform, at least not yet.[10]

The reluctance of the Ministry of Finance to implement necessary changes is difficult to explain. The answer lies partly in the nature of any bureaucracy: the institutionalization of turf, disdain for the abilities of other bodies that might replace it, and the protection of all powers vested in civil servants. The other part of the answer, however, is more Japanese. Three powerful bureaus within the Ministry of Finance are responsible for financial regulation: the Securities Bureau, the Banking Bureau, and the International Finance Bureau. The powers and influence of the three bureaus are roughly equal, and they offset each other. Each bureau is eager to maintain this delicate balance. If one bureau becomes more powerful than the others, the balance collapses. Equally, if one bureau, because of scandal or other reasons, loses part of its regulatory mandate, then the balance also collapses. The mentality at the Ministry of Finance is to keep the balance.

The scandals led to many proposals for regulatory reform, but virtually all were brushed aside. Though the Diet did pass a bill banning compensation payments for brokerage losses, nothing that truly threatened the system was adopted. There would be no independent regulatory agency like the Securities and Exchange Commission, no unfixing of commission rates to increase competition, no written rules backed up by the force of law to replace the system of administrative guidance. Nor would practices considered anticompetitive by foreigners be abandoned. Only excessive compensation payments were given up (and most Japanese believe that means will be found to circumvent this constraint). One observer, Takaaki Wakasugi, a Tokyo University professor of finance, believes that changes in the basic structure of the regulatory system will be extremely difficult to make:

> The creation of a stronger [regulatory] organization is necessary, but the most important thing is the way of thinking in Japan. The point is there are many similar things to [these scandals] in the business world. The securities industry was just unlucky that they were the ones caught. Creating a new regulatory organization is a small problem. There has to be a change of thinking. That change is going to take a very, very long time."[11]

"Japan is at a crossroads," said an angry David Mulford, U.S. Under Secretary of the Treasury for International Affairs, during an October 1991 visit to Japan. Either the Japanese government will take "dramatic steps" in financial regulation, he said, or it will be regarded as perpetuating an uneven, unfair marketplace in which scandals like the current ones can recur. Mulford, who has a reputation as one of the Bush administration's more active "Japan bashers," said that "it appears that the same non-transparent, anti-competitive approach will be followed" in the future.

Mulford's prediction is bound to be right, at least for the near future. The only way to change the Japanese financial system at all is to change it a lot. Big changes, like abolishing Article 65 or abolishing fixed-commission rates, don't come easily anywhere. The New York Stock Exchange strenuously opposed negotiated commissions in 1975, and no one in the City of London favored Big Bang when it was first proposed. In these cases, the governments initiated reforms through legal actions: in the case of Big Bang, the Bank of England wanted changes because it knew that without them, the cost of financing in the United Kingdom would remain high relative to New York and other markets, and Britain's continuation as a world financial center would be threatened. Big Bang led to a worldwide re-examination of home-country financial regulations and triggered many changes in them. These were mostly aimed at keeping up with and staying in alignment with regulatory standards and practices in Europe and America.

Japan remains the last holdout.

FURTHER DEREGULATION AND OTHER MISERIES

The situation, however, is not impossible to resolve. The Japanese process of financial deregulation is advancing little by little. It is like peeling an onion by removing one skin at a time.

Until the early 1970s, financial markets were totally regulated. The government set the rate for postal savings accounts and new issues of government bonds, and all other interest rates were arranged symmetrically around these. Foreign exchange controls were so extensive that even the amount of money a businessman could spend on a foreign trip was fixed. No company could finance abroad without applying several months in advance and waiting until the Ministry of Finance thought the coast was clear. Foreigners could only purchase, in aggregate, up to 25% of a company's stock, and virtually no foreign acquisitions were allowed. No Japanese individuals or institutions could own foreign securities or hold foreign exchange. Everything was regulated tightly and efficiently.

The 1970s, however, shattered this orderly world. First there was the collapse of the Bretton Woods Agreement, which resulted in floating exchange rates; then there was the oil shock in 1973. Next came the agonizing battles with the United States and the European Community over Japan's growing trade surplus and import restrictions. By the early 1980s, almost all the explicit regulations restricting cross-border capital flows had been repealed; they were replaced by administrative guidance. Interest rates too began to show some respect for market forces. The main problem facing the Japanese government was now recycling the money pouring in from its trade surplus. If exports were not to be restricted, then money couldn't be either. Capital controls would have to go, the yen would have to be internationalized (i.e., allowed to be used in transactions not involving Japan), and the domestic capital markets, awash with excess savings, would have to be opened up. Japan was peeling the onion back substantially.

The initial result was for more money to leave the country than came in, as Japanese investors purchased large holdings of foreign securities for the first time. That was all right, because it kept the yen weaker than it otherwise might have been until the Plaza Accord in 1985, when the dollar's rapid rise relative to other currencies was reversed.

David Mulford first came on the scene about this time, leading a U.S. delegation that insisted Japan open its capital markets to foreigners. This resulted in the creation of an "Ad-Hoc U.S.–Japan Committee" in 1982 to consider further deregulation and a schedule for implementation. The markets were already open in the sense that money could flow in and out without Ministry of Finance approval, but Mulford insisted that they were not open competitively. Foreign firms should be able to join the Tokyo Stock Exchange, he argued, and compete freely with Japanese firms for business in Japan. So the onion was peeled some more—stock exchange membership and investment trust management were approved in 1986, but the process was still not fast enough for Mulford, who continued to press the Japanese for more.

The Japanese also found themselves during the mid-1980s with a large budget deficit and a heavy schedule for selling government bonds. To these were added yen-denominated bonds of foreign issuers, called *samurai bonds*. Interest rates and underwriting allocations become more realistic as a result, and foreign underwriters were allowed in. Toward the end of the 1980s, the tax-free nature of income from postal savings accounts was changed, new instruments such as yen commercial paper were introduced, and other forms of market deregulation occurred.

There is still a long way to go, however, along the road to full deregulation. Foreign bankers in Tokyo still complain that underwriting practices are unfairly tilted toward the Japanese (though these have been improved), and that their operations are excessively burdened by administrative reporting and other requirements. Foreign fund managers are still prohibited from selling mutual funds in Japan. Surely they couldn't do any worse than one fund run by Nomura Investment Trust Company, which lost 92% of its value in the year ended March 31, 1992.

Forces Building from Within

In 1985, Japan had shed enough onion skins to be about as deregulated as the British were at the time (before Big Bang), and about a decade behind the United States. In 1975, the New York Stock Exchange had been forced to negotiate commission rates and to allow non-American firms to become members—an opportunity that the Big Four and many other firms promptly took advantage of.

The major regulatory development of the 1980s was the Big Bang in London in 1986, in which Britain forced negotiated rates, opened its exchange to foreign membership, and went a step beyond the United States, allowing banks to participate in the securities businesses. Thus, a new model for capital markets was created, and this model spread to Canada, Australia, France, Germany, and other countries, and was adopted by the EC for its 1992 banking directive.

Big Bang put the United States behind in the effort to modernize financial regulation. The Glass-Steagall law separating banking and investment banking was still on the books, but the Federal Reserve, absent any action by Congress, repealed it de facto in 1989 for those banks that it thought sufficiently well capitalized. This left Japan even farther behind the United States and Europe, despite two decades of step-by-step financial market deregulation.

At the end of 1991, Article 65 still remained in effect; however, on June 21, 1992, a bill providing for financial system reform, including provisions that would allow the banking and securities industries to enter each other's business, was passed by the Diet. The new law by no means provided for sweeping reform, though it did nudge the system toward greater competition and more open markets. Article 65 has been modified to permit banks to enter the underwriting business, but not the brokerage business (an impractical arrangement), through a majority-controlled subsidiary. City banks and securities firms also have been allowed into the trust banking business. Nonbanking players such as trading companies and manufacturers can form securities subsidiaries if they wish. Most Tokyo observers feel that the new bill is the product of much compromise and continuing bureaucratic control of the system, bearing only limited resemblance to the bill originally proposed. Asked about the limitations of the new underwriting provisions, Yoh Kurokawa, of the Industrial Bank of Japan, said, "The restrictions may be undesirable, but they will not have much effect on us for the time being as we are not in a position now to start up an aggressive underwriting business."[12]

Responding to complaints about the slowness of regulatory change, the Japanese, as usual, point out that onion peeling is their way and will effect the smoothest transitions possible. The Article 65 modifications that have been approved are an example—the changes will be adopted gradually, they say, over a few years' time. Commission rates are gradually being reduced, they also point out, especially to large institutional buyers, but there are many small firms that depend on commissions for their livelihood. Trading regulations are also being studied, they add, but administrative guidance is still the right way to handle these things in Japan. While the bureaucrats temporize, however, forces are building in Japan that will almost certainly accelerate the remaining reforms.

The weakening of the banks. Recognizing that much of their traditionally captive, core wholesale lending business has dried up, the banks are looking for new business areas to enter. Frustrated by Article 65 and intrabanking restrictions at home, their search has extended to overseas markets, but there they have found much the same problem—the only profitable lending business left is risky loans for real estate and highly leveraged corporations. Like their American counterparts, Japanese bankers have seen the shift of wholesale business into the securities markets at home and abroad. No other business seems as large, potentially profitable, and strategically necessary as the securities business.

The banks desperately need to improve the profitability of their basic banking business, but this is not easy to do in today's economic environment. Though the nominal profitability of Japanese banks has risen in the past few years (partly through deregulation of deposit and lending rates), Japanese banks have among the lowest banking spreads in the world, and among the highest operating costs. Their low margins have in part been the price for the many benefits Japanese banks have enjoyed over the last decades, including the opportunity to maintain the largest balance sheets in the world. Furthermore, their profitability has been supplemented by large capital gains in their securities portfolios. Now, profits on securities holdings cannot offer the support to overall bank earnings that they used to, and loan losses are building rapidly. Stripped of earnings from their securities portfolios, and with full accounting for nonperforming loans, Japanese banks are only barely profitable. This is a situation that can only get worse as new loan losses are reported in the coming years.

The Japanese banking system is coming under the same kinds of pressures that substantially weakened the U.S. money-center banks. The decline of wholesale banking profits sapped the vitality of those institutions during the 1970s and 1980s, even as they expanded their assets and lending activities. The same pattern of events seems to have afflicted the Japanese banks in the 1980s and 1990s.

Too many of Japan's bank loans, it now appears, went to finance the great bubble economy. These loans were made with the knowledge of the Ministry of Finance, which allowed them not only for the sake of maintaining bank profitability but also, no doubt, because the regulators themselves believed in the real estate and stock markets and did not fear losing the value of the loan collateral. Many bankers argue that Japanese banks are not as affected by bad loans as American money-center banks, though at this stage it may be hard to tell. Even if it were true, the fact remains that Japanese bank profitability, like that of the U.S. money centers, needs a boost. Maybe consolidation will help, but that seems doubtful. Mergers between Japanese city banks are beginning to appear more frequently, as more banks find themselves in need of rescue or revitalization; but the ability to slash overhead in Japan is minimal, and the banks already operate nationally, so there is little to be gained in opening new markets. Nor is the highly competitive, overseas wholesale lending business very promising. Only the vast securities business seems to offer the banks what they need.

Ultimately, profitability is an important element in bank safety and soundness regulation. If adequate profitability cannot be assured, then the banks risk becoming wards of the taxpayer. U.S. regulators learned this lesson the hard way. As in the United States, the claim is made in Japan that the banks could restore their profitability by having unrestricted access to the securities business. Also as in the United States, the legislature has allowed the pace of bank deregulation to rest with their regulators, which in each case are cautious because of the risk of banking failures. In both countries the speed at which competitive equality between banks and brokers occurs will be gradual. But as Yoh Kurosawa has said, with very few exceptions, the banks are not yet in a position to take full advantage of the regulatory relief that has been offered.

The growing power of securities firms.   While bank profits and credit ratings were sinking, the Big Four securities firms (until the scandals) were cleaning up. "Where," asked the banks, "is the balance in profitability between our two businesses that the Ministry of Finance is supposed to maintain? There is plenty of room in the securities business for us all."

The market crash was very hard on the securities firms, which had to endure enormous trading losses (the Big Four reported the value of their securities portfolios declined by almost $1 billion during the year ended March 31, 1992). They also suffered a quartering of trading volume, reimbursements to clients, defaults of tobashi trades, and other costly events. Only Nomura reported a profit for the year ended March 1992, and it was a very modest one. The share prices of the securities firms were all down about 45% for the year.

These things were bad enough, but all the major firms had sufficient capital (from large earnings in previous years) to absorb the losses without too much difficulty. What was not clear was whether the Big Four had enough political capital to absorb all the losses they had endured in the eyes of the public.

The firms had done the right things in atoning for their errors. They had made public confessions, sacrificed chief executives, and submitted to office closings and other penalties without complaint. They directed the Japan Securities Dealers' Association to draw up new regulations to prevent insider trading and market rigging in connection with new stock issues (which in any case were suspended for two years at the beginning of 1992 to help the market recover).

The Securities Industry Association also urged that steps be taken to revive the stock market. It proposed a new rule that would require companies to make a three-year pledge to pay out at least 30% of their profits in dividends (the average payout is now about 22%). It also suggested the rescinding of existing rules (designed to prevent market manipulation) that dampened trading volume and customer interest. It placed the most emphasis, however, on discrediting "program trading," or arbitraging between the cash market and the futures makets in various stocks and market indices; the Big Four charged that this practice had been the cause of the market crash in Japan, as well as of the market shocks in New York in 1987 and 1989. Foreign Tokyo Stock Exchange member firms are the only ones with the trading mentalities, and the technical understanding of index arbitrage, to participate in this lucrative business. The Big Four persuaded stock exchange regulators that the business ought to be stamped out, so in March 1992, new rules were introduced that doubled commissions on derivatives trading, required daily disclosure of proprietary futures trading, and threatened to impose stiffer capital requirements for index arbitrage. No one seemed to be mindful that a Nikkei futures contract already trades in Singapore, in which trading volume is rapidly increasing.

Despite these efforts at good citizenship, few in Japan believe that either the securities firms or the regulators have changed their ways. What they do believe is that shame and stigma have been carried away by those who resigned, that business will return to normal as soon as the market gets going again, and that there is no immediate danger of massive reforms such as the United States experienced in 1933.

But as the securities firms become more powerful, and the banks weaker, the "delicate balance" that the civil servants of the Ministry of Finance are charged with maintaining is in danger. In order to redress the balance it may be necessary to weaken one and strengthen the other: weakening the securities industry perhaps by allowing commissions to be either lowered further or deregulated altogether; strengthening banks by allowing them unrestricted entrance into underwriting and brokerage businesses. The central issue has little to do with whether the markets would be improved, or fairer; only that the great powers be balanced.

Deregulation from abroad. The Ministry of Finance, however, knows very well that negotiated rates, and full competition from banks in the securities business, are inevitable because of foreign pressure. Europe and the United States have established certain principles for dealing with each other, and Japan, that involve reciprocity. For the time being, while several countries adjust to new practices, there is no indication that either Europe or the United States intends to invoke existing reciprocity provisions that could cause Japan's international banking and brokerage licenses to be withdrawn. But in the end, the pressure will grow, and Japan will have to agree to allow universal banking in Japan; when this happens many other things probably will change at the same time.

The issue has already arisen. During the late 1980s, when European financial authorities met their counterparts from Japan, they endeavored to explain what was meant by the reciprocity provisions, and pointed out that since the Japanese were permitted to participate in universal banking business in Europe, European universal banks should be permitted to do full-service business (banking, securities, and investment management) in Japan. The explanation was followed by strongly worded requests to allow certain European (and later American) banking organizations to join the Tokyo Stock Exchange. So the Ministry of Finance provided an administrative loophole that allowed foreign bankers into the Japanese securities business. If the bank established a partly owned securities subsidiary in, say, Hong Kong, the subsidiary could open a Tokyo branch and then join the Tokyo Stock Exchange.

"What about us?" said the Japanese banks. "At least nine of our largest international commercial banking competitors have been permitted to join the stock exchange through offshore subsidiaries, but we have been left out." The same loophole was not extended to Japanese banks until mid-1992 because it would upset the delicate balance.

Foreign banks and securities firms had also been allowed into other business areas traditionally off-limits to foreigners, such as investment trust management and foreign exchange. And the way the financial business was changing outside Japan, it would not be long before even more requests were made, with the veiled threat of reciprocity behind them. These requests put great pressure on the Ministry of Finance to offer comparable opportunities to their domestic institutions.

Perhaps, the financial difficulties in Japan in the early 1990s carried with them a blessing in disguise. Maybe the turmoil caused by these events could justify what would normally have been an impossibly radical response: the declaration that, because of "changing world financial events not entirely to our advantage," it is necessary to abandon the old system completely and to reconfigure Japan's financial services industry along commonly accepted international lines.

It seems a great opportunity, but not many in Japan believe that the basic ways of thinking have changed enough yet for it to be taken up.

The Biggest Bang Yet

Sooner or later, however, Japan will experience a Big Bang of its own, and the effects will change everything. The Big Four will find themselves competing with at least a dozen formidable, well-capitalized, new competitors like Industrial Bank of Japan, Sumitomo Bank, and Mitsubishi Bank. These competitors will have substantial keiretsu cards to play, aggressive and well-trained relationship officers, and, in many cases, considerable know-how about securities markets. Initially, market share, not profitability, will be their beacon. Commission rates will drop almost instantly, as they did in London in 1986, to nearly nothing. The Big Four will find their profits draining away, and their high overheads and limited product lines will impede their ability to adapt.

The new leaders, of course, will have to become market makers on fully competitive terms. This will involve learning many new skills, developing the willingness and management capability to trade large blocks of securities rapidly for small spreads. To date, there is little evidence that any of the Big Four will be able to take these changes in stride. Shifting to fully negotiated rates will be hard enough for these firms, but to do so simultaneously with letting the banks into their business would be doubly difficult.

As Japanese institutional clients start to shop around more for the best rates and ideas, the Big Four will also begin to lose business to some of the aggressive, lean, highly competitive foreign firms that can offer greater trading skills and broader product lines—including derivative securities, block trading, indexing, and program trading. Several U.S. investment banks have learned how to operate very profitably in Japan over the past few years, precisely for these reasons.

Increased competition has been one of the primary goals of the American and European regulators who have pressed so hard for negotiated rates and removal of barriers between banking and investment banking. And their efforts are being justified by the results. As competition increases, commissions decline and innovation and client services increase. Financial markets thus become much more dynamic and beneficial to their users, though the value of many of these benefits comes out of the profits of the vendors. Success in a fully deregulated market depends upon the ability to change opportunistically while providing value to clients in the face of tough competition.

A final effect of deregulation is creation of market-wise clients. In free and competitive markets, clients do not watch to see which stock is going to be "supported" so that it can trade at 70 times earnings; instead, they learn to rely on market prices that reflect economic reality and good research, and they look to their businesses for profits, not the stock market.

The biggest changes, however, will come only when Japanese society demands that free-market conditions prevail throughout the commercial and political life of the nation. Japanese consumers tolerate a system that charges prices 40% higher than Americans pay for comparable goods and services and that robs them of the standard of living they have earned. Prices for land, for houses, for most ordinary consumer goods, and even for rice, defy common sense and rudimentary measures of value. Tatemae tells us that "Japan is an unusual and special place, and just because things are different in foreign countries does not mean they have to be that way in Japan, though gradual change does occur and this is healthy."

But many in Japan are becoming skeptical. Honne, the unspoken reality, is that "it's time for Japan to shed these remaining third-world practices, in financial markets and throughout business in general." It looks askance at the corruption and payoffs all around, and at a government that has failed to find an appropriate role for the country, apart from being the world's most aggressive economic animal.

Japanese citizens must ask if this is the way things ought to be run now that the postwar period is behind them and a new era of prosperity is at hand. In the Heisei—the era of the next generation—Japan will have to adapt again, as it did so admirably after the Meiji Restoration and again after World War II. The challenges are great, but Japan has never been a country unable to meet its challenges.

PART IV
BECOMING CHAMPIONS

In early January 1992, a group of U.S. bankers assembled to discuss the future. They shared the view that the worldwide recession would continue until mid-year or so, then ebb away only gradually. This prospect gave little comfort to those holding large quantities of nonperforming loans. They were also anxious about the American election coming later in the year. They were concerned that to recover his appeal to the voters, President Bush might come out with some sort of flashy economic program that would do little actual good, but would nevertheless increase the deficit further and panic the financial markets. Or his Democratic opponent might propose such a thing, and even win.

"Whichever way it goes," said one banker gloomily, "it's probably not going to help the economy or the financial markets very much."

"And that means it'll probably take us even longer to get this wave of bad loans behind us," another added. "And longer before we can be rid of the danger of being sunk by them."

"Not much chance for regulatory relief for a while either," said a third banker. "The Brady Bunch made a noble effort last year, but they couldn't get around Dingell and fell on their faces. I doubt they'll do much better now, assuming they even try. There aren't any votes in banking deregulation."

"Yeah," said the first banker, "but, thanks to the Fed, we do have ways around many of those old regulations. We can expand into other states under a variety of circumstances, and we can do securities business through Section 20 subsidiaries. And if we've been kept out of insurance, that may prove to be a blessing in the end."

"The real problem today," said another, "is that the economics of our business have changed so much, and things are now so competitive. We have to compete for funds to lend, paying out a lot of money for deposits that used to be free, and compete for loans with other financial players that aren't even in our industry, people who aren't regulated and constrained like we are. And whenever we do latch on to something good, our fellow bankers all try to horn in on it by cutting rates further. It's damn difficult now for us to get our lending spreads to cover both operating costs and the 'insurance premium' we need to cover our exposure to bad loans."

"And regulatory relief by itself isn't going to help these things much," commented another, "until we get the economics right."

"True, but our two basic banking businesses—retail and wholesale— now have very different economic structures. What's good for one may be bad for the other.

"Look," this banker continued, "to be successful in wholesale banking, you have to go where the clients are and put a couple of billion into the securities business—which is risky—and also develop capital market capabilities all over the world—which is expensive—and then you've got to trim way down to compete with real pros like Salomon Brothers or Goldman Sachs for small spreads on large volumes with large risk exposures. This business is very trading-oriented, very innovative, and involves a constantly changing line of products that are offered to some of the world's smartest customers. No wonder there are not many U.S. commercial banks busting their humps to get into this racket. Bankers Trust and J.P. Morgan, and I guess Citibank, have been at it now for about ten or fifteen years, but few others have really tried. Most of the rest of us are just beginning and are more than a little afraid that plunging headlong into the securities business could be a bigger mistake than lending money to Donald Trump."

"And in retail banking," added his colleague. "you have to be big to take advantage of the large economies of scale that exist in what is basically a huge, marketing-oriented data processing business. You also have to have the best technology, and an ability to develop totally new products and marketing ideas while keeping your costs down. Keeping the costs down means keeping the headcount down. The Fidelity Funds Group, for example, manages about $120 billion of retail assets—offering dozens of different products, or investment funds—with only about 5,000 people, one-tenth the number of people at NationsBank, which manages $120 billion of assets. NationsBank was formed after the merger of NCNB and C&S/ Sovran in 1991.

"Not many banks can face the economics of truly competitive retail financial services without major changes. Most banks are too small, uninformed, undercapitalized, and hard-pressed to spend the money it takes to beef up their consumer banking products. If they don't spend the money, though, they'll fall behind and their business will go to somebody else. So it's pretty likely we'll be seeing more of these big, cost-cutting mergers like NationsBank and Chemical, and more intra-regional consolidations (like Banc One) too, just to get the economics under control."

"Then, once you've done that and got your economics right, and have some good products to work with, you can buy up some more banks just to extend the franchise. That's what Bank of America is doing."

"But, either way, whether you do it or you don't, there are going to be a lot more mergers."

"Well, you can call 'em mergers if you want to," said one of the older bankers, "but I'm inclined to see them as eliminations. A lot more people and institutions are going to have to be eliminated from the industry before the economics of the banking system gets healthy again. That's hard on the folks involved, and there's bound to be resistance along the way. Much of it isn't going to be very pretty. Not a whole lot of today's bankers will survive, especially at the top, but those that do will be leaner and meaner and a helluva lot more competitive than ever before."

As the 1980s came to an end, U.S. commercial banks were in a difficult spot. They were being pushed into a corner of the marketplace, from which it was extremely difficult to compete. They faced a dilemma, one that involved making some tough choices.

They could specialize, focusing their activities on a limited number of businesses with the same economic characteristics. Through such specialization they could hope to improve their competitiveness and their performance.

Or they could become truly universal banks, by combining (probably through mergers) retail banking, wholesale and investment banking, and, as deregulation progressed, perhaps also insurance and other businesses. This has been a long-standing dream of many large money-center banks, a dream that many feel is not so far from being realized. Universal banking would offer increased stability through diversification, and would enable some important economies of scale to be developed.

The choice is a strategic one. Those who specialize usually find that what is required for success in retail and small to mid-sized corporate banking is quite different from what it takes to succeed in wholesale and investment banking. So they usually pick one or the other and then spend the next decade learning how to compete with the best firms in the business, especially those firms that are not banks. Retail-oriented banks, for example, have to compete with American Express, AT&T, and Sears Roebuck's Discovery credit cards, and with giant money-market funds like Fidelity and Dreyfus. Wholesale banks have to compete with the best of the U.S. and international investment banks. These nonbank competitors are powerful, flexible, aggressive, and well capitalized. They know what they are doing, and they have large market shares and aspirations for more. So far, only a few large American banks have chosen to specialize—Bankers Trust and J.P. Morgan each undertook a ten-year conversion to become combination wholesale and investment banks, with the principal emphasis being on the securities end of the business. The reborn Continental Illinois specialized in becoming a "business bank" for the Midwest. Banc One specialized in particular retail services, as did Bank of America after its troubles.

Those U.S. banks that opt to become universal hope to be able to achieve supereconomies of scale, and to cross-sell various products and services to all the customers of the bank. They aspire to dominant market shares at home and around the world. But the road to universal banking in the United States is full of obstacles. The U.S. system does not protect its banks from predator institutions operating in large nonbanking free markets within reach of banking customers. Large and active capital markets already exist, which offer lower rates and otherwise more attractive transactions; the business is therefore migrating from the banks to the capital markets. Neither of these problems is shared by European universal banks, at least not yet.

Banks cannot be specialists and universals in the European sense at the same time. The specialists, with all of their eggs in just a few baskets, are focused and competitive, but vulnerable to market changes and competitive challenges. Large universals gain safety from their size and large market shares. But their organizations are unwieldy and complex, and create difficult management, decision-making, and internal control problems. Such organizations can spend a lot of time arguing over which parts of the bank are responsible for what, and trying to decide which of their businesses are the most profitable, or the least profitable, and how to allocate capital and talent among them. They also find that if one part of the bank is experiencing losses or other problems, then the other parts are compelled to offer help, which may drain assets away from where they have been used successfully. Such interconnections may contribute to the stability of the bank, but they do little for its competitiveness. Even Europeans recognize that universal banking works best inside those countries that protect it; beyond their own borders they usually become specialists.

Banking regulators, acting in loose concert around the world, have already made their choice between stability and competitiveness. They have come down in favor of competitiveness. For some time now, regulatory changes have been in the direction of allowing market forces to run more freely. They provide for stability (to the extent needed—too much stability is a large public expense) through internationally accepted bank capital-adequacy standards, rather than through protectionism. In the still very imperfect world that economic policy makers and banking regulators have made, competitive effectiveness in the marketplace is essential to success, and lack of competitiveness over any sustained period of time can lead only to mediocrity and ultimately to the draining away of the strengths and market positions of key players. Undercompetitive banks are eventually eliminated by the system, either through failure or through acquisition. In the United States approximately 2,000 banks have disappeared over the past ten years as a result of this survival-of-the-fittest environment.

"How can you talk about 'survival of the fittest' when you have high residual protectionism for securities firms, insurance companies, and many local banks?" exclaimed one of the bankers at the meeting, described earlier. "The playing field may be getting more level than it was, but it's not level yet!"

"Steady," said one of his colleagues. "Nobody said anything about the system being entirely fair. We had it pretty good for quite a while. Now things are changing, and we've got to adjust, that's all. If we don't adjust, we're all in danger of not lasting out the century."

Though this process of competitive enhancement will naturally take some time to apply to all of the 12,000 banks in the United States, and to perhaps an equal number of banks in Europe and Japan, the effects have already begun to be seen in large, U.S. wholesale money-center and investment banks, which are currently experiencing dramatic changes.

The substantial reordering of wholesale banks and investment banks in the United States over the past several years is principally the result of sustained competitive effort by a small number of firms, which have recognized the opportunities presented by regulatory and economic change, and taken advantage of them. Competitive effort is a quality that combines aggressiveness in pricing with appropriate and sensible risk taking. The coming decade promises more of the same in the United States, judging by the weak state of many American banks and the de facto repeal of Glass-Steagall, which permits wholesale banks the opportunity to re-enter the securities business if they want to. American banks, however, have had a significant head start relative to their European and Japanese counterparts in adapting to the new, Darwinian competitive conditions. Those who have survived have been strengthened by it. These survivors will have at least a temporary advantage over those washing up in the next wave.

Many of the same conditions that apply in the United States today will emerge in Europe in the 1990s—customers and investors will judge banks more by the quality of their competitive effort and less by the strength of their historical relationships. In Europe too, competitiveness is advanced by specialization, not by universalization. Those that fall behind will be weakened and ultimately absorbed by others.

The Japanese have not been compelled to adopt a similarly competitive environment in their own country as yet. But the combination of financial strains inside Japan, and constant complaints by foreigners that Japan alone among the OECD countries has failed to introduce a fully competitive environment, should work to accelerate the double Big Bang that many observers expect for Japan. When this occurs, no doubt many further changes will follow, especially in the ordering of the financial power structure.

So, in the 1990s, no one will be able to rest on past laurels or on his market share. Everyone will have to develop fully competitive capabilities, or risk elimination. Yet genuine competitiveness is not an easy thing to achieve.

10
COMPETITION AND SUCCESS

When a company is small, it spends little time pondering competitive strategies. Partly, this is because the company knows what it's doing—and all its available time is occupied in doing it. Heavily regulated industries and those that don't change much also don't have to think a lot about strategy. But companies that want to grow and take advantage of market opportunities have to adjust their strategies continually. So do those that need to protect themselves against market changes that have opened the gates to new competitors.

Let's say a company does auto repairs for New York taxi fleets, a market in which three or four similar firms operate. The company's unspoken strategy is well defined by its service (auto repairs), its customers (taxi fleets), and its location (New York). As the company grows, however, it begins to consider expanding beyond the "cell" defined by the intersection of these three axes: customers, location, and services. It may decide to expand along the service axis by offering auto repairs to rental car fleets, or along the locational axis by exploring New Jersey or Connecticut, or along the customer axis by offering its existing customers special deals in purchasing bulk quantities of tires or batteries. Expansion is achieved by adding more cells to the existing matrix, and each move means a change in strategy.

Economists like Ingo Walter, who developed the client-arena-product (CAP) matrix approach to strategic positioning,[1] justify this strategy of organic growth. There are, for example, *economies of scale* and *economies of scope*, in which profits are increased per unit of production. Economies of scale can result from cell additions along the product and arena axes (i.e., selling more auto repairs by expanding the market to rental cars or to New Jersey, and thereby lowering the unit cost of operations). Economies of scope can be gained by adding more cells along the client axis (or selling new things like tires and insurance to existing taxi fleet customers, where the incremental cost of marketing is small). Most businessmen are quick to acknowledge that economies of scale are fairly easy to obtain in normal operating conditions, but economies of scope are not. We also know that even economies of scale can be lost forever to excessive overhead and the bureaucracies that result from expansion of a company's management and cost structure beyond an optimal point of efficiency.

The diversification of the risks associated with any closely related set of products, clients, or geographic markets can also produce gains by increasing the stability of profits. The CAP matrix clarifies where the risk-diversification gains may be.

There are other growth strategies to which the CAP matrix approach can be applied. Mergers and acquisitions result in the addition of a whole new colony of cells (cultures), some of which may be redundant and subject to elimination, thus providing cost savings. There is also the possibility of exchanging one whole colony of cells for another, as, for example, would occur if the company decided that auto repair did not produce sufficient returns and therefore sold the business and replaced it with an insurance brokerage firm.

Which axis you operate along depends on many factors. You will look for moves (i.e., organic growth, acquisition, disposals, and so forth) that appear to offer the greatest amount of incremental profit in the shortest time with the least risk. Of course, it may be hard to find the best moves because of the uncertainties inherent in your forecasts, or because you are playing the game with a complex mixture of economic and noneconomic goals in mind (e.g., you may think insurance brokerage is more prestigious than auto repair).

Some moves may be totally or partially blocked by a particularly tough competitor, or by legal or regulatory considerations. Some otherwise attractive cells may involve higher than normal costs of entry, or a higher risk profile. Some cells may be advantageously linked with other cells, others may not be. Your strategy will consist of the moves you decide to make, the changes you seek to initiate in the matrix. In many ways, strategy changes are the same as moves in the game of cell accumulation, in which the winner amasses cultures that maximize the goal-adjusted returns to the mover. This is somewhat similar to the Japanese three-dimensional, chesslike game of Go.

Strategy formulation can be a very complex process for large banking institutions, though it may be visualized usefully in terms of cells, cultures, and CAP matrixes. A worldwide universal banking strategy would involve expanding along a wide variety of wholesale banking and retail and consumer finance axes in several important countries simultaneously. Perhaps only Citibank has been bold enough to maintain such a strategy—most other universal banks define what they want to do in more limited terms, usually preferring to restrict retail services to their home country and their principal wholesale operations to the OECD and a few other countries. Those banks that specialize, for example, in investment banking may limit themselves to a considerably smaller number of cell cultures on the grounds that they can be better watched over and nurtured than a greater number of sprawling and overlapping cultures. No two financial organizations will have exactly the same sets of cell cultures; nor will they ever have exactly the same microstrategies with respect to particular cell changes, though there will, of course, be many similarities. The goals of all the players, however, are largely the same: to achieve maximum value of the player's franchise over the long term by adjusting cell cultures.

GETTING THE STRATEGY RIGHT

In 1975, Alfred Brittain III became chairman and chief executive of Bankers Trust New York Corporation, then the seventh-largest bank in the United States and the fifth-largest in New York City. At the time, the bank was trying to cope with serious loan delinquency problems, many related to real estate loans made in the early 1970s, when the oil price rise in 1973 sharply increased inflation and interest rates. Brittain and his colleagues continued to fight fires throughout the 1970s.

"There's got to be a better way," he must have said to himself one day. "The oil shock was bad enough, but it really destabilized our financial economy. It's true that Regulation Q has now come off, which has freed up interest rate ceilings, but now we've got to pay for our deposits, which really eats into our lending profits. And not only that, we're now facing a goddamn technological revolution in retail banking with these automatic teller machines and all. These things require a lot of computer power to support them and, for us—on a unit basis—they are very expensive."

So Brittain commissioned a strategic review.

In 1979, Bankers Trust was a 200-branch bank with total assets of $31 billion and capital of less than $1 billion. As in most banks at the time, loans accounted for 52% of assets, and deposits were 75% of liabilities. More than a third of its deposits were noninterest bearing. Net interest income after loan loss provisions was about $500 million, more than twice noninterest income. The bank earned $114 million after taxes, a 12.6% return on capital.

Goals Come First

In the strategic review that followed, the Bankers Trust executives were asked to assess their strengths, their weaknesses, and their goals for the future. They concluded that they had good relationships with large corporate clients in the United States and abroad, a well-regarded portfolio management and securities custody group, and a state-of-the-art trading capability in government and municipal securities. They also concluded that the expected capital investment necessary to maintain even their fifth-ranking position in New York retail banking was high, and the returns low. They were doubtful that even with appropriate levels of investment, they would be able to increase their market share at the expense of their larger competitors.

"We're fifth now, but in a few years we may get pushed lower," one of the reviewers said. "Why not specialize instead in something we're good at: wholesale banking and securities trading?"

"You mean get out of retail banking entirely, sell off our branches and everything, and put the money into wholesale?"

"Right, it's a radical idea—something nobody else has done, but it could work for us."

"Hang on a minute," Brittain himself interjected, "we can't go off half cocked on this. Before we try to decide whether to chop the business in half, we'd better be clear on what it is we are going to achieve by doing so. We need to define where is it we want to go—in economic and market share terms—and then see whether we can get there from here.

"But whatever we do, it's got to make sense to the stockholders. If we are going to change, it ought to result in an increase in our return on investment, and ultimately our stock price."

The executives involved decided that a risk-adjusted return on investment of 20% would be possible in an all-wholesale business, so that became an important goal. The key to achieving this goal was the risk-adjustment and measuring systems that had to be installed throughout the bank. There was no point in setting goals you couldn't monitor closely.

Another goal, they decided, was to redeploy capital from a weakening area of the bank's business to a stronger area in order to avoid a deterioration in the bank's return on investment. A third was to use specialization, focus, and competitive intensity to become one of the top three New York City wholesale banks. The plan was presented to the board, and though the details were sparse, it was approved.

Understanding Comparative Advantage

Brittain and his colleagues understood that, in competitive terms, they suffered a disadvantage in retail banking, which it would be wise to escape from, and enjoyed some advantages in foreign exchange and government bond trading, investing, and processing, which should be exploited. Some areas, such as corporate finance, were competitively neutral, and these in time would have to be reinforced. By shedding the weak and emphasizing the strong factors in its competitive makeup, the bank increased its competitive leverage.

Bankers Trust decided that it would redirect its business thrust to large corporations and governments, financial institutions, and wealthy individuals. The services it would offer were bank loans (which the bank would attempt to originate but not keep—it would sell participations in the loans to other banks), corporate financial advice and deal structuring, trading in securities and foreign exchange, and investment management and custodial services.

New capital was invested in the trading areas, then headed by Charles S. Sanford, Jr., who became president of the bank in 1983 and succeeded Brittain as chief executive in 1987. Among the initiatives in this area was the handling of corporate commercial paper, which after a prolonged legal struggle was opened up to commercial banks in 1984. Later, when the Federal Reserve first entertained the possibility of Section 20 securities affiliates for banks, Bankers Trust was one of the first to apply for permission to create one.

Once committed, the bank introduced organizational changes to ensure that the internal infrastructure would sustain an all-wholesale environment in which, increasingly, Bankers Trust's chief competitors would be J.P. Morgan and New York's finest (and toughest) investment banks. Decentralization and profit orientation came first. Titles were changed to de-emphasize hierarchy, and a loose, partnership-oriented management style was introduced. The duties of the former lending officers were changed; they became salespeople for the bank's full range of products and services, which for many of them required substantial retraining. New investment banking-like incentive compensation schemes were introduced to encourage individuals to generate profits that corresponded with corporate and departmental goals. Bank officers made efforts to replace the somewhat stuffy and old-fashioned banking culture of the past with a more entrepreneurial spirit. Employees were encouraged to accept the changes enthusiastically. Those who would not or could not do so were let go. New people, some with investment banking backgrounds, were brought in to shore up areas in which the bank lacked skills. A major bankwide reorganization and management acclimation effort was put into effect to accompany the strategy shift. Inside the bank, the objective of the changes was "do it better, and smarter, with fewer, but better-paid people."

But it still took about ten years to effect the change. The retail branches were not all sold until 1984. By this time, the risk-adjusted return on investment had risen to more than 16%, higher than that of any other major money-center bank, but well short of the goal. Noninterest income had tripled between 1979 and 1984, however; it was now equal to net interest income after loan loss provisions. Bank loans still accounted for about 50% of total assets (now more than $45 billion), reflecting the bank's lack of success in distributing rather than holding loans. Deposits, of which now only 18% were noninterest bearing, dropped to 58% of total liabilities. Without the branches, Bankers Trust had to purchase most of its lendable funds in the market.

In 1984, Alfred Brittain commented on the changes that were still occurring:

> Bankers Trust will combine the on-balance-sheet capability and service breadth of a commercial bank with the intermediary skills and entrepreneurial spirit of an investment bank. We call that worldwide "merchant banking."[2]

During the 1980s, Bankers Trust had to face several market-related problems; reserving more for third world debt, most of which was a legacy of the past; getting its fast-growing commitment to sophisticated trading activities under control (a substantial loss in trading foreign exchange options occurred in 1990); and coming to terms with financing LBOs and hostile takeovers, a field in which Bankers Trust became a market leader. The bank also needed to upgrade its technology systems to produce effective controls and efficient back-office operations and to support fully competitive trading and corporate finance activities. Bankers Trust installed a highly cost-efficient, all-purpose, bankwide system that would not have been possible at a large multiple-purpose universal bank.

By the end of 1990, Charlie Sanford, the first major U.S. bank CEO to come from the trading end of the business, could safely say that at last the strategic conversion was complete. Total assets reached $63.6 billion, of which loans (after credit provisions) were a little more than 30%, an amount considerably less than the 45% of assets that were devoted to securities and trading inventories. Total deposits had dropped to less than half of all liabilities. Borrowing against trading inventories rose to $25 billion, more than 40% of liabilities. Total capital exceeded $3 billion, providing a tier-1 ratio of 5.4% and a total capital ratio of 10%. Net income was $665 million, and the bank's return on capital was over 22%. At year-end, its stock price was 141% of book value, a rare situation in American banking at a time when the average money-center stock price to book value ratio was 83%. Like J.P. Morgan, Bankers Trust had emerged as a different kind of bank, a specialist in wholesale banking.

Noninterest revenues for 1990 were $2.3 billion (75% of total revenue), about half of which was from trading securities and foreign exchange. Fees and commissions were $559 million (down from more than $700 million the year before when Bankers Trust assisted in the RJR Nabisco LBO financing), and fiduciary services and funds management revenues were $468 million. These amounts were comparable to the revenue components of many investment banks.

A Strategic Checklist

For most banks, strategy changes are small and infrequent. If a franchise is operating at nearly optimal value, radical changes are counterproductive. If, on the other hand, a franchise is operating way below optimal value, radical changes may be necessary to restore the franchise value or to prevent further deterioration. The banking industry, however, is regulated, conservative, and for the most part, resistant to radical changes, even when they are necessary.

Bankers Trust's conversion was no doubt far more extensive than the brave Brittain and his colleagues had in mind when they decided to give up retail banking. Bankers Trust's decision differs from some of the other major strategic adjustments that have occurred in the banking field in that it was entirely voluntary. What all banks that have been through such changes, voluntarily or otherwise, have learned is that a lot of organizational change is necessary to effect even modest strategic changes. This is no doubt why so few strategic changes are attempted. Everyone knows that large organizational changes are difficult to go through and often don't seem to work. A strategy change requires a top-to-bottom shakeup which must be applied over a sustained period of time before it can work. During this period, which may last for years, there will be numerous opportunities for backsliding—times when you are tempted to take the heat off in exchange for a little peace and quiet—but there can be no backsliding if the transformation is to "take."

Bankers Trust started in the right place—with a review of its goals. It considered a lot of possibilities, and applied reality checks to its thinking on several occasions, but only one goal was changed explicitly, the level of return on investment. It knew that to achieve the higher return the bank would have to increase profitability, and this at a time of high competitiveness and market changes in its basic business that appeared to reduce profits, not increase them. To meet the goal, something different would have to be done. That something different would have to emphasize Bankers Trust's comparative advantages (of which there were then only a few) and minimize its disadvantages. The bank would need new skills too, and a climate would have to be established in which new talent could be attracted and retained. Once the new direction had been chosen new implicit goals would develop, for example, to increase trading and market making, to be innovative in corporate finance, and to learn how to market ideas better—to become "real" investment bankers.

At this stage, Bankers Trust had to make another choice. What sort of role did it want to play in the market? It is very difficult to fix a strategy until the role that goes with it is clarified. For example, did Bankers Trust aspire to being a world-class player in global financial circles? Or was it content to be only a major national player, i.e., a prominent U.S. financial services firm like the larger regional banks, or maybe an investment bank like Dillon Read? Other alternatives included seeking out a highly profitable niche player position, like Brown Brothers Harriman or maybe KKR. Failing all of these, the bank might consider becoming a merger candidate. Each role was a viable one. As it was, it chose to be a major national player with substantial world-class ambitions.

Even a firm that has addressed these issues still faces the toughest question of all. Do we have the money, the time, and the grit to implement the proposed strategy changes in such a way that we can be sure of producing something better at the end of the process than what we are giving up? Reorganizations are expensive; new investments have to be made, job termination settlement payments paid, and new talent acquired. Some mistakes might have to be paid for too.

Strategy changes also take time. Even a patently successful transformation, such as Bankers Trust's, took a decade. Perhaps no changes of comparable magnitude can be completed in less time—the organization has to be remolded and then hardened. Compensation and promotion policies have to be established, sometimes on a trial-and-error basis, new people have to be hired and trained, new leaders selected, and role models have to emerge. A company that does not have a generous amount of time to give to these processes may be better off selling the business to another compatible firm.

These are all issues of implementation. The best of strategies will fail if the implementation is not effective.

DOING IT RIGHT

During the summer of 1989, the management board of a large continental European universal bank met to consider the bank's future in the light of new regulatory and competitive conditions being introduced around the world. The bank was very secure in its home country, where banking spreads were high, competition light, and the bank's market share large. The home-country market was not growing, however, and as competition from foreign banks and nonbanks increased, the board expected a gradual decline in domestic profits, then considerably more than 50% of the bank's consolidated net income.

The profitability of the bank's international business was much lower than that of the domestic business, and in recent years it had deteriorated to practically nothing, after all additions to loan loss reserves had been accounted for. The bank operated wholesale and securities businesses in New York, London, and Tokyo, and a very successful private banking business in these and several other cities around the world. In New York, the bank had a grandfathered license to participate in investment banking that predated the International Banking Act of 1978. In London, it was active in the Euromarkets and had acquired a small brokerage firm in the run-up before Big Bang. This firm had nearly failed, and had to be given a substantial capital infusion soon after negotiated commissions came into effect. In Tokyo, the bank controlled a Hong Kong-based joint venture that had acquired a seat on the Tokyo Stock Exchange, though it had not yet made any money.

The chairman was concerned about the changing environment. "At present, we are one of the twenty or so top banks in the world," he said, "but this may not be so in ten or twenty years. Our domestic growth opportunities are limited. Overseas competitors are being introduced to all of our clients because of the new deregulation, but (except for private banking) we are not making comparable progress abroad. We need to redefine our corporate mission, our goals, and our strategy."

The group studied these matters and restated the bank's mission, goals, and objectives. It was no longer to be mainly a prominent national entity; its mission was now defined in global terms. Its goals were to maintain its status as one of the world's most prestigious and profitable banks. Its objectives were to shore up its international operations over the next ten years so that these too would be among the world's most prestigious and profitable by the year 2000. The plan was to treat Europe as the highest priority, the United States next, and only then to deal with Japan and the rest of the Far East.

Problems of Implementation

The word went out. Build up the international business, especially the investment banking part. In Europe there were only a few possible acquisitions, mostly second-tier English merchant banks, and the bank was leery of them after its experience with the English broker. There were some strategic alliances with other European banks to consider, but these mainly offered linkages to some other large, domestic-oriented retail bank, and were not of much use in developing investment banking. There was also the possibility of hiring stars away from some of the Anglo-Saxon firms, but the bank had never done this before and feared that language and cultural difficulties would negate much of the value in hiring leaders from outside.

Meanwhile, some of the senior wholesale lending officers were getting into the act. One wanted to buy a medium-sized commercial bank in Belgium, another to lead a large underwriting for a questionable client in France. Disputes broke out frequently and these were carried to the top. The firm's chairman felt it was best to get everybody involved with as much enthusiasm as possible, so most of the proposals were approved, though few were successful and some failed miserably. Many in the firm began to feel that it was too difficult to achieve rapid growth through internal expansion because of overlapping and conflicting authority, inexperience, and a traditional aversion to risky transactions. Expansion would have to depend upon business brought in through acquisitions.

Large acquisitions, however, were not likely to be approved, regardless of the changed mission of the bank. The risk of losing control of operations to executives from the acquired entity was too great. Also, if anything ever went wrong in a large acquisition, it could affect the bank's high-grade bond rating and its stock price.

"Look what happened to Credit Suisse when First Boston got in trouble, or to Midland Bank when it acquired Crocker National Bank in the early 1980s," some of the board members could be counted on to say. "The results were disastrous—large acquisitions are out, but you can probably get small to medium-sized deals through the board without too much trouble."

Meanwhile, in the United States, a young American MBA working for the grandfathered investment-banking arm of the bank, had an idea that he believed could really put the bank on the map in the states and make a lot of money too. The idea was for the bank to specialize in raising equity capital for American (and other) banks. Most banks needed new equity, and would for years. Raising bank equity capital was clearly a growth industry. It could be raised by selling new common stock, or various kinds of ingenious convertible securities or subordinated debt that counted as tier-2 equity capital under the BIS accords. It could also be raised through mergers or by selling assets to capture unrealized gains, and retiring debt with the proceeds. A full menu of highly profitable investment banking activities in the United States and overseas could be devoted just to raising equity for banks.

"The problem is," said a colleague, "we don't know much about bank equities; and many of them are pretty sick. We don't trade them or have any capability to distribute them (especially in the United States). Nor are we particularly competent in mergers or real estate deals or securitization."

"True," the MBA replied, "but those are things we can learn or hire people to do for us. And we've got three things going for us that the big American investment banks don't.

"First, we have terrific access to the top level of these banks, thanks to years of dealing with them as correspondents and in the interbank market. Second, we know banks and bank credits; we ought to be able to spot the sick ones early and avoid them. Third, we've got the bank's securities portfolios in Europe."

"They'll never let you within ten miles of those portfolios. They're not about to let them become dumping grounds for American mistakes."

"Look," continued the MBA, "I know the portfolios are sacred, but they have made risky investments before. If the top guys over there say, 'This is something we're going to do,' then the rest will do it.

"Say we set it up as a big in-house mutual fund to invest only in bank stocks. Only banks that had been prescreened would be accepted. The portfolio managers could invest their clients' money in a well-diversified single-industry play at a time when bank stocks are cheap. It would be voluntary, of course, and ultimately make a lot of money for them."

"OK, then what?"

"Then we go around to the top people at Citibank, Chase, whatever. Those on our list. And we tell them what we are trying to do. 'We want to buy a lot of your stock,' we say, 'in order to sell it in Europe.' We tell them that we are prepared to underwrite up to, say, $100 million of a domestic U.S. equity issue for them, providing that we are a lead manager of the deal. A few deals like that, and the phone will be jumping off the wall, we'll shoot up in the league tables, and people will start to take us seriously. Of course, we don't have to take down the full $100 million each time, we can either distribute it ourselves (in the United States and Europe), pass it on to the syndicate, or just sit on it for a while if we have to. We'll only have to worry about it though the first few deals."

"Man, that's pretty wild. Have you talked to London about it?" London was the headquarters for the bank's international investment-banking activity; the MBA's unit reported to London.

"They were pretty cool toward the idea. They said they didn't have much distribution capability either, and that they doubted the head office would go for it and weren't sure they wanted to push it. Also, they pointed out that at present they are invited into the international tranche of most U.S. bank deals, which are modestly profitable. The idea might irritate the American syndicate managers, they said, and cause them to cut us off. They worry about losing some piddly little syndicate business, even though over here we would be working on large, very profitable deals. And, they told me I had to see what the branch thinks." This was the New York branch of the commercial banking arm, which has a large lending portfolio in the United States, and is responsible for most of the relationships with the major banks.

"Did you talk to the branch?"

"Yeah, but they have a real not-invented-here problem. No idea of ours for how we can make a lot of money off their clients is going to appeal to them very much. They want to make absolutely sure we can deliver before we can even talk to any of 'their' banks, and their people will always have to be present whenever there is a discussion with one of them.

"Unless I can get all this worked out, London won't raise the issue with the head office. However, London did say that the head office might buy it if we said we would restrict ourselves to banks with double-A bond ratings; but there are only a handful of them and they're the ones who don't need new equity."

"A nonstarter, eh?"

"No wonder none of the big European banks, despite their exemption from Glass-Steagall, has ever amounted to anything in the U.S. investment banking market."

How Bankers Trust Would Have Done It

The European bank did not realize it was instituting a major strategy change when it "clarified its mission and objectives," and it included very few organizational changes in its new plans. This was its great mistake. Put in CAP matrix terms, the plan to focus on bank equities called for moves along all three axes. A new emphasis on marketing to banking clients was needed; the targets initially would have been U.S. banks, but plenty of other banks needed equity too. Ultimately the firm needed to develop the capability to handle a new product, equities, probably in cooperation with the head-office portfolio managers. Like most new capital market products, it needed to extend globally. Changes in the matrix as extensive as these would have involved many new responsibilities; leadership and authority questions would certainly have arisen and needed to be resolved before internal warfare broke out and killed the idea.

The European bank did not recognize that the new product idea was being developed right on the seam between the wholesale banking and capital markets businesses: between the old style of relationship-oriented banking business, and the new style of capital market innovation backed up by aggressive pricing and position taking. One of these needed to have the final responsibility to lead the effort to develop the new activity.

What would Bankers Trust have done if it had been in the European bank's place? Already oriented toward the new style of capital market activity, it would have previously appointed a head of Capital Market Services, and let that person confirm or replace subordinate heads of corporate finance and trading as necessary. There would also have been a head of American Capital Markets, reporting to the Capital Markets head. The young MBA's new idea would have been championed first by the capital markets units, whose leaders understood the bank's overall strategic goals and the urgency of realizing them. Compensated on the basis of goal realization, these leaders would have evaluated, promoted, and compensated their own subordinates in the same way. Those who didn't like the new system would have been gracefully retired. The firm would have worked to centralize investment banking in Europe and develop regional and national marketing and the capability to handle indigenous deals in particular countries. Under such an arrangement, disagreement over issues is not eliminated, but it is reduced and can be settled among like-minded executives.

In the case of the bank equities proposal, Bankers Trust would have congratulated the young MBA on his idea and helped him explore it at all the right levels. When the heads of American and European Capital Markets got wind of it, they would have considered whether it fit in with other plans then in the works, and if it did, they would have conferred with the heads of the private banking and portfolio management units and worked it out together. If they couldn't, then the matter would have been referred to the bank's chief executive to decide, and if he approved it, he would have made someone accountable for the results.

Bankers Trust would also have savored the opportunity to create a specialization in a potentially profitable sector of the capital markets where, if it moved swiftly and aggressively, the bank might secure a significant market share. If it worked, great. If it didn't, the idea could be abandoned with relatively little damage—at minimum, the bank would have learned something.

The Bankers Trust of old would not have acted like this. Bankers Trust today is an entirely different organization from the one Brittain was elected to head. The changes that revitalized it did not result from access to great supplies of capital, or from new customers and markets acquired through acquisitions, or from a technological innovation. They occurred because the bank wanted to change itself, and before that could happen the people who worked there had to be changed: they had to be inspired, retrained, motivated and compensated differently, and in some cases, replaced. If the people are not changed not much else will be.

MEASURING SUCCESS

Bankers Trust almost unquestionably has been successful in changing its strategy and in forming the culture needed to implement its new strategy effectively. Relative to other U.S. money-center banks, Bankers Trust has excelled in terms of profitability, creditworthiness, and stock price appreciation. Relative to these other banks, Bankers Trust has increased its standing, reputation, and influence. By the reckoning of most knowledgeable observers, as of the end of 1991, more than a decade after the strategy shift was adopted, Bankers Trust was the third-most-important wholesale banking organization in the United States, behind J.P. Morgan and Citibank.

But is that the right measure to apply?

Size and the League Tables

For years, the publication of annual rankings of commercial banks by size (total assets, profits, and so forth) has been an important ritual, even though not many changes were reported on a year-to-year basis within any single banking market. However, when the rankings were compiled on a global basis, the annual rankings changed considerably. The principal reason for this change was the varying exchange rates at which bank assets from other countries were converted into dollars. As the dollar weakened after 1985, U.S. banks slid down the list. Another reason for change was the rise of Japanese banks during the 1980s, when their total assets increased at double-digit rates of growth for several years. Thus by the end of 1990, seven of the ten largest banks in the world, ranked by assets, were Japanese.

As we have seen, not all of the asset increases of banks were to support wholesale transactions: many went to finance consumer borrowing and stock market and real estate purchases. Asset size also says nothing about the profitability or soundness of a bank, other than reminding us that the bank may enjoy some economies of scale, and be considered too big to fail by regulators at home. By itself, asset size is more a measure of stability and customer relationships than of competitiveness, particularly on an international scale.

In the early days of the Eurobond market, bankers found that their deals were being watched closely and reported on by an eager financial press. The press, in the form of weekly newsletters and magazines devoted to the international financial community (e.g., *Euromoney*), began to keep score of who did the most deals and then to publish the results for all to see. One banker compared the process to the weekly publication in the London newspapers of the standings of teams in the U.K. professional soccer league. These tables, which now cover many categories of financial market activity, are referred to everywhere as "the league tables." Most bankers hate them; they reveal the strengths of a few and the weaknesses of hundreds.

In the beginning, the tables only showed the rankings in Eurobond new issues. They were similar to tables published by *Investment Dealers Digest* in New York, but only included Eurobonds. Even though your firm might be making millions in secondary market trading, brokerage of U.S. shares to European investors, arranging cross-border mergers or stock issues, you would only get credit in the tables for Eurobonds. Later, foreign bonds were added; together these two make up "international bonds." Most professionals knew the tables were not useful predictors of a firm's overall profitability, its success in penetrating foreign markets, or its ability to develop future business potential, but those who read them (clients and head office superiors) believed they were good indicators of international market prowess and influence.

Because so many people believed this, the tables were the reason for many otherwise foolish competitive moves made by firms trying to increase their ranking. In the Euromarkets, banks sometimes decide to increase their market share and visibility by "moving up in the Eurobond tables." Such occasions are usually marked by a flurry of wrongly priced deals, in which the ambitious bank is forced to subsidize mispricing in order to accumulate market share. After a few issues, internal accountants tally up the losses and stop the process. Euromarket observers also have come to understand that league tables are not especially meaningful during times when great distortions exist; for example, the Japanese practice of issuing corporate bonds in the Euromarket to avoid restrictions in the Japanese bond market, and then selling the bonds back to Japanese institutional investors. Such roundtripping can hardly be viewed as a measure of international competitiveness on the part of the Japanese underwriters that lead these issues, but nonetheless, the league tables display Nomura and the others very prominently.

In time, the tables were broadened to include ranks in more categories—international equities, mergers and acquisitions, medium-term notes, and bank loans arranged. Shifting positions over a period of time give indications of changing competitive capabilities.

The league table rankings, together with the data describing the volume of financing in each category, have enabled the competitive dynamics of the world's first totally unregulated, wholesale financial marketplace to be analyzed scrupulously by academics, journalists, and market competitors alike. Academics have pointed out that statistical measures of change among market leaders show the Euromarket environment to be about twice as volatile for participating firms as the domestic U.S. capital market.[3] Journalists make headlines out of changes in market positions and glamorize some of the leading figures behind the changes. The firms themselves are constantly rearranging the data to show themselves in the best light possible when marketing their services to prospective clients.

If what we are looking for, however, is a rough measure of market influence and competitive ability of firms across a range of related wholesale services, we need to consider rankings in several different events. For example, by adding together the total volume of reported transactions led by different banks for comparable clients during the same time period, it is possible to judge the relative order of market penetration that each firm has developed, both in its home market and in the international market, and the competitive distance that exists between players. In this sense, a "pentathlon" (five events) approach to league table measures may actually give a better idea of the aggregate competitive power that firms, and types of firms, have put together over the years.

This approach seeks to assess the extent to which a variety of banks and investment banks have penetrated the market for wholesale financial services. For this purpose, we assume that other services offered to different customers—for example, retail banking services and asset management—can be set aside. The same sort of analysis, however, also could be performed for these service sectors, which no doubt would also show a significant degree of market penetration by nonbanking competitors.

Indeed, to focus the analysis, we can revert to the CAP model and identify a common set of clients (governments and corporations), a common set of products (capital raising and corporate finance), and a common arena (by country or by global data). This process is limited by the need to select the most actively utilized wholesale services, where individual bank participation can be clearly seen. League tables, for example, are not published for the annual volume of government securities or commercial paper distributed by individual firms (most issuers select several dealers to whom they auction off their securities at regular intervals). Rankings are not prepared for domestic securities markets in all countries. Also, the rankings are not reliable predictors of profitability as different profit margins apply to different services. Accordingly, not all firms seek to maximize their activity in every service; some choose, in effect, to drop out of certain services.

Rankings do not exist for the volume of secondary market trading in different securities markets. At a time when trading has become an extremely important segment for all banks and investment banks it is perhaps regrettable to have no reliable league tables for trading activity. However, trading is essentially an underlying activity that permits firms to become competitive in the primary markets (i.e., for new issues). Success in primary markets now has to presume success in secondary markets, where, if carried out well, such endeavors will also contribute significantly to a firm's overall profitability. In the long run, market leaders tend to be involved in most services that are important to their clients, and they develop what capabilities are necessary to be effective in offering these services. Also, they are usually among the most profitable firms in the industry. The pentathlon approach is a search for the market leaders and world-class players with the greatest impact on the market. Multiple indexing efforts using the best data give better information about competitive capabilities than do single-indexed data.

Scoring in the Pentathlon

Wholesale banking is no longer defined as the business commercial banks do with corporations and governments. It has become integrated with investment banking, as large segments of once-captive banking business have migrated through securitization processes into the securities market, a market controlled by investment banks, not commercial banks. How, therefore, does Bankers Trust look when compared to its new competitors?

In 1991, based on published league tables that record "full credit to lead manager" basis whenever possible,[4] Bankers Trust arranged $21.1 billion of international loans, $2.8 billion of U.S. private placements, and $2.5

billion of Euro medium-term notes (MTNs); it lead managed $2.1 billion of Eurobonds and international equities, advised on mergers with a transaction value of $2.3 billion, and maintained substantial amounts of commercial paper outstanding for its clients. All together Bankers Trust led more than $26.2 billion of U.S. wholesale financing transactions during the year (excluding the commercial paper, in which multiple dealers handling different amounts were involved), and about the same amount of international wholesale financing transactions, counting the syndicated bank loans in both categories. This compares with $31.8 billion of U.S. wholesale financing arranged by Chase Manhattan, $33.2 billion for Bank of America, $69.7 billion for Chemical Bank (with Manufacturers Hanover), $75.4 billion for J.P. Morgan, and $82.5 billion for Citicorp. Bank loans accounted for more than 70% of the total volume for all these banks except J.P. Morgan (62%).

Merrill Lynch, however, with $101 billion of U.S. underwritings in 1991, $67.6 billion of domestic MTNs arranged, $21.5 billion in M&A transactions, and $8.2 billion in private placements, led a total of $198.3 billion of U.S. wholesale financing transactions, or seven and a half times the amount posted by Bankers Trust and more than twice that of Citicorp. On the same basis of calculation, Goldman Sachs, First Boston, Lehman Brothers, and Morgan Stanley each had totals exceeding $100 billion.

On this basis, U.S. investment banks captured the top six rankings (accounting for 60% of the total volumes reported for the top twenty U.S. firms, and approximately 43% of total U.S. market volume). Only seven U.S. commercial banks were included among the top twenty firms, accounting for a total of 25% of the top twenty volume, and 18% of total U.S. wholesale transactions. U.S. affiliates of foreign firms (Credit Suisse, the Lazard group) in aggregate accounted for only 8.8% of the total market. For a table showing these data see Appendix I.

And, if an international pentathlon were to be formed by excluding domestic underwriting, MTNs, and private placements from the 1991 financing totals, and adding Euro MTNs to international loans, international bonds and equities, and global M&A transactions, then the international leader would be Credit Suisse/CS First Boston with $98.9 billion of transactions arranged. Goldman Sachs would be second ($87 billion), closely followed by Citicorp ($83 billion), J.P. Morgan ($72.3 billion), and Merrill Lynch ($66.7 billion). Barclays Bank would be eighth ($43.1 billion), and S.G. Warburg ninth ($42.2 billion). Of the top twenty, twelve were Americans (of which five were investment banks) with 43.7% of the total market, five were continental European universal banks (15.5% of the market), two were U.K. banking groups (6% of the market), and one was a Japanese securities house (1.9% of the market). Bankers Trust, by the way, appeared in nineteenth place. (See Appendix II.) A study based on 1990 results produced very similar ranking and concentration results, though individual firms appeared in different places.

The top six international firms comprised about 50% of the total volume of the top twenty, and 33% of total market volume. This concentration is somewhat less than that found within the U.S. wholesale market, where the total volume of transactions is somewhat larger ($1.8 trillion versus $1.4 trillion) than for the international wholesale market.

The top-twenty composite volume of transactions in 1991 was fourteen times greater than what it was in 1980, reflecting an exceptionally high annual compound growth rate of 30%. During this period, underwriting of international bonds and equities, MTNs, and M&A all developed considerably, and bank loans became less important. Also during the period, CSFB and First Boston became subsidiaries of Credit Suisse, Deutsche Bank acquired Morgan Grenfell and moved its capital market headquarters to London, Barclays Bank acquired Barclays de Zoute Wedd, Bankers Trust and J.P. Morgan transformed themselves into investment banking-type organizations, and Nomura Securities appeared as a financial powerhouse in Europe as a result of Japanese roundtrip issues. In 1991, six banks were included in the international composites on the basis of strong performance in a single activity (e.g., lending): Citicorp, Chemical Bank, First Chicago, Bank of America, and Chase Manhattan), but the rest were active in several categories.

The composite international tables show that asset size is not essential to effective competition. Some sort of minimum size is understood, of course, but otherwise there is no correlation between the largest banks in the world and competitive performance. None of the seven banks with total assets greater than Deutsche Bank, which ranked twelfth in composite performance, were included among the top twenty. Of the world's thirty largest banks ranked by assets at the end of 1991, only six were included in the top twenty composite rankings.

The tables also show that as a bank moves across its domestic borders into the international world beyond, it lays down much of the power it has based on domestic relationships. Across borders, banking business is done very differently, especially for large European universal banks. It is more competitive; good prices and new ideas matter. In this kind of environment, the Anglo-Saxon investment banking firms seem to have had an advantage over their larger, more traditional, slower-moving rivals. They represented eight of the top twenty composite firms, and two of the others (Credit Suisse and Deutsche Bank) scored well in areas serviced by Anglo-Saxon firms they had acquired. Among the Anglo-Saxons, several, including J.P. Morgan, Citicorp, CS First Boston, and Goldman Sachs, have made significant penetration into foreign markets for wholesale banking services, especially in the areas of mergers and acquisitions and Eurobonds and equity securities.

But so far, none of the investment banks or the large European universals has yet carved out as large a share of market outside its own country as it enjoys within it. And even such modest shares as these tend only to be obtained at great expense and effort over many years. Accordingly, many potential competitors prefer to stay at home or reduce their commitments abroad. Only those with considerable confidence and the strongest domestic positions make big plans for international business. Today these firms make up a small cohort indeed. Ten or so American firms, two or three British, two or three Swiss, two or three French, one German universal bank, and one or two Japanese.

11
THE NEW WORLD ORDER

The end of the Gulf War coincided with a deluge of events in Eastern Europe that brought about the end of the Soviet Union and Soviet-style communism in Europe. The war, which focused the attention of half the world on American military prowess and smart weapons, seemed a convenient way to make the point that the United States was still a mighty superpower, while the Soviets no longer were. As victor in the forty-five-year Cold War, the United States alone would now have the power to enforce order in the world.

President Bush proclaimed this new condition, one not seen since 1945 (and even then only briefly), a "new world order." What he meant was that a new time was upon us, a time when we could look forward to peace and stability in the world under American leadership and protection. Under these benign conditions, the Middle East would settle down, Western Europe would forge itself into a single economic community, Eastern Europe would be integrated into Western Europe, and the Soviet Union would be completely rebuilt along market-oriented, capitalistic lines.

It was not long, however, before Bush's new world order began to wobble and fall apart. The Soviet Union disintegrated into a dozen parts, each struggling to survive economically and raising fears in the West of misplaced nuclear weapons, civil war, famine, and massive migrations. Already warfare had broken out in Yugoslavia, Georgia, and Armenia. Czechoslovakia has been pulled apart, and minority groups were clashing with each other everywhere. The Ukraine declared itself independent and the new owners of the former Soviet battle fleet in the Black Sea. Communist economic power, once it could be freely observed, proved to be a mirage. It soon collapsed, leaving millions unemployed, inflation rampant, and conditions hopeless. Vast amounts of aid and food relief were required, but a world in recession had little in the way of excess savings to offer. Even the West Germans began to stagger under the load of carrying their eastern brothers. The whole region began to resemble an economic black hole, in which billions upon billions would have to be poured before any value could be returned.

Power of the sort needed to forge a new world order, however, requires money, and following a decade of growing budget deficits, the United States did not feel that it had a superpower's bankroll for foreign affairs. Most of the costs of the Gulf War had been paid for by the allies, especially Saudi Arabia, Kuwait, Japan, and Germany, the latter two being reluctant to participate in the military operations. Even without the Gulf War, U.S. financial aid to the former Soviet Union would have been modest. What money the U.S. government had was needed to pay for losses in taking over bankrupt banks and S&Ls, to provide unemployment insurance, and to invest in deteriorating physical and human infrastructure.

The Japanese felt they had been shaken down for their $13 billion contribution to the Gulf War and were not eager to be hit up again for the Russians, who less than fifty years before had mistreated their Japanese prisoners and seized their lands in the Kuriles. Besides, the Japanese had no money now either. Their great financial surpluses were finished, and the private sector was very doubtful about investments in either the former Soviet Union or its satellites. Japan's attention had to be centered on its collapsing financial economy and its trade problems with the Americans and the Europeans, both of which had worsened considerably after Bush's disastrous visit to Tokyo in January 1992.

It was difficult to see where the leadership was for forging a new plan to get the new world order back on its feet. The Americans, the Japanese, and the Germans were feeling pinched, and were unwilling to add the burden of new foreign aid programs to their overloaded domestic taxpayers. It was not long before editorial writers all over the world began referring to the "old world disorder," and noting that what was new was that there was now no order in the world at all, irrespective of the president's words.

Financial firms felt as if these remarks described conditions in their industry perfectly. After a decade of fantastic growth in financial services, with the introduction of many new products and services, the 1980s had come to a disappointing end. Banks everywhere were caught up in a tidal surge of loan losses. The situation was aggravated by a global recession in 1990 and 1991. Bank mergers broke out in the United States, Europe, and Japan as authorities tried to stem the tide by consolidation. Meanwhile, the threat to banking spreads from further deregulation and increased competition continued unabated. The move to a single market for banking services in Europe was right on schedule, to be effected by the end of 1992. These events put more stress on a system already pressured by the need to conform to the BIS minimum bank capital-adequacy standards, as well as by the growth of nonbank competitors, which were not similarly regulated.

The problems, however, were not confined to the banks. Nineteen ninety was one of the worst years ever for U.S. and British securities houses, and 1991 was even worse for the scandal-ridden Japanese firms. Wall Street, on the other hand, bounced back to a record year, despite the fact that empires like Maxwell's and BCCI had foundered, sending repercussions all over the world. Interest rates dropped and stock prices soared to record levels, bringing with them a record volume of new issues in the capital markets. Mergers and acquisitions died out in the United States, but they continued in Europe (though at levels forced downward by recession). And all Eastern Europe was hurrying to effect some kind of privatization with the help of clever but expensive advisers from the West.

Capital Market Realignments

A lot was happening at once. It was a chaotic time in which to consider strategic questions. Most of the major players kept their heads and looked around cautiously, not so much at the other players as at the playing field. What they saw was a global capital market bursting with activity—a capital market deep in the process of reconfiguration.

In the United States, banks were consolidating to reduce costs and expand their franchises. Large retail banking colossi like Bank of America were rising up and absorbing local and regional banks. Capital constraints continued to bind many of the major banks, but in the United States, for the first time in years, stock markets would take new issues of bank shares, and recapitalization could commence with large issues. Chemical Bank, for example, was able to sell $1.5 billion of new stock in January 1992, right after its merger with Manufacturers Hanover—just when it needed it. Many other banks would follow suit in efforts to rebuild the equity base of their firms. Others, weakened by the recession, would succumb to a merger or Fed-assisted liquidation.

Meanwhile, the securitization of assets formerly housed on the balance sheets of banks and insurance companies continued. The securities markets would pay higher prices for these assets than the banks and insurers, and as a result the migration continued at a record level. In addition to the expansion of money market funds and the issuance of mortgage-backed securities, the markets were absorbing large quantities of securities collateralized by other types of assets, especially automobile and credit card receivables. In 1991, nearly half of all private sector debt securities sold were asset-backed, more than $290 billion in total. This amount was about equal to the total volume of debt issues sold in the international bond markets that year ($260 billion).

Despite the failure of Congress to pass the administration's omnibus banking bill at the end of 1991, the event was only a setback—not a defeat—for those banks wishing to expand their franchises into other states or to venture into corporate underwriting. Out of more than 12,000 banks in the United States, only four or five were placing importance on securities underwriting and other investment banking transactions (through their Section 20 subsidiaries) as a part of their future coverage of wholesale markets. Only two such banks, J.P. Morgan and Bankers Trust, had decided to substantially narrow their focus and specialize in investment banking and its underlying securities trading. These two banks had established themselves by the end of 1991 as significant new competitors to the big investment banks, but few of the other large banks had done so. Most banks were planning to de-emphasize wholesale services altogether, specializing instead in smaller, regional companies and retail services. Those that wanted to cross state borders otherwise prohibited to them would have only to buy up a distressed bank or S&L from the FDIC on reasonably favorable terms to do so.

The silent work of deregulation continued. In 1982, Rule 415 had made U.S. capital markets, like the Eurobond market, accessible on a moment's notice, and companies could now put their securities offerings up for bidding where the best all-in price would win. Competition increased. Investment bankers could hold their breath and bid a lower rate for a company's business to gain market share and capture an important new client. Or they could search the world for the best financing conditions, which, together with a swap or some other form of synthetic security, would yield an attractive rate for the company without its having to be provided out of underwriter's compensation. Soon, all capital market activities were sufficiently linked as to be considered truly globalized, and markets became more closely integrated into a single pool of funds that could be accessed from all over the world.

Then the SEC passed Rule 144a in 1990, which provided for the sale of unregistered securities anywhere within the United States as long as the investors were large and sophisticated ones. In effect, this regulation integrated the U.S. private placement market with the registered securities market and the Eurobond market. The transference of the Euromarket's underlying nonregulated structure to the United States was now complete. The biggest beneficiaries were foreign issuers of securities, which began to trade more actively in the United States, where pension funds and other institutions were increasing their holdings of foreign stocks and bonds at a rapid rate.

Financing in the markets, which had gone to support the merger boom of the 1980s, was now turned to the task of rebuilding the equity base of American industry. In 1991 equity new issues were triple their 1990 levels, and they continued to grow in 1992. Also, the debt markets surged with new issues to refinance old debt with higher interest rates. Trading profits surged as the total volume of securities accessible to traders continued to increase. No longer did major securities dealers restrict themselves to domestic stocks and government, municipal, and corporate bonds; they now traded foreign government and corporate bonds, foreign stocks, foreign currencies, oil and gas and other commodities, and they dealt continuously in futures and options in these things. More than half of all non-interest revenues for many of the leading investment banks (and for the commercial banks in conversion to investment banks) were now derived from various trading activities. There was no longer much distinction between new issues and secondary market trading—it's all capital market activity. Accordingly, many of these trading–investment banking firms were now seen primarily as market counterparties, rather than as financial advisers.

Whatever their role, investment banks were seeking to cut costs further, and to repair some of the damage done to firms during the 1980s. After several firms that had been dramatically successful in the 1980s nearly failed in 1990, their parental rescuers and stockholders began to show concern for the sloppy, arrogant, and amoral approach that top officers took to managing these firms. After the Salomon Brothers market-rigging scandal, which brought in investment tycoon Warren Buffett, things began to change on Wall Street. Matching compensation to performance seemed a good idea. People in authority began to feel, "it's great having a star bank analyst like Thomas Hanley, but if the equity securities division of which he is a part can't afford him, he'll have to go." Paying bonuses of senior people in company stock, rather than in cash, seemed like a good idea too. Getting operating costs under control, putting risk management systems in place, and diversifying sources of capital were other steps that many firms took when they came up for air after the 1980s.

Wall Street firms have a history of cleaning up the mess only at the end of a long and profitable run of expanding markets, during which they feared chaos less than being left behind. What will happen during the next cycle is hard to tell, but the unsuccessful risk exposures of firms in the last cycle are unlikely to be repeated. Risk management is one of the skills that the more aggressive players are beginning to master, and this will more often than not result in better pricing of positions taken (so as to provide a suitable cushion against the risk of loss). Also, those firms with major public corporations as controlling shareholders (Salomon, First Boston, Shearson Lehman, Kidder Peabody) can certainly expect to be watched more carefully in the future and kept in line with acceptable risk parameters.

In Europe, perhaps the most important development is the increasing use of capital markets in general. The Eurobond market has continued to be active, especially for the issuance of bonds denominated in ECUs or European currencies, though few sizable local corporations are interested in the national bond markets. Equity markets, however, are showing many more signs of life. Deregulation of stock exchanges has resulted in lower costs of execution, better market making, more cross-border trading and exchanges of information and market technology. A growing awareness of derivative securities and their uses is also evident in London, Paris, Zurich, and Frankfurt. In 1990, $8 billion of international equity securities—mostly European—were brought to market, compared with less than $2 billion in 1985 and none in 1980. The prognosis has to be for a continuing increase in capital market utilization by European nonfinancial corporations, which have lagged well behind their U.S. and Japanese counterparts, as market integration continues around the world and the capital market practices and regulations of the three main financial regions converge further.

Improving markets encourage small and mid-sized companies to go public and thus create a market for their shares, or to raise new funds without becoming indentured to the hausbank. Good markets suck new issues into them, which further improve secondary trading markets and investor liquidity and awareness, and the process of transformation into a capital market-oriented system continues. Privatization efforts contribute to market improvement too, by increasing the supply of institutional grade investment securities that can be sold abroad as well as at home.

The more companies come to be held by the public, the greater the activity in the market for corporate control. Continental European markets have made many adaptations in the past few years to permit a much greater flow of mergers and acquisitions. Consequently, debates about the ethics and procedures of corporate governance have become more common. It is now generally assumed that in the near future a new European consensus on the rights of minority shareholders in contests for corporate control will emerge and be adopted by the EC. In 1991, for the first time, continental Europe's continuing activity in free-market mergers, acquisitions, and LBOs included at least four large contested deals.

The more chances that companies have to obtain lower cost or more innovative financing from the market, the more their ties to their traditional banking relations will weaken. This is an irreversible spiral, in which market opportunities draw one farther and farther away from one's illiquid beginnings. It may be quite a few years before the Continent reaches the level of market involvement that companies enjoy today in the United States and Britain, but the process has begun and is gathering momentum.

As markets develop further, European banks most oriented to securities transactions, such as Credit Suisse, SG Warburg, Deutsche Bank, Swiss Bank Corporation, BNP, Barclays Bank, and UBS, will benefit the most. They will be able to attract business away from traditional banking competitors without losing much business of their own; then will also have the chance to move to more profitable areas (mergers, equities, securitization, and derivatives) and participate more extensively in the secondary trading markets for corporate securities. Those that do not seize the opportunities promptly will experience an erosion of core business similar to that seen by many U.S. banks during the 1980s.

Many European banks, however, will see it as their first priority to position themselves properly in their own changing domestic banking markets. Many such markets are already overbanked (or overbranched), and further erosion of banking spreads could be fatal. The first response to these conditions appears to be consolidation within a single country in order to achieve economies of scale and sufficient bulk to fend off other banks, foreign or domestic, that seek to take away customers. Intramarket consolidations have been especially visible in Holland, Italy, Spain, and Scandinavia, and these have mainly involved retail-oriented banks with virtually no significant banking activities beyond their national borders.

The larger European banks must choose either to advance toward, or retreat from, extensive involvement in international wholesale lending. Some will want to follow their customers into other markets; others will reason that if they could have back all the money they have already paid out in international corporate and government lending and invest it instead in well-controlled domestic opportunities, they would gladly do so. For the most part, we are already seeing a division among those that are, or aspire to be, among the top twenty or so in the composite rankings, and those that are gradually pulling up stakes.

Also, the larger banks will have to face increasing involvement in Eastern Europe and the former Soviet Union. It may be that much has been learned from the Latin-American lending experience that could be applied to this area in order to reduce loan losses. So far, bank involvement in new facilities is limited to export and other credits that are substantially guaranteed by their own governments. Within a year or two, the banks will be pressured to put up unguaranteed funds. In the end, the banks will oblige, and begin a long and complicated period of making and working out loans to Eastern Europe. For many banks, especially the German, this will be a distraction. Much of senior managers' attention will focus on how to avoid being drawn too far into loan exposures they consider to be dangerous, and *they will* neglect other problems and other strategic opportunities.

In Japan, banks have been feeling battered since early 1990. Their traditional customer base has eroded, forcing them to find other ways to put assets on the books. So far, the other ways, such as lending to real estate and stock market speculators, have not proven helpful. Meanwhile, loan losses mount as the post-bubble economy sorts itself out, banking spreads come under pressure, capital is in short supply for many banks—a problem made worse by the plunging of Japanese stock prices—and further substantial deregulation is looming. Japanese banks will face further internal mergers (like Mitsui and Taiyo Kobe, and Kyowa and Saitama banks), as well as competition from new directions brought about by the lifting of regulatory barriers between banks of different types and by the changes to Article 65. Only a handful of Japanese banks (e.g., IBJ, Sumitomo) have undertaken serious preparations for the day of reckoning, when unrestricted investment banking activities will be possible. Preparation usually means establishing viable nonbanking activities outside Japan, either in London or the United States.

Japanese banks will need a two- or three-year period "to catch their breath, to adjust to all the changes and digest their portfolio problems at home and abroad," according to one senior Japanese banker. But when this process is complete, and the Japanese come hurling out of the penalty box, "I do not foresee their reverting to the herd-mentality behavior they exhibited in the 1980s." They will go off in different directions, he says, each trying to follow strategies that are best suited for it. Surely many of the present crowd of city, long-term, and trust banks now aspiring to international wholesale success will return home to business areas in which they have a better chance. Some will revert to retail services, in areas of the world in which there are many Japanese (Hawaii, California, Brazil), or withdraw only partially, leaving behind a specialty area like project finance or leasing. A few will remain in the fray and prepare to battle other large international wholesale banks for market share and profitability. These banks will have to master the business of investment banking to do so, something that has eluded Japanese banks so far.

The large securities firms may also have to lay low for a while, following the Nomura market-rigging and other scandals, though inside betting in Tokyo is for the penalty period to be rather short. Regulators claim they will watch things more closely "next time," but the same insiders doubt much will happen until Article 65 is totally repealed. Though the Japanese say they expect this within two to three years, few seem to be doing much about it.

The Japanese financial market has been, in its own way, rather open to foreign influences and transactions. Deregulation has been a continuous process for twenty years or more, and little by little progress has been made in removing regulations that restricted the free movement of capital, both within Japan and between Japan and other markets. Now, new ideas are applied fairly quickly in Japan (bonds with stock warrants, program trading, fixed-priced offerings, and so forth). The origin of these ideas is usually foreign; either they are picked up in the Euromarket or the United States and adapted for use in Japan by Japanese securities firms, or they are introduced into Japan directly by foreign securities firms located there. These introductions have helped modernize the Japanese securities markets, but there is still a long way to go to bring them up to the standards of the United States and London.

The Japanese markets continue to lag behind the others in terms of several important goals: utilizing sound investment management practices, accessing the new issues market for corporations, making markets in securities on some basis other than ramping up the latest hot-story stock, and introducing regulatory mechanisms that bring the country's financial regulations and practices into convergence with those of the major markets of the world.

Japanese securities firms have much to learn about modernizing their markets. So far they have had little incentive to change things, as profits have been extraordinary and competition limited to a handful of other Japanese firms. The foreign securities firms, now digging in in Tokyo, represent the real competition, and though the Japanese have been able to contain them for some years, many of them are now breaking out and competing effectively with the big firms for local Japanese business.

The securities firms will have to adapt to this condition or lose ground in their home market. They will have to learn how to handle the new products and how to compete effectively on the basis of good prices and valued innovation. Most people who know the Japanese know that when they are ready to compete, they will do so very effectively, though not necessarily profitably. At the moment, however, the Japanese know little about investment banking as it is practiced in New York and London, despite having been in the international securities business since its modern beginnings. No doubt this is because the management of the firms has been oriented almost exclusively toward the domestic brokerage business, of which there was always a plentiful and profitable supply. But with the bubble burst, zaitech winding down, significant institutional competition from the foreign members of the Tokyo Stock Exchange, lousy markets at home, and major deregulation staring them in the face (Article 65 and negotiated commissions), it may be time to shift their priorities. Such shifts will require moves along the client, product, and arena axes. For the Japanese, who suffer acutely from cultural blockages that make it very difficult to hire, motivate, and promote first-rate local executives, such moves are not easily made.

These firms passed through the 1980s without learning much about how to deal successfully with non-Japanese clients or products, though Nomura in New York, under former Kidder Peabody chief executive Max Chapman, has perhaps made the most progress, assuming anybody in Tokyo is listening to Max. Adaptation will be the challenge of the 1990s for the Japanese, as it will be for all the major players.

Another American Century?

The major changes that began in the financial marketplaces and in the competitive dynamics of banking in the 1980s are continuing. The economic philosophy of the governments of the OECD (and many other) countries is to generate economic growth through the maximum sensible exposure to free-market capitalism. No one is forecasting any significant degree of backsliding on this commitment, though European and Japanese governments have a history of weighing in on competitive issues to support their own teams. Deregulation and integration have been allowed to progress and have released and focused powerful market forces that have improved capital market efficiency globally. Deregulation has fostered a convergence of financial regulatory practices around the world, which has allowed non-banking and foreign firms in the United States, Europe, and Japan to gain greater market access. This has increased competition for market share, not only because fixed commissions and distribution structures have been eliminated, but also because new players have been allowed into formerly restricted national markets.

The basis of competition in many parts of the world has moved away from historical, single-bank relationships (hausbanks) toward multiple relationships based on performance. Thus the markets have been full of innovation and aggressive market making on the part of those seeking to improve their position or protect existing relationships. One of these innovations, which has been extremely successful in the United States over a period of less than a decade, is the securitization of assets formerly held on the balance sheets of banks and insurance companies. Thus, in the United States at least, a large part of traditional wholesale banking activity is moving off the balance sheets of large commercial banks into securities markets.

This movement is partly the result of a widening gap between bank lending rates and the market rates for these assets that are otherwise available. Although market rates are often competitive with the rates quoted by the banks with the best credit ratings, most American banks have so deteriorated in terms of credit quality that their own cost of funds has become too high to offer competitive rates on high-grade assets. American banks have suffered considerable credit-quality erosion from losses on loans to third world borrowers, real estate developers, and highly leveraged corporations. The American banks, however, suffered their wave of credit losses early in the cycle; European and Japanese banks are just now beginning to catch up with them in terms of credit exposure problems. Consequently, many Japanese and European banks have been downgraded by rating agencies over the past two years.

It is likely that these conditions will continue for several years in Europe and Japan, and that the pressure of attractive market alternatives to bank lending will accelerate during the 1990s. Events such as the completion of the single-market efforts in Europe, the integration of Eastern Europe with the West, and the reconstitution of the Japanese markets after its coming Big Bang will assist the process. Strategies will be revised, new approaches taken, mergers made, and firms restructured. Many firms will feel that it is too difficult and costly to attempt to become a fully equipped world-class player. A large number of firms around the world will review the pros and cons of settling instead for a major national-leaguer position, and be happy with it. Others may decide to become a specialized entity of another world-class player by selling out. Some, of course, will stick it out, seeking to become one of a dozen or so global banking champions.

Adaptation is the key to survival. It is the essential requirement for all of the players that aspire to world-class roles in the year 2000 and beyond. Adaptation presumes that there is an ideal prototype firm for the wholesale financial markets of the future and that most of the players are not yet there. Such a prototype would be a relatively lean, tightly managed but nonhierarchical securities and trading-oriented entity, with global relationships and marketing capabilities, adequate capital, and large numbers of talented, specialized personnel in place who are capable of making attractive profits and can train and develop others to replace them. Such firms will have to be able to develop a high tolerance for risk (and the ability to manage it), but also a deep commitment to serving clients before they serve themselves.

All firms will have to adapt, though some more than others. Some will benefit from starting positions that are advantageous, i.e., being "almost there" (CS First Boston, Goldman Sachs, S.G. Warburg), or possessing an existing market franchise that is almost as difficult to destroy as it is to duplicate (Deutsche Bank, J.P. Morgan, IBJ). Management, cultural, and financial bottlenecks will stymie many firms, and their adaptations will be slowed or in some cases prevented by them.

It is arguable that those adapting first will have a comparative advantage over the others. These firms will be able to offer the most up-to-date, responsive, comprehensible, and useful (i.e., the most competitive) services, engaging capital markets all over the world. These firms will have the latest ideas for sale and will benefit the users of their services the most, and thus they will attract more clients and business than the others.

The factor that sets such firms apart from the others may be their ability to get into the highly concentrated, top-twenty elite circle of competitors. The top twenty firms account for nearly half of the total revenues for global wholesale banking services (see Appendix II). Within the circle itself, the top five firms in 1991 accounted for market shares two and a half to three times greater than the shares of the bottom five firms. Those outside the circle end up with very small market shares.

Adapting to such an ideal firm prototype depends how far where you want to go is from where you start, and how rapidly you want to make the trip. How fast a firm decides to change is generally related to how much change it has to make, as well as to quality of the leadership on hand to manage the change.

Those with the greatest changes to make may be the Japanese banks. Little in their backgrounds has prepared them for the securities business, or for open, performance-oriented relationships. Their home markets have not given them much competitive strength that is useful abroad. They suffer from language and cultural problems, more so than similar European banks. Their experience as lenders may cause them to underprice financings in order to obtain business, but then lose money on it. Senior management in Tokyo, distracted by a rapidly changing, almost dangerous domestic banking environment, and many important regulatory changes on the way, may be unable or unwilling to learn the new requirements for international wholesale success, and therefore block or interfere with it. If major deal-failures during the transition period combine with other unhappy news, they may result in the de facto closing down of the wholesale business abroad, which in turn may adversely affect a bank's relationships with its major domestic wholesale clients.

Japanese securities firms should have a somewhat easier time than the banks because they understand the securities market environment, if not always all markets abroad. However, as they share most of the other characteristics of Japanese banks, they too will find it difficult to make such an enormous adaptation, not to mention making it quickly.

On a list ordered in terms of decreasing levels of difficulty in adapting to the new prototype, large European universal banks are next. The universals have several advantages as global competitors—they already know the securities business, especially the trading end, they manage money themselves and therefore have substantial placing power at their disposal, and being European, they are comfortable with the language and cultural differences in at least two of the three global markets. The universal banks, however, are stable, relationship-oriented, loan-making organizations with a majority of their earnings coming from domestic business. Such a structure is quite different from the structure to which it must adapt. The banks' boards of directors, mainly populated with people from the old structure, are very likely to see no need for change at all. Many of these directors are involved with domestic business and do not have much familiarity with the changing international environment, and they already find it difficult to understand or approve the risk exposures, reaction times, and profitability consequences of decisions that they must make to be competitive in the investment banking aspects. Indeed, many have had disastrous experiences (e.g., Credit Suisse, National Westminster) from investing too aggressively abroad. The boards of universal banks are not eager to see changes made that involve heavy exposure to unfamiliar risks, or radically different operating methods.

The universal bank most successful in making the adaptation required by the times is Credit Suisse, which has set up a holding company to simplify decision making (by having its decisions made at the subsidiary level,

CS First Boston). Though Credit Suisse got into international investment banking somewhat by accident with its original position in Credit Suisse White Weld, it deliberately extended its involvement through Credit Suisse First Boston, the acquisition by that company of a major stake in First Boston, and finally the takeover of all of CSFB and First Boston. Credit Suisse believed for several years that CSFB and First Boston would be more successful if it did not interfere with them, and they were left alone. Later, when First Boston got into serious trouble with its bridge loans, Credit Suisse stepped in, too late to prevent large losses and ultimately a downgrading of its prized Aaa rating from Moody's (to Aa-1) in January 1992. Credit Suisse changed the management, however, and restructured CSFB and First Boston into a holding company, CS First Boston. Now this subsidiary, which is responsible for all international investment banking (all international wholesale banking really), is run quite independently from the traditional universal bank by an American investment banker, John M. Hennessey. In February 1992, CS First Boston announced that it had earned $215 million for its fiscal year 1991, as compared to a loss of $500 million for 1990, and all three of its operating units had contributed to the profits.

The other large Swiss banks have not adopted the holding company idea (which is not capital-efficient in Switzerland) and still run the international investment bank at the board level, though increasingly decision-making authority is delegated to the banks' "international groups." These groups have not yet broken entirely free of local Swiss considerations in deciding strategic issues.

The German universal banks, with the important exception of Deutsche Bank, which acquired Morgan Grenfell to help with international acquisitions and money management, have not yet adapted very much. The Germans have been especially focused on bringing the eastern part of the new country under control and in sorting out their ongoing problems in Poland, Hungary, Czechoslovakia, and the former Soviet Union. Though the Germans realize that their traditional wholesale business in Germany is changing, they also believe that it is not changing fast and therefore the banks have time to watch how things develop before adjusting their internal structures.

The other European universal banks are ones with comparatively little securities market expertise, a full panoply of structural obstacles to adaptation, and in many cases industrial portfolios of their own to manage. Some banques d'affaires, like Paribas, have already adopted an investment-banking type of culture, and are quite adaptable. But most of the others do not appear willing to or capable of undergoing any sort of drastic change unless it is absolutely unavoidable. Many of these others prefer instead to form some kind of strategic alliance with similar banks in other countries.

The preceding also applies to British banks, except for Warburg and Barclays, which have already adapted considerably to the new requirements for successful wholesale banking in Europe. National Westminster, through its subsidiary County NatWest, is trying to keep up with Barclays, but it has not been easy. Other large British banks, like Lloyds, (premerger) Midland, Standard & Chartered, and Trustee Savings Bank, have either abandoned intentions to compete in the international wholesale banking business, or have yet to take it seriously. Most of the merchant banks, with the notable exception of S.G. Warburg, appear content to make their living inside the United Kingdom and have essentially opted for a niche role.

This leaves the American banks, which have been prominent in their presence on the top-twenty composite rankings since 1980. The large commercial banks, though somewhat active on the international scene, are fading and being replaced by investment banks and rebuilt commercial banks like J.P. Morgan and Bankers Trust. The most internationally active American banks in the past, Citicorp and Chase, both deeply weakened by poor domestic performances over the past several years, have withdrawn somewhat from the investment banking sector. Either or both, if they survive their present difficulties intact, may get back into the game in the future. If so, they will do so as those who have survived the worst and have learned a lot about competing.

Bank of America and Chemical, once powerful international lenders, have retreated from the field. They also are not focusing seriously on international wholesale banking at present. Both completed major acquisitions in 1991–1992 and have indicated a strong interest in domestic retail banking and cost cutting. Under these circumstances, their investment banking arms are unlikely to develop much beyond their present, rather limited, capability in the next four years.

The large American investment banks have the least amount of adapting to do to fit the new firm prototype. They have the shortest distance to travel, and the greatest ability to adapt quickly, based on a lifetime of adapting to changing market and competitive conditions. Firms like Goldman Sachs, Merrill Lynch, and Morgan Stanley have passed through the tumultuous 1980s virtually unscathed, largely because management was successful in controlling the firms under difficult conditions. High profitability during this period enabled the firms to attract excellent staff, put them to good use, and retain them. They were also able to attract all the capital they needed and invested much of it in information technology and other programs that would enable them to lower costs and manage the risks of the business better in the future.

Other top firms like First Boston, Lehman Brothers, and Salomon Brothers all experienced troubles in the 1989–1991 period, which resulted in substantial losses, replacement of top management, and a large number of defections by key employees. Yet these firms adapted to their changed circumstances quickly, and bounced back, regained profitability, and began again to increase their market shares.

Besides being adaptable, the successful investment banks also understand marketing and love to compete. They are completely uninhibited about calling a major company, which is not a client, in a territory where the firm is not well known to propose an idea that just came up. The caller expects to be rejected, but keeps trying. Sooner or later, he gets through and a deal is done. He wins the business because the idea was timely and well conceived and the new client could see the value in it.

In endeavors like these, the American investment banks are playing the part of the New Men of finance—the ones described by Walter Bagehot more than a hundred years ago, who made the City of London work by constantly challenging the Old Capitalists. The New Men had different ideas, or were more aggressive in quoting prices, or more willing to take down positions to help out the clients, or to provide information that the client did not have. The New Men had little money, but they did have a service orientation and a willingness to please. The Old Capitalists had lots of money, but worried about losing it and were reluctant to spoil clients with excessive services. The New Men sometimes overextended themselves and failed. But others replaced them in the game, eager for the chance to show what they could do. The Old Capitalists, who never stumbled because they were so cautious, soon found that they were losing business to the New Men (whose aggressive prices they would not match). When they were unable to stop the hemorrhaging, they withdrew from business and retired.

Does this mean that the next century will be one in which American men and women of finance dominate? Certainly there is some reason to think so, based on the continuous high ranking of U.S. firms since 1980 (and earlier) in the composite league tables described as being fair indicators of real market presence. Customary ranking of banks by assets, or deposits, or by preeminence in one or two special areas such as syndicated loans or Eurobond underwriting, does not give a full picture of the presence of a particular firm in the market for now-globalized wholesale financial services. American firms, as a group, stand well in the rankings despite a dismal close to the euphoric 1980s and the subsequent damage to individual banks and investment houses. Since the beginning, however, the list of high-ranking American firms has always been subject to relatively high levels of turnover.

The firms best able to succeed in these conditions are those that specialize in adapting and have already tuned their organizations to global competition. In that sense, despite the tough times many U.S. banks and some investment banks have been through during the past several years, American financial preeminence in wholesale banking services is likely to continue. The firms are stronger for having survived their difficulties and find great opportunity in the fact that the market for their services has spread widely in Europe, and to some extent in Japan. All expectations are for the spreading to continue. Meanwhile, banks from Europe and Japan will still suffer from problems in their own regions that may hamper their ability to adapt themselves to world competitive conditions, at least for a few years. All these factors point to increasing competitive strength among ten or so American firms.

However, it must be noted that these firms are losing their American identity. J.P. Morgan claims that now about a third of its professional employees are non-Americans, including its chairman and three of its five top officers. CS First Boston is increasingly hard to tag as American. Though its U.S. subsidiary, First Boston, is as American as Merrill Lynch, the rest of the firm is not, nor is its parent, nor are many of its board members. Morgan Stanley and Goldman Sachs each say that about a third of their employees, capital, and profits are non-American. Merrill Lynch hires hundreds of foreign nationals around the world. These firms are far more international in their makeup, their offices and representations, their clients and revenues, and their outlook than many of the most "international" of banks in Europe or Japan, including Deutsche Bank, BNP, and Industrial Bank of Japan. Warburg may be more advanced in this category than most the Americans, but not by much.

American-style wholesale banking and ultimately, no doubt, technology-driven American-style retail banking will become a model for the rest of the world, as long as competitive conditions are maintained and free markets are allowed to send capital to where it is appreciated the most. Universal banks are solid, but less competitive. If competitiveness over time is the principal factor separating those that are successful from those that are less so, then the American-style bankers should become the champions. But, if so, it is unlikely that they will be strictly "American." The firms will be groups of 10,000 employees or less, made up of professionals from all over the world.

Like Captain Kirk's starship *Enterprise*, the place will be a polyglot. But all its personnel will be trained alike and trained well. Such firms may then constitute the first in the new and true race of global bankers.

APPENDIX I U.S. Firms Wholesale Banking and Investment Banking 1991 ($ billions)

Firm	Underwriting (a)	Private Placmts (b)	Global M&A Advisory (c)	Intl Loans Arranged (d)	Med Term Notes Lead Mgd (e)	Total	% Top 20	% of Total Industry
Merrill Lynch	100.9	8.2	21.5		67.7	198.3	15.2%	10.9%
Goldman Sachs	71.2	13.0	36.0		25.2	145.4	11.1%	8.0%
First Boston	58.4	9.4	26.8	25.4	19.1	139.1	10.6%	7.6%
Lehman Bros.	69.1	5.6	21.1		15.6	111.4	8.5%	6.1%
Morgan Stanley	48.8	7.2	27.2		20.3	103.5	7.9%	5.7%
Salomon Bros.	46.3	8.1	21.8		11.9	88.1	6.7%	4.8%
Citicorp	4.7	5.5	2.2	70.1		82.5	6.3%	4.5%
J.P. Morgan	9.7	6.3	10.7	47.2	1.5	75.4	5.8%	4.1%
Chemical Bank (*)		5.8		63.9		69.7	5.3%	3.8%
Kidder Peabody	50.9	4.6	2.6		1.2	59.3	4.5%	3.3%
Bear Stearns	33.9	2.2			1.7	37.8	2.9%	2.1%
Bank of America		1.5		28.7	3.0	33.2	2.5%	1.8%
Chase Securities	3.3	4.1	2.4	22.0		31.8	2.4%	1.7%
Bankers Trust		2.8	2.3	21.1		26.2	2.0%	1.4%
Lazard Houses			21.0		0.6	21.6	1.7%	1.2%
DLJ	11.5	1.8	6.2			19.5	1.5%	1.1%
Prudential Securities	17.2	0.2	1.5			18.9	1.4%	1.0%
PaineWebber	11.1	3.0	3.9		0.3	18.3	1.4%	1.0%

APPENDIX I **(cont.)**

Firm	Underwriting (a)	Private Placmts (b)	Global M&A Advisory (c)	Intl Loans Arranged (d)	Med Term Notes Lead Mgd (e)	Total	% Top 20	% of Total Industry
Smith Barney	6.2	1.4	5.8		0.3	13.7	1.0%	0.8%
NCNB				12.5		12.5	1.0%	0.7%
Total Top 20	543.2	90.7	213.0	290.9	168.4	1,306.2	100.0%	71.8%
Industry Total	588.9	110.4	218.7	727.0	174.3	1,819.3		
Top 20 as % of Total	92.2%	82.2%	97.4%	40.0%	96.6%	71.8%		

(a) Securities Data Corp., full credit to lead managers (top 25)
(b) *Investment Dealers Digest*, March 9, 1992, Top 20 (full credit to lead manager)
(c) Securities Data Corp. (top 25), U.S. targets only
(d) IFR *International Financing Review*, January 4, 1992. Top 50 lead managers all loans and nifs, arrangers only
(e) *Investment Dealers Digest*, January 20, 1992. Top 15 agents, domestic programs (full credit to lead agent)

(*) Chemical Bank plus Manufacturers Hanover totals

APPENDIX II   International Wholesale Banking and Investment Banking 1991 ($ billions)

Firm	Intl Loans Arranged (f)	Intl Bonds Lead Mgd (g)	Intl Equities Lead Mgd (h)	Euro MTNs Lead Mgd (i)	Intl M&A Lead Mgd (j)	Total	% of Top 20	% of Industry Total
CS First Boston	25.4	23.0	1.9	16.7	31.9	98.9	10.31%	6.89%
Goldman Sachs		14.5	4.6	6.8	61.1	87.0	9.06%	6.06%
Citicorp	70.1	0.6		12.3		83.0	8.65%	5.78%
J.P. Morgan	47.2	7.6			17.5	72.3	7.54%	5.04%
Merrill Lynch		12.3	1.0	19.1	34.3	66.7	6.95%	4.65%
Chemical Bank(*)	63.9					63.9	6.66%	4.45%
Morgan Stanley		12.2	0.7	4.5	44.0	61.4	6.40%	4.28%
Barclays Bank Gp	32.9	3.0	0.4		6.8	43.1	4.49%	3.00%
S.G. Warburg	4.5	7.3	2.6		28.0	42.4	4.42%	2.95%
Salomon Bros.		8.0	0.9	2.1	29.6	40.6	4.23%	2.83%
Shearson Lehman		2.0	1.1	2.8	31.9	37.8	3.94%	2.63%
Deutsche Bank	12.5	15.6	0.2	1.3	7.4	37.0	3.86%	2.58%
First of Chicago	32.7					32.7	3.41%	2.28%
UBS	19.0	12.2				31.2	3.25%	2.17%
Bank of America	28.7					28.7	2.99%	2.00%
Nomura Securities		25.9	0.5	0.7		27.1	2.82%	1.89%
Credit Lyonnais	20.6	6.8	0.1			27.5	2.87%	1.92%
SBC	14.8	12.1				26.9	2.80%	1.87%
Bankers Trust	21.1	2.1		2.5		25.7	2.68%	1.79%

APPENDIX II (cont.)

Firm	Intl Loans Arranged (f)	Intl Bonds Lead Mgd (g)	Intl Equities Lead Mgd (h)	Euro MTNs Lead Mgd (i)	Intl M&A Lead Mgd (j)	Total	% of Top 20	% of Industry Total
Chase Manhattan	22.0	0.6			3.0	25.6	2.67%	1.78%
Total Top 20	415.4	165.8	14.0	68.8	295.5	959.5	100.00%	67.00%
Industry Totals	727.0	299.8	15.5	77.7	311.5	1,431.5		
Top 20 as % of Total	57.1%	55.3%	90.3%	88.5%	94.9%	67.0%		

(f) *IFR International Financing Review*, January 4, 1992. Top 50 lead managers loans and nifs, arrangers only
(g) *IFR International Financing Review*, January 4, 1992. Top 60 lead managers only Eurobonds and international issues
(h) *IFR International Financing Review*, January 4, 1992. Top 20 lead managers only international equity issues
(i) *Investment Dealers Digest*, January 20, 1992. Top 15 Review, January 4, 1992. Top 15 agents, Worldwide MTNs full credit
　　to lead agents only
(j) *Mergers & Acquisitions Magazine*, March 1992. Securities Data Corp (top 25) lead agents

(*) Chemical Bank plus Manufacturers Hanover totals

NOTES

Chapter 1

1. William Greider, *Secrets of the Temple* (New York: Simon & Schuster, 1987), p. 146.
2. Martin Anderson, *Revolution* (New York: Harcourt Brace Jovanovich, 1988), pp. 147–148.
3. Daniel Patrick Moynihan, *Came the Revolution* (New York: Harcourt Brace Jovanovich, 1968), p. 154.
4. Ibid., p. 135.
5. Ibid., pp. 151–158.
6. David Stockman, *The Triumph of Politics* (New York: Harper & Row, 1986), pp. 380–394.
7. Anderson, *Revolution*, p. 175.
8. Jeff Madrick, "Even B-Schoolers Say It's a Bummer," *New York Times*, July 7, 1991.
9. Roy C. Smith, *The Money Wars* (New York: E.P. Dutton, 1990), p. 30.
10. Frederick Lewis Allen, *The Great Pierpont Morgan* (New York: Harper & Row, 1948), pp. 140–145.
11. Federal Reserve Board, *Annual Statistical Digest*, 1989.
12. Edward I. Altman, "Defaults and Returns on High Yield Bonds—an Update through 1991," unpublished paper, Stern School of Business, New York University, January 1992.
13. *Historical Statistics of the United States: Colonial Times to 1970* (Washington, D.C.: Government Printing Office, 1975).
14. John Steele Gordon, "Understanding the S&L Mess," *American Heritage* (February–March, 1991).
15. Lawrence J. White, *The S&L Debacle* (New York: Oxford University Press, 1991), p. 65.
16. Ibid., p. 71.
17. Ibid., pp. 74–75.

Chapter 2

1. "Compensating deposits" were frequently required in the 1960s and 1970s by banks making loans to corporations. Typically about 20% of the value of the

loaned amount was to be retained on deposit with the bank, at no interest. This had the effect of increasing the cost of the loan considerably: e.g., in December 1970, the prime rate was 6.75%. Compensating deposits of 20% would increase the effective cost of the loan to 8.44% (6.75% / 0.8 = 8.44%), or 3.94% over the banks' passbook savings rate of 4.5%.

2. Lowell L. Bryan, "A Blueprint for Financial Reconstruction," *Harvard Business Review* (May–June 1991), pp. 73–86.

3. M. Myers, *A Financial History of the United States* (New York: Columbia University Press, 1970), pp. 38–50.

4. Harold Cleveland and Thomas Huertas, *Citibank 1812–1970* (Cambridge, Mass.: Harvard University Press, 1985), pp. 258–265; and George S. Moore, *The Banker's Life* (New York: W.W. Norton, 1987), p. 203.

5. Peter Grant and Robert McNatt, "Squandered Decade," *Crane's New York Business*, June 17, 1991.

6. Roy C. Smith, *The Global Bankers* (New York: E.P. Dutton, 1989), pp. 33–35.

7. Robert N. McCauley and Rama Seth, "Foreign Bank Credit to U.S. Corporations: The Implications of Offshore Loans," Federal Reserve Bank of New York, *Quarterly Review*, Spring 1992.

8. Roy C. Smith and Ingo Walter, *Global Financial Services* (New York: Harper & Row, 1990), pp. 722–751.

9. Philip L. Zweig, *Belly Up* (New York: Crown, 1985). Also see Mark Singer, *Funny Money* (New York: Alfred A. Knopf, 1985).

10. Testimony to the Subcommittee of Financial Institutions, Supervision and Insurance, Committee on Banking, Finance and Urban Affairs of the House of Representatives by Comptroller of the Currency C.T. Conover, September 18, 1984.

11. George G. Kaufman, "Are Some Banks Too Large to Fail? Myth and Reality," *Contemporary Policy Issues*, vol. VIII (October 1990).

12. Continental Bank Corporation, *Annual Report*, 1990, Letter from the Chairman.

13. *The Economist*, August 17, 1991, p. 26.

14. John W. Milligan, "Can Bank of America Become America's Bank?," *Institutional Investor* (March 1991).

15. John W. Milligan and Ida Picker, "The Collapse of Citibank's Credit Culture," *Institutional Investor* (December 1991), p. 45.

16. Fred R. Bleakley, "Weakened Giant," *The Wall Street Journal*, August 16, 1991.

17. *New York Times*, July 30, 1991.

18. Lee Burton, "FASB Alters Plan on Valuing of Securities," *The Wall Street Journal*, March 26, 1992.

19. William Dudley, "Banking's Burden," *Financial Market Perspectives* (January 1992), pp. 1–7.

20. Alan Friedman, "Expanding Away From Home," *The Financial Times*, December 2, 1991, p. 32.

21. *New York Times*, July 17, 1991, p. D6.

22. Charles McCoy and Ralph T. King, Jr., "Add Security Pacific to Bank America: The Result Is Clout," *The Wall Street Journal*, August 13, 1991.

23. David Hilder and Roger Lowenstein, "Merger of Two Big Banks in New York May Be the Start of a Wave," *The Wall Street Journal*, July 16, 1991.

24. Ibid.

25. *The Economist*, July 20, 1991, p. 16.

Chapter 3

1. Randall Smith, "How Salomon Muscled Aside Merrill to Become Lead Underwriter on Time Warner's Big Offering," *The Wall Street Journal*, July 19, 1991.

2. Kurt Eichenwald, "1990 Called Wall Street's Worst Year," *New York Times*, February 27, 1991; and Securities Industry Association, *1991 Fact Book*, New York, 1992.

3. *United States vs. Morgan*, et al., 1954 Southern District of New York.

4. *Economic Report of the President* (Washington, D.C.: Government Printing Office, 1990).

5. Securities Industry Association, *1991 Fact Book*, International Finance Corporation, Salomon Brothers, 1992.

6. Securities Data Corporation, Mergers and Acquisitions Database, 1991.

7. "Money Machine," *Business Week*, June 10, 1991.

8. "The Big Squeeze," *The Wall Street Journal*, August 12, 1991.

9. Statement by Warren Buffett, chairman of Salomon Brothers, Inc. to the subcommittee on securities markets of the House Energy and Commerce Committee, September 4, 1991.

10. Michael Siconolfi and Laurie Cohen, "How Salomon's Hubris and US Trap led to Leaders' Downfall," *The Wall Street Journal*, August 19, 1991.

11. Ibid.

12. Michael Siconolfi, "Salomon Unit Posts a Huge Increase in Quarterly Profit," *The Wall Street Journal*, July 24, 1992.

13. *Investment Dealers Digest* (March 1992).

14. Interview with John L. Weinberg, *The Wall Street Journal*, August 14, 1991, p. C20.

15. Sources: *1991 Annual Reports* of J.P. Morgan & Co., and Morgan Stanley group.

15. The Prudential Insurance Company of America, *1991 Annual Report*.

16. Jack Egan, "The Bank of the Future," *US News and World Report*, April 29, 1990.

Chapter 4

1. European Communities, "The Economics of 1992," *European Economy*, no. 35 (Cecchini Report) (Luxembourg: Office de Publications des Communautés Européennes, 1988).

2. Roy C. Smith and Ingo Walter, "Economic Restructuring in Europe and the Market for Corporate Control," paper presented at INSEAD, Fontainebleau, France, May 1990.

3. U.S. Department of Commerce, Bureau of Economic Analysis, September 1991.

4. KPMG Peat Marwick McLintock, *Management Buyout Statistics*, January 1991.

5. Securities Data Corporation, merger data file, January 1992.

6. Roy C. Smith and Ingo Walter, "European Industrial Restructuring and the Market for Corporate Control," in Karel Cool, Damien Neven, and Ingo Walter, eds., *Economic Restructuring in Europe* (London: Macmillan, 1991). The paper includes tables for buyer and seller companies. In each table approximately 70 industries (classified by two-digit SIC codes) were designated. U.S. and European industry involvement in M&A activity during the period were tested for statistical correlation by Pearson coefficients.

7. AP-Dow Jones News Service, March 19, 1992.

8. Security Data Corporation, merger data file.

9. Marshall I. Goldman, *What Went Wrong with Perestrioka* (New York: W.W. Norton, 1991), p. 224.

10. Ibid., p. 211.

11. *The Economist*, September 28, 1991.

12. Deborah Hargreaves, "Continued Sharp Fall Forecast in Soviet Oil Output," *The Financial Times*, November 6, 1991, p. 24.

13. Peter Gumbel, "Soviet Gold Levels Called into Question," *The Wall Street Journal*, October 1, 1991.

14. David Fairlamb, "Intrigue and Betrayal at Russia's Central Bank," *Institutional Investor*, June 1992.

15. Christopher Parkes, "East German Workforce Slashed," *The Financial Times*, April 14, 1992.

16. David Goodhart and Andrew Fisher, "Stirrings of Life in the East," *The Financial Times*, September 13, 1991.

17. "Kohl's Debterdämmerung," *The Economist*, April 4, 1992.

18. Richard E. Smith, "Bundesbank Warns Bonn to Curb Spending," *International Herald Tribune*, March 18, 1992.

19. *The Economist*, "Survey of Business in Eastern Europe," September 21, 1991.

20. Edward Balls, "EC Protectionism Threatens East European Growth," *The Financial Times*, April 13, 1992.

21. Richard Blackhurst, "Implications of the Changes in Eastern Europe for the World Economy" (Kiel, Germany: Institute for World Economics, 1991).

22. Horst Siebert and Holger Schmieding, "Restructuring Industry in the GDR" (Kiel, Germany: Institute for World Economics, July 1990).

23. *The Economist*, "Survey of Business in Eastern Europe," p. 28.

24. Leslie Coutt, "Treuhand Announced Record Sales in June," *The Financial Times*, July 23, 1992; and The Treuhandanstalt, November 1991, as quoted in "Hand of Kindness," *The Economist*, March 21, 1992.

25. "Czechs By Millions Invest $35 in Big State Sale," *New York Times*, January 21, 1992, p. A9.

Chapter 5

1. Charles P. Kindleberger, *A Financial History of Western Europe* (London: George Allen & Unwin, 1984), p. 470.

2. Andreas Haindl and Raymund Scheffrahn, *Swiss Banking in the 1990s*, Occasional Papers in Business and Finance, The New York University Salomon Center, No. 12, 1991, p. 5.

3. Ibid., p. 21.

4. Stephen Lewis and Franco Ricciulli, *Restructuring the Italian Banking Industry* (New York: Salomon Brothers, 1990), pp. 1–4.

5. Deutsche Bundesbank, Statistical Review of German Banking, August 1990.

6. Lewis and Riccuilli, *Restructuring the Italian Banking Industry*, p. 7

7. Christian Harm, "The Financing of German Industry by German Banks," unpublished manuscript prepared at New York University for the World Bank, November 1990, pp. 71–90.

8. Alfred Herrhausen, "Kontroverse über die Macht der Banken," *Verbraucherpolitische Hefte*, no. 5 (December 1987).

9. Ibid.

10. J. Bradford De Long, "Did J.P. Morgan's Men Add Value?," unpublished paper for members of the Cliometrics Society, June 1990.

11. Unpublished survey by Korn/Ferry International, New York, December 1991.

12. Jeremey Edwards and Klaus Fischer, "An Overview of the German Financial System," Council for Economic Policy Research, quoted in *The Economist*, December 7, 1991, p. 91.

13. Alfred Steinherr, lecture to a group of New York University students, Frankfurt, January 16, 1992.

14. Kindleberger, *A Financial History of Western Europe*, pp. 124–125.

15. John Evans, "East May Delay Germany's Thrust Abroad," *American Banker*, July 26, 1991.

16. Reuters, September 9, 1991.

17. Carlos García-Pont and Donald R. Lessard, "Alliance Networks in European Banking," unpublished manuscript prepared at MIT Sloan School of Management, September 1991.

18. Peter Grant, "Allfinanz—To Be Or Not to Be?," Address at 3d International Life Insurance Conference, London, March 19, 1991.

Chapter 6

1. William Dawkins, "Small Bang Fall-Out," *The Financial Times*, December 12, 1991.

2. Alice Rawsthoprn, "French Brokers Incur Losses of FFr600m in 1991," *The Financial Times*, April 15, 1992.

3. Marilyn Resener, "Paribas's Family Feud," *Institutional Investor* (June, 1990).

4. Jacques Neher, "Paribas Expected to Seek Bigger US Financial Role," *The New York Times*, July 23, 1991.

5. Interview with the author, February 1991.

6. Quoted in Madlyn Resener, "Will Jean-Yves Haberer Get the Last Laugh?," *Institutional Investor* (November 1991).

7. *The Economist*, November 16, 1991 and April 4, 1992.

8. Quoted in Resener, "Will Jean-Yves Haberer Get the Last Laugh?," p. 90.

9. Interview with the author, February 1991.

10. Siegmund Warburg related his strategy to me at a meeting in 1981, shortly before his death. I had just taken over as president of Goldman, Sachs International Corporation in London, and sought his advice on how, as an outsider, to penetrate the British market. He urged that whatever else I did while in London, I must "at all times be seen as a strong American banker, not a made-over British one."

11. Michel Fleuriet, "Mergers and Acquisitions: The French Experience," (Paris: Chase Manhattan Bank, 1989).

12. "Five Years Since Big Bang," *The Economist*, October 26, 1991.

13. Ibid.

14. Ron Chernow, *The House of Morgan* (New York: Atlantic Monthly Press, 1990), pp. 165–230 for the relationships with the other Morgans and the period leading up to the Guinness affair. See also Dominic Hobson, *The Pride of Lucifer* (London: Hamish Hamilton, 1990), pp. 20–30, 166–218. This "unauthorized biography of a merchant bank" is mainly about the modern Morgan Grenfell and the Guinness scandal.

15. Chernow, *The House of Morgan*, pp. 681–688.

16. Roy C. Smith, *The Global Bankers* (New York: E.P. Dutton, 1989), p. 214.

17. *The Economist*, November 30, 1991.

Chapter 7

1. Japanese National Commission, "Japan: Its Land, People and Culture," (Paris: Unesco, 1958).
2. *Money and Banking in Japan*, Economic Research Department, Bank of Japan, 1964, p. 5.
3. For the early postwar economic history I have relied mainly on John G. Roberts's exceptional history of the Mitsui Group, *Mitsui: Three Centuries of Japanese Business* (New York: John Wheatherhill, 1973), which covers this period in great detail, pp. 365–387; on William Manchester's *American Caesar* (Boston: Little, Brown, 1978), and on Kamekichi Takahashi, *The Rise and Development of Japan's Modern Economy* (Tokyo: Jiji Press, 1969).
4. Patrick Smith, "Letter from Tokyo," *The New Yorker*, October 14, 1991.
5. Roberts, *Mitsui*, pp. 373–374.
6. Ibid., pp. 430–435.
7. Bank of Japan, *Money and Banking in Japan*, p. 29.
8. Ibid., p. 81.
9. Karen Elliot House and Urban H. Lehner, "Miyazawa Sees Japan World Role Impaired," *The Wall Street Journal*, April 13, 1992.

Chapter 8

1. Goldman, Sachs & Co., Japan Economic Research, October 1991.
2. On the valuation of Japanese real estate, see Jeffrey A. Frankel, "The Japanese Cost of Finance—A Survey," *Financial Management* (Spring 1991). This may be the most definitive summary in all academic literature on Japanese cost of capital. Frankel appends a long and very useful list of sources to the paper.
3. Robert Thompson, "Japanese Golf Club Memberships in the Rough," *The Financial Times*, November 8, 1991.
4. *The Economist*, September 28, 1991, quoting a study by U.K. stockbrokers James Capel & Co.
5. K. French and J. Porteba, "Are Japanese Stock Prices Too High?" National Bureau of Economic Research paper (Washington, D.C., April 1989).
6. Goldman, Sachs & Co., Japan Economic Research, October 1989.
7. Bank for International Settlements, *Annual Report 1991*, Basel.
8. *The Economist*, August 31, 1991.
9. Ibid.
10. Charles R. Elliott, "Japan Weekly Commentary," Goldman, Sachs & Co., April 20, 1992.
11. "How Japan Will Survive Its Fall," *The Economist*, July 11, 1992.
12. *The Economist*, August 17, 1991.
13. "Deep in Bad Debt," *The Economist*, November 2, 1991.
14. Edward Balls, "Slowed Down to a Walking Pace," *Financial Times*, July 15, 1991.
15. Moody's Investor Services, "Outlook for Japanese Bank Ratings," March 13, 1991, and Standard & Poor's *Creditweek International*, "Japanese City Banks' Falling Profits," April 1, 1991.
16. David Atkinson and Jeffrey Hanna, "Japanese Banks—Valuing Stock Portfolios," (Tokyo: Salomon Brothers, September 1991).
17. U.S. Department of Commerce, *Survey of Current Business*, August 1991.
18. "When the Bridge Caught Fire," *The Economist*, September 7, 1991.
19. David Sanger, "Toshiba Rewrites a Hollywood Script," *New York Times*, October 8, 1991.

20. Sources: Japanese Economic and Trade Research Organization (JETRO); and James C. Abegglen and George Stalk, Jr., *Kaisha, The Japanese Corporation* (New York: Basic Books, 1985). JETRO's estimates of the percentage of Japanese manufacturing capacity outside Japan are based on sales of goods manufactured overseas divided by total sales.

21. *The Wall Street Journal*, January 2, 1992.

22. Jeffrey Frankel, "Japanese Finance—A Survey," National Bureau of Economic Research Working Paper No. 3156 (Washington D.C., November 1989).

23. Ibid.

Chapter 9

1. The early history of Nomura and the Japanese securities industry is well described in Albert J. Alletzhauser, *The House of Nomura* (Boston: Little, Brown, 1990), pp. 25–161.

2. James Sterngold, "Bills Coming Due for Japan, Inc.," *New York Times*, November 11, 1991.

3. James Sterngold, "Testimony on Brokers in Tokyo," *New York Times*, August 30, 1991.

4. Clay Chandler, "Nomura's Two Top Officers Will Resign," *The Wall Street Journal*, July 23, 1991.

5. James Sterngold, "Japan's Rigged Casino," *The New York Times Magazine*, April 26, 1992.

6. Steven Weisman, "Series of Scandals Have Japanese Debating If Country Has Grown Corrupt," *New York Times*, August 19, 1991.

7. James Sterngold, "Japan's Scandals: No Laws to Break," *New York Times*, July 15, 1991.

8. Clay Chandler, "Japan Forces a Rescue of a Credit Union at Heart of Giant Loan-Fraud Scandal," *The Wall Street Journal*, April 29, 1992.

9. James Sterngold, "Japan Hit By Another Scandal," *New York Times*, August 14, 1991; and Clay Chandler and Yumiko Ono, "Who's the Rags to Riches 'Bubble Lady' in Japan's Bank Scandal?," *The Wall Street Journal*, August 23, 1991.

10. James Sterngold, "Japanese Learn a Lesson in Bureaucratic Rule," *New York Times*, November 3, 1991.

11. James Sterngold, "Beneath the Rocks on Japan, Inc.'s Playing Field," *New York Times*, September 1991.

12. Statement by Yoh Kurosowa at an International University of Japan banking industry conference in Tokyo, May 12, 1992.

Chapter 10

1. Ingo Walter, *Global Competition in Financial Services* (Cambridge, Mass.: Ballinger, 1988), pp. 43–68.

2. Susan Crevoor, "Bankers Trust New York Corporation," Case No. 0–286–005 (Boston: Harvard Business School, 1985).

3. Roy C. Smith and Ingo Walter, *Investment Banking in Europe, Restructuring for the 1990's* (Oxford: Basil Blackwell, 1990), pp. 139–143.

4. The sources used were Securities Data Corporation, *Investment Dealers Digest*, *Mergers and Acquisitions*, and *International Financial Review*.

Index